Social Networks in Urban Situations

To Max Gluckman
point-source of our network

Social Networks
in
Urban Situations

*Analyses of Personal Relationships
in Central African Towns*

Edited by
J Clyde Mitchell

Published for the
Institute for African Studies
University of Zambia
by
MANCHESTER UNIVERSITY PRESS
1969

Published by the University of Manchester at
THE UNIVERSITY PRESS
316–324 Oxford Road, Manchester M13 9PL

ISBN 0 7190 1035 7

Distributed in the USA by
HUMANITIES PRESS, INC
171 First Avenue, Atlantic Highlands, MJ 07716
First published, 1969
Reprinted with minor corrections, 1971, 1975

Reproduced and printed by photolithography and bound in
Great Britain at The Pitman Press, Bath

Preface

This symposium arose out of a set of papers read to a seminar for fieldworkers at the University College of Rhodesia and Nyasaland in 1964 and 1965. Partly by accident and partly by design, a number of young researchers came to be studying various aspects of social relationships in Zambia and Rhodesia, several of them in towns. The potentialities of social networks as a tool for examining the structure of social relationships in 'modern' societies had interested us for some time and it was inevitable that several of the papers should have been organized around this topic. These papers were read at early phases of the fieldwork of the people concerned so that they had the opportunity of taking back to the field the fruits of the discussions we had had on the notion of social networks.

That several of us had been interested in social networks is not difficult to explain. Several of the staff at the University College had had close associations with the Department of Social Anthropology and Sociology at Manchester where John Barnes had been a Simon Research Fellow at the time when he was studying Bremnes and where he had developed his paper, published in 1954, which provided the point of departure for Elizabeth Bott's seminal study. The notion of the social network had remained a constant topic of conversation in the department in Manchester ever since Barnes had read his first paper on the topic to a seminar group there. It took some time, however, before the idea began to influence field enquiries. 'Bill' Epstein's fieldwork in Zambia had been completed before he was appointed lecturer in the Department at Manchester. The papers in which he makes use of the notion were thus based on a re-analysis of his field notes rather than on the conscious use of the concept while he was collecting his field data. Others engaged in fieldwork at the time had been influenced by Barnes's paper and Bott's book so that Phillip Mayer and his colleague Pauw was already analysing their material using social networks. In 1958 when I started some work in the African residential areas of Salisbury I tried myself to collect material on the social networks of different African families, but for a variety of reasons, the attempt was not very successful. But I did not lose confidence in the potential usefulness of the notion particularly in urban studies. The publication of Phillip Mayer's book in 1961 justified this confidence so that it was understandable that when a number of fieldworkers gathered at the Rhodes-Livingstone Institute in Lusaka and the Department of Sociology at the University College in Salisbury, they should have been alive to the possibility of exploring the idea of social network.

v

The thinking that has gone into this symposium has been the result of much discussion and argument: it represents substantially a collective effort and involved more people than those who have published papers in the symposium. In particular Mr Roger Wood presented fascinating papers about the development of social relationships among African farmers in an area of recent settlement in which he made considerable use of the idea of social networks. Since this symposium was to be concerned specifically with urban studies, however, his papers could not be included here. The group, centred on the Department in Salisbury and the Institute in Lusaka, broke up after November 1965; they are now widely scattered. Further close discussion, except among a few of us who had landed up in Manchester, was no longer possible and some of the contributions have developed beyond the form in which they were originally submitted. There are therefore some discrepancies and differences of opinion from one paper to another.

Furthermore, the papers of Bruce Kapferer, Pru Wheeldon, David Boswell and Peter Harries-Jones were written while they were still engaged in fieldwork and before they had had an opportunity of analysing their material fully. Subsequent analyses may well present different emphases and almost certainly a more sophisticated use of the ideas first put forward here. They show a considerable advance, however, on empirical data on social networks at present available and for this reason alone, irrespective of the intrinsic interest of the analyses themselves they are worth publishing.

Individual authors have expressed their gratitude to those to whom they feel personally indebted. As a group we feel particularly indebted to Max Gluckman who has been the main inspiration in many direct and indirect ways to the studies that are presented here. The ideas had their origin in the Department he established in Manchester, they were developed there under his stimulating guidance and continue to do so today. We also owe a debt to our colleagues who formed part of the seminar in Salisbury and whose observations and contributions we have probably incorporated without knowing their origins. I refer to Sister Mary Aquina, Dr Kingsley Garbett, Mr Peter Fry, Dr Norman Long, Mr Blackson Lukhero, Mr A. Sommerfelt and Professor Jaap van Velsen. We are also indebted to the many colleagues at Manchester who commented on and criticized the papers which Bruce Kapferer, David Boswell and I read at seminars in March 1966. We are also grateful to the Publication Committee of the Institute for Social Research (formerly the Rhodes-Livingstone Institute) of the University of Zambia under whose auspices the book is being published and to Mrs Barbara Hulme who has done much of the typing involved.

J. Clyde Mitchell

Contents

Contents

List of Figures

List of Tables

CHAPTER I

The Concept and Use of Social Networks[1]
by
J. Clyde Mitchell

Metaphorical and analytical usages
A colleague of mine who recently sent me a copy of a book he
had written, playfully inscribed in it: 'And these three things
abideth—class, role and network—and the greatest of these is network.' He was teasing me about our common interest in social
networks but his joke, like all jokes, had a serious core to it. It is
perhaps too early to say just how important the concept of social
network will be in sociology. Insofar as British studies are concerned, the use of 'networks', as an analytical rather than a metaphorical concept, dates only from 1954. Since then there have been
a few studies which have made extensive use of it but the idea
is becoming more and more popular.[2] This popularity seems to
have two quite different origins. The first derives from a growing dissatisfaction with structural-functional analyses and the
search, consequently, for alternative ways of interpreting social
action. The second is in the development of non-quantitative
mathematical ways of rigorously stating the implications entailed
in a set of relationships among a number of persons.
    The image of 'network of social relations' to represent a com-
plex set of inter-relationships in a social system has had a long
history. This use of 'network', however, is purely metaphorical

[1] The notions in this introduction have been developed in close association
with the contributors to this symposium and with others who have been
members of seminar groups in Salisbury and Manchester. In particular I would
like to thank Dr G. K. Garbett, Mr M. B. Lukhero, Mr A. Sommerfelt,
Dr J. van Velsen and Mr Roger Wood who were members of the Salisbury
seminar. I would like also to thank all those who took part in the Manchester
discussions and particularly to Dr André Béteille who discussed his joint paper
with Srinivas with me when he was in Manchester in 1966; to Dr G. K.
Garbett and Professor J. A. Barnes who guided me on matters of graph theoretic.
[2] Frankenberg (1966: 242) writes for example, 'Another helpful analogy
which I believe makes the first *major* advance in the language of sociology
since *role* is that of "network" ' (Original italics).

I

and is very different from the notion of a social network as a specific set of linkages among a defined set of persons, with the additional property that the characteristics of these linkages as a whole may be used to interpret the social behaviour of the persons involved. When Radcliffe-Brown, for example, defined social structure as 'a network of actually existing social relationships' (1952: 190), he was using 'network' in a metaphorical and not an analytical sense. His use of the word evoked an image of the interconnections of social relationships but he did not go on to specify the properties of these interconnections which could be used to interpret social actions except at the abstract level of 'structure'. Perhaps more often than not the word 'network' when used in sociological contexts is used in this metaphorical way.[1]

The danger in representing persons as nodes in a network, and the complex relationships between them as lines, had led Firth (1954: 4–5) to caution against taking a metaphor to be more than it is. Reader points out that as a metaphor the notion of 'network' subsumes, and therefore obscures, several different aspects of social relationships such as connectedness, intensity and status and role (1964: 22). But the metaphorical use of the word, however common it is, should not prevent us from appreciating that it is possible to expand the metaphor into an analogy, as Reader would say, and use the concept in more specific and defined ways.

One of the ways in which a metaphor may be transformed into an analytical concept is to identify the characteristics on which its heuristic usefulness rests, and then to define these characteristics in terms of general theory. Insofar as the idea of social networks is concerned it has been used in sociological writings in a variety of different ways ranging from the purely metaphorical, as we have already seen, to the precise and restricted way required in mathematical graph theory.

In graph theory a finite set of points linked, or partly linked, by a set of lines (called arcs) is called a *net*, there being no restriction on the number of lines linking any pair of points or on the direction of those lines. A *relation* is a restricted sort of net in which there can only be one line linking one point to another in the same

[1] In the same way that MacIver uses 'web' in the definition of society as the web of social relations (MacIver and Page, 1962: 5). A recent example of the non-specific use of the notion of network is in a paper by Adams (1967).

direction, i.e. there are no parallel arcs. A *digraph* is a relation in which there are no loops, that is there are no lines which link a point back to itself directly without passing through some other point. A *network* in graph theory is a relation in which the lines connecting the points have values ascribed to them, which may or may not be numerical.

In sociological writings the word 'network' may be applied indiscriminately to any of these somewhat different structures distinguished in graph theory. When Beshers and Laumann (1967) talk of 'a network approach to the study of social distance' in a recent paper for example, they are concerned with mobility as the passage of individuals through paths leading from an initial occupational category through intermediate steps to some terminal category. They use the transition probability of moving from one category to another, to represent a measure of the gap between the occupations. This is in accord with the graph theory definition of a network.

The notion of the social network that Barnes (1954) introduced in his study of a Norwegian island parish approximated to that of a digraph in that the connections between the persons were thought of in terms of single links (i.e. there were no parallel arcs) and loops were plainly inapplicable but there was no limit to the number of persons involved. Mathematical graph theory is not restricted to finite nets but in sociology, as we shall argue later, it is usually necessary for pragmatic reasons to work with an identifiable set of persons and the relationships that exist among them. The notion of network used by Bott (1957), Philip Mayer (1961), Epstein (1961), Pauw (1963) and Adrian Mayer (1966) is closer to the idea of a digraph since they restrict the persons in a given network to a finite number and they do not take particular account of the multiplexity of links of the persons in the network. The contributors in the book accept the finite nature of the network and also pay special attention to the multiplexity of links. For them, a social network is a net in which there are no loops but in which the arcs may be given values. In other words it is thought of as being finite, but there may be several links in either direction between the persons in the network and these links may be accorded different qualities or values.[1]

[1] F. E. Katz (1966: 203) defines networks as 'the set of persons who can get in touch with each other' and contacts as 'the individuals who comprise a network'

The interest in these studies focuses not on the attributes of the people in the network but rather on the characteristics of the linkages in their relationship to one another, as a means of explaining the behaviour of the people involved in them. This concept of a social network is similar to that of a sociogram as used by Moreno and his followers. Studies of sociograms developed mainly by social psychologists took such phenomena as clique formation, leadership, or task performance as their main problems (Festinger, Schachter and Back (1950); Cartwright and Zander (1960)). In these analyses they related the structure of friendship choices in a group to leadership or the performance of tasks. Out of these studies developed the identification of particular patterns of linkages—for example, the star, the wheel, the chain, the isolate, which could be used in the explanation of how test subjects performed the tasks they were set.

The application of sociometric methods to sociological field studies has been developed particularly by Loomis and his colleagues in the study of rural social systems (1953, 1967). There, is however, a difference between these studies which were based primarily on formal questionnaires and the studies which used the network concept as developed by Barnes and which have been based predominantly upon participant observation.

Another aspect of network studies developed by the social psychologists has been that of communication. Here the interest has been in the way in which rumours, ideas or information in general diffuse among a set of people. The chains of linkage along which the information can flow here have central importance. An example of the application of these techniques to a field problem is the study by Coleman, Katz and Menzel (1957) of the diffusion of knowledge of new drugs among a set of physicians in an American city.

The use of groups of subjects in experimental settings together with questionnaire methods to obtain data has led to the quest for methods of rigorous mathematical analysis of the characteristics of the linkages among the subjects.[1] These concerns, particularly

they are the members of the network set. It seems more in keeping with the common use of the word 'network' to refer to a network as the set of *linkages* among persons and contacts as the set of persons connected by these linkages.

[1] Procedures for analysing sociomatrices are discussed, for example in Zeleny (1941), Bavelas (1948), Luce and Perry (1949), Festinger (1949), Kephart

in respect of the flow of communication among a set of people who may know each other, have influenced the way in which sociological graph theory has developed. Witness, for example, the concern in digraph theory with directedness, connectedness, reachability, transmitters, relayers and receivers, strengthening, neutral and weakening points (Harary, Norman and Cartwright (1965)).

Barnes (1954), however, introduced the idea of a social network to describe an order of social relationships which he felt was important in understanding the social behaviour of the parishioners in Bremnes and which was not subsumed by structural concepts such as groups based on territorial location or on occupational activities. He later used the concept to draw the distinction between the type of social network which would characterize a community like that of Bremnes and the type which would be characteristic of a classical tribal society. The interest here is in the morphological features of the network itself and their implications for social behaviour rather than in the flow of communications through the network, though communication-flow is not excluded by Barnes's approach. This step whereby the relationship of the linkages in a network to one another is taken to be a salient factor in interpreting social action is one of the steps whereby the metaphor of a social network is expanded into an analogy and made analytically useful.[1]

This was demonstrated particularly in Bott's study of conjugal roles in London families (1955, 1956, 1957). In this study she correlated the morphological characteristics of the networks of

---

(1950), Luce (1950), Beum and Brundage (1950), Harary and Ross (1957), Coleman and MacRae (1960), Beaton (1966) and particularly Harary, Norman and Cartwright (1965).

[1] The significant point here is that in using the idea of 'networks' to interpret the social behaviour of any particular individual the behaviour of other people with whom he is not directly in contact must be taken into account. Nadel (1957: 16) when discussing the idea of 'network' expresses the notion thus: 'Let me stress that I am using the term . . . in a technical sense. For I do not merely wish to indicate the "links" between persons; this is adequately done by the word relationship. Rather, I wish to indicate the further linkage of the links themselves and the important consequence that, what happens so-to-speak between one pair of "knots", must affect what happens between other adjacent ones.' I personally would modify the 'must' to 'may' in his statement to avoid the implication of necessary functional integration.

the families she was studying with the allocation of conjugal roles within the family. The attractive feature of Bott's study was that her dependent variable (conjugal roles) was not patently connected with her independent variable ('closed' or 'open' networks of the couples). The elucidation of this unexpected relationship led to a set of illuminating hypotheses about conjugal role behaviour which have stimulated several subsequent enquiries (Udry and Hall (1965), Nelson (1966), Aldous and Straus (1966), Turner (1967)).

It is unfortunate, however, that this striking and stimulating study should have had the effect of associating the notion of social networks almost exclusively with conjugal roles. Where network ideas have been used specifically, they have been used to test Bott's original finding instead of to extend their application to other types of sociological problem to which, perhaps, their relevance appeared to be more obvious.[1] Several British social anthropologists, however, were able to see the significance of the ideas suggested by Barnes and developed by Bott, and have applied them to somewhat different problems.

Philip Mayer (1961, 1962, 1964) and his colleague Pauw (1963), for example, specifically used the idea of social network to elucidate the behaviour of different types of migrants and of settled townsmen in the South African town of East London. They have concentrated on the important point made by Bott, that the behaviour of people who are members of a 'close knit' group of friends is likely to be considerably influenced by the wishes and expectations of these friends as a whole, while those whose acquaintances do not know one another may behave inconsistently from time to time without involving themselves in embarrassment.

Epstein (1961)[2] on the basis of an examination of the social contacts of one of his African research assistants over a few days, suggested that Bott's division of social networks into 'closed' and 'open' types could be applied to different parts of a single personal network, the relatively 'closed' parts forming an effective network and the relatively 'open' part an extended network. He used this idea to explain how the norms and values of the local élites in a town percolated into the ranks of the non-élites with whom the

---

[1] Williams (1963) is an exception for although he deals mainly with kinship he clearly recognizes the importance of other types of networks in the rural community he studied.   [2] Reprinted at p. 77 below.

élites themselves had no direct contact. Subsequently, in a paper given to a seminar in Manchester in 1962, and published here (Chapter IV), he supplemented his earlier paper by showing how gossip which flowed along a chain in the network of a typical member of the social élite of Ndola was transmitted against a background of the norms and values of the social status of the people in that chain.

Adrian Mayer (1966) used the idea of a social network somewhat differently. He traced the chains of influence through which a candidate in an election solicited support and showed how the successful candidate was able to reach a particularly extensive body of potential supporters in this way. The contributions of Wheeldon, Kapferer, Boswell and Harries-Jones in this symposium all illustrate further extensions of the use of social networks in the Barnes tradition. Wheeldon (Chapter V) examines a challenge to leadership in a voluntary association in a Eurafrican community in a Central African town and uses the concept of social networks to show how the established leadership is able to bring pressure to bear upon their antagonists by means of their links through common intermediaries. Kapferer (Chapter VI) analyses a dispute that arises in a processing plant on a mine and shows how the parties in the dispute activate links with their fellows to mobilize support for their own particular point of view. Boswell (Chapter VII) describes how people in three different sets of social circumstances in Lusaka when they are bereaved utilize existing links with people to mobilize special help. Finally, Harries-Jones (Chapter VIII) shows how links based on common rural origin, kinship and proximity are used to establish the 'grassroots' organization of a political party in a Copperbelt town.

These applications of the idea of social network in the Barnes/ Bott sense, stem from a common origin and have been developed by the contributors to this book in common seminars and shared discussions. They therefore use the same basic set of ideas and postulates although each study in turn differs in the way in which these are used to interpret the field data. Each writer has used the concept as a means of elucidating some aspect of his field observations —however different the particular problems were in which he was interested. Social networks may be used to interpret behaviour in a wide variety of social situations and clearly are not limited to the study of conjugal roles alone.

Structuralism and social networks

An important point in the use of the notion of social networks in the interpretation of field data is that it is complementary to and not a substitute for conventional sociological or anthropological frameworks of analysis. It was introduced into British social anthropology in the first instance particularly because the conventional categories of structural/functional analysis did not appear to be adequate when anthropologists began to make studies outside the ordinary run of small-scale, isolated 'tribal' societies. When Barnes started studying his Norwegian island parish using the approach which was customary amongst British anthropologists in the 1950s he found this approach inadequate for his purposes. He distinguished in the first place two types of social structure in the community. The first was the territorial system in which domestic, agricultural and administrative activities took place. The second was the herring fishing industry in which men were engaged in activities for a relatively short time. These two 'fields' of social relationships, however, did not constitute the entirety of social relationships, for Barnes went on to say:

I find it convenient to talk of a social field of this kind as a network. The image I have is of a set of points some of which are joined by lines. The points of the image are people, or sometimes groups, and the lines indicate which people interact with each other. We can, of course, think of the whole of social life as generating a network of this kind. For our present purposes, however, I want to consider, roughly speaking, that part of the total network that is left behind when we remove the groupings and the chains of interaction which belong strictly to the territorial field and the industrial systems.

This field of social relationships Barnes saw as being made up of 'ties of friendship and acquaintance which everyone growing up in Bremnes society partly inherits and largely builds for himself' (Barnes, 1954: 43).

The framework in which Barnes was working at the time was heavily influenced by the structural approach, the most sophisticated examples of which were represented by the work of Evans-Pritchard and Fortes in the decade between 1940 and 1950. In this approach, reflected also in much American sociology at the same period, the behaviour of persons was interpreted largely in terms of their membership of 'bounded' groups and their involvement in social institutions or, at the other end of the scale, in small groups in terms of dyadic interaction. Thus F. E. Katz, pointing to the utility of the idea of networks in sociological analysis writes: 'There are conceptual gaps between micro-sociologists and macro-sociologists and between normative structuralist and behavioural interactionists.' He goes on to propose 'a way of looking at social networks in the hope that this may close some of the conceptual gaps' (1966: 199).

Structural/functional analyses represented a marked step forward in sociological analysis and provided a deeper understanding of behaviour than had been possible before, particularly when applied to small-scale localized societies. The 'institutional' structure of the Nuer or the Tallensi in terms of kinship, and its politico-jural extension the lineage, provided a coherent and systematic framework into which nearly all the daily activities of people and their relationships with one another could be fitted. But the inadequacy of this approach became apparent when social anthropologists began to direct their attention to more complex societies such as Bremnes, to urban communities in India and Africa, and to small-scale societies which lacked single pervasive structural characteristics in terms of which their morphologies could be depicted. Thus van Velsen who studied a 'stateless' society whose social relationships were marked by a lack of predictability and certainty, found the 'structural' approach inadequate. He notes that structuralist interpretations involve generalizations about the behaviour of people in terms of the positions they occupy in the social system but that these generalizations based as they are on abstractions ignore individual deviations from the pattern. These deviations, however, van Velsen argues are essential elements of social action and must be subsumed by the analysis. In his study he does this through situational analysis (van Velsen, 1964, 1967): in the studies presented in this book the notion of the social network is used instead.

There appear, in fact, to be three different orders of social relationships which are characteristic of large-scale societies—possibly of all societies—but particularly of urban social systems (Mitchell, 1959, Epstein, 1962). These are:

a. the *structural order* by means of which the behaviour of people is interpreted in terms of action appropriate to the position they occupy in an ordered set of positions, such as in a factory, a family, a mine, a voluntary association, a trade union, political party or similar organization.

b. the *categorical order* by means of which the behaviour of people in unstructured situations may be interpreted in terms of social stereotypes such as class, race, ethnicity, 'Red' and 'School' among the Xhosa in East London.

c. the *personal order* by means of which the behaviour of people in either structured or unstructured situations may be interpreted in terms of the personal links individuals have with a set of people and the links these people in turn have among themselves and with others, such as the social networks of the families in Bott's study.

These are not three different types of actual behaviour: they are rather three different ways of making abstractions from the same actual behaviour to achieve different types of understanding and explanation. The contention underlying the studies reported in this symposium, therefore, is that structural studies, even when supplemented by an account of the social categories which are meaningful in general social interaction are insufficient to explain the details of social behaviour. To do this an account of the social networks of the actors involved is essential.

The characteristics of social networks
Those who have used the notion of social networks in the interpretation of field data have found it necessary to distinguish certain features or characteristics of these networks as being germane to the explanation of the behaviour they have sought. The majority, so far, have concentrated on the nature of the links among people in the network as being the most significant feature. This is what Barnes has referred to as the 'mesh' of the network and Bott as 'connectedness'. It is the feature which Philip Mayer sees as distinguishing between the social networks of 'Red' and 'School' migrants, and the feature which marks off the effective from the extended network in Epstein's paper (Chapter III).

But as yet there seem to be no commonly accepted set of criteria which might be used to distinguish the characteristics of one type of network from another. This is partly because the study of personal networks requires meticulous and systematic detailed recording of data on social interaction for a fairly large group of people, a feat which few fieldworkers can accomplish successfully. Certainly the earlier writers who made use of the notion have not provided enough systematically recorded detail in their accounts to make it possible for readers to check their interpretations. Even in Bott's study, which so far has been the most thoroughgoing in this field, we are nowhere given the detailed information necessary to understand clearly the relationships that couples have with other couples in their 'network'. Her conclusions, therefore, cannot be checked. She does not, for example, list the couples involved in the 'close-knit' networks and indicate the precise linkages among them. Nor does Epstein or Philip Mayer, or Pauw do this. Epstein does in fact describe the contacts that his field assistant, Chanda, makes as he goes about his affairs in two specific days in Ndola but this is done in narrative form and the requisite data, for example, to allow a diagram of Chanda's network to be drawn, are not available. Philip Mayer discusses the 'closed-networks' in which 'Red' migrants are involved but does not, in fact, present us with lists showing us which of these live together in town, how many are in the rural areas and so on. Pauw lists the persons said to be in the 'networks' of three persons in his study but does not provide the data from which it is possible to check his estimate of the extent to which the networks are 'open' or 'closed'.

But this deficiency arises in part also out of the lack of a set of features which are commonly accepted among sociologists as most likely to be germane to the understanding of behaviour in network terms, and to which observers might systematically direct their attentions when they are in the field. Furthermore, even if such a list of criteria were available, there is no standardized way of recording the information about networks which will allow subsequent detailed and systematic analysis. The fieldwork required for a systematic check of the interconnections in a single network, as Bott points out (1957: 49), is likely to be onerous, this apart from such difficulties as defining what constitutes a 'relationship' meriting the recognition of a link between two people which may justifiably be represented by an arc in a graph.

From the work that has already been done on social networks, however, there appear to be several morphological and several interactional characteristics which are likely to be apposite in any attempt to describe social behaviour adequately. The morphological characteristics of a network refer to the relationship or patterning of the links in the network in respect to one another. They are *anchorage, density, reachability* and *range.* The interactional criteria on the other hand refer to the nature of the links themselves and are the *content, directedness, durability, intensity* and *frequency* of the interaction in the links. We may now consider each characteristic in turn.

a. *Morphological criteria*

1. *Anchorage.*[1] When Barnes originally wrote about social networks he had in mind the general ever-ramifying, ever-reticulating set of linkages that stretches within and beyond the confines of any community or organization. His notion about the 'mesh' of the network refers to the network as a whole and is not related to any specific reference point in the network. This idea is sometimes denoted by the phrase 'the total network'. But the idea of the total network must be a broad generalization. When Barnes, for example, makes the distinction between the total network of small-scale and large-scale societies by referring to the number of separate links that would be necessary to get from any one person and back to him, he is making a generalization about the characteristics of the totality of all links in that society. If this proposition were to be tested it would be necessary to trace the shortest paths of a large number of people in the community from themselves through others and back to themselves and to express the generalization as an average or median number of links. In practice, however, many difficulties would present themselves to a fieldworker who tried to designate the characteristics of 'mesh' of a total network as for example, the difficulty that in all societies the path from an individual back to himself via his parents would represent a universally minimum path of three steps. The idea of the total network is essentially a general heuristic concept: as with similar general concepts such as Gemeinschaft

---

[1] Graph theorists refer to the point source of a 'tree' as the 'root' of the graph (Ore, 1962: 59; Busacker and Saaty, 1965: 29). As I understand it a 'root' cannot have a positive indegree (i.e. cannot have links coming in to it) a restriction which would make the notion inapplicable to most social networks. In the absence of a better term I suggest the term 'anchorage' to refer to the point of orientation of a social network.

and Gesellschaft, when it comes to actual fieldwork it is always necessary to specify the context. In so far as social networks are concerned this involves isolating part of the total network and considering the characteristics of that part only.

The criteria to be used in partitioning the total network for detailed examination present a problem. The sociometrists normally work with a distinct group of subjects—the boys in a scout troop or the children in a classroom. But the problem for the sociologist is more difficult since he is concerned with the behaviour of individuals in a social situation which may be affected by circumstances beyond the immediate context. The person to whom the actor is orienting his behaviour may not be physically present though he would almost certainly be in the individual's personal network. The behaviour of a child towards another in a classroom, for example, will probably be conditioned by its knowledge that its mother knows the mother of the other. The network links in this case would need to extend beyond the classroom to the parents of the children. How far the links of a network need be traced depends entirely upon the field-worker's judgement of what links are significant in explaining the behaviour of the people with whom he is concerned. This implies that normally a network must be traced from some initial starting point: it must be anchored on a reference point.

The point of anchorage of a network is usually taken to be some specified individual whose behaviour the observer wishes to interpret. Which individual is taken will turn on the particular problem that the observer is interested in. Epstein took Chanda, Adrian Mayer took the Congress candidate in Dewas, Pauw gives several examples of networks centred on different types of permanent town-dwellers in East London. This has led to the specification of this type of network as ego-centred though the term 'personal network' may be more acceptable. Barnes, in his contribution to this symposium, argues that it is preferable to retain the word 'network' for the 'total network' so that for him the terms 'ego-centred' or 'personal network' are self-contradictory. Accepting the necessity of anchoring a network analysis on specified individuals, however, he calls the set of direct links of that person with others his 'primary star'. He then goes on to distinguish the primary zone, i.e. the primary star together with the inter-connections among the persons in the primary star; the secondary star i.e. the persons connected by two steps to ego, the secondary zone as the secondary star together with the inter-connections among the persons in the secondary star; and so on. One assumes that the order of the star or zone that needs to be taken into account to explain behaviour of ego will change from problem to problem. These concepts and terms clarify issues by identifying those aspects of the network which are likely to be significant for analytical purposes. The terms 'ego-centred' and 'personal networks', however, are so widely used that it is likely that they will be retained to signify the combination of stars and zones which the fieldworker wishes to designate as relevant for his purposes.

We have no experience yet with the application of Barnes's schema to empirical data, but other experience suggests that it will seldom be necessary to go beyond the second order zone to trace influences on the behaviour of individuals.

In interpreting the behaviour of the workers in the cell room of the mine he studied, Kapferer considers the direct links of workers with each other to be most significant. To avoid confusion with less specific uses of the word 'network' he calls this part of the network the 'reticulum'. Wheeldon is concerned with the links which connect the antagonists in the dispute she studies: the part of the total network that is anchored on the two persons concerned and which links them at the most through three intermediaries. Boswell looks at the 'action-sets' centred on the bereaved persons in his three cases and these provide examples of the use of third-order links in personal networks. Harries-Jones centres, in his study, on the leaders of the party cells in the township he studied.

The point of view taken in these essays is that a network is most conveniently anchored on an individual. Bott uses the idea of joint networks, i.e. relationships which a couple together have with some other person. Barnes (1954: 43) and Jay (1964: 137) both argue that a network may be considered as anchored on a group. Taking a group as the point of anchorage of a segment of a network, however, involves difficulties arising out of the fact that a group is itself an abstraction derived from a consideration of selected aspects of the total social behaviour of the people considered to be members of the group. A link connecting one group to another can only mean that the groups as wholes are in some sort of relationship to each other. A network anchored on groups in this way could be constructed but care would have to be taken to ensure that the links connecting the groups all represent the same level of abstraction.[1] A more cogent objection to the use of groups as points of anchorage for networks turns on the importance of the idea of multiplexity of social relationships[2] among people in a social network. The relationships that link the people who form a group are by definition single-stranded relationships, those in a network may be multiplex—a fact which might be important in explaining the social action involved. It seems probable that most of the propositions concerning the relationships among groups could be restated at a somewhat lower level of abstraction in terms of the links among the various individuals concerned. If this is so there is much to be said for the presentation of analyses of network relationships as being anchored on an individual chosen particularly because of the part he plays in the events being analysed.

2. *Reachability*. The degree to which a person's behaviour is influenced by his relationships with others often turns on the extent to which he can use these relationships to contact people who are important to him or alternatively, the extent to which people who are important to him can contact him through these relationships. This is the general idea of reachability in a segment of a network (Harary, Norman and Cartwright, 1965: 32). Reachability is also the basic idea underlying Barnes's notion of 'mesh' in his contribution to this symposium (pp. 62 ff. below). This concept should be differentiated, however, from that of density or 'completeness' which refers rather to the extent to which everyone in a set of ego's contacts knows everyone else. Reachability merely implies that every specified person can be contacted within a stated number of steps from any given starting point. If a large proportion of the people in a network can be contacted within a relatively small number of steps then the network is compact in comparison with one in which a smaller proportion may be reached in the same number of steps. The point may be illustrated by the following three hypothetical networks.

---

[1] The procedure here would be analogous to constructing a condensed digraph in which the groups would be represented by strongly connected components. See Harary, Norman and Cartwright 1965: 50 ff. An example is provided in Harries-Jones analysis pp. 335–36 infra.

[2] This concept is discussed below p. 22.

	A	B	C	D	E	
A	0	1	1	1	1	4
B	∞	0	1	1	1	3
C	∞	∞	0	1	1	2
D	∞	∞	∞	0	1	1
E	∞	∞	∞	∞	0	0
	0	1	2	3	4	10

(a)

	A	B	C	D	E	
A	0	1	1	1	1	4
B	∞	0	∞	∞	∞	0
C	∞	∞	0	∞	∞	0
D	∞	∞	∞	0	∞	0
E	∞	∞	∞	∞	0	0
	0	1	1	1	1	4

(b)

	A	B	C	D	E	
A	0	3	1	4	2	10
B	∞	0	∞	1	∞	1
C	∞	2	0	3	1	6
D	∞	∞	∞	0	∞	0
E	∞	1	∞	2	0	3
	0	6	1	10	3	20

(c)

The symbol ∞ indicates that the point at the head of the column cannot be reached from the point at the head of the row no matter how many steps are traversed.

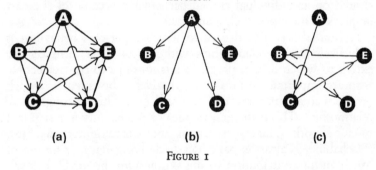

(a)   (b)   (c)

FIGURE I

The reachability in each network may be summarized by distance matrices, that is, in matrices where the number of steps taken to reach specified individuals appear in the intersection of the rows and columns for specified individuals, e.g. in distance matrix (c) A can get to E in two steps but to B in three steps. In matrix (a) A can reach all 4 points in one step: B, 3; C, 2; D, 1; and E can reach no point directly.

There are thus two distinct dimensions in the compactness of a network: (a) the proportion of people who can ever be contacted by each person in the network and (b) the number of intermediaries that must be used to contact others or, in other words, the number of links that must be traversed to reach the people concerned. I am aware of no measure which expresses the compactness of a graph by taking these dimensions into account. A somewhat crude measure may be computed by taking into account the proportion of points reached per person per step. For example in diagram (a) A reaches 4 points in 1 step, 3 in 2, 2 in 3 and 1 in 4 steps, an aggregate of 10 over all possible steps. B reaches 3 in 1 step, 2 in 2 and 1 in 3; C reaches 2 in 1 and 1 in 2; D reaches 1 in 1 step and E reaches none at all. Hence over the 5×4 possible steps an aggregate of 20 points are reached, an average of 1·0 points per step out of the possible maximum of 4 or a proportion of 0·25 points per step.

By similar reasoning in diagram (b) A reaches 4 points in 1 step, but no other point in subsequent steps. None of the others in the network reach any point in the 4 possible steps they may take. Thus the aggregate of points reached over all possible steps is 4, an average of 0·20 or proportion of 0·05 points per step. In diagram (c) A reaches 1 point in each of 1, 2, 3 and 4 steps; B reaches 1 point in 1 step; C reaches 1 point in 1, 2, and 3 steps; D reaches none and E reaches 1 point in 1 and 2 steps, an aggregate of 10 points over 20 possible steps or an average of 0·5 or a proportion of 0·125 points per step. Thus network (a) with an index of 0·25 is more compact than network (c) with an index of 0·125, and both are more compact than network (b) with an index of 0·05.

The sociological significance of the notion of reachability lies in the way in which the links in a person's networks may be channels for the transmission of information including judgements and opinions especially when these serve to reinforce norms and bring pressure to bear in some specified person. This is particularly important where links of this kind lead back to ego, a point which Bott, Epstein and Philip Mayer have all chosen to emphasize in their studies (see pp. 36–38 below).

3. *Density.* One should not confuse reachability, however, with density as Bott seems to do when she refers to the connectedness of networks. She defines 'connectedness'[1] as the extent to which the people known by a family know and meet one another independently of the family (1957: 59). She goes on to say: 'I use the word *close-knit* to describe a network in which there are many relationships among composite units, and the word *loose-knit* to describe a network in which there are few such relationships.' But the consequence of the 'connectedness' of the network

[1] The use of connectedness here for what is in effect density is confusing especially in view of the somewhat specialized uses of the word in topology and graph theory.

in her terms is the extent to which the norms of the family are or are not reinforced through intercommunication.

Much the same point is made by those who have followed Bott. Reader (1964: 22) for example, defines 'connectedness' as: 'lines of communication between those whom Ego knows and who know him, and know one another'. Epstein describes the effective part of Chanda's network as 'Those people with whom Chanda interacts most intensely and most regularly, and who are therefore also likely to come to know one another, that is to say that part of the total network which shows a *degree of connectedness*'[1] (1961: 57, my italics).

The implication here is that where the relationships among a set of persons are dense, that is, where a large proportion know one another, then the network as a whole is relatively compact and relatively few links between the persons need to be used to reach the majority.

Density, as Barnes calls it, is used in the sense in which completeness is used in graph theory, i.e. the extent to which links which could possibly exist among persons do in fact exist. In Figure 1(a) we may say that ten links are possible among the five persons involved if we count a link either from A to B or B to A as one link. In fact all these links exist and the network is complete or has maximum density. Barnes (see pp. 63–64 below) proposed a measure of density as

$$200a/n(n-1)$$

where *a* refers to the actual number of links and *n* to the total number of persons involved including Ego.

The fact that density and reachability are not directly related one to the other is illustrated by the density and degree of reachability in Figures 1(b) and 1(c). The density of each network would be $800/20 = 40\%$. The reachability in the two figures is different, however, 1(b) being somewhat less compact with an average of 0·8 points reached per step than 1(c) with an average of 1·0 points.

In sociological analysis our interest is primarily in reachability since norm enforcement may occur through transmission of opinions and attitudes along the links of a network. A dense

---

[1] By 'total network' Epstein means here all the personal relationships Chanda is involved in, not the 'total network' in Barnes's sense.

network may imply that this enforcement is more likely to take place than a sparse one but this cannot be taken for granted. The 'pattern' of the network must also be taken into consideration.

4. *Range.* Some people have many direct contacts while others have few. The first-order range or number of persons in direct contact with the person on whom the network is anchored is likely to be a significant feature of a personal network as Wheeldon and Kapferer show, if the emphasis is on mobilizing support for Ego.[1] Kapferer and Wheeldon use the idea of range in different ways. For Wheeldon range is made up of the number of people in direct contact with Ego combined with the social heterogeneity of the individuals concerned. A person in contact with thirty others of widely differing social backgrounds would have a wider range network than a person in contact with thirty people of the same general social background (p. 133 below). She does not attempt to quantify the concept but uses a broad classification in small-, middle- and large-range networks.

Kapferer (p. 224 below) incorporates some of the aspects of range in his idea of 'span'. The span of a person's network in Kapferer's paper is the proportion of actual links among a specified set of persons with whom Ego could possibly have contacts. Using Barnes's terminology (p. 59 below) it is the proportion of links taken up by Ego's primary zone of all the links among the specified set of persons. Kapferer's measure of span has direct relevance to an individual's mobilization of support in a dispute which is the core of the problem he is considering. Wheeldon is interested in the range of personal networks from the same point of view.

The relationship of range to other morphological and to interactional features of networks has not yet been fully explored. Pauw (1963: 191) remarks that the closed (i.e. relatively dense) networks of migrant labourers in East London, South Africa, comprise fewer units than the open (i.e. relatively sparse) network of a town resident. This we might suppose would be related in turn to the variety of contexts in which the person interacts with the people in his network but this has not yet been demonstrated.

In general it appears that there is probably a limit to the number

[1] Range here refers to direct contacts. The range could equally well refer to second, or any order contact if necessary.

of people with whom an individual might be in direct and regular
contact, but as yet there does not seem to be enough empirical
evidence available to provide an estimate of what it might be.[1]

b. *Interactional criteria*

As the adjective suggests, the morphological characteristics of
personal networks—anchorage, density, reachability and range—
refer to the 'shape of the individual's network'. They may be
equated with the structural aspects of social behaviour. At the
same time the behaviour of individuals vis-à-vis one another may
be perceived in terms of the characteristics of the interactional
process itself: content, directedness, durability, intensity and frequency of interaction. Some of these interactional aspects may be
crucial in understanding the social behaviour of the persons
concerned.

5. *Content.* From a sociological point of view the most important interactional aspect of the links in a person's network is that
which concerns the meanings which the persons in the network
attribute to their relationships.[2] The links between an individual
and the people with whom he interacts come into being for some
purpose or because of some interest which either or both of the
parties consciously recognize. We may speak thus of the content
of the links in a person's network. This content may be, among
other possibilities, economic assistance, kinship obligation, religious cooperation or it may be simply friendship.[3] The actors and
the observer in any social situation are able to understand the
behaviour of those involved because it is accorded a meaning in
terms of the norms, beliefs and values which they associate with
this behaviour. In sociometric studies, normally, the content of
the networks is severely restricted, frequently by referring only to
friendship or to leadership choices. Some sociologists also tend
to look at personal networks in terms of restricted interactional
contents. Barnes, for example, conceived the network as made up
of the 'ties of friendship and acquaintance which everyone grow-

[1] A general impression is that this limit in an urban environment may be about
thirty persons.
[2] Here the approach converges with that of the symbolic interactionists. See
for example Rose (1962).
[3] Content here has much the same connotation as Caplow's idea of 'ambience'
(1955).

ing up in Bremnes partly inherits and largely builds up for himself' (1954: 43). Later he says that 'the content of network relationships is what is left when we remove the groupings and chains of interaction which belong strictly to the territorial and industrial systems. In Bremnes society, what is left is largely, though not exclusively a network of ties of kinship, friendship and neighbourhood' (p. 43). In other words the total network would include the content of all social interaction—including that stemming from the territorial and industrial systems as well. The personal network, however, is confined in Barnes's analysis effectively to friendship, neighbourliness and kinship since the phrase 'though not exclusively' is not expanded in his paper. Bott (1957) apparently accepts this definition of networks since she talks consistently of networks in terms of friends, neighbours and relatives (pp. 58 ff.). These she describes as areas of informal relationships (p. 101) which she contrasts with the 'more specialized and formal relationships that are maintained with doctors, clinics, schools and so forth' (p. 102).

Other writers have also laid emphasis on the content of the links in personal networks. Thus Adrian Mayer (1966: 108) illustrates in a diagram the diverse linkages of the 'action-set' of the candidate in the election. The links between the individuals (sometimes groups) are distinguished by their content, i.e. these vary between one or more of the following: kinship, occupational, caste, State, economic, religious links, and so on. Mayer goes on to say that while the outgoing relationships may be diverse, the incoming links all have the same content—support for the candidate in the election.

The various contributors to this symposium who use the idea of 'content' have used it in slightly different ways. Epstein, whose paper was written much earlier than the others, describes it thus:

What we observe are a number of individuals conversing together, recounting experiences, exchanging news of acquaintances and friends, discussing personal matters or ideas and so on. Implicit in much of this conversation are the norms, values and attitudes of general or special application recognized in the society. An important part of such conversation is made up of gossip, that is discussion of the affairs and behaviour of other persons in their absence. Viewed then in terms of the content of interaction the network may also be seen as a series of links in a chain of gossip (1961: 58, p. 112 below).

Here content refers to the content of the *flow of communication*
through the network. Kapferer refers to this aspect of interaction
as *exchange* content (p. 212 below) which distinguishes it clearly
from the notion of content which Wheeldon uses in her paper
(p. 132 below). Here content refers to the *normative* context
in which interaction takes place such as kinship, friendship, common religious beliefs, economic obligation etc. It is to normative
content that I refer when I use the word 'content'.

The content of a link in a social network therefore is not directly
observable but must be inferred by the observer in the normal
course of study. The observer's abstracting the content of network links contrasts with the sociometric approach of using
questionnaire methods which deliberately specify the content of
the links between the respondents in the study. The use of observation to collect data on networks has consequently led to the
recognition of the importance of the concurrence of several contents in one network link. Network links which contain only one
focus of interaction are called 'uniplex', or more simply, 'single-
stranded' relationships. Those which contain more than one content on the other hand, following Gluckman, are called multiplex,
or more simply, multi-stranded or many-stranded relationships
(Gluckman, 1955: 19; 1962: 27).

The identification of distinct contents in a network link, however, involves problems which stem from the difficulties an observer has of attributing meanings to the behaviour of the actors.
In fact the sociologist abstracts the content of a network relationship from the actual behaviour of the protagonists involved in
terms of what seems to him to be reasonable explanatory concepts. The actors' perceptions of the meanings in a set of relationships are relevant data imparting 'rationality' to actions, but
they are not necessarily analytical concepts. The problem emerges
particularly clearly when we consider a 'single-stranded' relationship. It could be argued that from an actor's point of view no
relationship has only one content. This is true. The observer,
however, for his purpose may be justified in treating a set of
actions as being so dominated by one set of identifiable norms
that for all intents and purposes the relationship is single-stranded.
An employer-employee relationship may be so treated if sex,
ethnic status, socio-economic status, religious persuasion or any
other possible category of social interaction can be ignored as

unimportant. Equally a multiplex relationship implies that the observer finds it necessary to consider the co-existence of several different normative elements in a social relationship. The perceptions of the strands in the relationship, however, depends upon the analytic purpose of the observer.[1]

In Wheeldon's and Kapferer's contributions the notion of multiplexity in relationships linking people at one or more steps assumes considerable importance because the implication here is that people who are bound in many ways together are more securely bound to each other.[2] Kapferer expresses this by saying that multiplex relations are 'strong', that is, are more likely to result in a person's being mobilized for support than a person who has only single-stranded relationships with another, though it should be noted, that Kapferer's notion of multiplexity is based on exchange content and not on normative content which Wheeldon makes specific use of in her contribution. The idea of multiplexity also relates Frankenberg's notion of 'social redundancy' (1966: 278 ff.) to the personal network. The basic idea behind 'redundancy' is that in multi-channel routes alternative channels are available if any one channel should fail. A multi-stranded relationship is analogous to a multi-channel communication route insofar as effect on social behaviour is concerned, since people in a multi-stranded relationship interact with one another in many different contexts and are therefore less likely to be able to withdraw completely from contact with one another as people in a single-stranded relationship are able to do.[3]

In terms of graph theory, a multiplex relationship may be represented structurally as a set of parallel arcs linking two points, but in terms of the contents of these arcs, sociologically speaking, the separate component arcs might fruitfully be considered to be

[1] I am grateful to Peter Harries-Jones who raised the problem of uniplex relations with me.

[2] Compare this with Nadel's (1957: 71) formulation. 'The advantages of role summation (i.e. multiplexity) lie in the strengthening of social integration and of social control. For the more roles an individual combines in his person, the more is he linked by relationships with persons in other roles and in diverse areas of social life.'

[3] This seems to be the point behind Williams's discussion of the coincidence of kinship, friendship, neighbourhood, political and religious 'networks' in the rural parish he studied. See Williams (1963: 205 ff.).

links in different graphs as for example a graph of kinship links
or a graph of links of economic assistance. This has considerable
relevance when the relationship of the content of network links
to sociological abstraction in terms of institutions is considered
(see p. 45 below). The importance of looking at the *structural*
as well as the *interactional* aspects of network links is that the
influence through several links of dissimilar content may be
traced. For example, from the point of view of the social behaviour of the people in a personal network, the fact that A is
linked to B in terms of kinship and B to C in terms of occupational
ties, may or may not affect the extent to which A can enlist C's
services for some purpose or other. In his description of the electoral action-set in Dewas, Adrian Mayer deals with this point
explicitly, for the out-going links were often of a quite varied
character in second and third steps although the in-coming links
were always electoral support.

A number of points arise out of the coincidence of multiplexity
and morphological features of personal networks. One of these
is raised specifically by Srinivas and Béteille (1964: 167) who
write: 'Traditionally the village lived in a narrow world where
the ties of locality, caste, kinship and hereditary service led back
and forth between the same set of persons. Relations were multiplex in character, and the circuit of relations had a tendency to
become closed.' Barnes (1954: 44) had already suggested that the
social network in small-scale societies was characterized by a
tight mesh. Gluckman (1955: 19) had pointed out that in small-
scale societies relationships tended also to be multiplex. A question
which might well be investigated by the use of networks is the
degree to which one condition necessarily implies the other.

6. *Directedness.* Thus far we have been discussing networks
without specifying whether the relationship between the people
in the network should be considered either as oriented from one
to the other or reciprocal. The problem is particularly germane
in sociometric studies where frequently the topic of investigation
is friendship choice. A person may choose another as his friend
without having his choice reciprocated, so that the link between
the two is essentially a directed one. In some of the problems
which could be examined by means of social networks the directionality of the relationships would not be important, but frequently there is a lack of reciprocity in a relationship which lends

itself to a more accurate description in terms of a directed network link. In the action-set described by Adrian Mayer the content of the links was closely related to the direction of the relationship. In the networks considered by Barnes and Bott, however, the contents were largely kinship, friendship and neighbourliness, which could be taken to be reciprocal relationships so that directionality was not very important.

But clearly employer-employee relationships, or patron-client relationships which might easily constitute a link in some personal network, are not reciprocal in this way, so that the influence of one person on the other will differ according to the direction of the interaction. Here the question of directedness becomes relevant. In all the field-work papers in this symposium the direction of the flow of interaction is significant. In both of the situations described by Epstein the direction of the flow of information—attitudes about norms or gossip as the case may be—is significant, since the content of the information (as apart from the content of the interaction) is determined by the direction in which it flows in each case. Boswell's and Harries-Jones's contributions are examples of action-sets which depend upon directionality in the same way as that described by Adrian Mayer. In Wheeldon's and Kapferer's contributions the direction of flow of influence is clearly of considerable importance since in both cases the person's purpose was to mobilize the people contactable through his network in support against an antagonist.

In graph theory, relationships which are not reciprocal may be represented simply by asymmetric adjacency matrices, in which zeros are entered when a relationship is not reciprocated. If the absence of reciprocity is to be distinguished say from indifference, signed graphs could be used in which negative entries could represent the lack of reciprocity and zeros simply the absence of relationships. Where multiplex relationships are involved, however, additional difficulties arise since the direction of flow of interaction in terms of one of the strands of a relationship may be the opposite to the flow in terms of another. Financial aid, for example, may be reciprocated by political support. The reciprocity in terms of different types of goods and service is clearly of considerable importance in understanding social action in many spheres of life. In these circumstances a compound adjacency matrix consisting of the union of several separate matrices which reflect links in terms of specific interactional contents could be used for analytical purposes.

7. *Durability.* A network exists in the recognition by people of sets of obligations and rights in respect of certain other identified people. At times these recognized relationships may be utilized for a specific purpose—to achieve some object, to acquire or pass on some information, to influence some other person in a desired direction. The recognized rights and obligations are thus potential links in an action-set or communication-set (see p. 36 below) which may come into being for a specific object and disappear again when that object is attained or frustrated. But the underlying consciously appreciated expectations which people have concerning other identified people obviously persist over a longer period than an action- or communication-set, and may last, as in the case of kinship, for a person's lifetime.

The personal network, as used in this symposium, exists situationally in the sense that the observer perceives only those links of the total set of potential links which are activated and being used by the actor at any one moment, and which the observer considers are significant for the problem he is interested in.[1] At the one extreme there are the links in the action-set which are mobilized to cope with a particular crisis, such as the action-set described by Boswell which was mobilized to handle the funeral of the stranger woman whose daughter had died in hospital. This came into being for a specific purpose, lasted for a few days and then subsided into latency again when the purpose had been met. At the other extreme there are networks which are in constant use and are the means for innumerable transactions before and after the specific incident which is the point of the analysis. The action-set mobilized to cope with the funeral of the woman of élite parentage, also described by Boswell, is a good example of this type of network.

The underlying set of consciously recognized rights and responsibilities out of which a particular personal network may be realized or an action- or communication-set mobilized is itself

[1] F. E. Katz distinguishes between *actual* networks, i.e. the contacts which are latent or activated and are currently in Ego's network; potential networks, i.e. the *possible* networks of which Ego can be a member; and proximate networks, i.e. the persons with whom Ego is *likely* to establish contact (1966: 204). His distinction between latent and activated links is relevant here.

constantly changing as people build up new acquaintances, make new contacts or lose touch with others. This has been explicitly commented on by several writers. Bott (1957: 90), for example, makes the point that among her twenty families there were five who were in the process of undergoing a change in their network organization. Srinivas and Béteille say that 'a network even when viewed from the standpoint of a single individual has a dynamic character. New relations are forged, and old ones are discarded or modified' (Srinivas and Béteille, 1964: 166). We have very little empirical information on the way in which the latent network changes over time particularly through the life-cycle of the individual. Analysis of the social and geographical mobility of individuals could be considerably enriched by studies of the composition and structure of personal networks in different situations. A well-known hypothesis concerning the adjustment of families who have been rehoused on new estates turns specifically on the extent to which old network linkages become inutile and inoperative and the extent to which the families develop new links involving substitute rights and obligations in their new locations (Young and Wilmott, 1957: 106 ff.). It seems possible also that the expansion and contraction of personal networks at different phases of the life-cycle hold out considerable potentialities for understanding the domestic cycle, social maturation and similar problems.

Harries-Jones is able to provide some valuable data on the changes in a personal network where he is able to reconstruct part of the network of an individual concerned in a political struggle in the early 'fifties and show how it had changed in the succeeding decade during a time of dramatic political development (see pp. 335 ff.). More studies of this kind will be essential before the detailed empirical evidence will be available to allow generalization about the processes of change in networks.[1]

8. *Intensity.* The intensity of a link in a personal network refers to the degree to which individuals are prepared to honour obligations, or feel free to exercise the rights implied in their link to some other person. The intensity of a person's relationship with a close kinsman is likely to be greater than that with a neighbour, for example. Reader, who recognizes this component of the per-

[1] There are, of course, several studies of sociograms over time, but few of social networks as they have been conceived of here.

sonal network uses an almost identical definition as 'the "strength" of the ties which bind person to person, the willingness with which the parties are prepared to forgo other considerations in carrying out the obligations associated with these ties' (1964: 22).

Face-to-face interaction is not a necessary condition for the obligations entailed in a relationship to be honoured. There are many circumstances where an intense link with a person living some distance away may be an important factor in the behaviour of an individual. The ties of people who have recently moved to a housing estate with friends and kinsmen left in the area out of which they have moved, and the links which migrant workers retain with their homes provide examples of this. Srinivas and Béteille describe the relationship of migrants who have left a village with those remaining behind: 'Many of those who have left the village continue to influence its social life in a number of ways. Often they return at harvest time to receive rents and renew leases with their tenants. Several of them send remittances to relatives in the village every month. On occasions of birth, marriage and death they revisit the village' (1964: 166). Philip Mayer similarly emphasizes the role of rural kinsmen particularly in the life of 'Red' migrants living in town (1961: 90 ff.). The point here is that even if there is infrequent communication between an individual and the people who are in his network, the intensity of the relationships—that is the value with which the individual invests them—may be sufficient to make the people important elements in the individual's network.

Harries-Jones makes a distinction between two types of links based on common local origin which in fact turns on the notion of intensity. One set of links is with those people from an individual's home area to whom he acknowledges some obligation or feels free to call upon for assistance when he needs it. In other words the individual has intense relationships with these people. But they may not be immediately available to him when he needs help: some may live in the rural home area, some in another town and others in the town where the individual happens to be living at the time. The effective set of links with people of common local origin is with those of them who in times of need for support or services are living sufficiently closely at hand for him to be able to contact them personally or for him to be contacted by them personally.

Kapferer's notion of the 'strength' of a relationship, by which he means the ability of a person to exert influence over others, is also closely related to the notion of intensity. His proposition that the 'strength' of a relationship is related to the degree of its multiplexity, however, points to different origins of intensity in network links. Not all intense relationships are multiplex; there are some, like close kinship, for example, which in many societies are defined by virtue of moral obligations as 'intense' in their own right. This bears on Wheeldon's analysis of the way in which Armstrong prevails upon his antagonists to capitulate. Some of the links through which he operates are intense because of multiplexity and others are intense because of the moral value they are invested with as, for example, the relatively less multiplex kinship ties (see Figures 10, 11 and 12, pp. 163, 167, 169 below), but Armstrong achieves his ends ultimately by manipulating intense links.

Measures of intensity are obviously difficult to devise; and for the time being, we must rely on the assessment of the fieldworker for estimates of this important interactional characteristic of personal networks.

9. *Frequency.* An obvious characteristic of interaction in a network which is amendable to more simple quantification than the other characteristics so far described is the frequency of contact among people in a personal network. An aspect of this characteristic is the regularity of contact which Reader points to as a possibly significant factor in interpreting social behaviour (1964: 22). A high frequency of contact, however, does not necessarily imply high intensity in social relationships. Contacts with workmates may be both regular and frequent but the influence of these workmates over the behaviour of an individual may be less than that of a close kinsman whom he sees infrequently and irregularly, in the sense that if a man must choose between either meeting the wishes of a close kinsman or those of his workmates, he is less likely to frustrate his kinsman. Although counts of the frequency of contacts have been extensively used by 'interactionist sociologists' in the past, their relevance to network analyses seems to be marginal.

The observation, recording and analysis of personal networks

These characteristics of personal networks have all emerged as relevant in the course of studies of networks either in this symposium or in other analyses preceding it. No one study has taken into account all of these characteristics: one or other of the characteristics, rather, has been selected in one study as of major importance and another in a different study. In any systematic study of networks, however, it would appear that account would need to be taken of at least the cited characteristics as well as, possibly, of others not considered here. To record data of this range and in this detail requires not only a clear idea of what characteristics of networks need to be observed and recorded but also an intensity of fieldwork few research workers are able to achieve. The paucity of detail concerning networks to which I have already referred bears testimony to this.

The fieldwork may involve interviews, the use of questionnaires, or of observation both participant and non-participant. Bott used interviews in her studies. She reports that there were, on the average, thirteen interviews ranging from eight to nineteen of over an hour each with every family (1957: 21). The details were apparently recorded descriptively on schedules and subsequently abstracted in the form needed for her generalizations. Bott herself says: 'Before the analysis of networks can become at all precise it will be necessary to define degrees of intimacy and obligation of the various relationships.' She attempts to do this with regard to kinship but goes on to say:

> If possible it would be advisable to interview several members of a network, following the links of interaction from one to another, instead of relying on what each couple say about their network as I have done. Precise definition of connectedness would require quantitative analysis of the total network, of the independent network of husband and wife, of the joint network (the people with whom they have joint relationships) and of that part of the total network composed of kin, that composed of friends and that composed of neighbours. But the data of the present research are not consistent or detailed enough to permit such quantitative analysis (Bott, 1957: 61).

Using interviews has the disadvantage that the fieldworker becomes aware of the characteristics of the network only from the point of view of his respondent and is, therefore, precluded from checking the actual quality of the relationships. This could be prevented if the fieldworker were to interview every person that a respondent claims to be in his personal network. Clearly to conduct interviews of the same depth with all the people in a personal network would be an onerous task. Yet if any degree of validity for the accuracy of the data is to be claimed, there seems to be no alternative. Difficulties arise, also, with regard to the assessment of such characteristics as the intensity, the content, and the directionality of the relationships if the fieldworker using interview techniques must rely on the respondent's own estimate of them.

Sociometrists have used questionnaires successfully in collecting information for constructing sociograms. In the experimental situation in which this technique is used the choices are limited to persons within the group. This enables mutual and unilateral choices to be identified and used in identifying leaders and isolates. But the detail of information needed for the construction of a sociogram is limited. The content of the interaction is restricted almost entirely to friendship and characteristics of the interaction such as content, frequency and intensity are of secondary importance. It seems, therefore, that questionnaires should play a supportive rather than a major role in the study of more general sociological situations where contents may vary and other characteristics of the network are likely to be significant.[1] Harries-Jones's analysis of the local cells of a political party in Luanshya draws on survey material and demonstrates the fruitful way in which it may be used in conjunction with personal observation and knowledge of the situation.

In many ways, however, the most reliable and adequate information is likely to be obtained through direct observation. The observer over a period of time is able to make his own assessment of the interaction of an individual with others around him and to record its characteristics. This is the method Epstein used to gather information about the spread of gossip. He recorded the content of the conversation as he ran across it in general fieldwork. Kapferer used more formal and systematic observation in his study of the Cell Room. The situation was sufficiently limited for him to be able to watch the persons involved and to overhear most of the conversations going on. Special difficulties are involved

---

[1] Rural sociologists, in particular, seem to have used sociometric methods to identify leaders in the communities they have studied. See for example Loomis and Beegle (1950), Loomis (1967).

if the observer is a participant in the interaction, i.e. is one of the elements in the network. Here his own presence is likely to influence the situation. Nevertheless a good deal may still be accomplished as shown by the contribution of Wheeldon and Boswell, both of whom used participant observation.

Epstein, Wheeldon, Kapferer and Boswell in their contributions to this symposium have all made use of the technique of situational analysis, used by Gluckman in his study of social relationships in modern Zululand (1940). Harries-Jones's analysis is based primarily on direct observation, but instead of starting with a series of linked events as the others do, he presents his material more formally, setting out the structure and organization of the institutions involved before proceeding to show how personal networks based on 'home boy' ties, kinship and locality, provide the basis for the organization of the primary cells of a political party.

The situational approach on the other hand starts with the series of connected incidents—possibly trivial incidents. The analyst then sets out to show how these incidents may be interpreted in the light of the regularities in the social structure in which the incidents take place. These incidents are the passage of a research assistant during a day or two in Ndola, the gossip about a *cause célèbre* and how it reached the ears of a number of the African élite in Ndola, a challenge to the leadership in a voluntary association run by Eurafricans in a large town, a dispute on the shop floor concerning a 'rate-buster', and three deaths and the funeral arrangements made in connection with them. These sequences of incidents serve to raise, in dramatic form, the problems in the interpretation of the behaviour of the *dramatis personae* which the observers are then able to set about explaining.

The fieldwork upon which the analysis is based is, of course, much deeper and more extensive than mere presence when the incidents constituting the situation took place. It involves a detailed knowledge of the ecological and institutional background of the participants as well as familiarity with the 'history' of the situation. Thus although his opportunities of observation were sharply constrained by his position as a fellow mourner, Boswell was able to interpret the behaviour of the actors in the situation partly in terms of the institutional structure of mourning behav-

iour. But the explanation of the specific behaviour in the situation necessitated his tracing out and recording the characteristics
of the relevant networks of the actors.

These data are normally recorded in descriptive and narrative
form in the course of normal fieldwork. The characteristics of
the personal network must then be abstracted from the field
notes. But the interaction is often so complicated that even the
most gifted fieldworker stands to miss a good deal. Some system-
ization of the categories of information to be recorded would
obviously improve the quality of the analysis which can be made
on the basis of the observation. The use of a schedule setting out
the types of data that need to be recorded for each network
would no doubt fill some of the gaps. Recording the interaction
in diagram form in the field may also help to bring out the
characteristics of the network. The frequency of relationships,
for example, may be represented by heavy lines linking symbols
representing the actors, the different contents by coloured lines,
the direction of interaction by arrows in the lines and the intensity
by the relative distance between the persons in the diagram, a
technique suggested also by Reader (1964: 22). But in the end
the accuracy and reliability of the information will depend on the
ability of the fieldworker to observe and to note down what is
relevant for his purpose.

Recording the density and directedness of relationships in the
form of an adjacency matrix (Harary, Norman and Cartwright,
1965: 110 ff.) has the advantage that it ensures that the fieldworker
systematically checks all possible relationships in the network
so that it is collated in a form which makes possible subsequent
mathematical manipulation. Here the person on whom the network is anchored is placed at the top left-hand corner of the
matrix and the other persons in the network placed along the
vertical and horizontal axes in some order which is of interest
in the analysis. One dimension of the directedness, for example
the giving of economic help, is allocated to one axis and the
reciprocal, for example the receipt of economic help, along the
other. A 'one' is entered in the cell where a link exists, otherwise
a zero is recorded. The leading diagonal from the top left-hand
corner to the bottom right-hand corner, i.e. where the row and
column corresponding to the same individual intersect, is left
blank. A systematic check of each cell in the matrix will ensure

that all possible relationships have been enquired into—a procedure which is essential if the reachability and the density of
the network are to be made use of subsequently. Different matrices
may be used for different contents, thus allowing the study of
multiplex relationships by the simple superimposition of matrices.

Network data in matrix form are amenable to manipulation
by mathematical techniques based on graph theory provided always that the sociological assumptions do not violate the mathematical assumptions underlying graph theory. The use of graph
theory, pioneered by the sociometrists, holds considerable
promise for stating the properties of networks in formal terms
which should enable sociological deductions to be tested more
rigorously than previously. Formal mathematical procedures have
been developed to handle some properties of networks which
may be relevant for sociological analysis. Examples of such
properties are connectivity; clusterability; reachability; weakening, neutral and strengthening points; structural balance and so
forth (see especially Flament, 1963; Harary, Norman and Cartwright, 1965). These procedures involve operations on adjacency
matrices which may be tedious and tiresome especially if the
matrices are large and the operations are performed manually.
Computers can be programmed to perform the operations but
the difficulties in access to programmers and limitations of availability and costs of machine-time are an impediment to their
widespread use. Garbett's (1968) ingenious adaptation of the use
of optical coincidence cards for operations on adjacency matrices
makes available a cheap and simple device for the analysis of
networks containing as many as fifty persons.

The combined use of graph theory and probability mathematics provides an intriguing method of erecting model networks
with which empirical networks can be compared. Rapoport and
his colleagues in studying sociograms for example have developed
the idea of a 'random net' which is a model of the structure of
friendship choices in a given set of persons on the assumption
that friends are chosen entirely at random. This model network
is then modified on the assumption that certain constraints operate in the choice of friendships: for example, that if two people
are chosen by a third as a friend they are more likely than not
to choose each other as friends (Rapoport and Horvath, 1961;
Foster, Rapoport and Orwant, 1963). This device has been applied

to the study of the extent to which delinquent children tend to associate together in a school in America after having taken into account such 'biases' influencing friendship choices as mutual friendship, sharing friends and sex (Fararo and Sunshine, 1964).

So far there seems to have been very little traffic between sociological graph theorists on the one hand and fieldworkers on the other. Those interested in the properties of social networks which can be handled by formal mathematical procedures seem to develop sophisticated schemes which bear little reference to empirical data. On the other hand those who have looked at field data in terms of social networks have not drawn extensively on the concepts of graph theory and the procedures derived from them, to spell out the implications in their material. Harries-Jones in his contribution to this symposium is one of the few to make use of several notions derived from directed graphs in order to bring out some of the features of his field material.

Yet the potentialities of the use of model networks, such as 'random nets' to estimate the extent to which socio-economic status, race, ethnicity, sex, age or any other social characteristics influence the alliances and oppositions in a set of social relations, or of the formal properties of graphs to represent the characteristics of social networks such as clusterability, or connectedness, are considerable. In particular the possibility of using graph theory to derive indices suitable for use in sociological analysis is particularly inviting. So far there are few measures of this sort which are generally acceptable. One which has been used for a long time is the estimate of density which is simply the number of links that actually exist expressed as a proportion of the maximum number of links that could possibly exist. Barnes in his contribution to this symposium shows how a measure of this sort can be applied to describe the properties of different types of personal networks (see p. 64 below). Wheeldon uses a simple measure of multiplexity to distinguish different types of network and a rough measure of range which could easily be refined (p. 134 below). Kapferer employs measures of span, density, and multiplexity and classifies the personal networks of the workers in the cell room by the combination of these properties. He is able to show how these measures may be used to demonstrate the differential effect of networks of different types on the behaviour of workers in the cell room (pp. 215 ff. below).

There is obviously much to be gained by standardizing as much
as possible the types of measure which may be relevant in the use
of networks in sociological analyses, but it will take time before
the properties which are considered relevant will be commonly
accepted and agreed upon. Some progress in this direction will
be made by the adoption wherever possible of the terms and
concepts used in graph theory so as to achieve some uniformity
in definition and usage.[1] Sociological analysis, however, should
not be constrained by a lack of terms where these are clearly
necessary for analysis. Concepts such as multiplexity and intensity
which are not part of graph theory appear to be essential in the
use of networks in sociological analysis. Graph theory will no
doubt prove to be invaluable in elucidating some of the characteristics of social networks but it is essentially a formal logical technique. The notion of a social network on the other hand is a
sociological concept and as such has a much wider connotation
than a digraph.

Norms, networks and communication
So far sociologists who have used the notion of personal networks
to analyse their field material have done so in relation to two
different problems. The first of these relates to the flow of communication through networks, especially in relation to the
definition of norms,[2] in what we might call a communication-set.
This is one of the points which emerges from Bott's work when
she says: 'When many of the people a person knows interact with
one another, that is when the person's network is close-knit, the
members of his network tend to reach consensus of norms and
they exert consistent informal pressure on one another to conform
to the norms, to keep in touch with one another, and, if need be,
to help one another.' Correspondingly, 'when most of the people
a person knows do not interact with one another, that is when his
network is loose-knit, more variation on norms is likely to develop

[1] Barnes (1969), however, observes that the confusion over terminology
among graph theorists seems almost as great as that among sociologists over
networks. Hopefully books like that of Harary, Norman and Cartwright
(1965) and the useful paper by Barnes himself will encourage some uniformity
among the sociologists at least.
[2] Here the work of social psychologists such as Back, Festinger, Hymovitch,
Kelley and Thibaut who study the flow of rumour in experimental and other
groups is relevant. See, for example, Back *et al.* (1950).

in the network and social control and mutual assistance will be more fragmented and less consistent' (Bott, 1957: 60). It is also this process that Philip Mayer seizes upon in his analysis of the incapsulating process amongst 'Red' migrants in East London. 'The Red syndrome', he writes, 'which has been termed incapsulation, has one feature, a "tribal" type of moral conformism, stressing the superiority of the original undiversified institutions; such institutions make for multiplex relations and the close-knit type of network; and this again makes for consistent moral pressure and conservatism. The processes are two-way or circular ones. It is by refusing to branch out into new habits that Red migrants retain a basis for close-knit networks; while it is by keeping the networks close-knit that they inhibit cultural branching out' (P. Mayer, 1961: 292).

'In the other syndrome', he continues, 'more characteristic of School migrants, we find a culture which has been more tolerant in principle of the engagement in diversified institutions; accordingly, a tendency towards the single-strand type of relation and the loose-knit type of network. Again this produces two-way or circular effects. Cultural specialization makes for looser-knit networks, while the looseness of the network allows for cultural specialization. The School culture, with its institutional diversification thus carries within itself its own dynamic of change in the migrant situation' (P. Mayer, 1961: 292).

The flow of information is also the point that Epstein selects as the aspect of the personal network to emphasize in his study of networks in towns. In his argument the norms defined in the relatively dense part of the personal networks of the élite in the towns are transmitted to other parts of the community and particularly to the non-élite through extended links in the network (pp. 111-13 below). In the paper in this symposium he is able to document in detail how information—in this case gossip about an adulterer caught *in flagrante delicto*—flows along links in a network anchored on one of his informants. He was also able to show how the network through which the information percolates slants the story so as to reaffirm the norms of the people in the upper part of the social system 'giving them a sense of identity as a distinct social class' (p. 126 below). This study by Epstein relates Gluckman's (1963a) discussions of the social role of gossip to the specific network in which it takes place and serves to give greater precision to Gluckman's ideas. In her contribution Wheeldon provides another example of this process. She describes how opinion and points of view about a rift among office-holders in a voluntary association, flow through links in a personal network from one antagonist to the other, so that they do not have to come face-to-face with one another and suffer an open breach in their relationships.

Instrumentality and choice

A second way in which personal networks have been used is illustrated particularly by Adrian Mayer's paper (1966). This essay analyses the use that people make of network linkages in order to achieve desired ends. Here the linkages are used for the flow of goods and services rather than the flow of information. Adrian Mayer calls this type of network an action-set.[1] In his view a certain number of linkages which exist in the total network in a community may be mobilized for a specific and limited purpose. This mobilization implies some transaction between the person at the centre of the action-set (in this case the candidate) and the persons in the action-set. In Mayer's words: 'This transactional element distinguishes action-set linkage from network linkage' (1966: 122). In terms of the specific situation that Mayer describes the transactional elements were in particular what he calls 'patronage' and 'brokerage'. In patronage the support is bartered for some specific promise: the resources had to be husbanded and awarded to influential people who would bring many votes with them. Brokerage on the other hand meant mediating between a person in the action-set and some other person with whom the candidate has special contacts. Mayer outlines the characteristics of the Dewas electoral action-set as follows:

a. many different out-going links were mobilized but the incoming relationships were all the same, viz. electoral support;
b. the links were sometimes based on group membership, e.g. members of the same wrestling gymnasium or a group of religious worshippers, but they might have been distant kinship or caste membership. Some links were between employer and employee, creditor-debtor or storekeeper-customer;

[1] Harries-Jones discusses Adrian Mayer's concept of action-set on p. 301 below.

c. it contains intermediaries or paths of linkages leading out from
    ego;
d. it is a bounded[1] entity, unlike the total network. It ends with
    the voters in the ward; and finally
e. it is not a permanent entity, it exists only until the election.

Adrian Mayer's conception of an action-set may be considered
as a special kind of instrumentally-activated personal network.
Both Boswell and Harries-Jones describe similar instrumentally-
activated networks in this symposium. Specific persons or categories of persons are called upon to provide goods, perform
services or contribute support for the person who is at the centre
of the network. In one of the cases that Boswell describes, those
who were mobilized were members of the Anglican Church,
people from the same tribe or merely people who had been
together at the hospital at the time of the death of the daughter
of the woman concerned. Harries-Jones shows that the political
party cells in the Luanshya African township drew upon neighbourhood, tribal and kinship links. A point of substance here is
the criterion used to include a person in any specified network.
Adrian Mayer in discussing the lateral links in an action-set (the
feature which would contribute towards 'density' in the action-
set) writes: 'lateral links are defined in terms of the relevance to
the criterion governing the formation of the action-set. In this
case only the lateral links connected with ego's election are
relevant. This is not to deny that there are many lateral *network*
ties linking people in the action-set, which are not used by ego
or his intermediaries to achieve their ends. We must distinguish
between the potential material of network links, and those links
which are actually used in the action-set's constitution. The lateral
linkage in an action-set does not indicate the complete pattern of
interaction between members' (Mayer, 1966: 111).

An action-set, therefore, is delineated in terms of the specific
transaction that brings it into being. A personal network on the
other hand denotes a set of linkages which exist simultaneously on
the basis of different interests and which persist beyond the duration of any particular transaction. An action-set may be looked
upon as an aspect of a personal network isolated in terms of a

---

[1] Barnes argues cogently (p. 66 below) that the term 'finite' is more apposite
here than 'bounded'.

specific short-term instrumentally-defined interactional content: the personal network itself is more extensive and more durable.

Certain difficulties arise, however, in identifying the limits or extent of a personal network. The first of these is that of determining the number of steps in the links radiating out from ego that need be taken into account to establish the 'boundary' of a network. Clearly some limit must be put on the number of links to be taken as definitive for any specific network; otherwise it would become co-extensive with the total network. This difficulty is resolved by fixing the 'boundary' of the network in relation to the social situation being analysed: the analyst traces links from ego to the constituents of the network and among the constituents themselves in as much as the links are necessary and sufficient to throw light on the problem being studied. I have suggested that in practice it seldom seems necessary to go beyond the second-order zone (see p. 19 above) but there can be no general rule and the 'order' of linkages traced must be determined by the canons of what can be taken to be an adequate explanation.

A second problem arises out of the fact already referred to (see p. 26 above) that not all of the potential links that a person may have with another need be activated at any particular moment. The relationship an individual has with some person may be dormant or latent until it becomes the basis of some social action. This is illustrated particularly by kinship relationships in towns. Kinsmen of many different categories probably exist in towns but they become recognized as *kinsmen* only when the content of the relationships becomes realized, i.e. when a person is able to claim services or aid in terms of the bond, or on the other hand respond to an appeal to him in terms of a kinship relationship. We need thus to distinguish between potential links in personal networks and those that are actually being used in social interaction.[1] As before the network must be defined operationally. The individual builds up a network in terms of his interests in whatever situation he finds himself and these interests, and the actions he takes in terms of them, define the effective links in a personal network. In this sense all personal networks have an instrumental basis to them.

[1] Williams makes the same point in distinguishing 'effective' from the 'non-effective kin' (1963: 168).

Recruitment to networks

The existence of relationships which are potentially links in a personal network but which do not necessarily become used raises a problem about the way in which an individual recruits members to his network. Empirically it is clear that individuals recruit people to networks on the basis of many different relationships and that, further, the types of relationship they use for recruitment to networks varies with their social situation and their social position. The fieldwork papers in this symposium illustrate this. Wheeldon's contribution shows that in the inter-ethnic community she studied, personal networks were located almost entirely within the community itself though there were some links across the colour cleavage to Europeans. Since the community itself was small people were able to know a large proportion of its members personally. People were recruited to networks particularly through kinship links and through common membership to voluntary associations. In the much larger, transient and more anonymous African townships other more universalistic types of links, appropriate to the specific urban circumstances, were used in personal networks. One of these is the 'tribe', that is an ethnic category, and by extension the joking-tribe. The stranger woman in Boswell's case of the lonely escort utilized links of this sort, together with membership of a church, to build up an action-set to cope with the emergency she found herself in.

But people who have lived in a town for any period build up relationships with people in many different social contexts and these people may become part of a social network. In the funeral Boswell describes of the woodcutter killed in a motor accident the people mobilized in connection with the funeral were recruited from kinsmen, neighbours, fellow tribesmen, joking-tribesmen, business associates and members of the political party to which the dead man had belonged. The social network here reflects the variety of social relationship some particularistic and some universalistic in which this settled townsman had become involved. Also in the funeral where the deceased woman was a member of a well-known family in Zambia, the persons who were in the network mobilized for the occasion were almost entirely kinsmen but did include a few fellow-tribesmen, joking-tribesmen and clansmen, and a colleague or two of her brothers, almost all of them old schoolmates in high-status occupations, illustrating here the effect of social position in the composition of the network.

Kapferer examines social networks in a strictly circumscribed situation—the workplace—paying attention to the content of the social exchange between workers, as well as the normative content of the links. Apart from the actual job activities the exchanges involved conversation, cash assistance, personal services and joking. The normative context of the links among the workers however included tribal allegiance, joking-tribe and kinship categories (not actual kinship) and age, showing how even in a fairly restricted situation network links may be built up on many different bases. The workplace network, however, is only part of the personal network of each worker and an individual may have dealings with some of his workmates outside the work situation (i.e. the link in the network is multi-stranded), or he may not. But the wider social context is reflected in the composition of the personal network. Kapferer has been able to show in material not yet published that the type of network which workers in the municipal townships generate is different from that generated by workers living in the mine township. The network of the individual in the mine township contains a high proportion of people who work with him, several involving the wives as well as co-workers. But in the municipal areas the network is recruited from a wider variety of social categories and is therefore less dense. This difference may be related, Kapferer argues, to the greater mobility of the municipal areas and the greater occupational differentiation in it. The well-known distinction that Epstein draws between the unitary structure of the mine townships as against the atomistic structure of the municipal township (Epstein, 1958: 191) is here being spelt out in network terms.

Harries-Jones shows how a political association is built up at the lowest level from links pre-existing in the community. The relationship which was mainly utilized in building up the action-sets was that of having a common 'home' origin though this was often grafted on to putative or real kinship ties. But one of the points that Harries-Jones raises is the degree to which the obligations incumbent upon being a 'home-boy' are mandatory upon a person. The social category of 'home-boy' may exist as a set of norms applicable to a person with defined attributes. When two people interact in terms of these norms each becomes part of the other's personal network. But he argues that obligations to a 'home-boy' are not always honoured and more research is needed to establish in which social circumstances they are honoured and in which rejected.

Potential members of a person's network may thus be defined as a category of people who in terms of the general norms of values of the community might be expected to provide ego with some specified type of service or support or alternatively who might expect ego to provide them with some specified type of service or support. The relationships may imply considerable specificity such as support in an election between a candidate and some party supporter for example, so that the content of the network link is single-stranded and defined solely by the norms of the recruitment category out of which the network member was drawn. On the other hand the relationship may be diffuse and imply services and support of a general nature such as implied by neighbourliness or kinship.

But the potential relationship need not necessarily be activated and so become a linkage in a personal network. For this to happen the people concerned must become involved in some social action —some social exchange or transaction which converts the possible into an actual social linkage. There is an element of individual choice, therefore, in the make-up of any person's network in the sense that the individual seeks to establish and maintain contact with a number of persons in terms of his interests in them while he sees no point in extending casual contacts with a large number of others. Equally he may be morally obliged to accept the approaches of a number of other people but will maintain contact with only those that he must.

Each personal network, therefore, will be unique though obviously influenced by such factors as the social position of the person concerned and the social situation in which he is placed, the stage of the life-cycle he is at and a number of purely idiosyncratic factors relating to the individual's personal history. But we are interested in a systematic not an idiographic understanding of social behaviour. We must therefore consider the procedures by which unique linkages in personal networks may be examined within a framework of systematic sociological analysis.

Abstraction and structure

Since the links in a social network may be social contacts in terms of such a variety of different interests, it is almost certain that some of the links may simultaneously be part of groups or social categories in a larger context of interaction such as membership of a workgroup or membership of an ethnic group. Srinivas and Béteille made an important point in this connection which illuminates the relationship between the institutional structure of a community and the total network. They write:

It seems evident that the kinship network in India is relatively close-knit as compared, let us say, to the economic or political network. It may be that the same forces which lead to an extension and loosening of the economic and political networks also lead to the shrinkage and tightening of kinship networks in contemporary India. Territorial dispersal and mobility lead to the extension of economic and political ties: they often also lead to a shrinkage of the network of *effective* kinship relations based upon reciprocal obligations.

We have now been led to a point at which it is necessary to talk in somewhat more abstract terms. From viewing the concrete networks of interpersonal relations of a number of individual actors we have been led to talk about networks pertaining to different institutional areas. We can now speak about economic networks, political networks, ritual networks and so on. It is evident that when we speak, say, of an economic network we are making an abstraction. A concrete network of interpersonal relations cannot be wholly economic in its constitution, except in the limiting case. Generally such relations have economic components which have to be abstracted from their concrete matrix and then put together.

The economic system may be viewed as a network of relations regulating the flow of goods and services. The political system may, likewise, be viewed as a network of relationships regulating the flow of command and decision. It must be pointed out that the links in networks of this kind are unitary in character, as opposed to concrete networks of interpersonal relations where the links are usually composite or multibonded.

Economic, political and ritual networks of the kind described above would correspond to what Marion Levy characterizes as 'analytic' as opposed to 'concrete' structures. Thus a network of economic relations provides an understanding of the organization of production in a society, and a network of political relations provides an understanding of the distribution of power. Such networks in a complex society cut across the boundaries of communities and corporate groups, and in fact, serve to articulate them to wider social systems. And once we shift from the individual actor and his network of concrete interpersonal relations to the productive system and its corresponding network we move from the 'subjective' network of the actor to the 'objective' one of the observer (Srinivas and Béteille, 1964: p. 167).

An analysis of the structure of a community or organization in terms of its social institutions, therefore, is an abstract representation of its component systems of relationships. But the sort of abstraction an observer makes, as Srinivas and Béteille point out, determines the sort of structure he erects. Institutional analysis involves abstraction of a specified type of content from the links in a network of multiplex relationships in real life, and the representation of these relationships in systematic and summary form. The sequence of abstraction, after the initial act of observation, is from actual behaviour to multiplex linkages in networks, from multiplex relationships to what Barnes calls 'partial networks', that is in terms of a single specified content, and from partial networks to the institutional structures.

The fieldworker analyses his observation and is able to show how, amongst a specified number of people, relationships are built up in terms of a variety of normative contexts. A meets his obligations to B and C in terms of kinship norms and also because they are neighbours. B and C claim support from D and E whom A does not know, because they are their workmates and because they attend the same church. At this point the fieldworker can start building up a picture of the relationship among the people he is studying by constructing a network with multiplex links. Having done this he is able to examine the relationships of A, B and C as kinsmen abstracted from their neighbour statuses, that is he constructs a partial network. It is only at this point that he is able to compare relationships in partial networks based on kinship content in different areas and contexts and at different times to state the relatively enduring relationships which represent the structure of relationships among kin, and the set of systematized norms that constitute the institution of kinship. Regularities in the partial networks based on workplace association or religious associations likewise provide the basis of the construction of the structure of industrial relations or of churches and of the institutions associated with these structures.

It is at this point that the process of abstraction may be related to the concept of 'role'. In terms of the social network a role is the behaviour to be expected between two people in the light of a designated content of their link. The content of interaction, it will be recalled, refers to the meaning which actors attribute to their relationship in terms of its specific *raison d'être*. Content, through its meaning for the persons involved, in role theory thus becomes the normative framework of the role relationship encompassing the expectations of ego and alter of each other. The concept of role, therefore, becomes relevant in networks at the level of abstraction involving partial networks: role relates essentially to *dyadic* behaviour in terms of the content of the partial network.

A role-set by definition must be located within a partial network since the relevant alters in the role-set interact in terms of a common normative content that articulates their relationship. The role-set concept, however, remains essentially dyadic in that the roles in the set, although linked by their common institutional context, are conceptualized in isolation one from the other. The essential idea behind a social network on the other hand is that the variations in the behaviour of people in any one role relationship may be traced to the effects of the behaviour of other people, to whom they are linked in one, two or more steps, in some other quite different role relationship. A man may quarrel with a kinsman because the latter is linked through a workmate to an adamant political opponent of the former.

The flow of pressures and influences through a network in this way provides a means of examining the notions of functional integration in social systems. This may be approached by considering a classical problem in sociology; the differences between small-scale or 'tribal' societies on the one hand, and large-scale or 'modern' societies on the other. In small-scale societies where social relationships are typically multiplex a single social act may be construed in terms of roles in several different institutional contexts. A sacrifice at an ancestor shrine, for example, could be an act simultaneously within a kinship, a religious, an economic and a political context. The partial networks constituting the basis of an institutional analysis of the whole social system can thus be abstracted from a relatively small number of social actions. Conversely an institutional analysis subsumes a large proportion of the social actions in the community.

It is this coincidence of contexts or multiplexity of relationships which provides the basis for the notion of institutional integration and by implication, therefore, of equilibrium which characterizes the notion of a social system. This follows from the observation that if a person interacts with the same people in differing social contexts it is likely that his behaviour in one context will be affected by his behaviour in another. The multiplexity of the relationship leads to a strain towards consistency in behaviour. But the essential point is the extent to which the co-existence of different contexts in relationships among people is logically necessary, as against merely a matter of happenstance. The notion of multiplex links among the persons involved in a social network allows us to dispense with the *assumption* of institutional integration and 'equilibrium' and to approach the interrelationship of institutions rather as an empirical matter involving the extent to which partial networks must necessarily coincide in specified links between persons.[1] This presumably is the import of Reader's observation: 'Since, moreover, the "network" can be studied without reference to social or physical boundaries, the method seems at last to escape from presuppositions of closure and equilibrium' (1964: 20).[2]

The fortuitous as against the necessary coincidence of links in social networks enables us to understand the behaviour of persons in specific situations. Epstein's description of the course of the struggle between the Mineworkers Trade Union and the Tribal Representatives on the Copperbelt in 1957 illustrates this. Some Tribal Representatives were also members of the Mineworkers Union and revealed to the Trade Union officials the companies'

[1] This is in line with a recent trend in which the validity of the notion of functional equilibrium which has dominated sociology for the last twenty years is being challenged (see Buckley, 1967). The notion of 'structural balance', however, applicable to signed graphs, i.e. those in which the links connecting points may be designated as either negative or positive, provides a means of examining the inconsistencies in relationships among a given set of people. In this sense it provides a way of studying equilibrium, or the lack of it, in designated sets of social relationships (see Davis, 1963; Harary, Norman and Cartwright, 1965, Chap. xiii). The use of 'structural balance' to analyse empirical data, however, is rare: it remains largely a toy of the lecture-room theoreticians.

[2] See also his definition of ego-centric models: 'Starting from the social individual rather than from society, and involving only minimal presuppositions of structure and equilibrium. Such are role-theory and "network" models' (1964: 14).

intention to try to persuade mineworkers through the Tribal
Representatives to return to work during a strike. This led to an
open conflict between the two bodies and the eventual dissolution
by the Companies of the system of tribal representation (Epstein,
1958: 98–101). The chance coincidence of trade union links with
those of being a Tribal Representative here made it possible for
the Trade Union to acquire information which was important in
its struggle for power.

Many writers (e.g. Gluckman, 1962: 8; Barnes, 1954: 44;
Frankenberg, 1966: 257 ff.) have indicated that one of the characteristics of large-scale societies is the large number of single-
stranded relationships in them. The relative weakness of institutional integration in these societies is directly connected with the
paucity of multiplex relationships for there are few circumstances
in which people in large-scale industrial communities meet one
another constantly in a variety of social settings.[1] Instead their
activities in one sphere of life are comparatively isolated from their
activities in some other sphere. In social network terms the con-
stituent links of partial networks are largely independent of one
another and do not coincide.

This seems to be true particularly of social relationships in
towns and it is here, where the model of a functionally integrated
social system has proved inappropriate, that the approach to understanding social behaviour through the structure of the social networks of the people concerned has proved most useful (Mitchell,
1966). It is no accident that Bott, Adrian Mayer and Philip Mayer,
and Epstein, Barnes and the other contributors to this volume,
should have turned to the notion of the social network in their
quest to understand behaviour in the social situations they studied.
For the structure of social relationships of the rural parishioners
of modern Norway, the families in London, the local politics in
an Indian town, or the activities of contemporary African townsmen accords so little with the structure of communities commonly
described in anthropological writing, that some other approach
seemed essential.

It should be clear that this does not mean that the analysis

[1] Morris and Mogey (1965: 145 ff.) try to use the notion of networks to define
the 'neighbourhood' in studies of housing estates in England. Their promising
attempt, however, is hampered by their inadequate appreciation of the salient
characteristics of social networks.

of social relationships in terms of social networks is a substitute for an analysis in terms of social institutions. The two types of analysis start with the same basic empirical data but proceed to make abstractions in different ways. An institutional analysis utilizes partial networks to erect a logically coherent structure of norms and behaviour patterns as for example, the kinship system, or the religious system. Its success depends upon the simplifying process by which only a single aspect of the complexity of human behaviour is considered at a time. The network approach on the other hand deliberately seeks to examine the way in which people may relate to one another in terms of several different normative frameworks at one and the same time and how a person's behaviour might in part be understood in the light of the pattern of coincidence of these frameworks or 'contents'.

Because social networks ramify across and between institutions they provide a means of examining the inter-relationships of the behaviour of people in different contexts, a feature which the very abstraction necessary in institutional analysis precludes. Institutional analysis by its very process of abstraction must minimize the connection *between* institutions. In so doing it allows the analyst to represent a vast set of actions in terms of a common normative frame work in highly compact form. The relationship of one institution to another, however, must remain a postulate.

An analysis using social networks on the other hand, through the notion of multiplexity allows the behaviour in terms of one normative framework to be related directly to that in another. The interconnection between institutions, if it exists at all, can be demonstrated empirically in this way: it is not a postulate of the procedure.[1]

Networks and institutional analyses by their different assumptions and procedures in fact complement one another. The chance combination of normative frameworks in a network structure accounts for the individuality of a community while at the same time, a systematic institutional analysis is not precluded by it. In

[1] This is consistent with Blau's conception of the interpenetration of social structures. In discussing over-lapping memberships of groups in fact he writes: 'the networks of social relations that define their structures are interpenetrating, and the boundaries between them are neither sharp nor fixed . . .' (Blau 1964: 284). Note, however, that Blau is using 'network' here in a metaphorical way and not in the specific sense used in this book.

this way the uniqueness of particular empirical communities can be comprehended through the structure of network linkages within them, while at the same time their features may be seen in terms of the universal characteristics of social institutions in general. By concentrating on situations in towns in a region where institutional analyses have achieved some degree of sophistication, this book aims to provide some examples of how network and institutional analyses might be combined.

CHAPTER II

Networks and Political Process[1]

by
J. A. Barnes

Introduction
In the study of national politics we usually concentrate our attention on the working of social institutions that are specifically and explicitly political—parliament, parties, elections and diplomacy. At this level, where we have to look for data on political forms and processes is clear, however much we may argue about the interpretation of these data. But once we leave the national level, we have to hunt more carefully for the raw material of politics. It is easy to see that processes of alliance, challenge and compromise, trials of strength and allocation of rewards, similar to those seen at the national political level, operate within the region, district and village, and inside clans, companies, churches and other non-territorial groups; even within the family somewhat similar processes are at work. In this sense, then, there is something usefully described as politics even though it is not national politics. But these lower-level, or local-level, political processes occur within institutions that fulfil many functions that are not political. Political behaviour is here intimately bound up with actions that are aimed at other non-political ends, and can be isolated from these other aspects only analytically, not in terms of space, time or personnel. For example, the typical African village council is a multifunctional body, concerned with administration, justice, and even religion as well as with the specifically political task of the resolution of struggles for power; at any moment of time it may be serving any or all of these functions. Hence in looking at local politics it is inconvenient to concentrate narrowly on the social

[1] This paper was presented to the Wenner-Gren Symposium No. 32 on 'Local-Level Politics', Burgwartenstein, July 1966. It is published also in Swartz, M. J. (Ed.) *Local-Level Politics* (1968) Aldine Press. We are grateful to the author, the editor and the publishers for their permission to allow it to be republished here.

processes at work in specialized political institutions, for there may not be any. We have instead to take the view of politics implied in the expressions 'academic politics', the politics of sport, church politics and the like, and to seek wherever we can find them those processes whereby individuals and groups attempt to mobilize support for their various purposes and to influence the attitudes and actions of their fellows. In the words of Fallers (1963: 312), 'the polity or political system is viewed, not as a concretely distinct part of the social system, but rather as a functional aspect of the whole social system: that aspect concerned with making and carrying out decisions regarding public policy, by whatever institutional means'. At the local level either these political processes are carried on within an institutional framework ostensibly intended for some other purpose, such as the cult of the ancestors, the playing of football, or the celebration of marriage; or they cut across the institutional divisions of society and succeed because relationships established in one context are utilized in another. In this paper I am mainly concerned with politics in the second, unspecialized, sense, and with political process again in its second, transinstitutional type of manifestation. With these limitations in mind, I shall look at an analytical tool that several writers have found useful when writing about local politics, the concept of the social network.

In 1953 I read a short paper in which, *inter alia*, I mentioned the idea of the network (Barnes, 1954: 43–44), an idea I had picked up from my elders, principally from Fortes' book, *The Web of Kinship* (1949). I used it to describe how notions of class equality were applied, and how individuals made use of personal ties of kinship and friendship, in Bremnes, a community in Norway. Bott (1955, 1957) and others made use of much the same idea in different contexts and it appears that it may be useful in examining many kinds of social situation. A. C. Mayer (1966) has recently reviewed some of the relevant literature and has applied a refined version of the concept in his analysis of an election campaign in India. These and other reports show that the concept is useful in describing and analysing political processes, social classes, the relationship of a market to its hinterland, the provision of services and the circulation of goods and information in unstructured social environments, the maintenance of values and norms by gossip, structural differences between tribal, rural and urban societies, and so on. There is also a large body of writing on the use of the idea of a network in the study of industrial organizations and small groups (cf. Harary, 1959).

Perhaps because of the diversity of contexts in which the idea of a network has been applied, there is already a good deal of confusion in the literature, for each analyst reads a different interpretation into the writings of his predecessors and introduces new refinements to suit his own particular problem. I must take some of the responsibility for this, for what I wrote seems not to have been clear. I wrote as briefly as possible, saying only what was strictly necessary to describe the delimited Norwegian social scene I was examining. I did not distinguish between the distinctive features of all networks (in contrast to dyadic relationships, groups, categories and the like), and those features that happened to be present in the Norwegian network I described. Some readers assumed that these specific and local features must be present in all networks, and have introduced modifications to fit empirical situations where these features are absent. Other readers have misunderstood what I meant by the total network, perhaps because I did not give any reference to Radcliffe-Brown, from whom I had taken this idea. In this paper I will try to sort out some of these issues. Since my earlier article seems to have been written too elliptically, I shall guard against repeating this error by spelling out the issues as I now see them in what will probably be unnecessary detail. This paper is therefore largely a reluctant exercise in unapplied methodology.

There are four questions that can be asked. First there is the historical question: who said what, and what did he mean? I shall ignore this question, for Mayer and Mitchell (1966: 54–56) have reviewed the literature in social anthropology and this need not be done again yet awhile. Second, what are the useful concepts we need to be clear about? Third, for what kinds of analysis are they needed? Fourth, what names shall we give to these concepts? The last question should be trivial, but unfortunately it is not. Far too much of our time is wasted in arguments about names, but we cannot be sure that we are merely wasting our time unless we can distinguish between arguments about facts and ideas and argument about names. It is probably always going to be difficult to make this distinction in the social sciences, since the same terms have to do duty as technical terms and folk-concepts (cf. Barnes,

1962b: 407–9), but the distinction has to be made. Where possible I shall suggest ways of measuring characteristics, not only because this is one way of giving precision and comparability to our enquiries, but also because it is easier to argue about quantified concepts. They can be clearly seen for what they really are, analytical constructs, and not mistaken for Platonic essences.

We construct analytical tools not because they look beautiful but because we have a job of work to do with them. In particular we take measurements not for the joy of counting or to provide computer fodder but in order to prove or disprove some hypothesis. The kind of measurements we take is determined by the kind of hypothesis we are trying to test. The notion of network has been developed in social anthropology to analyse and describe those social processes involving links across, rather than within, group and category limits. The inter-personal links that arise out of common group membership are as much part of the total social network as are those that link persons in different groups, and an analysis of action in terms of a network should reveal, among other things, the boundaries and internal structure of groups. While there are other ways of discovering groups, the network concept is indispensable in discussing those situations where, for example, the individual is involved in 'interpersonal relations which cut right across the boundaries of village, sub-caste and lineage' (Srinivas and Béteille 1964: 166). It is appropriate where enduring groups such as parties and factions have not formed, and where individuals are continually required to make choices about whom they should look to for leadership, help, information and guidance. It helps to identify who are leaders and who are followers, or to demonstrate that there is no enduring pattern of leadership.

Given the network, the principal contrast drawn by almost all writers is between close-knit and loose-knit networks. Thus Bott (1957: 60) argues that the more close-knit the network the greater the degree of segregation between the roles of husband and wife. This proposition has been expanded by Frankenberg (1966), who constructs a continuum of societies characterized by varying degrees of 'social redundancy'. Srinivas and Béteille say that one effect of social change in India has been the transformation of close-knit networks into loose-knit ones, whereas in South Africa P. Mayer (1961: 289) contrasts the close-knit network of the 'Red' migrant with the loose-knit network of the 'School' migrant. A. C. Mayer (1966: 110–11) associates what he calls 'hard' and 'soft' electoral campaigns with short-path and long-path action-sets, a contrast probably parallel to that between close-knit and loose-knit networks. To test these and similar propositions, and to see in what other situations comparable phenomena occur, we need a standardized procedure for measuring the extent to which any designated portion of a network is 'loose-knit' or 'close-knit'; in other words we need a measure of the local density of the network. Hence in this paper some possible measures of network density are examined.

The total network

We turn then to the second question. What analytical tools are available? We can begin with a picture of a society containing a plurality of actors, some of whom have some kind of relationship to others. This presumably is what Radcliffe-Brown had in mind when in 1940 he talked of social structure being a 'network of actually existing relations' (Radcliffe-Brown, 1952: 190). As a definition of social structure, this statement has been the subject of considerable controversy which is not relevant here. The fact remains that there are people in the real world and some of them impinge on others. The notion of one person impinging on another is left vague, deliberately. The kind of analysis we are concerned with at any time will determine how broad or how narrow a meaning we give to 'impinging', whether we are concerned only with positive rather than negative relationships, with direct rather than indirect interaction, and so on. In this paper I am concerned only with symmetrical relationships, so that if A impinges on B then always B impinges on A, but the concepts discussed can be elaborated to deal with nonsymmetrical relationships if required (cf. Luce, 1950: 169–70). In other words, I discuss only undirected graphs; the study of directed graphs lies beyond the limits of this paper (Harary and others, 1965). The minimum requirement is that given any two individuals, there are two logical possibilities; either they 'impinge' on one another or they do not. If they do impinge on one another, we say they are 'adjacent' (Harary and Norman, 1953: 39). Given then an array of facts about real people and their relationships with one another, we try to comprehend these facts by making a model containing persons, some of whom are in social relationship with some others. Strictly speaking, no social relationship 'actually exists' in the same sense that you and I and other real people exist. But these social relationships are 'actually existing' in the sense that they form part of a model that we seek to make as close as possible to empirical reality in all relevant particulars, rather than to some idea in someone's mind. They are part of a model that explains what actually happens, not what people think happens or might happen.

In building the model, the crucial empirical fact is that every real person impinges upon, or comes into contact with, several other people. This entails that in the model the corresponding social relationships linking persons do not form a simple chain or single star. Instead we find that if we try to represent the model in two dimensions, with points for persons placed conveniently so that they can be linked by lines showing social relationships, the lines criss-cross one another often, and they often form closed circuits. The resulting pattern looks slightly like an untidy net and is appropriately called a network. Similar patterns are studied in electrical and communication engineering and the arrangement is closely analogous to a topographical graph, as understood in mathematics (Cherry, 1957: 26; Ore, 1962: 1–2), with persons corresponding to nodes, junctions or vertices, and the links between them to edges. The term 'network' has been used as the name, or part of the name, of various generically similar concepts in graph theory, such as 'communication network' (Flament, 1963, Chapter 2) and 'transport network' (Berge, 1962: 71), but no single definition for the term appears to prevail (cf. Hockett, 1966: 256, f.n. 56). It seems legitimate to use it here for a broadly similar sociological concept. The O.E.D. gives as one meaning of 'network' 'an interconnected chain or system of immaterial things', and there is even an English folk-category, 'the old-boy network' (Frankenberg, 1966: 253), used to describe the interconnected links of patronage and communication that run between men who were pupils at the same exclusive school. Whether or not this network may usefully be identified with 'social structure' is neither here nor there; whatever it is, it is a first-order abstraction from reality, and it contains as much as possible of the information about the whole of the social life of the community to which it corresponds. I call it the total network. Figure 2 shows a portion of a hypothetical network. The portion

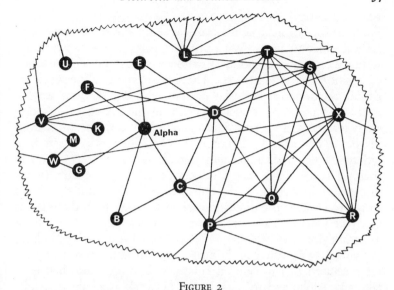

FIGURE 2

Typical arbitrarily delimited portion of a total network

contains nineteen persons, each of whom is adjacent to some other persons included in the portion or lying outside it.

By 'partial network' I mean any extract of the total network based on some criterion applicable throughout the whole network. Thus for example the cognatic web of kinship forms an easily identifiable partial network. The networks of marriage, the political and religious networks discussed by Cohn and Marriott (1958), and Mayer's political network (1962: 275), are other examples of partial networks. It seems to me preferable to use the term 'network' only when some kind of social field is intended, for there has been much confusion about ego-centric and socio-centric extracts from the total network. In my usage we can never speak of an ego-centric network, and I shall suggest special terms for ego-centric extracts or properties of the network. This is contrary to the usages followed by Bott, Mitchell, Epstein, Jay and others, who also differ among themselves. But we are all agreed about the total network, and to my mind any other kind of network ought to resemble the total network in structural form.

Stars and zones

For purposes of analysis we can carve up the total network in several different ways. We can select parts of the network for scrutiny on a basis of position or form or content. The criterion of position is best taken first. The links in the total network are dyadic relationships between persons, and one obvious way of isolating a position or social locality in the network for closer study is to take any person Alpha and to look at the network from his point of view. Each member of the network sees it in a different light, as Srinivas and Béteille (1964: 166–67) stress in their reference to the actor's 'subjective' definition of his network in contrast to the observer's objective definition. But they seem to me to confuse the discussion when they say that 'there are as many networks as there are actors in a social system'. Let us keep 'network' for a set of concrete interpersonal relationships linking individuals with other individuals, and introduce new terms for actor-centred or ego-centred concepts. The first step then is to take any Alpha and to look in the network at all those dyadic relationships of which Alpha is one member. We then have a set of relationships which may be pictured as radiating from, or converging on, Alpha. If I understand Mitchell correctly, this is what he means by a 'bounded ego-centric network'. It seems better to avoid the term network in this sense and instead to refer to an extract of this kind from the total or partial network as Alpha's *primary* or *first-order star* of social relations, by analogy with a *star subgraph* as defined by Ore (1962: 12). The persons who are adjacent to Alpha I call Alpha's primary or first-order contacts. If Alpha is a contact of Beta, then Beta is a contact of Alpha. I have arbitrarily chosen one of the nineteen persons shown in Figure 2 as Alpha, the marked person of reference, in Figures 3 to 6. In Figure 3, this Alpha is shown with his six primary contacts B, C . . . G. The term 'star' has been used by Moreno (1953: 720) and his followers as meaning an individual who is comparatively often chosen by his fellows in specified contexts (e.g. Forsyth and Katz, 1946: 345), while Harary and Norman (1953: 8, 42) mean by star a connected graph without articulation points or *biconnected graph* (Berge, 1962: 198), but I think there need be no confusion with the several usages.

Most writers who have used the network as an analytical tool have been interested in the fact that for any Alpha, some of his

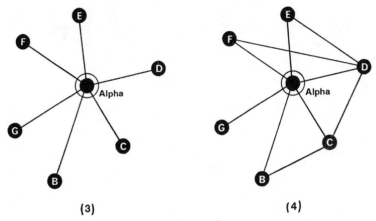

FIGURES 3 and 4

(3) Typical primary star (4) Typical primary zone, with density 48 per cent

contacts are adjacent to one another. It is here that the notion of density or completeness appears. The next level of complexity would therefore seem to be the set of all relationships between two persons, each of whom is either Alpha or one of his contacts. An appropriate name for this set is Alpha's *primary* or *first-order zone* of social relations. Figure 4 shows the links between our Alpha and his first-order contacts B, C ... G, together with the links of B, C ... G among themselves. The measure of density in the zone, mentioned in the caption, is discussed below in the next section.

If Beta is a contact of Alpha, we may expect some of Beta's contacts to be contacts of Alpha and others not to be adjacent to Alpha. Yet Alpha has, as it were, indirect access to all Beta's contacts, for he can get in touch with them through Beta. More precisely, we can say that Alpha has second-order contact with them. We may call the set of all relationships between two persons, one of whom is either Alpha or one of his first-order contacts, as Alpha's *second-order star* of social relations. Similar definitions may be introduced for higher order stars if these are needed. Alpha's *n*th-order star is made up of all social relationships between two persons, one of whom is either Alpha or a contact of Alpha of order $(n - 1)$ or less. Figure 5 shows the second-order star of our Alpha, with his first-order contacts B, C ... G, and his second-order contacts, P, Q ... X.

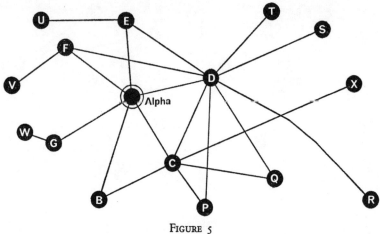

FIGURE 5
Second-order star

Likewise we can define zones of increasing magnitude based on any Alpha. His *second-order zone* is made up of all the existing relationships between two persons, each of whom is either Alpha or one of his first- or second-order contacts. In general his *n*th-order zone contains all links between two people each of whom is either Alpha or a contact of Alpha of order *n* or less. Figure 6 shows our Alpha's second-order zone.

Alpha's second-order zone contains, among others, all the relationships in his əscond-order star, and that in turn contains, among others, all the relations in his first-order zone. In general, the *n*th-order star forms part of the *n*th-order zone which forms part of the $(n + 1)$th-order star.

For simplicity zones and stars have been presented as extracts of the total network. However, the same definitions may be applied to any partial network, and it is here that these analytical tools are likely to be of more use. Thus for example in studying how conformity to the norms of social class is maintained, it may be useful to look at the first- or second-order zones in the partial network of social class relationships centred on any potentially deviant Alpha. In studying a segregated political field, such as church politics, we can look at the partial zones based on church leaders and extracted from the partial network of relationships between church members.

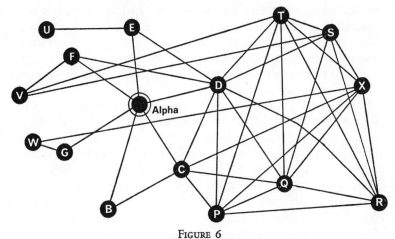

FIGURE 6
Second-order zone, with density 32 per cent

Density

These zones and stars are defined with reference to some person Alpha and are therefore ego-centric and not socio-centric constructs. One contrast drawn both by Bott and myself has given trouble because of its uncertain status as either ego-centric or socio-centric. In her book and earlier articles Bott wrote of loose-knit and close-knit networks, and I distinguished between networks with large and small mesh. I think we meant the same thing, but neither of us suggested an exact measure of the characteristic. Bott's study was based on twenty families, none of which was in significant contact with any other in the sample. Hence in effect she saw each of twenty discrete sets of relationships through the eyes of only one married couple. Hence her qualities of loose-knit and close-knit must refer to the properties of these sets of relationships defined with reference to the central married couple in each. On the other hand I was concerned in my analysis with only one network, to which all of my informants, or rather my models of my informants, belonged. Moreover, in my crude analysis, I was concerned only with the network as a whole and not with differences in mesh between one part of it and another.

In a recent popular article on the family, Bott (1964: 102–3) writes of a contrast between communities and social networks, and says that in Western society the trend is for networks to replace communities. Here she seems to have silently and, I think, regrettably changed the meaning she gives to 'network', for it is clear that in her earlier usage, as in mine, there is always a network in any society, however rich in group and community activity it may be. The trend she mentions is better described as a movement from dense to less dense networks.

Some hypothetical and highly artificial examples may help to illustrate the characteristic we both were aiming at. To take a limiting case, imagine a society in which everyone is in direct contact with everyone else. We can go by direct links from Alpha to Beta to Gamma and back to Alpha, where Alpha, Beta and Gamma are any three different members we like to choose. Hence the network is of uniform mesh, and the mesh is as close as possible. At the other extreme, consider only one particular kind of social relationship between members of a society, the link between proselytizer and convert. We then have a partial network in which the mesh is uniform and maximally large. Alpha converts Beta and Gamma; Beta converts Delta and Epsilon, while Gamma converts Eta and Zeta. Whatever path we trace out from Alpha we are never led back to him, for the network always ramifies and never anastomoses. In the language of graph theory the network constitutes a 'tree'. A third and intermediate example of a network of uniform mesh is given by a hypothetical society dominated by the horror of homosexuality. No-one is permitted contact with anyone else of the same sex, but everyone is in direct touch with all people of the opposite sex. If Alpha is a man, he is in touch with any woman Beta, and she is linked to any other man Gamma, who is in contact with any other woman Delta, and thence back to Alpha. In this network, whatever link we take initially we can get back to our starting point in four moves.

In these hypothetical examples the mesh is uniform throughout the network, and we can characterize the network as a whole as either close-knit or loose-knit or of some intermediate mesh. However, since we are concerned with 'actually existing' social relationships, we have to deal with networks that vary in mesh from one part to another. We therefore need a measure of the extent to which a network is close-knit or open-knit in the vicinity of any member Alpha. None of the various measures of connectivity used by topologists, small group theorists and others are appropriate here. A star or zone is always connected, for by its method of construction there is always some chain (in Berge's terminology; semipath according to Harary and others), of unspecified length, between any two of its members. In general, through each of Alpha's primary contacts there passes one or more cycles (semicycles) of minimal length; the mean or median value of these lengths is a measure of the 'mesh' of the network in the vicinity of Alpha. Probably easier to compute is a measure of the extent to which a zone approaches completeness, the state where each member is in direct contact with every other. We define this measure, the density of the zone, to be the proportion of the theoretically possible direct links that exist in fact. If we assume that in the three hypothetical societies just mentioned each person is adjacent to ten other persons, then these measures have the values shown in the table. For ease of calculation we assume that in the 'no homosexuality' society, the population is ten men and ten women.

Society	Mean length of shortest closed paths	Density per cent	
		First-order zone	Second-order zone
'Everyone knows everybody'	3	100	100
'No homosexuality'	4	18	53
'Proselytizing'	∞	18	2

The failure of the measure of first-order zone density to discriminate between the last two societies in the table, despite their radically different form, might suggest that this measure is unlikely to be useful. However its utility may be small only at the lower end of its scale. In general, if Alpha is adjacent to m persons, this measure cannot be less than $200/(m + 1)$, however sparse the network. This measure of density, divided by 100, is identical with the ratio of actual to potential relationships proposed by Kephart (1950: 548) for interpersonal links. It should not be confused with the 'proportion of connectivity' used by Coleman (1964: 448, 454) for directed graphs; this is a measure of the extent to which any member is ultimately connected to every other, not of adjacency.

The first-order zone shown in Figure 3 contains Alpha and six other persons. The maximum possible number of links is therefore 21, and only 10 are present in fact. Hence the density of the

zone is 1000/21, i.e. 48 per cent. The second-order zone shown in
Figure 6 contains Alpha and 15 other persons. There are 38 links
present, compared with a maximum possible number of 120. The
density is therefore 3800/120, i.e. 32 per cent.

Clusters

In his study of social life in an African town, Epstein (1961: 57–59)
draws a distinction between what he calls a person's effective network and his extended network. This nomenclature does not fit
the usage followed here, but the distinction is important. The
contrast is between those primary contacts of Alpha who are
adjacent to one another and those of his contacts who are not.
If Alpha is a member of the élite, then according to Epstein's
evidence, he and his effective network, or effective circle of
common friends, by their gossip determine and uphold a set of
appropriate norms and values which is then disseminated to the
wider public through Alpha's other friends. Clearly there will in
practice not always be a simple division of all of Alpha's contacts
into one portion, each member of which is adjacent to all other
members, and another portion none of whose members know
one another. There may be intermediate configurations, as shown
in Figure 4, where Alpha, C, D, E and F have several links between
them but where no four persons are all adjacent to one another.
The term 'clique' is available for sets of persons each of whom is
adjacent to all the others (cf. Harary, 1959: 391), and it seems useful to keep Epstein's term 'cluster' for something different. His
original use of the term may be widened slightly to refer to a
set of persons whose links with one another are comparatively
dense, without necessarily constituting a clique in this strict
sense. To identify a cluster as a relatively dense area of the network we need a measure of density that is based on all members
of the cluster rather than on a single person of reference, either
central or peripheral. The notion of density used earlier for ego-
centric zones seems applicable here. We can take any set of persons
in the network and see to what extent the relationships between
them are dense. It should be possible to discover which clusters
of persons, with, say, five or more members, contribute to the network, say, 80 per cent or more of the theoretically possible links
between them. These values, 5 and 80, are fixed arbitrarily and
experience may show that more useful distinctions can be made

when the parameters are given other values. For any person Alpha, by examining the network to which he belongs we can discover all the distinct clusters of which he is a member.

In Figure 2, the comparatively dense web of links between them suggests that C,D,P,Q,R,S and X may form a cluster with seven members. Of the 21 possible links between them, 17 are present, giving a density of 81 per cent. The seven-member set therefore just satisfies the required condition for a cluster. Alpha is linked to two of the members of this cluster, C and D, and we can test to see whether the addition of Alpha to the set brings the density down below the cluster mark. It can be seen from Figure 7 that with Alpha added to the original seven-member set, we have 19 links present out of 28 possible, giving a density of only 67 per cent. Thus Alpha is not a member of the cluster. Similarly we can see that V and L are not members. On the other hand, by adding T we obtain 23 links out of a possible 28, giving a density of 82 per cent. Hence we can say that T is a member of the cluster. We cannot go on to say that these eight persons are the only members of the cluster, for several of them are in touch with other persons who are not included in the portion of the network shown in Figure 2. In general, we cannot study the whole of a total or partial network and have to limit our enquiries to a delimited portion. We must

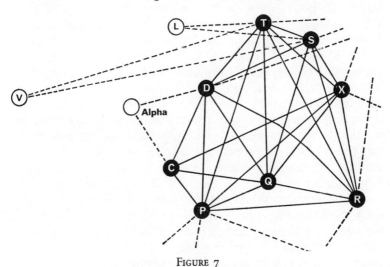

FIGURE 7
Cluster with eight members, density 82 per cent

expect that the boundaries we draw for purposes of study may cut through several clusters. To determine who belongs to these partially-exposed clusters, we have to trace out those links that run from persons in our sample to persons outside it.

Not all members of a cluster make the same contribution to its density. Thus for example in the cluster shown in Figure 7, Q is linked to all the other seven members; D, P, R, T and X each have six links; S has five and C has only four. We may describe Q as a core member of the cluster and C as a peripheral member. We may also describe Q as an essential member, for if we remove Q, the density of the set formed by the remaining seven members drops to 76 per cent, which is below the critical value of 80 per cent. None of the other members of the cluster is essential in this sense. There is parallelism here with the distinction in graph theory between weakening, neutral and strengthening points (Ross and Harary, 1959: 141; cf. Flament, 1963: 39–40). Likewise our use of an arbitrary threshold for cluster density is similar to the procedure suggested by Hubbell (1965) for the identification of generalized cliques.

Boundedness and finiteness

A. C. Mayer (1966: 100–2) has discussed the somewhat confused notion of 'boundedness' as he finds it in the writings of Bott (1957: 58–59), himself and myself. I have drawn a contrast between bounded groups and unbounded networks (Barnes, 1962a: 8). Mitchell (1966: 54) writes of personal networks and stresses that the network has to be treated as if it were bounded, whereas Mayer (1962: 276, f.n. 15) refers to a network that is unbounded only within 'the kinship frame of reference'.

Several writers have also referred to networks as finite or infinite. Here there seems to be both clarity and agreement. A finite network is one containing a finite or limited number of persons, whereas an infinite network contains an indefinitely large number of persons. If bounded and unbounded are to be nothing more than synonyms for finite and infinite, we should drop these terms as unnecessary. If the terms are to be retained, we must give them meanings different from finite and infinite. I have not always followed this rule, and a discussion of where I went wrong may help to clear up the confusion.

When I wrote that a certain partial network in Bremnes had

no external boundary, I was mixing two distinct statements that should have been separated. Firstly, the Norwegians in Bremnes were consciously members of a world society and saw virtually anyone in the world as approachable directly or indirectly; indeed, one of the aims of the foreign missionary movement in Bremnes was to approach as many distant individuals as possible. Hence the number of people in the total network of which the inhabitants of Bremnes were a part was of the same order as the total population of the world. This is finite in fact, but its actual magnitude in this context is not significant; it makes no difference whether it is ten billion or a hundred billion. Hence for purposes of analysis we can treat the Bremnes portion of the network as if it were part of an infinite network. With some other societies, this heuristic assumption would not be legitimate. For example, in pre-contact Tikopia, the absence of links to other island populations and the perceptibly limited size of the population on Tikopia must, I presume, have been significant in many contexts of social interaction. A model of an infinite network would therefore seem inappropriate here.

Secondly, whether or not there were boundaries in the Bremnes total network, and whether or not these boundaries were perceived by the inhabitants of Bremnes, I could for the limited purposes of my analysis ignore them. For instance, it might have been true when I did my study that no social relationship of significance to the people of Bremnes crossed the Iron Curtain and that therefore the Bremnes social network was bounded, at least in that direction. Whether or not this was true was irrelevant to the particular analysis I was making and this also I could ignore. A boundary implies a contrast and a discontinuity; any given person is on one side of the boundary or the other. When we speak of membership of a group we are aways making this contrast, for there are not only members but also non-members with whom the members are contrasted. The model I made of the Bremnes network was unbounded, in that I did not have to consider any person who was definitely outside the network. In principle, everyone in the Bremnes social universe could be reached from anyone else via a sufficiently long path through the network.

I then went on to discuss the Bremnes class network and showed how every person made his own division of the rest of the people

in the network into three sets, superiors, equals and inferiors, even
though each link in the network was one of ostensible equality.
Mayer is right to note that these 'classificatory sets' are bounded,
for the contrast between the three sets is inherent in their definition; there is a boundary or discontinuity between one set and
another. But the sets are infinite, for there is no limit on the
number of persons in each set or on the number of links between
them.

There are thus two distinct characteristics pertaining to any
total or partial network. The network is either finite or infinite.
There are a limited number of persons in a finite network, and
this fact is significant for the flow of interaction going on in the
network. In an infinite network, the fact that in reality only a
finite number of persons are in contact with one another is ignored
for purposes of analysis, and we examine a delimited area of what we
can treat as a network stretching on for ever and ever. Secondly,
the network is either unbounded, or partially bounded, or
totally bounded. If it is unbounded, everyone in the social
universe is in the network and there are no persons outside it.
If there is a boundary, there are some persons known to exist
who are not in the network or who can be reached only by a very
circuitous route. The notion of a boundary, or discontinuity,
is more relevant to partial than to total networks. Thus for instance if we take the partial network formed by peer relationships
in a community, then there will be boundaries or discontinuities
between any individual and his parents and between him and his
children. The esoteric culture of peer groups does not cross these
boundaries, even though by taking a long series of links between
an individual and a slightly younger peer we might be able to
establish a path through the network between a man and his son.
Mayer (1962: 276, f.n. 15) argues that it is impossible to have an
unbounded total network in a finite population, but I think this
is not so; just as the Einstein model of the physical universe is
finite but unbounded, so the total network of any completely isolated society is finite (or can be treated as finite) but unbounded.

If we examine any network, whether it be bounded or unbounded, finite or infinite, total or partial, and concentrate our
attention on a particular person as a point of reference, then we
discover the various ego-centric properties of the network. This
is quite different from saying that the network itself is ego-centric;

it is not. In particular, if we examine the network in the vicinity of this person, say within Alpha's second-order zone, then we have under scrutiny what we may perhaps regard as a 'bounded' portion of the network. But it is clear that the zone is bounded only because we have defined it to be so, and not because the network of which it is a part may perhaps be bounded. When Mitchell argues that in analysis we must treat the network as if it were bounded, I think he means, in the terminology used in this paper, that for practical purposes we can look only at an analytically-delimited portion of the total network, such as a zone or a star; he does not imply that the total or partial network to which it belongs is necessarily bounded. Since the limits of the zone are limits of analytical convenience, while the limits or lack of limits of the network reflect a condition of reality, it seems best to use different words to express these two different ideas.

Action-sets and action-sequences
This long exposition of the principal formal properties of networks of social relations has not taken us very far along the road towards the study of political process. I have been led to spell out these properties at such great length only in the hope that if we can agree on concepts and measures, we can go on to discuss empirical evidence from different contexts that is truly and not merely nominally comparable. Fortunately the next analytical distinction we have to make does begin to clothe these bare logical categories with the stuff of political action.

Mayer argues that I have used the word 'set' in two distinct ways and have led Bott and others to confound two distinct concepts. I find Mayer's discussion not entirely clear, but his main point is important, relevant, and was not made by me. The distinction he draws is between the network of social relations, persisting, as it were, in latent form through time, and the 'action-set' that emerges in a specific context for a specific task. Mayer's discussion, like my 1954 discussion of the network, is tied to a particular body of ethnographic data, and some of the characteristics of 'action-sets' which he deduces may not be found in all possible action-sets. An action-set has an originator Alpha who takes the decision to act to achieve some specific goal. Alpha activates some or all of the social relationships in his primary star, and those first-order contacts he has activated respond by activating in their

turn some or all of the relationships in their primary stars. Those
of Alpha's second-order contacts who are alerted in this way
respond by activating some of the relationships in their primary
stars, and so on. The process continues until Alpha's goal is
achieved. This is how I understand Mayer's concept, though he
does not put it in these terms.

The contrast between the network of social relationships and
the delimited constellation of relationships that are activated on a
specified occasion for a specified purpose is valuable, but the concept of 'action-set' needs careful handling if it is to have precise
meaning and yet be widely applicable. In Mayer's example the
originator was not an 'average' person in the community but
someone atypical, the local Indian Congress municipal candidate
or his Jan Sangh rival. The occasion was an election in 1961 in
Dewas town and the purpose was the securing of votes. Mayer
notes that in the action-set he studied, the relationships activated
were based on a variety of criteria, some of which were group or
category membership. The action-set contained many relationships several links removed from the originator, it did not
persist as an entity after the election was completed, and the
terminal respondents, the voters reached by the action-set, did not
form a group. The action-set had low, but not minimal, density
for a few persons in the set were activated via more than one path,
but the action-set was much less dense than the network from
which it was drawn. Mayer distinguishes between 'lateral linkages', chains of activated relationships converging on some intermediate respondent, and 'multipronged linkages', chains converging on a terminal respondent. He suggests that action-sets
may be compared in terms of the lengths of chains, and types of
cross-linkages, and relates differences in these two characteristics
to the types of election strategy employed by two candidates, the
loyalty of their supporters, and the promises they made.

In many contexts of social life we observe sequences of action
spreading through a network that invite analysis in terms of these
action-sets. But it is clear that often there is no obvious single
originator to a series of actions, and there is no obvious point at
which any sequence may be said to end. Nevertheless, the notion
of an action-set may still be applied, in modified form. Suppose
we look at any person Alpha who has been involved in a sequence
of actions. By confining our attention to Alpha's primary star,

we can record from which of his primary contacts stimuli or pressures to act come to him, and also which of his contacts, if any, Alpha activates in response to these stimuli. In other words, we can see which routes action-sets take through Alpha. It may be possible to link particular purposes with particular routes; the routes may tend to run in a certain direction, or there may be an equal frequency of routes taken in opposite directions.

Mitchell suggests ways in which the relationships that make up a network may be categorized in terms of content, frequency, durability and directedness (pp. 20 ff. above) and makes the important distinction between a network as a potential medium for the flow of information and gossip, and for the execution of transactions. The same kinds of formal analysis would seem to be applicable in examining the flow of gossip as in the study of action-sets and action-sequences, but the results are likely to be different. Both Epstein (pp. 113 ff. below) and Bott (1957) are concerned with the transmission of information and moral judgements within the network. The presence of cycles (semicycles, circuits) in the social network is a necessary, though not sufficient, condition for there to be cycles in the gossip paths. It is manifest from the studies of Epstein and Bott, as well as from a great deal of work in social psychology, that cycles in gossip paths have a direct effect on the achievement of consensus and the application of diffuse or organized sanctions against deviation from this consensus. On the other hand, as shown by Mayer's example, cycles may have much less significance in transactional paths and are likely to be few, however dense and cyclical the corresponding network may be.

Yet this contrast should not be pushed too far, for it is possible that the particular purpose examined by Mayer, electoral support, may be relevant. It seems intuitively obvious that an action-set aimed at securing electoral support in a society with universal adult franchise would be most effective if it ramified as rapidly and as widely as possible, so as to reach many voters with paths as short as possible. Other types of transaction may be best carried out through action-sets containing cycles. As a limiting case, consider the actions that are set in motion when a man goes mad. One of his primary contacts has to take the decision to recognize this fact, and hence in formal terms he is the originator of the action-set. But the action-set is likely to be recruited with reference to the madman, and it is several of his primary contacts who are likely to act in concert to make arrangements for him to be cared for medically. In many cultures, these are actions that are handled 'discreetly'; in other words, persons who are not primary contacts of the madman are kept out of the action-set as far as possible. The transactional links are closely centred on the madman and in the crisis it is possible that some of his primary contacts who had not previously been adjacent to one another have to make contact. The significant action, or much of it, takes place within the madman's primary zone, yet the inter-action with the madman himself does not have quite the same purpose as the interaction between his friends, for he is categor-ized as 'mad'. Here then we have an action-set of quite a different form from that considered by Mayer, and there are other possi-bilities. Action-sets aimed at the provision of substantial material resources may perhaps take the form of a few links each connect-ing the originator to dense portions of the network where his several clusters of friends can act in concert to come to his aid.

Partial networks
One other conceptual issue needs clarification. In my 1954 paper I divide the total network of Bremnes society into three 'fields' which I call the territorial system, the industrial system, and the remaining 'network of social ties between pairs of persons arising from considerations of kinship, friendship and acquaintance' (Barnes, 1954: 48). Within this third, unnamed, field I distinguish a sub-category, the class network, which Mayer (1966: 99) calls an example of a classificatory set. My aim in making these divisions was to discriminate between those relationships which were subsumed by the framework of bounded institutionalized groups or categories, such as the hamlet, the parish, the factory workshop, the missionary society and the ship's crew, and those relationships deriving from the ever-ramifying web of cognatic kinship, affinity and friendship. The class network has already been mentioned and need not detain us further, but I can now see that it is confusing to leave my third field unnamed. Mayer shows that the action-set he studied contained many relationships derived from common membership in political parties and in territorial, religious, occupational and caste groups and categories, as well as other relationships between kinsmen. Some links in the

action-set were patron–client or broker–client relationships. Likewise Srinivas and Béteille (1964: 166) mention an action-sequence
in which various links between father and son and lawyer and
client, as well as between fellow businessmen, were invoked to
secure a university place for a young student. These empirical
findings suggest that the non-institutional third field may not be a
useful analytical category, in that action-sets may seldom if ever be
systematically confined to it. Only part of the non-institutional
field forms the class network, for some non-institutional relationships are between persons who do not perceive themselves as
equals. Hence the non-institutional field may be a redundant
category.

It is well known that in many contexts individuals seek to
establish wider relationships with persons whom they meet in a
restricted institutional context. For example a man may start to
drink with someone he has previously known only as a workmate, he may recruit another workmate to his political party and
may seduce the wife of a third. In analysing these instances we
usually say that we now have a plurality of relationships between
the pair of men, one relationship (workmate) pertaining to the
industrial field and another (drinking companion, fellow member
of a political party, or cuckold) lying outside it. In Mayer's case,
however, it seems that Congress party workers approached their
contacts by a simple appeal to their membership of kin factions,
or of religious sects, or to their common attendance at a wrestling
gymnasium, and did not seek to secure the municipal votes of their
contacts by becoming their friends (Mayer, 1963, 1966). In other
words, the existing relationships were sufficient in themselves,
even though the purpose for which they had been activated, the
securing of votes for the Congress candidate, was irrelevant to
most of the relationships. If this phenomenon is found elsewhere,
as I guess it may be, then it would seem best to take the whole
of the total network as the universe from which any action-set
is drawn, rather than to focus our attention on the non-institutional partial field.

Other partial networks may be useful units of analysis. We have
already mentioned the class network and the web of cognatic
kinship as partial networks of analytical value. In societies where
role segregation is ritualized to a greater extent than in Mayer's
case, it may not be possible to secure action in one context by

appealing to a relationship appropriate to a different context. It may then be useful to look at the network of relationships within a religious cult, or between participants in a system of exchange, in isolation from relationships of other kinds. Likewise the bounded partial networks found within groups provide an essential part of the data needed for a study of the working of these groups. In studying these partial networks, we have available the concepts of partial star and partial zone discussed earlier.

We could perhaps look at all those relationships in the total network that are 'personal', that is to say, that derive from a person's status as a friend, patron or the like, rather than from his membership of any group. These relationships constitute a partial network, and it might seem appropriate to call this the 'personal network'. But Mitchell uses the term 'personal network' for those localized extracts of a network that I have called a star or a zone. I therefore suggest that the term 'personal network' be dropped. A partial network consisting of relationships not deriving from group membership might be termed an 'idiosyncratic network'.

Tribal and industrial societies

It has been suggested that network analysis is nothing more than a formalization of the social drama method of analysis developed by Turner (1957) and others. Both analytical methods are certainly concerned with choice in social action, in the problems of why in a specified context a man chooses one course of action rather than another, why and when and how he selects one contact out of many possible and appeals to one principle rather than to others. Yet if we try to construct the social network for a traditional tribal society of the kind studied by Turner in central Africa, we soon discover that it is all too easy. Everyone has some kind of relationship with everyone else in his vicinity and the network is maximally dense. Although the various relationships in the network vary in content, intensity, symmetry and indeed in every possible respect, there are everywhere relationships of one kind or other; there are no real strangers. In the populous urban communities studied by Epstein (1961), A. C. Mayer (1963, 1966), P. Mayer (1961), Mitchell (1966) and others network analysis is made feasible because in every person's social environment there are many strangers with whom he has no significant interaction at all. In small-scale societies this is not so. The typical state of affairs in tribal societies is expressed in a remark once made to me by an oldish Ngoni man whose immigrant origin I had just discovered. He commented: 'There are very few people here who know that I am really a stranger.' Between the tribal and urban extremes there are many intermediate types. For instance, the rural semi-industrial society of Bremnes lies well between the two extremes.

In tribal society, the pattern of relationships in the total network reveals its institutional structure, for the relationships are not all of the same kind and the various kinds are not distributed at random. But under tribal conditions the denseness of the network leaves no room, as it were, for the addition of those idiosyncratic relationships of friendship with strangers, or even of patron and client, that help to fill in the relatively sparse urban network. In the limiting tribal case we have our hypothetical society in which 'Everyone knows everybody'. Yet even in this society originators of action must be selective; they cannot mobilize the whole society every time anything needs to be done. The analysis of action-sets provides a way of systematically plotting the choices made, even though the complexity, or multiplexity, of the relationships linking the various persons in a tribal community make the isolation of any single originator, or single purpose, or definite end to a chain of action, all difficult to determine. An analysis of the directions and kinds of flow of action-sequences through members of the society may provide a way round these difficulties.

Relationships between persons in tribal society are typically multiplex, to use Gluckman's term (1955: 18–19), whereas in urban industrial society they are typically single-stranded. Networks in tribal society are typically dense, whereas in industrial society they are typically sparse. Mitchell (p. 24 above) asks if there is any connection between these two facts. Part of the answer would seem to be given by a consideration of the action-sequences going on in the society concerned. We may make the contrast in this way. In an urban society, Alpha originates action with his contact Beta for purpose 1, with Gamma for purpose 2, with Delta for purpose 3, and so on. In a tribal society, Alpha makes contact with Beta sometimes for purpose 1, sometimes for purpose 2, sometimes for purpose 3, and so on. He treats

Gamma, Delta and his other contacts in the same way. Hence
Beta, Gamma and Delta have more in common with one another
in the tribal example than in the urban example. We may argue
that therefore the chance that they are in direct contact with one
another is greater in tribal than in urban society.

All I have been able to do in these remarks is to suggest ways
in which our language of discussion about networks might be
clarified, and ways in which we might give precision and quantification to our descriptions of empirical situations. The remarks
themselves have been largely free of empirical content, and I have
talked about what might be done rather than demonstrated what
can be done from my own work. Many social scientists argue
that it is usually a waste of time to discuss elaborate analytical
tools that have not been tested in practice. I support this view,
but would defend myself on this occasion on the ground that the
tools I have discussed have already been used and have become
blunt. I have just tried to sharpen them a little.

CHAPTER III

The Network and Urban Social Organization[1]

by
A. L. Epstein

Introduction

In any social field much of the raw data of observation relates to behaviour that in itself is random or haphazard: the order imposed upon the material is achieved only after patient sifting and analysis on the part of the observer. Over the years social anthropologists have been able to develop concepts and other tools of research for isolating and examining the social regularities in pre-industrial communities. In this field they have in fact made considerable advances, though it might be said, in very general terms, that their task has been eased by the nature of pre-industrial society itself. When we turn to anthropological studies of modern urban communities a very different picture obtains. To say that custom is king may be a misleading characterization of primitive society, but in no circumstances at all could it conceivably be applied, say, to the urban communities now rapidly emerging all over Africa. Here the dominant characteristics—high population density, ethnic heterogeneity, increasing social and economic differentiation and a high degree of occupational and residential mobility—are more likely to foster the impression of a society inchoate and incoherent, where the haphazard is more conspicuous than the regular, and all is in a state of flux. It is not surprising then that in this field of study there is as yet little consensus amongst anthropologists on aims and methods, and that we should still be at the beginning of our quest.

The general problem I am raising emerges most strikingly in a town like Ndola. Ndola began as a small administrative post, railway junction and trading settlement. It has not yet come to

[1] Reprinted from 'The Rhodes-Livingstone Institute Journal', No. XXIX, June 1961: 29-61.

develop any major industry, and still possesses no single large-scale employers of labour such as are found in the neighbouring mine townships of the Copperbelt. Ndola's recent expansion has rested therefore in its ability to develop its original specialized functions and provide administrative, commercial, and transport and communications services for the Copperbelt as a whole. As an administrative centre Ndola serves as the headquarters of the Western Province, which embraces the whole of the Copperbelt as well as considerable areas of the rural hinterland. In virtue of its situation Ndola also provides the vital road and railway link between the towns of the Copperbelt, as well as the Belgian Congo, and the south. As a communications centre of increasing importance it has become the main depot of various bus companies and haulage contractors: garages, motor-repair shops and body-builders abound. Again, the goods-yard established to handle the heavy traffic in freight provided the facilities which have encouraged the emergence of Ndola as an important wholesale and distributing centre. Firms of importers have their warehouses, and other business concerns of many kinds have offices or agencies in the town. Ndola has become a rendezvous of commercial travellers who use the town, which now possesses a fair number of hotels[1] and guest-houses, as a base from which they can cover the Copperbelt. Thus Ndola reveals a greater diversification than other Copperbelt towns, and this process has been intensified in the rapid growth of the town in the post-war years, when the European population increased about sevenfold in the course of a decade.

But the general condition of flux associated with rapid growth and diversification is exhibited perhaps most markedly amongst the African inhabitants of the town. All told there are probably about 50,000 Africans living in Ndola today. Some—still a very small proportion—were born and brought up there; others have been continuously resident for the past fifteen or more years; but the great majority are newcomers who have come to live in Ndola within the last five years. They have come from other towns, and from the many tribal areas of Northern Rhodesia as well as from the neighbouring territories of Nyasaland and the

---

[1] The first African hotel in the Territory was opened officially in the Ndola Municipal Location towards the end of 1955.

Belgian Congo. Ethnically mixed, the African population also shows a concomitant diversity of culture which is expressed in the wide range of languages spoken, in the distinctive and sometimes exotic modes of dress of different tribal groups, and in differences in manner and behaviour. Ndola's African population is not only mixed, it is also highly mobile. There is a constant coming and going of people. Individuals move from one part of the town to another. This continuous circulation of people within the town is partly accounted for by various legal provisions which place the responsibility for housing Africans in the town on the employer and tie housing to the job: when an African gives up or loses his job he also loses his house, and has to move elsewhere. But the growth of the town itself also exacerbates the tendency towards circulation, for as new housing areas are established new residents move in from the older parts of the location, and their vacated houses are taken over by those coming from parts of the location marked down for demolition. Then, again, people leave and go to other towns or return to their villages in the reserves, while all the time yet others are moving in at such a rate that the number of Africans in the town has doubled itself in the space of only a few years. In these respects of course Ndola does not differ greatly from the other towns of the Copperbelt. What distinguishes Ndola is the obvious absence of any single large-scale organization that would provide a common framework of behaviour for a substantial proportion of its inhabitants in the way that a mine administration tends to structure the social life of Africans in a mine compound. In my study of Luanshya I used the term 'atomistic' to contrast the fluidity of the Municipal location with the 'unitary' structure of the mine compound. [For detailed discussion of this see Epstein (1958).] There is perhaps even stronger justification for applying the same term to Ndola.

Yet despite the apparent confusion of the urban scene, it is equally patent that the Africans who live in Ndola do not compose a mere aggregation of individuals nor a disorganized rabble. As a town Ndola exists to serve certain specialized functions, and complex economic and administrative institutions have been built up which ensure that the tasks necessary to these functions are, in the main, effectively carried out. Thus economic and administrative organization introduce at least a minimum of

social order. It also becomes apparent that within this framework
the Africans have elaborated a complex system of organizing
social relationships among themselves. One of the most striking
ways in which this organization manifests itself is, despite the
continuous coming and going of people, the apparent ease with
which strangers to the town are able to discover their friends and
kinsfolk, or husbands and wives to trace their deserting spouses.
The fact is that each individual African is involved in a network
of social ties (see Barnes, 1954, and Bott, 1957) which ramify
throughout the urban community and extend to other towns and
to the tribal areas. The immediate aim of this paper is to demonstrate the importance of the network in urban social organization,
and to indicate some of its characteristics and functions.

The procedure I propose to adopt is to set out *in extenso* and
without comment an account based on a number of texts prepared
for me by an African which records his movements around the
town and the contacts he made with various people in the course
of a number of days. This method may be considered to impose
a heavy burden on the reader, and some may object to it on other
grounds too. My justification for following this course is that
in the first place it illustrates vividly the random or haphazard
character of much of urban social life. However, I am not primarily concerned with the texts merely as illustrative material;
rather I take the behaviour they describe as the unit of analysis
through which I seek to establish other sets of regularities present
in urban life. In this respect the present paper looks towards
the development of a methodology or systematic approach to
the anthropological study of urban communities. The detailed
evidence of the narrative which follows puts the reader in a
position to check my own analysis and, where this is inadequate,
to suggest alternative and more satisfactory intepretations of the
material.

Chanda's social contacts in Ndola
It was shortly after noon when Chanda[1] left off work. He decided
to do a little shopping in town before returning to his house in

[1] I acknowledge here my thanks to my informant for his assistance, even
though I find it necessary to refer to him by a pseudonym. To help the reader
I have given all the other characters who appear in Chanda's account common
English names.

Kabushi Suburb. On the way to town, and just by the African Hospital, he met a woman who had just arrived in Ndola on the bus from Fort Rosebery. She was of his own tribe, a Lunda of Kazembe, and he greeted her. At first she did not recognize him, for it was a long time since they had last met when Chanda was on a short visit to his rural home. He introduced himself as ShiChomba, father of Chomba, and said that he was the former husband of Agnes K of Mulundu. At length the woman realized who he was and apologized for having forgotten him. 'Now I remember you well,' she said, 'because your daughter resembles you so much.'

After some further conversation, in which they exchanged news of friends and acquaintances, Chanda bade the woman farewell and set off again on his bicycle. Near the Government Offices (the 'Boma') he ran into his friend Thompson. Thompson was employed by the Municipality as an African Health Assistant. He was one of a small group of African assistants whose duty it was to maintain regular inspection of the location and ensure that people there adhered to the standards of hygiene laid down by the European authorities. Thompson at this time was having an extra-marital affair with a girl called Paula who was Chanda's classificatory sister. As they greeted one another a co-worker of Thompson called out from behind to ask if he were going home, but Thompson replied that he had met his 'brother-in-law' who would persuade his girl-friend to be nice to him. 'You have to keep in with your brother-in-law if you are to have a good "friend",' he added. Thompson accompanied Chanda to a store where the latter bought a broom, and then they rode off together in the direction of the location.

At one of the main road junctions they found many African cyclists heading for the location. They had just knocked off and were rushing for lunch. Thompson remarked: '*Mulamo*, better get off the road with these people riding crazily like this. You know, *mulamo*, they are running for lunch and then come back very soon. Some are allowed only 30 minutes and will be back at two o'clock—but people like ourselves, we get home without having to sweat. Then we have a wash and rest awhile before eating —but not they. They will just eat quickly as soon as they arrive, and I am afraid that some won't even find their wives at home. This time women like going out for charcoal and firewood in the bush. These poor fellows sweat very much. . . . There are some who don't even get home for lunch. They leave their houses very early at 5.30 in the morning and don't see their wives and children again until late in the evening. They have no bicycles—I wonder why they can't one day stop drinking beer and start saving money to buy a bicycle. . . . Their wives commit adultery very much during the day. You know, *mulamo*, their wives cook *bwali* (the traditional Bemba dish of porridge) with chicken relish and take it to their boy friends while their husbands die of hunger. Ah well, let them suffer: it is their turn now for when we were going to school they thought we were wasting our time, and laughed at us. . . .'

At length they reached the location. Then, near the market-place in Kabushi Suburb, someone called out to Thompson, using the appropriate greeting for a man seen returning from work. They stopped and Thompson spoke to the man, whom Chanda did not know. The stranger told Thompson that his father had had to leave his job on the mine at Luanshya because he was no longer considered fit to work. As they parted and went on their way Thompson remarked: 'You know, it is as though those who have stayed in the villages would bewitch us because we no longer visit them. Let's go, Chanda, that man is a real *lichona*.'[1] They approached the Bottle Store where Thompson noticed a Southern Rhodesian girl passing by. 'She's an Ndebele,' he said. 'If you want I'll call her so that you can "play" her.' 'But she does not know me, and anyway I don't speak Ndebele so how shall I coax her?' Chanda enquired. 'You know I've been in Bulawayo, and I know how to approach them; they're easy-going people,' Thompson replied. 'Moreover, you look very smart, *mulamo*, she wouldn't deny you.' But Chanda seemed unconvinced. He reminded Thompson that only recently the latter had jokingly threatened to expose one of Chanda's own peccadilloes. 'And is that Ndebele not also a woman?' he asked. 'No,' said Thompson, 'because she is not related to me, nor is she your tribeswoman. Such women are our "ration" here in town.' The two men parted and agreed to meet later in the day.

When he reached his house Chanda found that his wife was not at home. His next-door neighbour said that she had gone to

[1] A vernacular expression used of one considered to have severed his ties with his village completely.

Bwana M'kubwa, which is about six miles outside Ndola. This news upset him, for his wife had said nothing about going out. He was suddenly afraid that the Mobile Police Unit which was based at Bwana M'kubwa might have arrested her and taken her away. He spoke to another neighbour who assured him that there was no cause for alarm. She told him that the first neighbour was of the Nsenga tribe who had probably misunderstood what Mrs Chanda had said as she knew little Bemba. Eventually his wife returned and prepared food. Later he went off to deliver a message to a teacher at the school in the Old Location. He returned shortly and he and his wife spent the rest of the day quietly at home. . . .

The following day was a Saturday and Chanda went into town early in order to do some shopping. Outside the butcher's shop he met a young man called Godfrey. Godfrey was a Lozi. He and Chanda had once worked together for a short time when Chanda was employed as a clerk in the Public Works Department in Ndola. At the moment Godfrey was unemployed and looking for work. Chanda asked him to accompany him to a shop where Chanda bought some meat pies which they proceeded to eat on the spot. They were joined by another young man, a Lala by the name of John. John expressed surprise at seeing Chanda in Ndola, for the last time they had met they were both working in Luanshya, the nearest town, about twenty miles away. John, indeed, had been carpenter's assistant to Chanda's elder classificatory brother who still lived there. John had come over to Ndola and found work with a European as a house-boy, but at present he too was unemployed. Chanda introduced John to Godfrey and while they were chatting together another man came up and greeted Godfrey in Lozi, which neither of the others understood. The Lozi was an African detective stationed in Ndola and when he departed Godfrey commented: 'That man is very cruel—he arrests people very much. He will stay near the butchery because he knows that the butchery-boys steal much meat and then sell it privately. See him standing there by the back-door. . . .' John looked around. 'Does he also arrest "loafers", that old man?'

Together the three young men walked along the main street of the town. As they reached one of the oldest established and best known of the European stores Chanda was hailed by an orderly in the Public Works Department on his way to the Post Office to collect mail. 'Hallo, hallo, Mr Chanda. Are you well, my father?' He also greeted Godfrey. 'And have you still not found work?' he asked. Then he explained to Chanda: 'This man, father, suffers greatly through unemployment, and it's all the fault of Leonard T., that fellow you used to work with in the P.W.D. He led Godfrey astray. . . .' The orderly was about to embark on his story when a Land Rover pulled up outside the store and two Government Messengers got out. They immediately recognized the P.W.D. orderly and greeted him warmly. Chanda noted that all three were of the Aushi tribe in the Fort Rosebery District. Chanda was introduced to the newcomers and soon they were giving him news of a number of his friends temporarily engaged on a job there. At length the messengers went into the store to buy shot, but there was none in stock and they drove off. Chanda bade his friends farewell and set off home.

When he reached his house he found that he had visitors. His wife's grandmother Ella had just arrived from Fort Rosebery. With her on this occasion was her younger sister Rose, and Alice, the elder sister of his wife, both of whom were also living in Kabushi Suburb. Although she was a grandmother, Ella still looked very young and, indeed, prided herself on her youthful appearance: she regarded herself as a 'modern' woman and was still working as a nurse at the Fort Rosebery Hospital. She began to tell Chanda how when Laura, his wife, was a girl she had paid for her schooling. She had hoped that Laura would not marry early, but would continue her education at a school in Southern Rhodesia. But then when Laura was in Lusaka her mother had forced her into marriage with some Lala fellow whom she didn't love. When next she went to Lusaka, Ella continued, and saw Laura's mother she was going to tell her something . . . and not even to write a letter all the time! While they were talking there was a knock at the door and Chanda's sister Anne, who was on a visit from Elizabethville in the Belgian Congo, came in. Chanda made the introductions, and began to explain something of his family tree. Ella soon interrupted him: 'Do you know, Shi-Chomba, that this is your own grandchild you have married?' She went into a lengthy account of the way they were all related, and finally concluded: 'You *machona*, you never bother to write letters to those who remain in the village. One day when you go there you will find yourselves lost for those you left behind will already have gone.' They all laughed and agreed it was so. 'But time is short, grandmother.' Laura went and prepared food for the guests. Chanda sat apart and read the newspaper. . . .

Early next morning Chanda set off to visit his friend James who lived in another part of the town known simply as the African Suburb, and whose wife had just given birth to a baby. James had worked with Chanda's elder classificatory brother Michael on a carpentry course given at a mission station in their home district. Michael had introduced James to Chanda when he had come on a visit to Ndola a few years previously. James was employed as a carpenter in the Public Works Department where Chanda himself at that time was a clerk, and the two became very close friends. On his way to the African Suburb Chanda passed through the Old Location and called on another friend, a 'home fellow' from the Luapula Valley whom Chanda had known from boyhood. His friend was not at home; a younger sister's husband who was staying in the house said he had gone to Chingola and would not be back for a fortnight. Chanda did not stay, but rode off for the Suburb.

James' wife was standing in the doorway when Chanda arrived at the house. He spoke to her in Bemba, using the special greeting customarily addressed to a woman who has just given birth to a child. They spoke a little about the baby, and then she told him that her husband had gone off to another house where there was said to be beer. Chanda left and eventually found James with another fellow whom he didn't know, but who also lived in Kabushi. They entered a house where beer was for sale. But it was not to their liking so they moved to another house. But here they did not even enter because the owner of the house would not allow them to park their bicycles nearby for fear the police would suspect the presence of illicitly brewed beer and come and arrest them. James said: 'Let's go and look for beer at Maria's—though I know she will have taken it to *mikotokoto*', referring to those small clearings in the bush where beer is taken for sale in order to avoid the attentions of the police.

James had guessed aright. Maria greeted Chanda with an excited outburst: 'Good heavens! ShiChomba. I'd almost forgotten you, it's so long ago. . . . So you're back in Ndola again?' Maria was a friend of James' wife and remembered Chanda from the time he himself had lived in the African Suburb. They bought beer and then another 'home fellow' called George came in. They sat drinking and chatting until an Ngoni man interrupted and begged Chanda for a cigarette. George told Chanda not to be foolish, the fellow was a born scrounger: when he knew he was coming to drink beer he should have bought a packet of cigarettes for three-pence at a tea-room. 'If you give him cigarettes next thing he'll be begging for beer.' George continued to abuse the Ngoni, but none of the company intervened. Altogether there were six Ngoni and nine Bemba women present, as well as a number of Ngoni, Lala and Bemba men. But they were mostly older people. George joked: 'The beer is no good for here we are in the bush with only a lot of "old girls"—there's not a young 'un among the lot you could have some fun with.' He made some further ribald remarks and rose to go. James was keen to go on to the African Township at Twapya, a mile or so further along the road, where there was certain to be more beer, but Chanda said he had no more money and, after escorting his friends part of the way, he returned to Kabushi.

It was still quite early, so before going home he decided to call in and see his sister Anne. Anne was staying with a classificatory sister who was married to a businessman called Martin. At Martin's house there were a number of visitors including Martin's own elder sister and a classificatory brother, and another man whom Chanda didn't know but whom he identified as a 'Kasai'. Martin introduced him as a friend, adding that he had been in Northern Rhodesia so long that people no longer recognized him as a 'Kasai'. 'He speaks Bemba very well, and his face and manner do not reveal him as a Kasai.' Martin himself had just returned from a business trip to Elizabethville, and after a while Chanda asked him whether he had seen Anne's husband Jackson there. Martin replied that he had and had delivered Chanda's letter to him, but Jackson had said he was unable to answer it for the moment. 'But why can't he write us a few lines?' Chanda asked. Martin explained that Jackson was busy: he had just bought a new vanette, and he spent his time moving between the various Government offices to have his documents endorsed before he could put his vanette on the road. 'Oh, that is very good—that he is a rich man.' Chanda appears to have been suitably impressed, and he quickly changed the subject. 'What about the "fever coat" I asked you to buy me?' he demanded. 'You know last time I went I found the coats all right,' Martin replied, 'but you hadn't given me the correct size so I didn't buy you one. This time they were all finished. I tried hard to find you one, but I failed. Most of the ones I saw were of inferior quality which you, *mulamo* (brother-in-law), as a gentleman could not wear.' 'Oh, then I am unlucky,' Chanda said. Shortly afterwards he left and went home.

A short while after these events Mrs Chanda had to go to Bancroft, the new mine township near Chingola, for a few days. Chanda saw her off at the bus station and then rode off to town to collect some photographs of himself which he had had taken recently. Returning home later, and passing by the Beer Hall, he ran into a number of close kinsmen who had just arrived in Ndola from home. They were talking to Crawford, an official of the African National Congress, who was based at Ndola, the Congress headquarters for the Western Province. Chanda, who had himself been a branch official in the movement when he was living elsewhere on the Copperbelt, knew Crawford very well, but now he learnt that they were also kinsmen, for it soon emerged in the course of the introductions that Crawford was Chanda's classificatory father, although they were of different tribes and came from different parts of the country. Neither had known previously of the relationship, and now they both expressed their pleasure in its discovery. 'So you are related to Francis, my brother-in-law here,' Crawford exclaimed. 'You know,' he went on, 'Francis' sister is married to my own brother. Now it is good that our relationship is revealed today. That is why we get on so well together. It is the blood of kinship. Very fine, indeed.'

Francis, who worked for his maternal uncle as book-keeper, clerk and bus conductor, had come down to Ndola with one of his uncle's buses which required servicing. Now he insisted that Chanda give him a lift back to the garage on his bicycle. Passing through the town, Francis pointed to one of the offices and explained: 'This morning I went to those people to place an order for a new bus from Johannesburg at £3,000. You know, father, the ladies and the African clerks were looking at me very much and nodding their heads when they saw me signing the indenture papers with the manager. They saw me as a very high chap. . . . One of the European ladies gave me a cigarette. You know, father, I had two bottles of beer in the morning before I came into town so when I was talking I was very careful that my language was moderate.' 'Yes, indeed, you made an impression,' Chanda commented. 'It was a landmark.' At the garage Chanda produced the photographs of himself. Francis looked at them and exclaimed with a gasp of astonishment: 'Yaa—you look just like a European, father, truly. I know you are not coming home (i.e. to the village) any more because you are very particular about things. . . .'

The following afternoon, a Sunday, Chanda dressed up properly and set off for the Welfare Centre to watch the football match between teams from Ndola and Mufulira. But at the entrance to the ground he met his sister-in-law and her husband Robert on their way to the Beer Hall together with another elder sister of his wife. They enquired after Mrs Chanda and the baby and when he told them that she had gone off to Bancroft they upbraided him for not having informed them before. 'Who is there to sweep up the house, and fetch water for your bath? You did wrong by not telling us,' they said. Robert then invited Chanda to accompany them to the Beer Hall.

At the Beer Hall they found seats in one of the chalets and immediately Chanda found himself being introduced to a large number of people whom Robert addressed as brother, maternal uncle and so on. Together they all set to drinking the large supply of bottled beer which Robert had provided. Robert himself was a Lamba of the Ndola District. He had married Alice nine years ago. Once he had visited his wife's kin in the Kawambwa District, and appeared to have been greatly impressed by what he saw there. He began to tell his relatives how well he had been treated in Kawambwa, and sought to persuade them to go there in search of wives who would be respectful and docile. All present seemed to be growing increasingly drunk. Alice asked Chanda, who tended to become intoxicated rather quickly, why he was drinking so little and sat there so quietly. Chanda replied that he was perfectly all right; he was afraid to say much lest in an unguarded moment he let something slip which might give offence to his freshly introduced affines. A Bemba woman sitting nearby agreed, and said it was always wise to watch one's step when drinking with one's in-laws. But Robert, carried away by his theme, began singing lustily: 'I am a man grown old in the town who has married a beautiful lady of Kawambwa, and that's where I'm going to settle,' until his wife grabbed him by the shoulder and quietened him down. At six o'clock the Beer Hall closed and, as it was raining, Chanda made his way back to Kabushi and went to sleep.

Analysis of Chanda's social relationships

Chanda, from whose own written accounts I have built up these 'sketches from urban life', is a young man in his early thirties. He comes from the Luapula Valley where his father is a village head-man in the Lunda kingdom of Kazembe. Chanda spent his boy-hood in the Valley, and received an elementary education at a mission school in the Kawambwa District. On leaving school he accompanied an older relative to Elizabethville where eventually he got a job as a clerk in a European firm of importers and exporters. After some years he decided to return to Northern Rhodesia. At Luanshya he was employed as a filing clerk with a Medical Research Unit on the mine there. More recently he had worked as an assistant in an African store and tearoom at Bancroft before he decided to come to Ndola again where he was employed as a typist-clerk.

Chanda is not a typical urban African; for, as Ellen Hellmann (1949: 271) remarks, there is no such person. Nevertheless, run-ning through the accounts I have presented of his activities in Ndola we may discern and pick out a number of motifs, recurrent themes in the overall pattern of the social life of the town. I should note at once that the events recalled in these accounts all took place at week-ends when Chanda was off duty and free to enjoy his leisure. Yet we are also reminded on a number of occasions of the paramount need for a job in this community. The African of the towns no longer lives on the produce of the soil he has cultivated himself. Although a great many African women in Ndola do prepare gardens in the areas of bush which fringe the town, the produce of these gardens remains at most a valuable supplement to a diet of which the basic items are bought with cash. The urban African is essentially a wage-earner, dependent for his livelihood on the opportunities and services provided by the others, particu-larly Europeans. He has come into an urban world in which, as Louis Wirth (1956: 123) has aptly put it, the clock and the traffic signal are symbolic of the basis of the social order. Employment of some kind then is a necessity in the town, while the reflections of the Health Inspector on the African workers scurrying back to the location at lunch-time also demonstrate how the kind of work one does not only shapes the daily round, but also affects the regard in which a man is held by his fellows. The effective func-tioning of a town demands a complex division of labour within a

single economic order. Thompson's remarks also suggest important social divisions within the community which are based in
occupational differences and expressed in significant differences in
patterns of behaviour and ideology. When he wondered why
African labourers did not save instead of squandering their money
on beer his observation was not necessarily valid; nevertheless he
was giving clear expression to the same kind of 'middle class'
attitude which elsewhere views improvidence and thriftlessness as
amongst the chief characteristics of the English working class.

Where so much depends upon having a job, unemployment
must count as a major hazard in African urban life, though it is
not yet the chronic sore it has become in other more industrialized
societies. Although no reliable quantitative evidence is available,
there are ample references in the contemporary records to the
incidence of unemployment amongst Africans during the economic depression of the thirties. Undoubtedly the ability of many to
return to their villages in the tribal areas and live once more off
the land mitigated the general hardship, but the widespread distress of the period is recalled in the word *cipoyoyo*, a vernacular
term coined at the time and still commonly used in referring to
the slump.[1] After the war Northern Rhodesia entered upon a new
expansionary phase, and for some years now Government Labour
Officers have consistently reported a general demand for labour
in excess of the supply.[2] Full employment of course does not mean
that there are no unemployed. There appears to be a considerable
amount of transitional unemployment, particularly in the building industry as one contract comes to an end and others have yet
to begin.[3] There is also a very high labour turnover due to personal
and other causes, and young men like Godfrey and John, referred
to in Chanda's account, who give up or are dismissed from one
job may have to wait some time before finding another, and may,
as the P.W.D. orderly remarked, 'suffer much through unemployment'. As I have indicated, there has been no serious unem-

[1] Dr V. W. Turner tells me that among the Lamba of the Ndola District the
onset of the slump in the closing of the opencast mine at Bwana M'kubwa still
marks an important point in dating events.

[2] I refer to the situation as I knew it in 1956.

[3] Mr A. A. Nyirenda found in an independent study carried out in Lusaka
that many bricklayers there who were temporarily unemployed sought a
livelihood by selling in the African market. I do not know whether this
practice was followed in Ndola. See Nyirenda, 1957.

ployment throughout the period of my various field-studies. At the same time, the possibility of unemployment is always present as a potential threat to the personal security of the African in the town, a threat, moreover, to which he is especially vulnerable in certain respects. Since a strong body of official and unofficial European opinion still insists on regarding the African worker primarily as a temporarily displaced tribesman with only minimal rights and responsibilities in the town, no provision yet exists for social insurance schemes and the payment of unemployment benefits. Secondly, wages are generally paid on a 'ticket' basis, the ticket normally being completed in just over a month. But few families ever manage to make their wages stretch over the whole period so that they rarely have any savings behind them to withstand a spell of temporary unemployment or other emergency. On top of all this, houses are tied to jobs in such a way that loss of employment is likely to involve immediate eviction[1] with its attendant problems of moving furniture and possessions and finding temporary accommodation for wife and children.

The risk of unemployment does not of course affect equally or in the same way all categories within the African urban population. Obviously the pressures of the urban system do not weigh so heavily on the younger men who are still bachelors or have only recently married, and are relatively recent arrivals from the rural areas; and it is within this category that the highest rate of labour turnover is found.[2] Nevertheless the various factors just outlined above do underline the economically dependent status of the African in a Northern Rhodesia town. Socially and politically, it is also an uncertain status. While there are a number of ordinances whose provisions aim to protect the interests of the Africans, there are also various administrative measures designed to control the

[1] Under the terms of the African Urban Housing Ordinance the Location Superintendent has a discretion to allow an unemployed man to remain in possession of the house for a further month provided he can pay the rent himself. In my experience, few Africans are aware of this provision and my impression is that so great is the demand for housing that in any case the discretion is rarely exercised.

[2] See also Mitchell, 1951, where the evidence suggests that newcomers move about during the first five years of their residence on the Copperbelt and then settle down in one town. This is also reflected to some extent in African trade unions where the greater the stability of labour the stronger is the tendency to join a union. See Mwewa, 1958.

movement of the African population, the general effect of which
is to make even more manifest his insecure position in the towns.
Thus while local authorities are required by law to set aside special
housing areas or locations for their African residents, no African,
for example, may lawfully remain in such an area for more than
twenty-four hours without the special permission of the Location
Superintendent. In recent years there has been an increasing concern in many quarters about the growing incidence of violence
amongst Africans in the urban areas, which is commonly attributed to the presence of large numbers of 'loafers' believed to be
residing illegally in the locations.[1] In Ndola, accordingly, raids for
'unauthorized persons' are carried out regularly by the location
police. During my stay in Ndola one such large-scale comb-out
was undertaken by the Mobile Police Unit based at Bwana
M'kubwa at the request of the Location Superintendent. Such was
the manner in which they carried out their task that for days
afterwards I continued to hear of women who were said to be
sleeping in the bush for fear of arrest. At the next meeting of the
Urban Advisory Council the African leaders vigorously protested
against the provocative and offensive behaviour of the police.
They drew attention to the fact that women who were in possession of the correct residence permits had been arrested and subsequently fined in the African Urban Court because they were not
in possession of marriage certificates. Such arrests were of course
illegal since there was no law in force in the Territory which
required the compulsory registration of marriage amongst Africans. The District Commissioner, in reply, explained why the

[1] During 1955 there were widespread reports of stoning incidents in which
cars were attacked by riotous mobs after accidents involving Africans, frequently irrespective of the race of the driver and whether in fact the particular
car had been involved in the accident or was merely stopping to offer assistance.
In a similar sort of incident at Chingola some 2,000 Africans rioted after an
African worker was accidentally killed by a moving crane. Different interpretations will no doubt be placed upon these events, but it is at least clear that they
cannot be satisfactorily explained by an easy reference to the presence of loafers
alone. While it is true that many of those arrested for their part in the Chingola
riot were 'unauthorized persons' living on the mine compound without permission, they were not 'loafers' for they were in employment elsewhere in the
town. Parasites and rogues who live on their wits there may be—as there are in
every town—but my own view is that the dimensions of the 'loafer' problem
as commonly conceived are grossly exaggerated. What emerged plainly from
the Chingola incident were the dimensions of the housing problem.

Mobile Police Unit had been called in. The police as a whole was under strength, he said, but occasionally it was possible to borrow a platoon from Bwana M'kubwa for a couple of weeks. The Location Superintendent had gone away on a short leave, and he himself did not know what instructions had been given. However, the District Commissioner continued, as soon as he heard about the question of marriage certificates he got in touch with the Officer-in-Charge and told him to withdraw the instruction. The District Commissioner said that he was very sorry for what had happened; there had been a misunderstanding of the instructions to the police. When he sought to reassure the Advisory Council that the same mistake would not be made again, one member was quick to point out that a raid of precisely the same kind had been carried out at the same time in the previous year.[1] It was the possibility of such a raid that sprang to Chanda's mind when he returned home one day and was told by his neighbour that his wife had gone to Bwana M'kubwa.[2] In a Northern Rhodesia town the African is never a full and free citizen as that term would be understood elsewhere.

Environment is a relative concept: its bounds are never set, but what it shall include varies according to the social units isolated for purposes of analysis. Viewed then from the standpoint of the Africans dwelling in the location, the themes I have been discussing so far may be described as environmental constants: they refer to institutions and policies operative within the urban system over which the African has little direct control, but which impinge upon him at every turn. Economic organization and the local system of administration will vary of course according to the kinds

[1] After the meeting the District Commissioner commented to me that the Advisory Council had his full sympathy. On the other hand, he explained, one couldn't let the police down too badly. The whole business had put him in a very difficult position!

[2] In this generally unsettled atmosphere it is hardly surprising that Africans should sometimes appear unduly credulous and ready to believe the worst, and that the wildest rumours should receive widespread and ready acceptance. At the time of the arrests the rumour soon got around that Government was rounding up the tax defaulters and dispatching them to work on the great dam being built at the Kariba Gorge. Amongst Africans the area was commonly regarded as a 'death-trap' and for a week or more the clerks were scarcely able to cope with the long queues of Africans coming hastily to pay their overdue taxes.

of economic function that the town has come to serve, to the aims and practice of central and colonial governments, to the presence and role of minority groups, and so on. But whatever form these take, the economic and administrative institutions of the town form the major part of the new social environment to which the urban African has to adjust. They provide a basic institutional framework moulding and at the same time circumscribing the pattern of social relations amongst Africans in the town.

Within the limits set by this environment there are also areas of greater or lesser autonomy in which other sets of social uniformities are to be found. The first of these relates to the pattern of social relationships amongst Africans in the town. Here again Chanda's accounts provide a useful point of departure. These accounts show Chanda in personal interaction with a wide variety of individuals. The nature of his association with these people differs greatly in degree and kind. Some are purely casual and fleeting encounters as when he accompanied his friend James to the beer-drink at *mikotokoto*,[1] though it is noticeable here how he at once categorized the company in terms of its mixed tribal composition. In other cases, although the people were previously unknown to him, they fell into an acknowledged social category which required some modification of his behaviour. Such was his introduction at the Beer Hall to the kin of his wife's sister's husband, whom he at once treated as his own affines in accordance with tribal custom, although they were in fact of a different tribe and one, moreover, which enjoys low prestige in the towns. In yet other cases the encounter was again casual, but friendly interaction took place on the basis of a former relationship, as with the orderly or the young man Godfrey who had once been fellow employees with Chanda in the Public Works Department; or the effect of the meeting was to reaffirm ties which were still in existence, but temporarily dormant or inactive as in the case of his kinsmen who had just arrived in Ndola from the tribal area. Finally, there was a range of people he interacted with regularly, and with whom his relationship was relatively intense.

Each person within the total range of contact thus had a different role in relation to Chanda. For the most part, though not entirely, these roles reflect and emerge out of the different forms of grouping that operate within the urban field. It is obviously

[1] See above, p. 85.

beyond the scope of the present paper to embark on a detailed analysis of these groupings; all I shall attempt here therefore is to indicate them and sketch them in a preliminary fashion. To begin with, there are the social relationships associated with neighbourhood and locality. Social ties are brought into being by the mere fact of physical contiguity and proximity. There are parts of Africa where the housing of the urban population proceeds relatively free of Government or Municipal and other controls, and the African citizen has some degree of choice over how and where he should live. But in a town like Ndola choice of this kind is more restricted, for the responsibility for providing African housing is shouldered mainly by the local authority, while the actual allocation of houses is controlled by the Location Superintendent. The usual procedure in applying for a house is to approach the Location Office through one's employer. Since the housing shortage is so acute the newcomer will probably have his name added to a list, and may then have to wait for some months or even longer before he is housed.[1] Through this system of allocation the new occupant of a house has no idea what sort of neighbours he is going to have. Although the system does allow of a certain amount of selection of house-holders by the authorities, the Municipal Council does not follow a policy of attempting to concentrate members of certain tribes in particular sections of the location. Any one section or ward, therefore, will show considerable diversity amongst its residents in terms of tribal origins, and to a lesser extent in terms of occupational and other criteria. In short, one is rarely in a position to choose one's neighbours or one's neighbourhood.

Nor is it always easy to ignore or to isolate oneself from uncongenial neighbours. Houses in the location are small and their physical proximity imposes a certain minimum of cooperation. In order to reach one's own house, it is often necessary to cross a neighbour's yard. There is a communal water tap for each section and there are slabs for washing clothes. Here the women gather and have to take it in turn to fetch water or do their chores. The water taps are a frequent source of quarrels, but they also provide an opportunity for people to learn about one another, to make new

[1] In the meantime, a residence permit, renewable weekly at a cost of threepence, entitles one to reside legally in the location with friends or relatives. The whole situation lends itself readily to graft and all manner of intrigue.

friendships etc., and they become a focal point of chatter. The neighbourhood is socially a more important unit for women than it is for men. Men go off to work during the day and do not have the opportunities to form the same attachments within the immediate neighbourhood as the women, who spend more of their time around the house. Many African women still spend most of their time outside the house itself: they prepare the vegetables, cook their meals, and do their washing up in the open. In this way they see their neighbours doing exactly the same sort of thing and they carry on conversations together. Often they will pop over the fence, so to speak, and do their chores together. Neighbours help one another in a variety of ways: they borrow money from one another, or items of foodstuff if they should suddenly run out, or they may put up your mother-in-law if she should come to stay with you, and you consider it would be a breach of the in-law taboo to have her sleep in your own house. Beyond this, sets of adjoining houses become small gossip clusters in which the affairs of the neighbours are made known, discussed and criticized. Neighbours tend to know a good deal of one's private life and movements. Whenever a man returns home and finds his wife absent, as did Chanda on one occasion, his first recourse is to one or other of his immediate neighbours.

The boundaries of the neighbourhood are of course necessarily vague and, at its further reaches, neighbourhood shades into locality. Each part of the town, and each division or ward of the location is distinguished by the name conferred upon it by the local authority.

But as I have shown elsewhere (Epstein, 1959: 244) the Africans themselves also invent and employ other names to express the special character or value which a given locality has come to enjoy in their own eyes. Furthermore, in casual social intercourse, as when Chanda found his friend James in the company of a man from Kabushi whom he did not know, individuals are categorized according to the locality in which they live.

At the time Chanda prepared his accounts for me he had only recently moved into a new house and his neighbours do not figure prominently in them. In terms of numbers at least, the most important single category of persons with whom he interacted was composed of a varied body of kinsfolk. The *extent* of kinship, using that expression to cover the number of actual personal contacts with kin, is most striking. Nor of course do those individuals mentioned in the text exhaust the full extent of Chanda's kinship connections. There were a number of other kinsmen living in Ndola whom he saw more or less frequently, and there were many others visiting the town who would call on him, or whom he would encounter unexpectedly on the way. In Luanshya, too, he had an extensive kin connection and whenever the opportunity afforded he would make the journey there by bus or bicycle to visit them. But what is equally if not more striking is the *range* of kinship, that is, the nature and degree of spread of kinship ties, which may be seen plainly in the skeleton genealogy I have

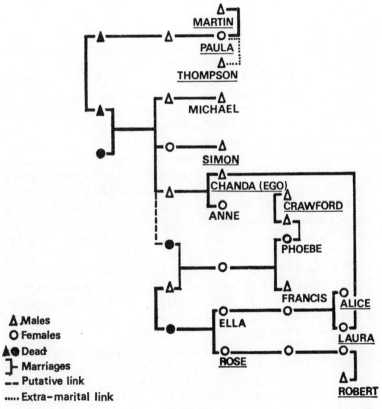

FIGURE 8

Skeleton genealogy of Chanda's kin

prepared to link those persons who find a place in his narrative. None of Chanda's immediate kin was in Ndola. Two sisters were living in Elizabethville, and another two elsewhere on the Copperbelt. His father and his three brothers lived at home in Lunda country. Nevertheless, even in Ndola he remains surrounded by kinsmen for he recognizes and maintains close links with those to whom he claims relationship, however remote, in both the male and female lines as well as by ties of affinity. In this way he speaks, for example, of Paula, the daughter of his father's father's brother's son, as his sister, and is addressed as father by the slightly younger Francis whose maternal grandmother was a classificatory sister of Chanda's own father.

It seems clear that a classificatory system of kinship of this kind performs the same general function in an urban milieu as it does in tribal society. More accurately, perhaps, it serves a dual function. On the one hand, it reduces all possible relationships of kinship to a limited and readily manageable number of categories of kin to whom behaviour is adjusted according to the appropriate kin relationship. On the other hand, it allows and even provides for the extension of these patterns of behaviour to an indefinite number of persons with whom actual genealogical connection may be extremely remote. In this respect, therefore, and in this sense, kinship provides one of the most important principles for ordering social relations amongst Africans in the towns. At the same time, kinship involves more than a mere indication of the appropriate forms of behaviour to be adopted in social intercourse. The recognition of ties of kinship involves also recognition of reciprocal responsibilities, obligations and privileges. At this time, for instance, Chanda's burdens were particularly heavy. He was keeping at his home and feeding his patrilateral cross-cousin Simon and his wife until Simon got a job and house of his own. A conversation with Thompson, whom he met one day at the Location Office in Kabushi as they were returning from work, illustrates the difficulties he was facing.

'*Mulamo*, I know you are in a fix,' Thompson began after Chanda had shown some reluctance to accompany his friend to the Beer Hall. 'You are very worried about your financial state. Your sister (meaning Anne) has come for a very important matter, asking for 10,000 francs to buy a plot of land in Elizabethville where all your sisters in the Congo can live with their families.

Your wife's grandmother is here too. And you need money for your rations and pleasure, and I understand you also have a very high account at the stores in town. So if you go home this time you will feel very sad. To make you forget all this, the best thing is to come with me to the Beer Hall so that you feel a little happy.' Chanda elaborated on his distress. 'Where can I ever find the 10,000 francs my sister is looking for?' he asked. 'If it were just clothes she wanted, it wouldn't be so bad, but she only wants money. When she wrote a letter from Chingola she didn't say anything about all this, just that she was coming here. 10,000 francs is nearly £150. I don't know what to do.' 'I understand fully the troubles you have,' Thompson replied. 'Moreover, you keep a lot of people at your home. But let us just go and drink some beer.'

The ties of kinship impose onerous obligations which are frequently resented and even on occasion ignored; but the responsibilities are also matched with privileges. If Chanda found his duties to kinsfolk irksome at times, he also knew that in other situations and at other times he would be able to claim from them hospitality and support. Thus when his wife was away on a short visit to Bancroft he was entitled to ask her sisters to come and help in cooking for and looking after him and, indeed, they upbraided him mildly because he had not told them that Laura had gone and he was staying on his own. From others, too, he was able to demand favours even if sometimes, as when Martin failed to bring him back a jacket from Elizabethville, he was sadly disappointed. In the towns, where social relationships are so often casual and transitory, and where the status of the African is so fundamentally uncertain and insecure, the maintenance of widespread ties of kinship helps to ensure that there will always be someone around one can rely upon for support and assistance now and for the future. Ties of kinship of course alter in their degree of intensity as the result of absence and the movement of people, but the ties themselves are permanent and enduring for they are fixed by the system of descent. The wide extent and range of kinship recognized in the towns thus introduces an important element of stability into what is an extremely fluid situation.

Where kinship appears to serve such important social functions in the towns, it is not perhaps surprising that its values should spill over into and colour other social relationships. Thus the modes of address and forms of behaviour appropriate between particular categories of kin are readily extended to unrelated persons, and close relations with neighbours and friends are frequently translated in this way into the idiom of kinship. What is even more illuminating as illustrating the high value that attaches to kinship are those cases where the parties to an already existing relationship are later found to be kinsmen as well. Such discoveries are usually made in the course of social introductions, which are frequently accompanied by a detailed recital of ancestry and family connections, and they will be received with expressions of deep pleasure. For example, when it emerged that Chanda was married to a girl whom he could properly call his grandchild, everyone present immediately chorused approval: they saw the link of kinship as lending additional strength to the bonds which already united them. The tracing out of Chanda's tie of kinship with the Congress leader Crawford was greeted with a similar display of approbation. In neither of these instances was the discovery likely to affect the behaviour of the parties to one another in any noticeable way. Nevertheless, the establishment of the kin tie was seen as something valuable in itself, lending to the relationship a tone it had previously lacked.

The nature of this 'additional' element emerges most clearly in Crawford's case, and offers a clue to understanding the value which kinship comes to assume in the urban areas. As mentioned earlier, Chanda had known Crawford already for some considerable time. Indeed, they were quite close friends and often drank beer together at the Beer Hall. But when he met his kinsman Francis together with Crawford one day, Francis at once explained that Crawford's own full brother, a schoolteacher in the Kawambwa District, was married to Phoebe, Francis's sister and Chanda's classificatory mother.[1] Chanda therefore immediately recognized Crawford as his own classificatory father. But what is important to note is that recognition did not involve any change in their behaviour towards one another. Chanda did not now treat Crawford with the respect due to a member of the senior adjacent generation, even allowing for the fact that in the matrilineal systems in which they had both been reared the relationship of

[1] The relationship involved here has to be understood in the light of the principles of positional succession, and the identification of alternate generations described by Cunnison, 1956.

father and son is much easier than in a patrilineal system, where it is the father and not the mother's brother who exercises authority over his children. On the contrary, their behaviour remained that of friends and equals. Indeed, this was emphasized by Crawford himself when he remarked: 'We play together, share our gifts, and so on just as friends and yet we are related by blood. . . . Ah, this is fine, indeed.'

Of course even in the routine of ordinary life under tribal conditions the intercourse of kinsfolk often lacks formal precision. On the other hand, among the tribes, kinship frequently provides a basis for the formation of corporate groups, for common residence, claims to land, and so on: as such, it is articulated with the whole political and social system of the tribe. In the towns this condition does not obtain at all; here, moreover, it has to be remembered that the urban African population is made up predominantly of men and women of working age, i.e. up to about 40, and that members of the senior generation are conspicuously absent. Thus kinship relationships under urban conditions are in a sense largely 'de-structured', and kinship consists essentially in broad categories of persons who stand in different degrees of relationship of blood and affinity to one another, but who tend to treat one another as equals and recognize a general obligation to help one another. This does not mean that the appropriate forms of behaviour as between, say, adjacent generations or affines are overlooked or minimized; what it means is that the further one proceeds beyond the range of immediate kin, the greater is the tendency to regard all kin, whatever their actual genealogical connection, as falling within the same broad category. It seems significant that in modern Copperbelt parlance such persons are spoken of as being related *mu cibululu*, a term now used by all tribes to express the notion of kinship which derives via 'Kitchen Kafir' from the Afrikaans word *broer*, meaning brother. The deep value which attaches to kinship in the urban context lies in the fact that at its furthest extension kinship becomes synonymous with and gives expression to the fundamental values of brotherhood.

Closely related to the ties of kinship, though really of a different order, are those which stem from membership of a tribe. Every African in Ndola is a member of a tribe, and the veriest tot will answer without hesitation if asked what tribe he belongs to. All told, there are probably some fifty and more tribes represented in the population of the town. They are drawn mostly from the Northern and Eastern Provinces of Northern Rhodesia, but important sections also come from the Western and Central Provinces, and from the neighbouring territories of Nyasaland and the Belgian Congo. The tribes themselves are scattered indiscriminately over the whole location, though here and there about the town small tribal pockets may be found. Thus the small settlement known as the Sanitary Farm, which is slightly apart from the location, is composed almost entirely of Luvale, and amongst other tribes is commonly regarded as the haunt of sorcerers and ghouls. To all Luvale, irrespective of the jobs they actually do, the collective term *Nyamazai*, scavengers, is contemptuously applied because the Luvale alone of all the tribes have shown willingness to undertake the work of night-soil removal. Luvale and Lunda from the Mwinilunga District are also said to be concentrated in various contractors' compounds around the town, and in the African Township at Twapia which caters for petty traders and other self-employed Africans, but I did not check these statements carefully in the field.

Although in the main they are thus interspersed and intermingled, the tribes are also set apart from one another by language, custom, and other marks of distinctiveness. A wide variety of tribal languages are spoken in the town and these are often mutually unintelligible. In the Urban Court or in other contexts where Africans of different tribes have to come together recourse has frequently to be made to interpreters. In these circumstances, misunderstandings of the kind attributed to Chanda's Nsenga neighbour are common. On the other hand, most Africans I have known well showed a remarkable ease in acquiring the tongues of other groups (see Epstein, 1959). Customs, too, particularly those relating to dress or adornment, serve as important diacritical indices which readily disclose one's tribal identity. Even physical appearance may be a relevant factor, as is suggested in Martin's introduction of his Kasai friend to Chanda, though it is also apparent from Martin's remarks that what are physical characteristics and what cultural may not always be easy to determine. On the basis of these and other criteria, tribes become important categories of social interaction amongst Africans in the towns, as Mitchell (1956) has shown. Support for this view of urban tribalism is to be found throughout Chanda's account. Whenever he comes into the presence of strangers, as at a beer drink or on encountering the Government Messengers from Fort Rosebery, he reacts at once by placing them in a category in terms of the distinguishing characteristics that have come to be associated with their tribe, and he adjusts his behaviour accordingly. But Mitchell was able to carry his analysis of this categorizing process much further: he was able to demonstrate how, despite the large number of tribes represented on the Copperbelt, the whole of the African urban population was in fact broken down into and contained within a very limited number of broad tribal categories. Knowledge of an alien tribe, its language, culture and system of internal relations are related to geographical and social distance. Neighbouring tribes may be acutely aware of the hostilities or cultural and historical differences which divide and separate them from each other; but such matters lie beyond the ken of the remote outsider living in another part of the country. His knowledge of the distant tribes is likely to be fragmentary, so that he tends to overlook or to be unaware of their internal differences and to bracket them all together, treating them as a single tribal entity. In this way, for example, the Bemba of the Northern Province ignore the considerable differences that exist between the tribes of the Eastern Province, and in the towns lump them all together as Ngoni, the dominant tribe of the region. In the same way, all Africans from the Belgian Congo who seek work on the Copperbelt are known locally as Kasai. For a long time I had myself lingered under the impression, fostered by African usage, that the term Kasai referred to a specific tribal group; it was only late in my field-work that I came to realize that the usage was only a further illustration of the categorizing process.

Tribalism in the sense just defined operates in a wide range of situations, but its influence is most noticeable perhaps in the field of personal interaction. Kinsfolk apart, a man like Chanda finds his most intimate associates among those he calls 'home-fellows' or fellow tribesmen. These are the ones he will put himself out to go and visit, and with whom he prefers to sit and chat and drink beer. In the urban context Lunda of Kazembe are associated with the numerically preponderant Bemba, with whom they share a common language and many common customs and traditions. Chanda has a number of friends, like Thompson for example,

who are Bemba, but he appears to have no close friends outside
the range of Bemba-speaking peoples. But, as in the case of kinship, tribalism involves more than a mere delimiting of the range
of interaction. Membership of a tribe also imposes an obligation,
vaguely defined though it may be, to give mutual aid and support.
Amongst fellow tribesmen one is always at home, for all share
certain common interests which set them apart from or in
opposition to the other tribes amongst and with whom they live
and work in the towns. At the same time it should be stressed
here that tribalism is always situational; it does not operate
equally or with the same degree of intensity over the whole field
of social relations in which the urban Africans now participate.
The young man Godfrey was linked with the African detective
as a fellow Lozi; but he associated himself with alien tribesmen in
their common opposition to the other in his role of policeman.

One concept that finds repeated expression throughout Chanda's
account is that of prestige. In broad terms prestige refers to the
esteem and regard which are accorded to a person (or group) in
virtue of his personal qualities, his special abilities, or his general
mode of behaviour and way of life. In the Ndola context some of
the marks by which a man of prestige is known are indicated in
Chanda's account of his visit to his brother-in-law and in his
conversations with Francis. He had called on the former in order
to see his sister, he said, but it is likely that he was more interested
in learning whether Martin had brought him back a 'fever coat'
from Elizabethville. A number of observers of the Northern
Rhodesia scene have already remarked the importance which
Africans attach to matters of dress. At this time it seems that the
'fever coat'—a long, loose-fitting jacket—was particularly prized,
and possession of one would have enabled Chanda to cut a considerable dash. Here then prestige accrues to the African who
dresses smartly in the 'European' fashion. Again, Chanda himself
acquires prestige because of his light complexion—'you look just
like a European'—and because in his mode of dress and in other
ways he comports himself like a 'gentleman', one of the many
terms now in common use on the Copperbelt to convey the
notion of superior social status (cf. Epstein, 1959). On the other
hand, in other contexts and in other company, his incapacity for
consuming large quantities of beer might count against him and
stamp him as something less than a full man. Evaluation in terms

of prestige extends even to the tribes themselves: this is clearly reflected, for example, in the boasts of the Lamba who had married 'a beautiful lady of Kawambwa', for the Lunda in general have a reputation for sophistication, while the Lamba are collectively designated as *bapwapwa*, a term of contempt originating in the alleged propensity of the Lamba for eating the lungs (*pwapwa*) which is commonly regarded as 'dirty' meat.

   In this context then prestige emerges as a pervasive concept in the sense that it enters into almost every social activity and into every social relationship; or re-phrasing it more forcefully, there are very few facets of human behaviour which may not be seized upon in evaluating prestige. This is perhaps what one would expect for the general fluidity of the urban situation, the heterogeneous and differentiated character of the African urban population with its concomitant diversity of norms and standards of behaviour, and the marked emphasis on achieved as against ascribed status create a set of conditions in which the struggle for prestige becomes a major preoccupation of the new urban-dwellers. Accordingly, the criteria of prestige are extremely varied, often ill-defined, and frequently inconsistent. There is therefore no one single principle which embraces all the various criteria of prestige, and no single prestige system which comprehends the whole community. In this sense prestige may be said to be 'particular' in that its conferment always involves reference to a particular situation and to a particular set of people. In another sense, however, prestige is 'general', and it is important that the two usages of the term be kept distinct. By 'general' I mean here that despite the variability in the components that enter into the whole notion of prestige, certain of these will tend to run together in clusters, and have widespread recognition throughout the community. Thus white-collar occupation, secondary school education, smartness in dress and appearance, a well furnished house, etc., are in themselves important and independent criteria of prestige. When they run together—as frequently they do—they mark out readily the man of acknowledged superior status. It is this 'clustering' which has enabled Mitchell and myself to speak (Mitchell, 1956; Mitchell and Epstein, 1959) of the 'European way of life' as providing a scale in terms of which the African urban population is stratified. In other words, such clusters or configurations provide the basis for the emergence of social classes as a further important category of social interaction. Social classes arise out of conscious-ness of kind: amongst the members of a class there is a ready and mutual acceptance of one another as social equals; they interact more frequently, exchange visits, develop common interests and activities and even distinctive modes of behaviour which mark them off clearly, at least in their own eyes, from other classes. It was precisely in these terms, for example, that Thompson and Chanda saw themselves as set apart from the scurrying African labourers who had once laughed at them for wasting their time in school.

Thus prestige in its 'general' aspect provides a working model of the class structure which the Africans themselves employ in a wide variety of situations. But it does not follow from this that in practice the lines of demarcation between classes can always be rigidly drawn. The fact that 'general' prestige is built up around a cluster of criteria allows of different combinations and permuta-tions which may make 'class placement' in fact extraordinarily difficult. This lack of rigidity in turn serves to promote and intensify the struggle for prestige within and between the strata, so that increasingly refined, 'particular' criteria of prestige come to be invoked to advance one's status. Thus while 'general' prestige provides an overall framework for categorizing the urban popula-tion in terms of class, in terms of actual social interaction 'parti-cular' prestige becomes increasingly important in marking in-clusion or exclusion from class membership. The variety and diversity and the general pervasive character of the 'particular' criteria of prestige thus opens the way to a complex pattern of changing allegiances and cross-cutting ties both within and between classes.

We have already had occasion to remark on the high degree of diversification as a characteristic of urban communities. With this process there goes too an increasing segmenting and specialization of social interests. A further mark therefore of urban communities is the development of various kinds of formal association for the protection and furtherance of those interests. Indeed, it is a com-mon assumption in the literatrure of urban sociology that, with the progressive displacement in uban society of 'primary' by 'se cond-ary' groups the association comes to have overriding importance in the social organization of the town. In recent years this view has been increasingly challenged (see Dotson, 1951; La Piere,

1954): certainly there is little support for it to be found in the Ndola material. Thus throughout Chanda's account there is mention of only one association, the African National Congress—and even then the reference was incidental. Here Chanda's lack of emphasis on the associations accurately reflects the relatively limited extent to which social relationships amongst Africans in Ndola are organized through membership of these bodies.

Apart from the churches, to one or other of which the vast majority of Africans in Ndola give at least nominal allegiance,[1] those associations which affect potentially the largest number of persons are the African National Congress and the various African trade unions. The African National Congress is a political body organized on a territorial basis, with a central headquarters at Lusaka and local branches throughout the country organized on a provincial basis. Ndola is the headquarters for the Western Province. Congress claims to represent the voice of African opinion in the Territory, and since its inception in 1949 has organized a number of campaigns to rectify African grievances or to protest against 'measures considered detrimental to African interests'. Despite the widespread popular support the Congress has enjoyed, it is a loose-knit organization, in some respects extraordinarily haphazard, with a very small registered membership. Indeed, the concept of a regular membership has very little meaning when applied to a body like Congress. Anthony Sampson's description (1958: 41) of the African National Congress in South Africa is equally appropriate to Northern Rhodesia: 'there are times of sudden indignation in the locations where nearly everyone claims to be a Congressman, others when Congress appears to consist of only a hard core of enthusiasts'. The activities of Congress are intermittent, and as a political association Congress acts to organize the community only in spasmodic eruptions and for specific purposes.[2] So far as trade unions are concerned, the analysis which I offered (Epstein, 1958, ch. 4) of the 'location' unions in Luanshya

---

[1] Most of the major denominations of organized Christendom are represented in the town. Roman Catholics constitute the largest single group, while in recent years the Watchtower sect (Jehovah's Witnesses) has emerged as an influential and highly organized group. There has been little of an African separatist movement in the Territory.

[2] This refers of course to the time when this paper was written and does not take subsequent developments into account.

seems equally relevant to Ndola. There are a number of African unions in the town, but with the possible exception of the Municipal and the Railway Workers' Unions, they are small, poorly organized and ineffectual. Indeed, in a few cases the organization has so broken down that it is only in a nominal sense that one can speak of the union as continuing to exist. Finally, there are a number of recreational bodies such as the Football Club or the Ballroom Dance Society, and the tribal dancing teams of the kind described by Mitchell in his paper on the Kalela dance. Conspicuously absent in Ndola is the profusion of tribal associations, mutual aid or burial societies, and the variegated assortment of social clubs reported so frequently of other urban communities elsewhere in Africa.

The apparent paucity of associational life in the town, and the general role of the associations in the community raise problems which lie outside the scope of the present paper. What is important in the present context is that they involve a very different mode of ordering social relations from those considered hitherto. Typically the association has a clearly defined formal structure, and to this extent the relationships in which the members participate are themselves 'structured' or formalized. However, the associations too have a categorical aspect. Voluntary associations tend to arise out of the interaction of persons who see the formally constituted body as the proper or more effective way of furthering the avowed aims and interests they hold in common. Once established, the association may extend further its membership and so come to include many strangers, but all members now interact consistently within a new structural framework. On the other hand, interaction within the association also gives rise to new sets of ties which continue to operate outside this framework. Thus Chanda knew Crawford primarily as a leader in the African National Congress, but when they met casually at the Beer Hall and drank together their behaviour reflected a categorical rather than a 'structured' or formalized relationship. In precisely the same way relationships developed within an institutional setting such as at school or at work provide a basis for friendly social intercourse of a different kind outside that setting. Apart therefore from the more specific role that they play in the political, economic and other sectors of urban life formal institutions and associations have a further importance in providing a major principle of recruitment to the network of social relations in which every urban African is involved.

Effective and extended sectors of Chanda's network
In the preceding section I have used the account of his activities presented by Chanda to illustrate the random character of much of urban social life. I have also tried to show that within this extremely fluid field there are also elements of regularity, and here too I have made use of Chanda's material in illustrating some of their properties. Briefly, I have drawn attention to the importance of various categorical and formalized relationships in urban social structure. But Chanda's material also has a further and more direct bearing on our problem, for it draws immediate attention to another principle around which social relations are ordered. As I have already noted, Chanda's accounts show him interacting on a personal face-to-face basis with a fairly wide range of people to whom he is linked in varying ways: he acknowledges certain general obligations towards most of them, and he treats them in the main as his social equals. Together these persons represent a section—in all likelihood a fairly limited one—of the total range of his social contacts in the town. However, they do not in any sense constitute a group for they lack any co-ordinating organization. They do not even form a collectivity for they have no corporate existence whatsoever: all they may be said to possess in common is the social tie which links each of them individually to a central figure, Chanda. Chanda, that is to say, is in touch with a number of people, some of whom may be in touch with each other, and some of whom may not. Barnes (1954) speaks of a social field of this kind as a network, and I find it convenient to follow his usage.

A network in this sense is always egocentric: it exists only and is defined with reference to a particular individual. As Barnes remarks, each person sees himself at the centre of a collection of friends. It follows therefore that the network is always 'personal', for the set of links that make it up are unique for each individual.[1] Chanda has his network, but the individuals who compose it are each also at the centre of their own. Many members of their networks will be unknown to Chanda as indeed is evident throughout his account. In parenthesis, it may be remarked that even his wife

[1] See, however, Barnes's discussion of this point in Chap. II, p. 57 above.

has her own network. While there are many kin and friends who form part of their common network, she has her own range of contacts which she maintains independently of her husband. This is consistent with their highly segregated conjugal roles suggested by Chanda's material in which his wife is never once mentioned as accompanying him on his visits.

A network is made up of pairs of persons who interact with one another in terms of social categories, and who regard each other therefore as approximate social equals, ignoring in this context the slight differences in social status there may be between them. Since it is essentially 'personal' the network allows of many different configurations, and these in turn may provide the basis for a typology of networks. Thus in handling problems of urban family structure in London, Elizabeth Bott (1957) attempted to relate variations in conjugal roles to different kinds of network. Briefly, she distinguishes between close-knit and loose-knit networks. A close-knit network is defined as one in which there are many relationships between its component units: in a family which has a close-knit network many of its friends, neighbours and kinsfolk will know one another. In Bott's terms, such a network has a high degree of connectedness. By contrast, a loose-knit network exists where friends, neighbours and kin are not known to each other and the degree of connectedness is therefore slight.

Applying Bott's distinction, Chanda's network would appear to be of the loose-knit variety. However, closer examination of the data suggests that this may not be an adequate formulation. To begin with, not every link in the network possesses the same density; as we noted at the outset, Chanda does not interact with everyone in the network with the same degree of intensity. There are those around him with whom he has close ties and who are also more closely knit together than others. There are others again with whom his ties are more or less close, but whom he sees less frequently and who are strangers or have only tenuous links amongst themselves. Thus there may be a relatively high degree of connectedness amongst those with whom Chanda interacts in terms of social class, or amongst those he counts as kin, but as between the two categories themselves the degree of connectedness may be slight. In short, the network may not be connected in its totality, but highly connected in its parts. Those people with whom Chanda interacts most intensely and most regularly, and who are therefore also likely to come to know one another, that is to say that part of the total network which shows a degree of connectedness, I propose to speak of as forming the *effective* network: the remainder constitute the *extended* network.

Barnes has observed (1954: 46) that it is only pairs of persons who are directly in contact with one another in the network who regard themselves as approximately of equal status; but he also points out that each person in the network does not necessarily regard everyone else in it as his equal. In the *effective* network the tendency of course is for status differentiation to be minimized; but in the *extended* network, although interaction takes place between approximate social equals, the likelihood of some status differentiation being recognized is much greater because of the different social categories from which the network is recruited. For example, when Chanda meets Thompson, or the orderly in the Public Works Department, or his wife's sister's husband Robert, he reacts to each of them as his social equals. Thompson himself, however, who is part of Chanda's *effective* network, knows neither the orderly nor Robert, and he would regard them both as his social inferiors, in the one case because of the orderly's lowly occupation, in the other because Robert belonged to a tribe that ranks low in popular esteem on the Copperbelt, and because he was a lorry driver to boot. The *effective* network then consists of clusters of persons fairly closely knitted together. The limits of such clusters—to use Barnes' term—are vague, but in some situations they show an exclusiveness so marked as to suggest the existence of groups in the strict sense, and point to recognizable divisions within the community. The *extended* network, on the other hand, which makes greater allowance for the gradations of social status, tends to cut across such divisions. The network as a whole, therefore, provides a covert or informal structure composed of inter-personal links which spread out and ramify in all directions, criss-crossing not only the whole of the local community, but knitting together people in different towns and in town and country.

In exploring the social system of Bremnes, Barnes was concerned with the concept of the network as one amongst a number of possible tools for use in the analysis of the phenomenon of social class. Elizabeth Bott has also used it for somewhat similar purposes. For Bott the network of friends, neighbours and relatives mediates between the family and the total society: perception of the society as a whole, and in particular of the class structure, is thus related to experience within this primary social world. More immediately, however, Bott was concerned with the concept of the network in explaining variations of conjugal roles within the family. It seems clear that all of these uses would be equally valuable in probing the social system of a town like Ndola. However, in concluding this discussion of the network I want to suggest that the concept may also have considerable relevance to the discussion of other problems arising within the urban field, such as the question of social control. For example, Mitchell (1957) has expressed the feeling that African marriage on the Copperbelt is gradually assuming a character of its own. He then raises the question what mechanism, in lieu of the kinship system, operates to enforce the norms of married behaviour, and suggests for answer that it lies in the African Urban Courts. The role of the courts is clearly important here, but I suggest that a fuller understanding of the growth of new norms of married behaviour, and the pressures towards acceptance of them may be found in the operation of the network.

The evidence to support the view I am putting forward would take us far beyond the limits of the present paper. Here therefore I am able merely to sketch in the general argument. In the discussion hitherto I have treated the network simply as a series of links in a chain of personal interaction: nothing has been said of the content of the interaction. When we follow a young man like Chanda through these various links what we observe are a number of individuals conversing together, recounting experiences, exchanging news of acquaintances and friends, discussing personal matters or ideas and so on. Implicit in much of this conversation are the norms, values and attitudes, of general or special application, recognized in the society. An important part of such conversation is made up of gossip, that is the discussion of the affairs and behaviour of other persons in their absence. Viewed then in terms of the content of interaction the network may also be seen as a series of links in a chain of gossip.

In common parlance gossip is frequently associated with idle chatter: in sociological analysis, however, it represents an activity of considerable importance (see Colson, 1953a). Much of gossip is condemnatory; but this implies the existence of some norm in terms of which one's character or behaviour is evaluated and condemned. In this sense the function of gossip is the reaffirmation of norms of behaviour held in common by those who participate in it. A further property of gossip is that its victims are rarely seized upon at random. In the words of Oscar Wilde's epigram, there is only one thing worse than being talked about, and that is not being talked about. To be talked of in one's absence, in however derogatory terms, is to be conceded a measure of social importance in the gossip set; not to be talked about is the mark of social insignificance, of exclusion from the set. In other words, gossip denotes a certain community of interest, even if the limits of community can only be vaguely defined. It is within the *effective* network that gossip is most intense, and the marriages, affaires, and conjugal relations of those within the *effective* network are among its major themes. In this way continuous gossip leads not merely to the reaffirmation of established norms, but also to the clarifications and formulation of new ones. When we recall, too, the importance that attaches to prestige in this society, so that breach of the norm is also likely to involve loss of esteem in the eyes of neighbours and friends, the importance that the network may assume as an instrument of social control readily becomes apparent. Given, too, this emphasis on prestige, the ensuing struggle to which it gives rise must be expressed in the continuous adoption of new norms and patterns of behaviour, for only in this way can those who already possess high prestige ward off the challenge of their competitors. I suggest that new norms and standards of behaviour will tend to arise more frequently within the *effective* network of those who rank high on the prestige continuum, and that through the *extended* network they gradually filter down and percolate throughout the society. From this point of view the network would also appear to have importance as an instrument in examining the processes of social and cultural change.

Network content, norms and urbanism

Thus far in this paper I have been discussing social regularities in terms of social relationships, and the ways in which these are ordered within a particular kind of institutional framework. It remains now to consider a quite different set of uniformities also amply illustrated in Chanda's account. These may be regarded

as behavioural constants, regularities to be perceived in the actual
modes of behaviour of Africans in the towns: they relate not to
the form but to the content of social relationships.

These behavioural constants consist in customs and usages, and
the values and attitudes which they express. Many of these derive
from indigenous African tribal culture. Such are the custom of
teknonomy, as when Chanda is addressed as ShiChomba, father
of Chomba, and the continued expression of traditional standards
of courtesy in modes of greeting and address, as when he was
addressed by the Public Works Department orderly as 'father' or
when Chanda himself greeted James' wife in the customary way
on seeing her for the first time after the birth of her child. Or
again, tribal custom is exemplified in the occasion when Chanda's
wife provided food for her female visitors, while he himself
sat apart reading a newspaper. Amongst most, if not all, of the
Northern Rhodesia tribes men and women normally eat separately, and the custom is still widely followed in the towns. But
while traditional practice and belief are often present at the core
of a given behavioural complex, particular customs may be
considerably modified under urban conditions, or perhaps survive only in fragmentary form. Finally, Chanda's accounts provide many instances of customs and modes of behaviour which
are specific to the town. They are the expression of African
urban, as distinct from or even opposed to tribal, culture. A good
illustration is to be found in the incident involving the Ndebele
girl, which argues a certain free-and-easy approach to extra-
marital relations, an attitude which is also evident, incidentally,
in Chanda's acquiescence in his friend's liaison with his classificatory sister. In certain circumstances urban Africans will express considerable concern about the extent of 'adultery'[1] in
the towns, and can on occasion condemn profligacy as roundly
as would any traditional guardian of tribal mores; but in everyday
life sexual laxity is taken lightly and, indeed, is accepted by many
as one of the more amiable aspects of the urban way of life, provided of course that one's affaires remain undetected or one is not
oneself the injured party. On the other hand, the acceptance of
'laxity' is not the same thing as condonation of promiscuity. The

[1] The word adultery is commonly used to translate a vernacular term—
bucende in Bemba—which covers heterosexual relations of any kind which take
place outside marriage.

urban areas have their own code of sex behaviour which includes norms for the regulation of extra-marital relations. Thus the Ndebele girl was fair game for Chanda because she was of an alien tribe; but more important is Thompson's comment that she could not refuse Chanda because of his smart appearance. In general, Southern Rhodesian girls have a reputation for sophistication. Many of those who come north are relatively well-educated, speak some English, and have a sense of dress which ranks them as more desirable than the local womenfolk. The implication of Thompson's remark was that such a girl could not demean herself by consorting with any Tom, Dick or Harry around the location, but a man of prestige, of high social status she would not refuse. Similarly, for Chanda himself the liaison would have been quite 'legitimate', and would have caused no stir so long as it was not discovered by the girl's husband or by his own wife.

Reference to the concepts of prestige and social status has been made on a number of occasions throughout this paper, and we have also had occasion to note some of the marks by which a man of prestige is known. Here therefore it only remains to observe how the notions of prestige and status as they have developed in the towns also provide norms of behaviour which different individuals can appeal to, and manipulate in handling their own relations. For example, Chanda was obviously disappointed when he learnt that his brother-in-law had not brought him a 'fever-coat' from Elizabethville. I suspect that Martin had not done so because he knew too well Chanda's propensity for purchasing goods well beyond the range of his pocket, and his chronic inability to pay his debts. But Martin was too diplomatic to say so openly. Instead he explained that most of the ones he had seen were of inferior quality and unworthy of a 'gentleman'. Since it was in precisely these terms that Chanda liked to see himself, there was little he could say in reply, and he was compelled to hide his chagrin.

The persistence in the towns of tribal customs and values, the abandonment or modification and adaptation of others, and the emergence of specifically urban customs, usages and attitudes raise complex problems of a somewhat different order from those considered earlier in this paper. They raise questions about social and cultural change, and the relationship between them. It was in fact the emergence of these problems rather than the nature of urban society itself which first drew the attention of anthropologists to the towns of Africa. Thus there developed a tendency in these studies to view the urban situation against a model of the tribal system, with a consequent failure to grasp that the new patterns of behaviour were also frequently specifically urban responses. Today there is an increasing tendency to accept, as a point of departure, the assumption that urban life everywhere shares certain common characteristics, and that these provide the basis for a minimal definition of urbanism. It then follows that the social life of urban Africans will more closely resemble the way of life developed amongst urban dwellers in other parts of the world than it will the traditional folk-ways of the tribe. This must not be taken to mean that the African who comes to the towns at once abandons his tribal culture. It is of course clear that the African who leaves his tribal area to seek work in the town will take with him a whole set of customs, values, attitudes, beliefs and so on: not only will he continue to utilize these in the town, but their persistence in the urban milieu may in turn influence the ordering of social relationships there. However, the point is that for the urban African the town is something given, a datum, with which he has to come to terms and to which he has to adjust. In other words, the problem of cultural continuity has to be set firmly, in the first instance, in the context of the urban social system, the major elements of which I have sought to outline in this paper, and secondly, in the context of the wider system which consists in the interrelations of town and country. Urbanization is one of the most notable features of our age, and all over the world new towns are rapidly growing up, or ancient cities being transformed. For the most part they draw their populations from amongst peoples of widely differing cultures who hitherto had followed a peasant or tribal way of life. These towns differ widely amongst themselves, and yet, as towns, they may be expected to share many structural resemblances. In terms of the argument presented here, I suggest therefore that these emerging urban communities provide for the anthropologist a potentially fertile field for exploring the interrelations of structure and culture.

CHAPTER IV

Gossip, Norms and Social Network

by
A. L. Epstein

Introduction

In an earlier paper (Epstein, 1961)[1] I sought to draw attention to
the value of the concept of the social network, as enunciated
by Barnes (1954) and later used by Bott (1957), in the analysis
of problems of urban social organization in modern Africa. I
pointed out there how each African urban-dweller may be regarded as the focal point of a number of social relationships,
defined in terms of different roles, some deriving from the tribal
system, others a product of the wider social system that has
developed in recent years. From this point of view it followed
that the social structure of the town could be viewed, at least in
part, as made up of a complex series of links in a chain of innumerable dyadic interactions. The further argument, which I
was not at that time able to develop in detail, was that when the
content of such interaction was also taken into account, the concept of the social network also helped to shed light on some of the
problems of social control in African urban society: how norms
of behaviour come to be set, how they are maintained or
sanctioned, and how they come to be diffused. The aim of
the present paper is simply to document this argument, and at
the same time to clarify a number of points made in the earlier
analysis.

The incident

In the first paper the procedure I adopted was to follow my informant in his movements around the town, and trace out the
nature of the various social contacts he made over a limited
period of time. The emphasis there was on the network seen
simply as a series of social linkages. Here my concern is more
with the content of social interaction: in this context the workings
of the network principle seem best brought out in charting the

[1] Reprinted as Chap. III above.

involvement of a number of persons in an incident, of no great significance in itself, which I recorded in the course of field-work in Ndola. The background to this incident was as follows. After I had been in Ndola for some time I decided to select two areas for intensive study, one a section in the Old Location, the other a section in Kabushi, and I was able to arrange for one of my African research assistants to live in each. I hoped in this way to be able to carry out formal interviews intensively over a period of time, as well as to achieve some approximation to the conventional anthropological ideal of participant observation, if only vicariously. One day my assistant in Kabushi called in the ordinary way at one of the houses in his section. He was met by a young lad who explained that he was the younger brother of the occupier, whom I shall call Charles, and that Charles was at present out of Ndola. When my assistant asked whether Charles would be back soon, the lad appeared reluctant to answer, and my assistant departed.

The reasons for Charles' absence emerged shortly afterwards. It appeared that he had been found committing adultery with a girl called Monica, who was the wife of Kaswende. Kaswende was at this time employed as a lorry driver by a firm of brewers which supplied bottled beer throughout most of the country. Kaswende's duties therefore often took him on long journeys, and he was frequently absent from Ndola for days at a time. During these absences Charles and Monica used to meet at Kaswende's house. Somehow Kaswende's suspicions became aroused and before his departure on one trip he asked his younger brother to keep an eye on Monica. One evening when Kaswende was absent the younger brother called at Kaswende's house. He received no reply, so set about forcing his way in. Charles thought that the best way out of this awkward situation was through the window; but the window-space in Kabushi houses is somewhat tiny and, as he was scrambling through, he lost a shoe which was taken by Kaswende's younger brother. When Kaswende eventually returned to Ndola he was of course duly informed, and he immediately sought out the adulterer. Confronted with the evidence of the shoe Charles was forced to admit his guilt, and Kaswende gave him a severe thrashing. He warned Charles, moreover, that the matter hadn't ended there, and that he would beat him again whenever he saw him. Kaswende turned out to be a man of his word, and he assaulted Charles on two further occasions. Charles then decided to leave Ndola, and I heard later that he had found a job in one of the other towns of the Copperbelt.

There is of course nothing peculiarly urban nor indeed African about an act of adultery, and there is certainly nothing very unusual in the circumstances of the present case. Cases of adultery in the towns of the Copperbelt are indeed legion (cf. Powdermaker, 1962: 164–69). Thus at Ndola one young African woman had agreed to keep a daily journal for me in which she would record her daily activities—whom she met and what they discussed, etc. Each day brought its regular tale of somebody's adultery until out of a mixture of tedium and embarrassment I felt compelled to ask her to stop. In any case, at this stage of my research I had already spent a considerable amount of time attending sittings of the African Urban Courts and recording the cases heard there, a substantial proportion of which were grounded in complaints of marital infidelity. Why then should I linger on the present case? What aroused my interest was not the incident itself, but rather that within a short space of time I heard the story from a number of different sources. This suggested that the affair was known to, and possibly had been discussed by, quite a wide range of people. It occurred to me that this was something worth looking into in order to try and trace out at least some of the story's ramifications.

The 'Gossip' network

I myself received the story in the first instance from my assistant in Kabushi, Ponde. Ponde first came to Ndola in 1947 to attend a course on social welfare, and it was at this time that he first met Charles, who was then working in one of the location tea-rooms. Subsequently, they came to know each other better, for both were keen footballers and belonged to the local club. However, they were acquaintances rather than friends, and although they both lived within the same section of Kabushi, Ponde had not visited Charles' house save for the occasion mentioned earlier. Ponde, in fact, did not hear the story 'in the course of his work', but from his side-neighbour in the section, Besa. Besa was a young man in his early twenties. His parents had brought him from Bemba country when he was a child, and he had gone to primary school in Ndola: in fact he had not been back to his rural home since then. At this time he was employed as a market-supervisor. Besa and Kaswende, the husband in the present case, had been class-mates at school: they had grown up together and were still close friends. One day Ponde was being visited at his house by a close friend Simon, an African Welfare Assistant. They were discussing the case of adultery of a mutual friend when Besa came in. After Simon's departure, Besa told Ponde the story of Charles and Monica.

I also received the story independently from Margaret whom I had come to know through her husband, a senior African clerk and a member of a number of African bodies. He was quite well known throughout the Copperbelt. Both Margaret and her husband were Bemba from the Luwingu District. Margaret had attended school at Mindolo, then the only boarding school for African girls on the Copperbelt. Margaret knew the story at first hand from Monica herself, with whom she had been at Mindolo. Margaret had also heard the story from Mrs Mutwale while they were combing out each other's hair one day. Mrs Mutwale and her husband came from the Luapula area. He was an accounts clerk in town, and said to be earning unusually high wages for an African at that time. Mrs Mutwale was another product of Mindolo, and as Margaret was telling me this she commented:'We Mindolo girls like to go about together, and don't like to go about with others.' Margaret in turn had related the case to a number of other women as well as to a young man called Nicholas who held a supervisory position under the Municipal Council. Nicholas also came from the Luwingu District, that is from the same area as Margaret and her husband. There was some element of a joking relationship between Nicholas and Margaret whom Nicholas addressed as sister-in-law, although there was no traceable connection between himself and Margaret's husband.

Finally, I heard the story again from my second assistant, Phiri. Phiri was a townsman, born and brought up on the mine compound at Mufulira, where his parents were still living. He himself had first met Charles in 1947 when they boxed against each other at a scout's Jamboree. They met again when Phiri came to join me in Ndola. The introduction on this occasion was made by Monica, who was herself a Mufulira girl. Monica and Phiri had in fact grown up together as children and, although they were of different tribal background, Phiri told me that he had always

regarded Monica's family as being in some way vaguely related
to his own. He himself had actually heard the story of Kaswende's
case while visiting Monica's mother who was then living in one
of the settlements a short distance out of Ndola. It appears that a
preliminary meeting of the parties had been arranged to discuss
the whole affair. Monica's brother, however, refused to attend the
gathering because Monica herself was not in Ndola at the time—
she had run away. Phiri was present when the brother arrived to
inform his mother of the latest developments. Later Phiri was to
hear the story again from Nicholas. They were good friends and
with a few others formed a regular drinking group at the Beer
Hall. Nicholas confided to Phiri that he was rather worried about
the whole business because he himself was indirectly involved.
Monica, he explained, had a friend and confidante called Alice.
Charles and Monica used sometimes to meet at Alice's house, for
Alice's husband was a businessman who was out of town from
time to time. But at length Alice grew fearful that her husband
might come to learn of her part in the intrigue and, what was
worse, come to have doubts about her own moral rectitude. Alice
therefore arranged to find another rendezvous for her friends. But
in the end her secret could not be contained. Returning from one
of his trips her husband found some clothes belonging to Monica
in the house. Somehow he divined what was going on, and he
chased Alice from the house, saying that she could go and live on
the money she had earned in adultery. It was these circumstances
which led Nicholas to disclose his fears to my assistant, for at this
time Alice was his own mistress, and he was afraid that his affair
too would be publicly exposed. He spoke bitterly against Margaret
whom he accused of being a great gossip-monger and always
spreading false stories about him. As a result he was having a
troublesome time with his wife who was threatening to divorce
him. Finally he told Phiri that he was no longer on speaking terms
with his 'sister-in-law' Margaret.

What these events reveal is how the discovery of an apparently
trivial act of adultery triggered off a chain of gossip, and even
came to affect the relations of a number of people. I should add
that my own attempts to trace out the path of all this gossip were
less than systematic and far from complete. In order to avoid over-
burdening the text with detail I have not included in my account
all the names which appear in my field-notes; on the other hand,

I did not discuss the matter with all those whose names I have mentioned. Each of these presumably was involved in yet another 'gossip set', so that the story was probably known to a much wider range of people than I have been able to indicate. Margaret remarked to me, indeed, that it was known all over the location (*uwaishibikwa ku mushi onse*). This may have been an exaggeration, but it does not affect the main point that in a town like Ndola, whose African population is so young in terms of urban experience and so heterogeneous in terms of tribal origins, occupation, and church affiliation, a considerable number of persons can be shown to be inter-connected through their common interest, expressed in gossip, in a case of adultery. Not every such case of course that occurs in the town will be the subject of so much talk. My research assistant Phiri was quick to point out that had the affair involved some of the people living in his section of the Old Location little more would have been heard about it. Why then the interest in the present case? For answer we need to look at the way in which social relationships are organized in the town, and at the norms of behaviour which inform those relationships.

In tracking down the sources from which my informants heard the story, and the others to whom they in turn passed it on, I have merely followed the links making up a number of individual's personal networks. I have treated the town, in Barnes' terms, as a social field within which each person is in touch with a number of people, some of whom may be in touch with each other, and some of whom may not. Each person's network, as I showed in my earlier paper, is built up in different ways: it may include neighbours, fellow members of some formal organization or association, or others drawn from the categories of kin and tribe and so on, each of which represents a distinct principle of social organization in the town. But while it is possible to isolate these various principles for purposes of analysis, what is striking is the way in which in the reality of social life such principles are often found operating simultaneously. In other words, any given dyadic relationship tends to have built into it a number of different and, for this reason, sometimes conflicting roles. For example, although Ponde and Charles were neighbours in the sense that they belonged to the same section and lived fairly close to each other, the neighbourhood principle had never been activated, and their relationship had its sources elsewhere. In the case of Ponde and Besa, however, the neighbourhood principle was stronger, but here too other roles affected the character of their interaction and defined their relationship. When Ponde moved into his house, Besa was already living in the section. They soon struck up a friendship, and since Besa was still a bachelor he used to drop into Ponde's from time to time to share a meal. Both were practising Roman Catholics and they took to attending services together. In this way Besa came to be introduced to Ponde's friend, Simon, and to Simon's sister, to whom he eventually became engaged. From this time he began to address Simon as brother-in-law, a mode of address he then 'extended' to Ponde whose relations with Simon were so close that to Besa it appeared as though they were brothers: in fact they were unrelated, being of different tribes and from different parts of the country (though they belonged to the same linguistic group). This translation of social ties which have grown up between unrelated persons into the idiom of kinship is seen also in the case of Nicholas and Margaret, and Phiri and Monica.

In these instances the use of kinship terms serves to buttress or give 'tone' to a relationship that is already quite close. On the other hand, the greater the number of roles present within a single dyadic relationship, the greater the opportunities for division within that relationship. Thus attendance at the same school and membership in the same religious body were each important bases of association within the network, but they sometimes ran counter to each other. Ponde and Phiri, for example, had been close friends at secondary school, where they had also known Margaret's husband. In Ndola they shared many interests in common, including an enthusiasm for football. But they had been brought up in different religious denominations, and their views in matters religious differed radically: sometimes they had heated arguments which threatened to disrupt their friendship. In matters of politics there were associated differences of attitude and conviction too.

Norms and the gossip network

In defining the character of a network then one has to take account of a number of variables: the role-components that enter into the network, the degree of 'mesh' or consistency between these roles, and the relative weight or intensity of each particular link. For even where relationships are built up out of the same role-components it does not follow that they are of equal 'quality'. The intensity of a relationship may be gauged in some measure by the frequency of interaction, but even more so by its content. Every social relationship involves the idea of exchange, and what helps to define it are the kinds of information, views and talk which are interchanged. Hence, as Gluckman (1963a) suggests, the closer the bonds of relationship the more intimate or even esoteric the gossip, and the more trite or meaningless it will appear to outsiders. For one of the functions of gossip for those who are party to it is to define or reaffirm the norms regulating behaviour amongst themselves, and marking themselves off from others. Here, I think, we have the key to the amount of gossip that gathered round the affair of Charles and Monica. This gossip did not consist in a bare recital of the 'facts' of the case: implicit in the telling was an evaluation of those 'facts'. Unfortunately, I did not gather any version of the story from Kaswende or his friends and kin. From the accounts which I did receive, however, the 'slanting' was quite plain: there was little expression of sympathy for Kaswende or even recognition of his position as an injured husband. Thus Ponde's comment was that the marriage of Monica and Kaswende was a strange one, and that many people had wondered at it. Many asked how a girl like Monica should have come to marry a man like Kaswende. The point was, Ponde then explained, that Monica was widely regarded as a very beautiful girl whereas Kaswende was quite an unprepossessing fellow. Moreover, he added, Monica was more highly educated than her husband, and could have found any number of men who would have been pleased to marry her. Phiri, who had known Monica from childhood, was able to explain some of the background. Monica had at one time been engaged to a man with whom Kaswende went about. Then she contracted venereal disease and had been very ill. Kaswende had been struck by her beauty: he sought medicines for her, and in the end she was cured. In gratitude Monica's parents were quite happy that Kaswende should marry their daughter. But Monica was less pleased with the arrangement. She found, moreover—or so rumour had it—that Kaswende was impotent, and it was said that the child she bore was not his. She had then started going around with other men so that Kaswende would be forced to divorce her.

The clear implication of all this was that Monica had married a man of inferior social status, and I took up this and other points with my assistants on a later occasion. I pointed out that as a senior driver Kaswende must have been earning relatively good wages, and thus in a good position to provide his wife with those things to which I knew African urban women attached importance. My assistants were quick to reply that although Kaswende was indeed quite well off, his manner of dress was really quite poor. In a word, Kaswende lacked those qualities such as education and 'civilized' taste which are necessary to confer prestige in modern Copperbelt society (Mitchell, 1956; Mitchell and Epstein, 1959). Here, too, presumably lies the explanation for Kaswende's unwillingness to divorce his wife. When I asked why he had not done this earlier in view of his wife's previous infidelities, Ponde replied that it might have been because of her beauty. What he had in mind, I suspect, was not so much Monica's physical attractiveness for Kaswende as the prestige which could accrue to a man of Kaswende's stamp who could boast such a beautiful wife.

The exchange of gossip, I have said, denotes a certain community of interest: it marks off the 'set' from others of whose intimate affairs they are ignorant, or which they would consider too unimportant for their concern. Through such gossip is expressed the norms of behaviour specific to the 'set'. Both of these points emerge in the present discussion. Although much of gossip tends to be condemnatory it is worth noting that in all the talk I recorded about the affair of Charles and Monica I heard no word spoken in condemnation of the act of adultery itself. None spoke maliciously of Charles or charged him with breaking up a home: on the contrary, as I have indicated, the sympathy appeared to lie with Charles rather than the injured Kaswende. This must not be taken to mean that all my informants condoned adultery. The standards of sexual morality on the Copperbelt may be permissive, but they are far from promiscuous. In any case, the point here is that marital fidelity is a norm of general application, accepted by all in theory if not in practice, and is not specific to any particular group or category within the population. Moreover, while an element of 'spice' is probably a necessary ingredient of a good deal of gossip, it is not the 'spice' alone which is of interest to the 'set'. What is important is their own social position and

that of the person who is the subject of their gossip. If we examine
the social characteristics of those involved in the present account
it will be seen that we are dealing mainly with those who fall
within the upper ranges of the prestige continuum (Mitchell and
Epstein, 1959). All the men whose names appear in the account,
save for the husband Kaswende and Besa, the market-supervisor,
were white-collar workers holding relatively responsible and
highly paid jobs. Besa himself aspired to a similar position, and his
constant problem was how to achieve a style of life on the miser-
able pittance he received from his job at that time. As for the
subject of all the gossip, the central figure was undoubtedly
Monica herself. In terms of the modern standards of the Copperbelt she was one of the most sophisticated, smartly turned out
and beautiful girls in Ndola. By virtue of her education and her
grooming she embodied in her own person many of the norms
and values which serve to define the prestige system of these new
urban communities (Mitchell and Epstein, 1959). Monica herself
thus belonged to the 'upper crust' of Ndola African society, but
as a member she was also bound by its rules. The fact that she had
had an affair with Charles did not in itself call forth any special
censure, for Charles belonged to the same social stratum. What
was criticized and made the subject of discussion was that she had
married someone of lesser social status. The gossip of her friends
who made up her own social network (or at least a section of it)
provided a re-affirmation of the values which they held in common, and which gave them their sense of identity as a distinct
social class. Thus the material presented in this paper relates mainly
to a type of network in which the various role-components
are subordinate to or merge in that of class; we have been concerned in the main with a 'class network' (see Figure 9). Had the
fieldwork been more systematic it might have been possible, and it
would certainly have been instructive, to plot the points at which
gossip tended to peter out, or cross the 'class boundaries', and to
note the changes in the character of the gossip as it did so. But
this does not upset the main argument. Mitchell and I (1959) have
argued the difficulty of postulating a contemporary class structure
in African urban communities for, while the prestige scale is relatively clear-cut, it does not yet provide a basis for the recruitment
of corporately acting groups. On the other hand, the present
analysis shows how, through the mechanism of the social network,

social classes or status groups in the Weberian sense are able to emerge, how they come to articulate the norms of behaviour which define their distinctiveness, and develop means for re-asserting their validity when they appear to have been challenged.

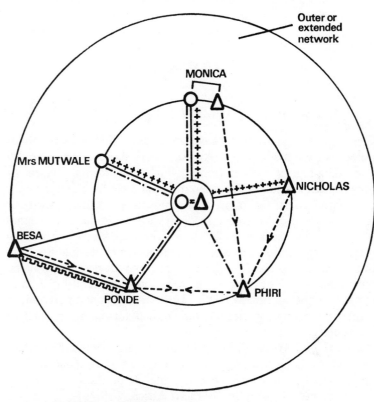

------- Same tribe or linguistic group

—·—·— Attended same school

++++++ Attended same church

ᴜᴜᴜᴜ Neighbours

-->-- Chain of gossip

FIGURE 9

Section of 'class network' (centred on Margaret) showing the interlocking chain of gossip

CHAPTER V

The Operation of Voluntary Associations and Personal Networks in the Political Processes of an Inter-ethnic Community[1]

by
P. D. *Wheeldon*

Introduction
One of the most important contributions which social anthropologists have made to sociological theory has been an increased
understanding of how societies which lack formal organs of
government are able to maintain order, and establish and sanction
the relative social positions, rights and duties of their members.
Most such studies have been made in rural pre-industrial societies
in the non-Western world. One of the exceptions is Frankenberg's (1957) study of a Welsh village in which he analyses how
the political processes of the selection and disposal of leaders,
the reconciliation of opposed interests, and the establishment and
reinforcement of norms, take place through the operation of
formal voluntary associations rather than formal governmental
institutions.

Here I endeavour to use the ideas which Frankenberg developed, together with a growing body of theory regarding the
operation of personal networks, to analyse political processes in
a small minority group in Southern Africa.

The Coloured community is one of the four distinct groups—
Europeans, Coloureds, Asians and Africans—which are together
involved in the characteristic caste societies of white-dominated
Southern Africa. The term 'Coloured'[2] or 'Eurafrican' is gener-

---

[1] The fieldwork on which this paper is based was carried out over a period of
approximately four years, but was most intense from February 1964 to October
1965. A Rockefeller Foundation grant made it possible for me to conduct a
Social Survey for one month during this period. I am indebted to those students
who helped to collect the survey data.
[2] The term 'Coloured' is used in Southern and East Africa for people who are

ally used to denote persons who are visibly descended from two or more of the other racial groups. The present analysis arises out of research undertaken in the Coloured community of approximately 3,300 members in what I have called Middlebury. In 1961 the European population of Middlebury was approximately 89,000 and the African population 215,000.

The founding members of the 'Coloured' community arrived from the Cape at the same time as the first European settlers. Although the community is still very small it has always expanded relatively fast, not only because the natural birth-rate within it is high, but also because it is constantly absorbing new recruits who are the result of local cross-racial unions. In the past the distinction between the descendants of the early settlers who call themselves 'Coloured' and the latter who may prefer to use the term 'Eurafrican' has been socially significant. Today, however, these differences are less important as marriages have created bonds between Coloured and Eurafrican families. For the sake of convenience I shall, in general, employ the term 'Coloured' because this is the term most generally used both inside the community and by outsiders to distinguish its members from the other racial groups.

On the whole Coloureds occupy an intermediate range of semi-skilled manual and lower supervisory jobs. Men are concentrated particularly as manual workers in the light metal and related industries, and many are plant and machinery operators of varying degrees of skill. Women are employed in light industrial work, domestic work, often as supervisors of African labour, and unlike men, are moving increasingly into higher status white-collar jobs.

During the research period the approximate median annual cash earnings of the different racial groups in the society are as shown overleaf:[1]

---

of mixed racial parentage, as distinct from people of 'pure' African, European or Asian descent.

[1] The actual figures quoted here are derived from a census taken shortly before my research began. A comparison of the census data for Southern Africa over several decades shows that even though the actual incomes themselves may vary, the ratios between the earnings of the different racial groups is virtually constant.

Table I
Population of Middlebury

Whites	Asians	Coloureds	Africans (urban)
$2,790	$1,815	$1,125	$300
R1,860	R1,210	R750	R200
£930	£665	£375	£100

These wage scales are a reflection of the general social and political status of the four groups vis-à-vis one another.

This disparity between African and Coloured wage rates is a reflection of the fact that many Coloureds, although not all, hold jobs which are subject to a degree of special protection. In Government, the Municipality, and in some branches of industry, a number of posts and occupations are informally designated as 'Coloured jobs'. This is largely because Coloureds, who do not have a distinctive culture of their own and share many of the attitudes of the Whites, are felt to be more capable than Africans of doing 'European-type' or 'advanced' jobs. They are paid at lower rates than Whites of roughly equivalent skill, but are to a great extent protected from the inroads of African advancement.

In the wider society, Whites explain their political and social dominance of the total society in terms of their cultural inheritance, which they claim is superior to that of both Asians and Africans. Coloureds, who share much of this ethos, would like to be accepted into White society. But most members of White society do not accept Coloureds as being of equal status to themselves despite these cultural similarities. Thus the dilemma for Coloureds is that they feel that they are excluded from White society on the basis of unjust racial criteria, but these very criteria are what protect their own superior economic and social position vis-à-vis Africans. This structurally determined ambivalence in Coloured political attitudes is greatly exacerbated by the fundamental and increasing opposition which exists between Blacks and Whites. Both individuals and leaders within the Coloured community try to avoid too direct an involvement in the party politics which are an expression of this power struggle. People say: 'We are too few to be politically effective, so it's better to keep out of party politics.'

That the community is indeed politically ineffective in the

wider society is demonstrated by the fact that it has no representative assemblies, courts, or independent economic organizations;
it even lacks the bodies which epitomize local autonomy in most
small communities, the School Board and the Village Management Board. Jobs, houses, education, health care and social welfare assistance are all controlled by individuals and institutions in
White society. Also, because of the community's short history and
the shallow genealogies of most members of middle age or more,
it has few powerful family groups extending over a number of
generations which may build up and preserve permanent economic and other interests. This does not mean, however, that
the community does not engage in politics. Sommerfelt (1958:
174) has defined political activities as 'particular manners of action
adopted by individuals or groups for the purpose of maintaining
or promoting their rights vis-à-vis others to culturally defined
benefits'. This definition can be applied to a large number of
formal voluntary associations which operate within the community and particularly to community development associations,
sports clubs and unions, and some churches.

These associations have, in general, three functions; they provide a focal point for the organization and expression of specific
interests within the community and between different sections
of it; they provide a platform from which some community
needs may be made known to powerful individuals and organizations within the White community; and they provide a series of
institutions in which the politically ambitious can acquire prestige
and influence. Many of them are short-lived, particularly if they
are not bound by responsibility for capital equipment, or by
significant connections into White society. Much of the underlying stability of political relationships tends to be centred on
individual leaders rather than institutions. This is possible because
the community is so small that most people know something
about one another, and many relationships between individuals are
multiplex.[1] Thus despite the fact that the community is part of a
'complex' society, it is more fruitful to view its internal organization in terms of the concepts of a 'stateless society' as described
by Colson (1958: 10) and van Velsen (1964: 312, 318) than in
terms of the institutional analysis of many urban sociologists and
political scientists.

[1] For definitions of the terms 'multiplex' and 'simplex' see page 132.

I analyse, thus, the way in which individuals participate in and manipulate one important voluntary association—since it is this interaction which contributes towards political processes within the community. In order to do this I have used the concept of the *network*.

Aspects of the concept of network

Each individual in a society has social relationships with a large number of friends and acquaintances. All these relationships together constitute what has been called a personal network. A number of writers, Barnes (1954), Bott (1957), Epstein (1961), Jay (1964), Srinivas and Béteille (1964), and Adrian Mayer (1966) have evolved rather different criteria in order to differentiate between these complex network relationships. I distinguish the following aspects of the concept.

1. *Content*. Relationships between individuals differ in their content and complexity. If the situations in which people habitually see one another are clearly distinguished it is possible to separate, very crudely, the *strands* which contribute to their relationship.

For example, if A sees B at work, if they belong to the same football club and are both members of the ratepayer's association, then I describe their relationship as having at least three strands, or to use Gluckman's terminology as being 'multiplex'. But if A sees B only at work then the content of their relationship is likely to be largely determined by this fact and it can be described as a single-stranded 'simplex' relationship. Some of these strands are more important than others in contributing to a close network relationship. In the Coloured community important strands arise out of membership of the same kinship group; work group; premarital peer group; sporting association; community service organization. Less important strands are the result of common membership of a welfare association; a church; or a neighbourhood. It may be possible to give these strands values, but for the purposes of the present paper I shall treat them as of equal value.

2. *Range*. The situations which I have described above do not necessarily result in the establishment of network relationships between participants. All they provide is an area of recruitment for such relationships. The problem is, thus, why do people

activate some latent network relationships and not others, and how many do they appear, habitually, to make 'live'?

Social psychologists have answered this question in terms of an analysis of the psychological characteristics of the individuals concerned. Certainly, personality does affect the kind of emotional contacts, and hence network relationships, one person is able to establish with another. But in the Coloured community certain elements in the social structure may narrow or extend the limits within which an individual has to work. For example, people who are not members of large families themselves and who do not marry into a large family, tend to have small-range networks unless they become actively involved in a great many community associations. Conversely, some occupations, and particularly teaching, provide an opportunity for the rapid extension of a person's network if this is desired.

In the analysis of my fieldwork I have, where possible, classified individuals in the community in terms of the range and character of their network, and related this to their observed actions in specific situations. I have not been able, as yet, to quantify this concept of range, and refer simply to small-, middle-, or large-range networks.

The range of a network is affected by two elements. These are, firstly, the absolute numbers of people with whom ego is observed to have a personal relationship, whatever its nature; and secondly, the numbers of people in his network who do not belong to broadly the same socio-economic group as himself. All the individuals at all social levels who were consistently referred to by other informants as being 'people who are influential', or 'people who I go to when I need advice' had large-range networks. These resulted in part from their active membership of, firstly, extended kinship groups, and secondly, an unusually high number of voluntary associations, through which they meet people of different socio-economic class than themselves.

3. *The effective and extended elements of a network.* Epstein has distinguished between two areas of a network. The effective area he defines as: 'Those people with whom [a person] interacts most intensely and most regularly, and who are therefore also likely to come to know one another, that is to say that part of the total network which shows some degree of connectedness'

P. D. Wheeldon

(Epstein, 1961: 57). The extended network by contrast would be those with whom a person interacts less intensely and less regularly, who are unlikely to know one another so that the network linking them would be relatively 'open'. On the basis of observation and survey material I have evolved crude quantitative criteria for distinguishing between these areas of the network. People with whom ego has a relationship in which may be distinguished three or more strands are part of his effective network. But people with whom ego has a relationship based on only one or two strands fall into his extended network.

There are other differences between social relationships which fall into these two categories which will emerge during the case study, and I shall return to an analysis of these later.

Aspects of leadership and network in the community

The Coloured community of Middlebury, like many others which have been described, has within it a group of about 80 to 100 people who are usually described as leaders or 'people one can respect for the things they do', this description often being qualified with the statement 'some of them are proud about nothing, of course'. Members of this high status category have some of the following social characteristics—membership of a family which is generally regarded as 'nice' (although this opinion is never unanimous); owning a 'respectable' business; holding a professional or white-collar job; attaining a supervisory grade in a trade or industry; keeping a well-paid job for a long time; being elected to executive positions in several formal voluntary associations. Among this group of 80 to 100 people there were six who were named again and again, both in general conversation, and in response to a formal questionnaire, as 'leaders'. When informants were asked to define the difference between 'influential people' and 'leaders' they frequently described leaders as individuals 'who know almost everybody in the community and are prepared to try to help them, and who know many Europeans too'.

The social characteristics of these leaders are given in Table II.

All six leaders occupied high status jobs, and A's job had the added advantage that he could dispense patronage if he wished to. All were also members of large families. Only two were active members of a church. Columns 5, 6 and 7 indicate the

Table II

Social Characteristics of Six Leaders in the Middlebury Inter-ethnic Community

| 1 | Sex 2 | High Job Status 3 | Kinship Married Born 4 | Membership of following groups | | | | Total 9 | Network Range 10 | European Contacts 11 |
				Sports Club 5	Wider Vol. Assn 6	Other Vol. Assns 7	Church 8			
A	M	2	M	1	—	2	—	5	large	many
B	F	1	B/M	1	—	6	1	9	v. large	v. many
C	M	1	M	—	—	2	1	4	medium	some
D	M	1	B/M	2	3	4	—	10	v. large	v. many
E	F	1	B	2	1	3	—	7	large	many
F	F	1	M	—	—	7	—	8	v. large	v. many

number and general character of the formal voluntary associations in which they were involved. It appears that having a very large-range network is correlated with being a member of many formal voluntary associations, as is having many contacts in the European community.

One of the leaders is Mr Armstrong who became chairman of the Coloured Community Civic Associations to which I refer later. He described his life in the community as follows:

I got my job because I had a good record at school. My mother always told us kids to get our papers, and as soon as they took Coloureds as apprentices I signed on, and worked at night until I qualified. The pay isn't as good as it could be but it is better than most jobs open to Coloured people, which are just dead ends, you know. I've got some nice friends [Coloureds] at work too. Then I met my wife at a big wedding—one of her sisters—you know Mrs . . . was getting married. We got married as soon as I got my papers. We are a very close family now, we see a lot of each other and we help each other when we need to. I get on very well with two of my brothers-in-law. I used to play football with one of them even before I knew my wife. That was just after I moved to Middlebury when I was young and fit.

My wife has always worked too, except when the babies came, and we've both been active in welfare work. I'm a member of [three associations listed] and I'm a Church councillor. I'm also chairman of the Coloured Community Civic Association and I'm involved with a multi-racial committee to sponsor multi-racial sports. I started it, really. My wife is our [Coloured] representative on the Federation of Women's Associations and she is trying to improve the facilities of our park. Well, its just an open place really, she wants to make it a proper park with equipment for the children.

We both have to say 'No, we are doing too much already' sometimes, people keep wanting us to join or start new things.

Our friends are not all Coloured people. We visit many European friends, but the people I see most of are . . . ., ..., ..., ..., [who is married to his sister], who live in this part of our suburb, and who also work for the Civic Association and for the good of sport.

We know most of what goes on in the community because we go out so much and meet so many people. And lots of people come to us for advice about their problems. Sometimes I, or the wife, can help, or know somebody else who can. Really, the house is almost like a clinic sometimes.

What is my contribution to the committees I work for? Well, its difficult to say, mostly its helping the community get on its feet. We are poor and many people have not had a good education and my experience is that if we want to improve our facilities we have to get European help to raise the money; we just haven't got enough here in the community. Usually if something new is being started, and they ask my help I ask Mr . . . or maybe somebody like Mrs . . . both of them have worked very hard to pull the community up—and they can tell me where to go for advice, or else they ask their friends who are interested to join a new committee for that purpose.

I can't always do much for a new committee myself because I'm so busy, but I can try and get the right kind of people who will work hard to contribute.

The process by which an individual builds up a large-range network seems to be as follows:

1. He joins a sports association—as an official if he does not play the game in question. In time, if he is congenial and able he will be elected to the Union which regulates play between several clubs. He may also become involved in the organization of inter-racial sport and thereby meet prominent men in other communities.

2. He maintains good relationships with the members of his own and his wife's kinship groups and observes the ideals of reciprocity regarding practical help and emotional support in a crisis.

3. In time he will be asked to join civic organizations of various kinds, most of which have some European members who usually see these organizations as representing the Coloured community. If he is congenial, hardworking and reasonably reliable he may, in due course, be elected to an office within the association.

4. If it is observed that he has developed useful contacts, he may be asked to sponsor new associations which would benefit from his contributions or those of his friends.

In other words, the contacts which a leader has incorporated into his network extend the range of that network almost infinitely. Through them he may, given the limits of the situation, meet people who have power in formal political institutions or voluntary associations, or who may exercise indirect influence on such powerful people.

Mr Armstrong's statement can be compared with that of Mr S . . . who is not an influential. He is a storeman in a large firm and earns an average wage. He has always lived in Middlebury and now rents a small council house which he shares with a wife, four children and a younger brother who is separated from his wife's mother (who is unmarried). According to the distinction on page 133 he has a lower medium-range network. He said:

I got my job through my brother-in-law who works there. The pay is bad but I don't want to change because I know where I am there, and the wife works too, of course. I live in a Council house and its all I can do to pay the rent there, so I don't want a bigger one though the children all sleep in the same room. If I was desperate for a bigger house I suppose I'd go to Mr Armstrong and ask him to go with me to see the Housing Officer. I was at school with Mr Armstrong but he has classy friends these days.

No, I don't know any Europeans really except Mr . . . and Mr . . ., who I work with. My friends are my neighbours and my relatives. I've got four brothers. I used to play football after I left school, but I'm too old and I don't want to waste time being an official. Yes, I know most of the Coloureds who others think are important [names given] but I couldn't call them friends really, I would have to be in a bad way before I would crawl to them for help, I'd even rather go to the Welfare—after all, the Welfare is supposed to help us if we are out of work, or have trouble. It helped me in 1961 when I was out of work for 8 months.

My closest friends are my brother who lives almost next door and Mr . . . whose house is at the back of this one. I see a lot of the wife's relatives too. Her younger brother lives here.

If we are sick they help, or if we go away on holiday they look after the house.

Thus Mr S's intimate friends and relatives provide help in many situations. In a serious crisis he has sought aid from government institutions, and the relevant agencies generally deal sympathetically with the needs of Coloured persons at this income level. If neither of these sources of assistance were adequate he would be likely to activate network contacts which are usually dormant, and ask Mr Armstrong for help. In so doing he would establish what I term a patron–client relationship. All members of the leadership category have many such relationships in their networks.

During the course of my discussions with informants about leadership and voluntary associations in the community, I frequently heard several very similar stories which were said to relate to a number of different people. The most frequent of these is embodied in the following statement:

Do you know Mr X . . . and Mrs Y . . .? [both Coloured]. Mr X . . . is supposed to be a respected leader of the Coloured community. Well, he was thrown out of the . . . association because when they wen to the book to find the money it wasn't there. Mrs Y . . . was very angry about it and she saw to it that Mr X . . . was thrown out of the committee. They didn't make it public of course, he said he had to resign because of pressure of work. But everybody knew the real reason, though they didn't want to say so out loud. There was a lot of talk. My neighbour [who it emerged was his wife's sister's first husband] says he doesn't believe it, but he was on the . . . association himself, but we don't see much of him. I believe it's true.

Sometimes a rider is added to the effect that Coloureds cannot be trusted to look after money honestly; either because the community is so poor compared with the European community that the temptation of extra money at hand is too much; or because Coloured people did not get the same kind of education as Europeans, and therefore were not taught how to look after money properly. These accusations are levelled with particular frequency against people who are felt to be politically ambitious, and beginning to be successful in realizing their aspirations.

Another set of stories incorporates allegations against the sexual morals of people to whom one's informant is, at that time, opposed. The status of prominent people in particular is frequently queried on these grounds. Sexual behaviour is measured against an ideal which holds that women should be virgins and men should not 'play around' too much before marriage. Both men and women should be completely faithful to their spouses after marriage, and marriages should be stable.

In fact, reality does not reflect these norms to any large extent[1] and as memories of breaches are very long it is possible for many people to be attacked in these terms. The norms are also not universally applied; one's enemies are described as sexually promiscuous, but the sexual breaches of oneself, one's friends, and one's supporters are 'forgotten' for the moment.[2]

[1] This aspect of the domestic organization of the Coloured community will be dealt with in another paper.
[2] That is, accusations of this kind are sociologically similar to accusations of witchcraft in many African societies.

As I said earlier, the community is small, and most people in it know one another by sight and reputation at least. There are few high prestige formal voluntary associations which embrace significant interest groups in the community. Thus individuals who are or who wish to become influential are forced to co-operate with one another in a number of such associations. It is almost impossible for people who have quarrelled openly to avoid the awkwardness arising from inescapable and continual face-to-face confrontations. This affects the conduct of the affairs of voluntary associations and the relationships between individuals in two ways, both of which will be illustrated in the case history which follows later.

Firstly, the kind of accusations I have described are almost never made to the face of the person who is being accused, and are seldom made to a known intimate of such a person, that is, to somebody who is part of the effective network of the accused as Epstein has defined it. But gossip which incorporates these accusations is passed on to people who are known to fall into the extended part of the accused's network. These people often, in turn, pass the gossip on to individuals who are ego's intimates, but are usually unwilling to reveal its source, except through vague hints. Ego will usually deny the truth of these accusations, and attribute them to the malice of one of these persons whom he suspects are opposed to him. But he will seldom go directly to the person whom he believes is 'slandering' him and attempt to clarify the matter, since this might result in an open breach between two people who have to cooperate in formal situations. Instead, ego will in turn comment unfavourably upon the person whom he believes to be his enemy to somebody who is likely to pass on the comment because he is an acquaintance, but not a close friend of his enemy.

The next steps in this process of accusation and counter accusation depend upon the progress of the original conflict. If it falls away then the dispute between ego and his enemy is likely to become dormant. If it persists or increases then other network contacts may be asked to intervene and help avoid open breaches between the participants.

Secondly, the way in which members of important formal voluntary associations conduct themselves is closely observed, widely discussed and frequently criticized. Executive members of associations who have to make decisions which they know will not be universally popular tend to be deliberately vague both about the matters at issue, and the decisions taken. As in rural Wales (Frankenberg, 1957) committee discussions are long and often difficult to follow; a vote is seldom taken; it is frequently almost impossible to ascertain, at the meeting, what decision has in fact been reached (though this may be interpreted afterwards in private); minutes may be obscure or non-existent; members frequently absent themselves from meetings which they fear will be acrimonious. This deliberate obscurity extends to relationships between voluntary associations, particularly if they compete with one another at one level of organization, but have to cooperate at a higher level. An example is sports clubs whose general rules and inter-club fixtures have to be coordinated through a Union. In such situations there is continual confusion about who has been invited to attend a particular meeting; what time the meeting is to be held; when it is to be held; what is on the agenda; whether an agenda was sent out at all, or in time; whether those who attend are merely representatives or observers; whether they have the right to vote; and whether their views are binding on the association from which they came. Committees are also frequently perfectly willing to abandon, re-interpret or reverse their own earlier decisions. The effect of this obscurity is to expand the range of choices open to the committee as a whole, and to individuals and factions in it. Conflicts are not allowed to emerge explicitly, and differences of opinion may then be publicly interpreted as 'mistakes' or 'misunderstandings'.

The chief organizers of these formal voluntary associations often feel, with justification, that they are surrounded by committee members who would not support them in a crisis. When, for example, a chairman feels particularly vulnerable and threatened he will frequently persuade friends who are part of his effective network and with whom he has a many-stranded relationship, to join the association and give him enough reliable support and practical help to tide the association over a period of conflict. An important part of this help may consist in acting as a cushion between the chairman and dissident factions on the committee, and it cannot thus be assumed that many-stranded relations always result in the freer flow of information. However, such intimates are frequently recruited from his kinship connections and if the conflicts in the association make it impossible for it to continue, then this failure may be explained in terms of the nepotism or favouritism of the chairman.

A small number of Whites are also involved in some of these associations. They are members of a larger and more impersonal community where relationships between members of committees are seldom as intimate as is general in the Coloured community. They frequently interpret the way of doing business which I have described as a reflection of the 'innately devious and inefficient Coloured mentality' and see the Coloured community as rift by jealousies. This interpretation also reinforces the conviction of many Whites that European culture is superior to that of any non-white group, whatever its aspirations. Many Coloureds themselves accept this negative evaluation of their forms of social organization as was demonstrated during a social survey in which many people said in response to the question 'Do you think there is a Coloured or Eurafrican community?' said 'No, we can't organize ourselves' or 'We hate to see our own people get ahead' or 'We always fight amongst ourselves, not like Europeans who get on with things.'[1]

I would argue that this way of organizing interrelationships is, rather, a function of the size of the community. Its members are forced into mutual interdependence in a number of different situations and wish to avoid open cleavages which might endanger future cooperation.

Some people in the community were noted for their forthright attacks 'to the face' of those they criticized. But such criticism was confined to people with whom their relationship was relatively remote in that it usually contained only one strand. They were observably much less direct, whatever the intensity of their feelings, in their comments to people with whom their relationship was multiplex.

In general, I observed that those individuals who persisted in open opposition to other people or groups within the society had very small-range networks. There were thus fewer channels through which they could be persuaded to accept more widely held views.

[1] White formal voluntary associations are not, in reality, free of friction and competition. Nevertheless, an idealized picture of the frictionless operation of White Society is widely held in the Coloured community.

The Community Civic Association

Many of the points I mention in the introduction emerged in the analysis of one of the community's most important formal voluntary associations, the Community Civic Association, which has been active for almost two decades. It was founded with the stated aim of furthering sport and the provision and maintenance of recreation facilities of all kinds. So far as its organization and importance for the community is concerned, the Association has passed through a number of phases which are typical of community service organizations of this type, and I describe them below.

The foundation. Two contradictory accounts of the foundation of the Association exist. That there are different accounts is significant since both of these reinforce the stereotypes which Whites and Coloureds hold about each other and their relative roles. Both are myths in the sense in which Malinowski (1922: 326–28) used the term.

A White informant, Mr Evans, gave me the following account which was echoed in various ways by other Whites who had also been involved.

The Coloured people are very nice, you know, but they don't seem to be able to arrange their own affairs. They are so jealous of one another, they are always fighting, and then going to outsiders to ask for their help in sorting out the mess. This Association was founded because some prominent Coloureds decided they wanted to improve their recreation facilities, but they couldn't decide among one another how to organize to get them. So Mr Borman and Mrs Yardley [both now elderly and no longer actively involved in associations in the community] came to me and asked me to form a committee. Well, I felt I could make a real contribution here, as they face a lot of difficulties, economic as well as personal, and I agreed to help them out. I was often sorry later because I found them, even the most prominent people, so unreliable. They wouldn't help even when I showed them the proper way to do things. But with time they learned to organize themselves a bit. I've resigned now, but I'm glad I could help them. Things aren't going so well these days I hear. They are really very nice people you know, much easier to talk to than Africans, even though they are so unreliable.

A Coloured informant said:

We wanted to improve facilities for our youth who are quite a problem because it is difficult for them to get jobs and they hang around the streets doing nothing all day. So a number of the most prominent people in the community got together and decided we would get some Europeans to patronize the affair. Mr Evans knew Mr Borman [who managed a garment factory in which many Coloured women worked] through the church and Mrs Van Bern knew Mrs Yardley because they worked together in the Child Guidance Association. So they asked them to come and be patrons and help us raise money. You need a lot of Europeans for a while when you start something which is going to need money because our community is too poor to contribute much.

A fairly large committee was established which contained three Whites—Mr Evans, Mrs van Bern and a representative of the Department of Social Welfare. In addition there were the five Coloureds who had originally mooted the idea and a number of other younger Coloureds including Mr Armstrong, who were already active in other associations and it was thought would do some of the practical work involved. Mr Evans was able, by a burst of activity, and through his extensive personal network to obtain at very little cost a shelter which could be used as the base for the organization of sports, and the holding of functions.

There was a vocal element within the community, but not represented on the committee, who opposed the whole idea. They explained this opposition on the grounds that it was the responsibility of Government to supply recreation centres, and that the shelter was so inadequate that it demonstrated that that was all the Europeans thought that they (Coloured people) were worth. The founding members of the Association say that the opposition was really based on resentment of the success of the whole venture and its sponsors. It provided a useful set of contacts which could be incorporated into the networks of committee members and hence widen their spheres of influence. It also provided, for the first time, an institution in which almost all sections of the community could become involved.

The running of the old facilities. Once the shelter was established its founders were faced with the responsibility of maintaining it, which involved a number of tedious small-scale repetitious jobs. When this became clear the composition of the committee changed:

a. All the White members except Mrs van Bern who was a book-keeper, and experienced in the financial side of running such associations, disengaged themselves.

b. The prominent older Coloured members who had started the idea spent less and less time on the affairs of the Association.

As a result, the committee members who remained involved were the younger men and women of the community who were ambitious; who had had the social and personal characteristics which were basic to the building up of an extensive personal network; and who were establishing new contacts through participation in this, and other, voluntary associations.

During this phase the most important contemporary cleavage in the community, that between Coloureds and Eurafricans, intruded into committee affairs. At that time large numbers of people who were first generation Eurafricans were joining the community, and its older members, many of whom came from the Coloured communities of the coast, which had been established for generations, felt their economic, social and political status was threatened.[1] At least twice during the early years, violent disagreements on this question, which had little to do with the manifest functions of the committee, led to open breaches, many of which persisted for years. The White participants, when they discuss this period, say they made a crucial contribution to the survival of the Association and the unification of the community, because they persisted in their attempts to emphasize common interests, and so bridge the gap between the two factions within the community. The following statement is typical.

Of course they [the Coloureds] fight all the time. They wanted to spend hours talking about whether the committee should be called Eurafrican or Coloured and putting forward claims that one section or another was being given preference. In the end we had to call ourselves just the 'Association'—not 'Coloured'. It was all pretty discouraging, let me tell you, because if a small community like that can't be united, what hope have they? However, I said this split was all nonsense and persuaded them to come back together and get on with the job they were there for.

Certainly the Coloured and Eurafrican cleavage has become

[1] The minutes of earlier community associations which existed during the period 1910–1945 refer repeatedly to the 'threat' Eurafricans pose to 'Coloured standards'.

much less deep since the foundation of the Association. I would, however, attribute this largely to the fact that the economy expanded rapidly for many years and was able to absorb many Eurafricans at status and wage levels established by Coloureds. Also intermarriage became increasingly common and in time many network links were established between members of the two sections. Thus in time open disagreements became more destructive, and techniques were evolved to avoid them. Mrs van Bern described this change in the following way.

The Secretaries in the old days weren't very experienced. [It emerged that the office was usually held by Coloureds who were better educated than most Eurafricans.] They used to try to put everything into the minutes, even the rows, which had nothing to do with the work of the Association. I used to look at the minutes in draft because I typed them out, and suggest that irrelevant things be omitted. Nowadays the trouble is that the Secretaries don't always mention even the relevant things!

Mr Armstrong, one of the active young community members, described events from his point of view.

There were lots of fights and I will admit that in those days feelings ran high. But in the Association a good deal of the trouble was caused because some of the Europeans, *not* Mrs van Bern or Mr Evans, kept interfering and telling us how to run things. Of course, we did need their help so we tried to avoid open fights. But I spent a lot of time trying to keep tempers cool, I can tell you. The Europeans said we were irresponsible about attending meetings. But lots of people in the community said: 'Well, if the Europeans don't want to listen to what we have to say, let them get on with running things *their* way'.

It is observable that a number of other associations in the community have lapsed, or 'gone dormant', because Whites are felt to be too dominant in their affairs, and community members have not resigned, but simply withdrawn from participation. In fact, the minutes of meetings held during this period indicate that local attendance at meetings was often poor, particularly when only routine business had to be dealt with. The few core Whites were, on the whole, regular in their attendance, and performed many of the day to day tasks which were essential for the survival of the Association.

Raising funds for new facilities. The ten years after the foundation of the Association were ones of general economic prosperity and growth. During this period a special suburb for Coloureds had been established by the Municipal Council, and the major proportion of the Coloured population of Middlebury now lives there. Feeling grew that this new community needed expanded facilities, on the spot.

All members of the committee realized, however, that it was beyond the powers of the small body which had existed until then to raise the large capital sum involved. Accordingly, Mr Evans, who had been active in the Association since its foundation, and who had extensive contacts both through his job, and through a long career of notable public service, persuaded a number of prominent members of the White business and financial community to join the Association and, in particular, to serve on a Fund Raising Sub-Committee. The Coloured membership of the Association was also expanded, as a number of young men and women who were already actively involved in either sports clubs or welfare committees, were invited to join the Civic Association.

An intense and high-powered campaign was organized by the members of the Fund Raising Sub-committee, and in due course greatly expanded and attractive sports facilities and a community hall were built. During this phase the specially recruited White members of the Association were overpoweringly important and the Coloured members of the Association participated with diffidence in the decision-making process. They did, however, run a series of small fund-raising events in the community which, although they were not very significant in the whole financial structure, stimulated interest in the project, and made it possible for local people to become involved. They also provided a series of situations in which three of the leaders of the middle generation in the community, Mr Armstrong, Mr Bronson and Mr Carruther, could compete with one another. They are contemporaries in their late thirties and competition amongst them, although not open, was keen, and was minutely observed and commented upon.

After the new facilities were completed the specially recruited White members of the Association gradually withdrew from its affairs. The Association then consisted of the few Whites who had remained active since the beginning, and many of the leading members of the middle generation of the Coloured community.

Some of these had been more or less active members of the
Association since its inception.

The administration of the new facilities. The maintenance and
running of these new facilities requires a good deal of administrative competence, as well as time. As their running costs are also
considerable an on-going fund raising organization became necessary soon after they were completed. Newly emerging leaders
in the community argued that this input of time and effort had
to come from the community itself, particularly since few outsiders were prepared to undertake such time consuming routine
tasks. Large sections of the community were affected by how these
facilities were run, and those responsible for making decisions
about these were observed with a critical eye and their performance was widely and freely commented upon behind their
backs.

Soon after the facilities were opened to the public the magnitude
of the task of running them became apparent, and it was agreed
that particular areas of responsibility had to be clarified. After
discussion it was agreed that a three-tiered form of organization
should be adopted. This is outlined below, with the title by which
I shall usually refer to each committee, in italics.

The Community Civic Association

1. *The Executive.* This is composed of the chairman, vice-
chairman, secretary and treasurer. It is empowered to take urgent
decisions but must refer these to the Association for ratification.
It does not meet regularly.

2. *The Association.* This body, from which the Executive is
elected, must take all major decisions, and must meet at least once
each calendar month to do so. It has 20 members, elected at an
advertised Annual General Meeting, each of whom also serves
on at least one sub-committee.

3. *The Sub-Committee:*

a. *The Use of Buildings Sub-Committee.* This is usually chaired
by the chairman of the Association. It decides which applications
for the use of buildings should be accepted and recommends what
fees should be charged. It is also responsible for keeping the buildings in good repair.

b. *Use of Sports Fields Sub-Committee.* This is usually chaired
by the vice-chairman of the Association. It attempts to cooperate

with sports unions and clubs in the organizing of the fair distribution of limited facilities.

c. *Running Funds Sub-Committee*. This organizes both on-going activities (e.g. children's movies) and special fund raising occasions (e.g. jumble sales, or junior dances).

d. *Community Activities Sub-Committee*. This attempts to encourage new activities in the community such as adult education, lectures, or badminton, but does not accept direct responsibility for running these activities.

e. *The Treasurer's Sub-Committee*. Chaired by the treasurer of the Association, it collects all fees, door money, etc. and checks the balance sheets of other sub-committees.

When the Association was reorganized in this way three important Coloured leaders were elected to various crucial offices. These were Messrs Armstrong, Carruther, and Mrs Bronson who were all of approximately equal age and status. They maintained friendly surface relations with one another, but their rivalry not only in this association, but also in two others, frequently emerged during discussions about apparently unrelated matters. For example, there was a good deal of controversy about what fees should be charged for the use of the new facilities, and what organizations should be permitted to use them regularly. The problem was a real one, and it was related to the question of the extent to which a small and relatively poor community could be expected to maintain such an expensive plant from its own resources. Since this was far from clear, and could only be established through trial and error, there was considerable scope for disagreement. All the Coloured members of the Association agreed, at this stage, that low fees should be charged to ensure that the facilities were widely used. White members of the Association, who still effectively held the purse strings, argued that the facilities must pay their own way from the beginning, as it would reflect badly on the community as a whole if the project got into financial difficulties.

Events in the national sphere also had an effect on the relative influence of individual leaders in the community. Elections were imminent and it was known that some form of representation for the Coloured community was a live if small-scale issue. It was widely rumoured that Messrs Armstrong, Bronson and Carruther had each been approached (among others) by the party in power as possible community representatives. Heightened competition between them was observable at meetings of the Association and also became apparent in increased friction between the sub-committees of which they were prominent members.

Ultimately Mr Armstrong was nominated by the party in power as a representative of Coloured interests, and appeared to receive a good deal of community support in this office.

On the Association the relative status of the three competitors was immediately re-defined. In the past its Coloured members had refused to elect their chairman from the community because, it was said, this would cause 'too much bad feeling'. Instead, a White had regularly been elected. Now, Mr Armstrong was elected chairman after the next Annual General Meeting.

His two unsuccessful rivals, Mr Bronson and Mr Carruther, were elected vice-chairman and secretary respectively. The Whites who remained on the committee became much less important. Thus for the first time the community possessed a facility of real importance which was to be run by Coloureds with almost complete independence.

The post-independence conflicts: the interim period

During the first year in which Coloureds were in control of the Association a number of fundamental differences of opinion between individuals and groups emerged. Clearly in any formal association there are likely to be divergent interests. But, for reasons I described earlier, in this community formal voluntary associations provide almost all of the situations in which ambitious individuals can acquire prestige and influence. As a result, disagreements about policy matters are much exacerbated by this underlying interpersonal competition. Everyone is well aware that this is happening and discussions about mundane and apparently unimportant matters tend to become very prolonged and emotionally charged.

The first of these conflicts of principle which also embodied an indirect challenge to the newly established Coloured leadership arose out of an old disagreement about the financial policy of the Association. During the period when the Executive was dominated by Whites the Coloureds had been virtually unanimous in their opposition to the Executive policy embodied in the phrase 'keep the Association self supporting', which meant that economic fees were charged for the use of the various facilities under the Association's control. But once Coloureds controlled the Executive they no longer opposed this policy so vigorously. They agreed instead that they, as experienced and responsible officials who had extensive contacts with Whites in the commercial world, realized—as their opposition did not—the extent to which the Association represented the Coloured community to the outside world. Their opposition, who were younger men and women without established positions, wished for the social prominence which could be derived from active membership of certain committees. They argued that members of the Executive were so much in touch with White views of the situation that they ignored the feelings of Coloured people in this matter. There was much popular support for their campaign to reduce hiring fees, which was greatly resented by those who were responsible for keeping the Association afloat financially.

The second conflict, which did not emerge nearly so explicitly during formal meetings of the Association, was expressed indirectly whenever the issue of official cooperation with associations of various kinds in other communities was raised. For several years an increasingly vocal opposition towards African advancement had been expressed in the White, Asian and Coloured communities. The dilemma for Coloured people was whether they should support continued White domination which involved occupying, apparently permanently, a subordinate but protected position in the total plural society; or whether Coloureds should support a non-racial society and risk losing a number of important economic privileges should the *status quo* be upset. This was an issue on which most people were reluctant to commit themselves and clear cut views were seldom publicly expressed. Most members of the Executive, who all held relatively well paid and secure jobs, were in favour of encouraging cooperation between the races, but their opponents on the Association, who were on the whole younger and less secure, were opposed to it.

As a result whenever it was suggested that a multi-racial venture of one kind or another should be held the idea was shelved, not explicitly, but through long delays while everyone discussed whether the Association should get involved, who should represent it, and where such meetings could be held. By the end of the year meetings of the Association were frequently very tense.

The conflict between these two groups, of whom Mr Armstrong and a Mrs Forward were clearly the focal points, was particularly obvious whenever there were discussions about how the sports field owned by the Association should be used, and by whom. All the young leaders who were described earlier were very active in various sports clubs and were ardently partisan in the disagreements which inevitably arose between these clubs and the Association. Mrs Forward and her supporters, although they were a relatively small group on the Association, had a good deal of unorganized but vocal support in a number of other clubs and associations in the community.

As a result of this conflict of interests, the Use of Sports Field Sub-Committee had not been very effective (from the point of view of the Association) in regulating the way in which these facilities were used, or in collecting the fees which were owed by sports clubs to the Association and used to maintain these facilities.

This division was frequently explained in terms of the natural opposition which exists between the young and the old. The young challengers of this period described themselves as 'young people who don't spend all their time on outside activities, and are in touch with real community feeling'. Several years earlier, before Mr Armstrong had been recognized as the representative of the Coloured community, he and his friends had described their opposition to their elders in almost exactly the same terms.

At the end of the year the usual public Annual General Meeting was held. It was not well attended, but the chairman commented on the fact that the youth of the community appeared to be showing an interest in the Association's affairs. He attributed this to the fact that young people were involved in the sports activities of which the Association was a part. Mrs Bronson, who as secretary had been increasingly inactive during the year, tendered her resignation and suggested that since the duties of the Association were now so onerous all the returning members should be re-elected *en masse*. She also suggested that the powers of co-option which the Executive already possessed should be generously exercised. These proposals were not opposed, and were therefore adopted. The various sub-committee reports followed, and were discussed in a desultory way. It was suggested from the floor that the hiring fees were too high. The reasons for this were explained by the treasurer and chairman, and the meeting was then adjourned.

It emerged afterwards that a member of the Executive had asked Mrs Bronson to suggest this mass re-election, in order to avoid a public demonstration of the support which various members of the Association might get or fail to get. The many young people present were known to be opposed to the established leaders. Mrs Bronson only agreed to make the suggestion because she did not expect to be involved in the Association's affairs during the next year.

Social characteristics of the participants

The social characteristics of the participants, and particularly the kind of networks they had built up, had an important effect on their actions in the conflict I shall describe shortly. As I said earlier they were divided into two groups, one of which (the Established Leaders) coincided to a large extent with the Executive, and their opponents (the Young Leaders) who occupied some important offices on sub-committees but who were not represented on the Executive. These social characteristics are summarized in Table III.

Additional network information:

Mr Arthur Armstrong, whose own kinship circle is small, has married into a large and active leading family several generations deep. Members of this family are well known outside the community through participation in a number of non-racial associations of all kinds. The kinship element in his network is very important since he is able to call on his kinsfolk for support. His network is very extensive indeed, and contains many influential people.

Mr Charles Carruther has only a medium range network in the community since he does not live in any of the three main suburbs in which the Coloured population of Middlebury is concentrated. He has many European friends but is not personally well known in the community.

Mrs Frances Forward immigrated to Middlebury as an adult after completing her professional training. She has not, however, been able to get a job in which her training is useful, and is a supervisor in a white-collar occupation. She has few kinship links in the community as her husband is also a relatively recent immigrant and is not active in voluntary associations.

Mr Edward Euston belongs to a large but geographically scattered

Table III

Social Characteristics of some of the Participants in the Community Civic Association

	Education 1	Occupational Status 2	Income 3	Kinship Contacts Birth 4	Kinship Contacts Marriage 5	Associations 6	Network Range 7	European Contacts 8
THE ESTABLISHED LEADERS								
Mr Arthur Armstrong	U/S	high	good	small	v. extensive	6	v. large	v. extensive
Mrs Barbara Bronson	L/S	medium	medium	large	medium	4	large	some
Mr Charles Carruther	P/S	medium	medium	small	v. small	2	medium	v. extensive
Mr Graham Games	U/S	high	good	small	small	4	large	many
Mr Harold Hadley	P	v. high	v. good	v. small	v. small	4	medium	some
THE YOUNG LEADERS								
Mrs Frances Forward	P	medium	medium	v. small	medium	2	small	few
Mr Edward Euston	L/S	medium	medium	large	medium	3	medium	few
Mr Dennis Donen	U/S	medium	medium	v. large	v. large	3	v. large	some

1. *Education.* All the people listed are relatively well educated. L/S = Lower Secondary School. U/S = Upper Secondary School. P/S = Post School but not professional training. P = Professional Training.

3. *Income.* All office bearers in the Association and its sub-committees appeared to have higher than average incomes. This classification is relative to the average for the Association and not the community as a whole.

4. 5. *Kinship Contacts.* On the whole, membership of what I have described as a 'small family' is the result of being first generation Eurafrican oneself, or of having parents who are Eurafricans. Many kinship contacts are usually the result of being a member of a family which has lived in the community for at least three generations.

6. *Associations.* I have included in this count membership of sports clubs, unions, community service associations, and active membership of churches, recreation clubs, the P.T.A.

sibling group holding jobs of widely varying status. His network is of medium range but contains few influentials within the community and none outside it.

Mr Dennis Donen has lived in Middlebury all his life, as has his wife. Both belong to large families several generations deep and know 'almost everybody' in the community but only a few people outside it.

Mrs Barbara Bronson had retired from the committee, and no longer attended meetings of the Association (see p. 152). She did, however, become involved in conflicts which emerged later (see page 170 and Figure 12).

The struggle for leadership

At the first monthly meeting after the Annual General Meeting the people who had held Executive office in the previous year were re-elected. The chairman proposed that Mr Graham Games be elected to the vacant secretaryship, and as no other nominations were received this was agreed. Mr Games is a close friend of Mr Armstrong and a distant relative by marriage. He is excluded by the conditions of his job from direct participation in politics, but is an active member of several associations. He is an influential person in the community and has a large-range network.

The newly elected Executive exercised their powers of co-option, as suggested at the Annual General Meeting, and asked a number of additional people to join the Association's various sub-committees. Many of these were relatives of members of the Executive and particularly of Mr Armstrong. Several of these extra people were assigned to the Use of Sports Fields Sub-Committee, which had been the focal point of opposition to Mr Armstrong. Mrs Forward remained the secretary of this committee and Mr Donen and Mr Euston remained chairman and treasurer, respectively.

These moves had three consequences. Firstly, the Executive was better able to ensure that the Association's decisions about the use of sports facilities could be enforced. Secondly, the relative strength of the young leaders on the Association was reduced. Finally, the young leaders' assertion that they represented the youth of the community was off-set by the fact that many much younger people, who did not support their views, had been added to the Association.

For several months it appeared that the competition between the established leaders and their young challengers had been reduced. The issue of what fees should be charged for the use of facilities was discussed exhaustively again, at all levels of the organization. Decisions on this matter involved a review of the whole financial structure of the Community Civic Association, and the services it provided. The advice of the few remaining White members of the Committee was constantly sought on this issue. In time it became clear that they were being cast in the role of outsider—scapegoats, or as Frankenberg (1957: 18) has defined the concept, as 'strangers'. As the Whites became more deeply involved in these complicated financial discussions they were generally presumed to be the source of financial decisions which were very unpopular in the community in general. Although members of the Executive were well aware of the necessity for these decisions, they did not publicly emphasize the fact that they agreed with them.

A new scale of fees was formally adopted in due course, with little apparent opposition within the Association. However, as soon as they were publicly posted several formal protests were lodged by the clubs of which the group of young leaders were active members. The other members of the Association were well aware of the fact that this was an organized continuation of the old conflict. The established leaders expressed outrage at the involvement of outside bodies in Association affairs. An uncommitted member remarked:

Europeans always say that their committees are kept separate from one another. I agree with this, but its not always easy because if you get involved with a man in one club its not easy not to get involved in another club too. This always seems to be happening in our community and it leads to lots of trouble.

A second source of conflict arose out of the accounting procedures used by the Sports Fields Sub-Committee. The Executive argued that these were not adequate and should be replaced by techniques suggested by the Finance Sub-Committee, whose chairman was the treasurer of the Executive. The office bearers of the Sports Fields Sub-Committee (Mrs Forward, Mr Donen and Mr Euston) rejected these suggestions on the grounds that they represented an attack on their own honesty and because they were too time-consuming. An alternative suggestion, which was that the collection of certain monies should be handed over to outside experts was also rejected.

The crisis. Again, relationships between the Executive and the young leaders and particularly between Mr Armstrong and Mrs Forward became very strained. Ultimately a public crisis was precipitated by a letter to the chairman of the Association from the chairman of one of the important affiliated clubs of which the young leaders were all members. This letter alleged:

1. That the Association had been packed by members of the chairman's family, who acted in his interests rather than in the interests of the community.

2. This favouritism was demonstrated by the fact that for the popular and therefore lucrative Christmas dance, the use of the sports pavilion had been granted by private agreement to the Joint Committee for Adult Education rather than the General Sports Union with which this club was affiliated.

The letter implied that this favouritism was one of the results of the chairman's persistent interest in multi-racial activities even when these were detrimental to the development of loyalty to the Coloured community as such.

3. The letter also contained some generalized allegations of general and financial inefficiency.

This letter, which was addressed to the chairman, was first discussed, formally, at a meeting of the Executive which he called specially to consider it. It emerged that several members of the Executive were already well informed about this letter and the circumstances surrounding its composition. Though none of them were members of the club from which it had originated, several people seemed to know that although the letter appeared to have emanated from its secretary, in fact it had been instigated by Messrs Euston and Donen and had been drafted by Mrs Forward, all of whom had acted, it was rumoured, without discussing the matter with the remainder of the club committee.

The specific allegations it contained were also discussed and it was pointed out that the booking which had been questioned was an annual event and had been so for some years. The Executive was unable to produce evidence of this, however, as the allocation had originally been decided by the Use of Buildings Sub-Committee, chaired by the Executive chairman, which had not kept regular minutes of its meetings for some time. The decision was reported in the monthly minutes of the Association simply as 'Booking'—the allocation of the sports pavilion for Christmas which was recommended by the Use of Buildings Sub-Committee was accepted. This lack of precision was explained by the Executive as simply a mistake, but the young leaders interpreted it as a deliberate attempt by the established leaders to obscure decisions which they felt might be unpopular.

The more serious allegations of nepotism and inefficiency were also discussed. The members of the Executive agreed that they had been leaning very heavily on the help of relatives but that this had been the only way to keep the Association going during the last year—when there had been so much work to do, and so much 'difficulty' in the Association and between the sub-committees. The problems of running not only this activity but others in the community was described in the following statement, made by a member of the Executive at this meeting.

The trouble with our community is nobody wants to do the hard work. They always say they'll do something and then you get there and find they haven't. With people you know well on a committee you can say to them at breakfast, or on the way to work, have you done so-and-so, or you can drop around after work and help them, or remind them. Young people specially, and you know we have to train the young people to take over—you can say to your own relatives 'do this', but if you say that to the daughter or son of somebody you don't know well, then they get all offended and say you are trying to be a boss, and 'who do you think you are?' Members of one's own family and friends are reliable, and other people are not. Other people always talk behind your back too, and say they will not do what they've been asked to do, but they won't say this to your face, and you don't know where you are. In the family you can talk straight.

At the end of the special meeting the Executive stated that they could not lead the Association successfully if they had to continue to function in this atmosphere of perpetual distrust and 'street corner talking against us all the time'. They stated that they would offer their resignations *en masse*, at the next monthly meeting of the Association, and leave it to the Association to decide what to do.

After this formal meeting was adjourned the discussion of this whole affair continued in the members' homes, and the matter was soon being analysed widely within the community. The issues and actions of the protagonists were heatedly canvassed, particularly by members of the effective portion of each one's network. Within a short period two different and opposed views of the matter emerged. Each incorporated the same factual material, but interpreted it differently. For example, Mr Armstrong's intimates saw his direction of the Association as hardworking and efficient.

He looks into applications to use the facilities to make sure that the Association will get its money, and there isn't trouble about bad debts. And he gets so little help from the other sub-committees (I'll mention no names) that he has to keep going to his family and friends and getting them to help, or nothing would ever get done. He is fighting for the good name of the community and should be helped for that reason.

Within the networks of Mrs Forward, Messrs Donen and Euston the issues were described this way.

We don't like to make personal accusations, but you really can't help it in this case. The chairman and his friends and relations are always sticking their noses into the affairs of sports bodies and other committees in the community, and asking to see balance sheets and constitutions which are none of their business. And he isn't really interested in the good of the community, all he's interested in is his own personal leadership. We are trying to help him with the hiring of the buildings and facilities, but he interferes all the time and says we aren't doing a good job—and he says the accountants say we aren't looking after the money properly. He is really trying to destroy our good names because he does not like any competition from the younger generation with new ideas.

Over the next ten days earlier attempts by the Executive to confine the conflict to the Association were abandoned. These two versions of the affair were extensively discussed by most of the relatives, friends and acquaintances of the chief protagonists, and ultimately hundreds of people in many networks were involved. By the end of this period it became clear that the version which had been initially held by Mr Armstrong's intimates had been generally, though not, of course, universally accepted as 'what really happened'. This was because of two factors—both of which can be analysed in terms of the character of Mr Armstrong's network as well as his personality.

a. As I have stated earlier, his personal network was a very

extensive one which had been built up over years through active
participation in a large number of voluntary associations. He was
generally liked and respected, though also envied, and people who
had known him personally thought he would have been motivated by a concern for the image of the community as well as by
personal ambition. Mrs Forward and Mr Euston were not nearly
so widely known and people were therefore unable to assess the
likelihood of their claims in personal terms. It was assumed, however, that they also were motivated by personal ambition.

b. Mr Armstrong's network contained a large number of influentials, as he knew all the prominent members of his own
generation in the community. Many of the most active of these
were people whom he met constantly in other situations, and with
whom, as a result, he had developed many-stranded relationships
of considerable strength. Also, most of the Whites in the Association were people whom he met in other voluntary associations,
and some of them were his personal friends, whom he entertained
and was entertained by. These influential contacts were incorporated only marginally into the networks of the younger leaders
because they met them only in the context of the Association and
not elsewhere.

Although the public view was that Whites who were members
of the Association could not be entirely impartial in their assess-
ments of the situation, it was agreed that they were less involved in
the situation than insiders, and also that they were experienced
members of other committees, and hence were more likely than
most people to know how executive officers and other members
of formal voluntary associations *should* behave.

The uncommitted members of the Association observed the
reactions of prominent people, both Coloured and White to the
two versions of recent events which was presented to them. Most
influentials in the community were reluctant to commit themselves publicly because as I have already suggested (pp. 140 ff) a
withdrawal of cooperation in all situations in which the protagonists meet in daily life, would severely disrupt the social life of the
community. However the general impressions they gave was that
Mr Armstrong should be supported on this issue. This view was
expressed by the White members of the Association with less
equivocation, and was widely repeated.

The view of the Whites in this matter was interpreted by the young leaders as further evidence that Mr Armstrong and his supporters were more interested in gaining favour with Whites than they were in providing their own people with what the young leaders described as 'real leadership'. They could not define this term with any clarity, largely because their attitudes to European participation in community affairs was itself ambivalent. Mrs Forward the most isolated, and the most ambitious and vocal of the group expressed it in these terms:

I think Arthur spends too much time on getting Europeans to help the community. What he really wants is to get to know them socially, he's not really interested in the community's good. Actually I know lots of Europeans too and some of my good friends are Europeans, but I don't try to pull them into community affairs all the time.

An analysis of her network showed that in fact the only Whites she could be said to know at all well were those she had met through participation in two voluntary associations, and these relationships were thus single-stranded and almost completely impersonal. Those Whites she knew in her job could not be described as influential in the wider White community since they were of low supervisory occupational status, and had no contact with Coloured people outside the work situation.

The healing of the breach
After it had emerged fairly clearly that the majority of both the Association and the community supported the Executive rather than their rivals, a process of compromise and reconciliation began. Pressure was brought to bear on the young leaders to persuade them to retract and apologize for their accusations.[1] Ultimately, the young dissidents were prepared to abandon their attack, not only because the pressures to which they had been subjected were considerable, but also because they had clearly failed to gain much public support. In addition, during the discussions and investigations of the Association's affairs which they had instigated, the techniques they themselves employed to deal with the finances under their control, which had already incurred the censure of the Treasurer's Sub-Committee, were openly and critically discussed by ordinary members of the Association for the first time.

[1] The network channels through which these influences worked will be discussed in the next section of the paper.

The young leaders stood to gain a good deal if they were seen to be reconciled to the established leaders of the Association. If they continued to oppose adamantly there would be less chance in the future of their becoming members of the other Community associations in which the established leaders were influential, and their own progress to community wide influence would be halted.

It was also important for the Association as a whole that this rift should appear to be healed. It would reflect badly on the established leaders if they were believed to confirm and hence reinforce one of the stereotypes which a large number of Coloureds held about themselves, i.e. that Coloureds are unable to work together because they are too jealous of one another, and that Coloured associations frequently 'go dormant' because there are disputes about the proper handling of their funds.

The resolution of the conflict, and the bringing of the young challengers back into the fold could not be done at a public meeting, or even at a sub-committee meeting, since this would be too public an acknowledgment of the breach. In fact, it was notable that during the period of most heated discussions and accusations, no official committee meetings of any kind were held. Some reconciliation had to be effected, and without bringing the protagonists face to face, otherwise the possibility of reconciliation might well be permanently lost.

The operation of networks in this situation. The negotiations were conducted through a number of persons who were members of the networks of two or more of the chief protagonists and were hence able to act as intermediaries between them. The young leaders did not all agree to withdraw their accusations simultaneously, but capitulated individually over a period of several days. And the swiftness and completeness with which they were prepared to capitulate was a reflection of the different character of their networks. In the description which follows I refer to the operation of network links which came to my attention. It is likely that there were others of which I was unaware.

Armstrong-Donen

Mr Donen it will be remembered, had a very large-range network. He had many common linkages through kinship, common membership of voluntary associations, and common friends, with

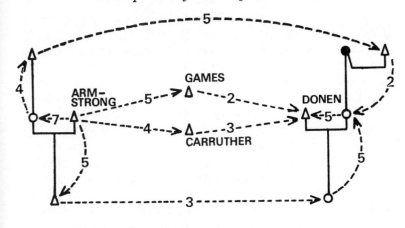

——————— Kinship relationship

---3--- Network relationship showing number of strands in the relationship

------> Direction in which influence was brought to bear

FIGURE 10

Armstrong–Donen

Mr Armstrong. That he was a member of the young leaders, and not the Executive, may be attributable to the fact that he had recently come into conflict with Mr Armstrong in another formal voluntary association in which they were both deeply involved; also, he was younger than Mr Armstrong and a mutual friend told me that, 'He thinks Arthur blocks his way ahead by inspecting what he does all the time.' Pressure was brought to bear on him through linkages, represented in Figure 10, all of which are part of the overlapping segments of his and Mr Armstrong's networks.

1. *The links through kinsmen of the senior generation*

The Donens and Mrs Armstrong had known each other all their lives. The two wives had many friends and even a number of distant relatives in common. Each identified herself with her husband's views in this matter, and criticized the other's husband, but they were both very concerned to avoid an open breach. When they met in public they ignored the whole affair.

Soon after the row started Mr and Mrs Armstrong went round to Mrs Armstrong's father's house in order to discuss the matter. Mrs Donen's step-father who was a close friend of the old man, was also there, as was usual. The two old men had heard rumours of the dispute, and after a while the conversation came around to the matter. The behaviour of the participants was not discussed specifically, but the old men were asked how they thought people *should* behave in an Association of this kind. Both of them had been members of clubs of various kinds in their youth, and Mrs Armstrong's father had been very active in a number of community associations in the early days. The old men said that they had observed that Coloured people were jealous of one another, and this often led to fights, but they agreed that such quarrels should be confined to the Association in which they arose, and were prepared to censure committee members who 'talked about them outside'. They said it was all right to talk to your 'real friends' but it was bad to talk to 'just anybody'.

After a while Mr Armstrong and Mrs Donen's step-father left. Mrs Armstrong told her father that her husband was very disturbed and hurt by this attack, and that the whole family felt it was an attack on their loyalty to the community.

Shortly afterwards Mrs Armstrong's father dropped around to visit Mrs Donen's step-father and told him how upset all the Armstrongs were about this although they didn't want to show it. Mrs Donen's step-father, although he was not at all close to his daughter, feared that this relationship with his old friend might be threatened, and went to see his daughter for a short visit and urged her to persuade her husband to 'stop all this quarrelling over nothing' and emphasized how angry all the Armstrongs were about the accusations which had been made. Mrs Donen was uneasy about passing on this message, as she feared that her husband would regard her as a 'traitor' if she did so, but she had been finding that her friends at work were identifying her with her husband's views and 'talking about' her, and wished to have the conflict resolved. So Mrs Donen passed on to her husband the information she had about the considerable depth of indignation the Armstrongs felt and also told him that people were 'looking at' her and 'talking about' her.

Mr Donen's wife was in a particularly acute intercalary position in this dispute, in that she represented her husband to outsiders but the outside view to her husband, and was keen to alleviate the tensions inherent in such a position.

2. *Links through kinsmen of the junior generation*

Mr Armstrong's two teenage sons are members of several of the junior associations in the community, and particularly the athletics union, and a popular electric guitar ensemble. They are widely known and date many of the prettiest young girls in their age group. One of these is Mr Donen's daughter who very much resented the intrusion of the quarrels of her elders into her own social life. She said she didn't have lots of young boy cousins like other girls, and didn't want to be fighting with possible boy friends just because her father was. She urged her mother to ensure that her father 'stopped fighting with people'.

In both these cases the message was passed through a considerable number of intermediaries. In general, information which passes through four or more people is much modified. But in these cases Mr Donen was given a relatively clear and accurate picture of the views of Mr Armstrong because each network link in the set contained a large number of strands; because the people involved were emotionally close; and because all of them found that the conflict adversely affected relationships in other parts of their networks.

3. *Links through mutual friends:*

a. Mr Games is a member of Mr Armstrong's effective network, but his relationship with Mr Donen contains only two strands arising out of marginal participation in relatively unimportant voluntary associations. When Mr Games met Mr Donen at a sports match and urged him to stop 'saying things' about Mr Armstrong, Mr Donen rejected this advice on the grounds that 'though he is a good friend of the Armstrongs he's got nothing to do with me, really, and shouldn't interfere in my affairs'.

b. Pressure brought to bear on Mr Donen through Mr Carruther, was, however, more effective. He had been an influential member of the Association in the past but by the time of this conflict, had more or less withdrawn from active participation in its affairs. Several members of the Association (including an important White) urged him to interfere, and he reluctantly agreed to do so. His relationship with Mr Armstrong included four strands, two of which had been important in the past, but were now dormant. His relationship with Mr Donen, although it contained three strands, was becoming closer because their wives were very close friends.

Mr Carruther uncompromisingly supported the Executive in this issue, because as he explained, he had 'seen too many good associations breaking up like this'. He urged Mr Donen to 'stop fighting with the Executive'—and said, by implication, that competition within an association was normal, but that he very much disapproved of 'taking the fight outside to the street-corners' as this 'got everybody talked about and didn't do anybody any good'.

Mr Donen was much more inclined to take this advice seriously than he had been that of Mr Games.

The result of this pressure was that Mr Donen very quickly decided that he did not wish to continue the conflict. He went to Mr Carruther's house and told Mr Carruther that the statements he had made about the Executive in general, and Mr Armstrong in particular, had been misinterpreted. He said he had not really wanted to become involved in the affair at all, and although he had discussed their grievances with Mr Euston and Mrs Forward, he had not known they were going to send a letter of accusation, and had been horrified by the extreme attitudes expressed in the letter they had written.

He also said that since he had really had very little to do with the matter there was no point in going to Mr Armstrong directly and saying this, as then they might quarrel. Mr Carruther agreed and assured Mr Donen that Mr Armstrong would understand Mr Donen's real attitude if Mr Carruther explained it. There was no suggestion that he should make a public withdrawal of the accusations made by the group of which he had undoubtedly been a member.

Armstrong-Euston
Mr Euston did not agree to withdraw his accusation for several days. This was partly because he had a forceful personality and was ambitious, and would have gained prestige had the accusations of his group been generally accepted. He had a medium range network and was most active in a young sporting and party-going crowd in the community, who were not represented on the

Association. Although he was a skilled craftsmen he had no steady jobs and was felt by many leading members of the Association to be a little unreliable. His network bonds with both his supporters and his opponents in this conflict were not very strong and he was insulated from pressure and gossip to a much greater extent than Mr Donen had been. Pressure to conform was, however, exerted.

1. *Pressure through kinship bonds:*

a. Mr Armstrong's daughter, who was at school with Mr Euston's shy young son, and also a member of the same 'Rock Group', indignantly told many mutual friends that Bob Euston's father was 'awful because he's been passing remarks about my father'. Bob Euston asked his father what this was all about and was clearly distressed by the possibility of more 'whispers about' him.

b. Mr Hadley, who had much the same kind of family background as Mr Armstrong, had recently married into the same

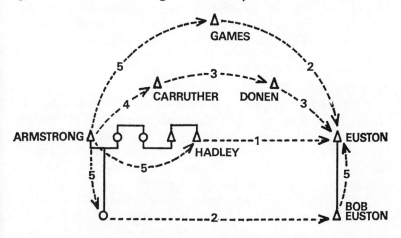

——————— Kinship relationship

– – –3– – – Network relationship showing number of strands in the relationship

– – – – –> Direction in which influence was brought to bear

FIGURE 11

Armstrong–Euston

large extended family. He was a new member of the Executive but felt himself to be identified with the older members in so far as the accusations against them were concerned. He dislikes tension and is a perceptive and articulate man who, because of his job, cannot participate directly in party politics. He argued that it should be possible to get at the 'real root' of the accusations. He discussed this problem with Mr Armstrong and Mr Games and several of the influential Whites in the Association, and argued that ambitious younger people in the community should be encouraged to make a contribution, but they should also be warned that 'it is always better to keep your own business to yourself. In this community people always watch what you say, and if you talk to just anybody there is always trouble. Europeans may be different.'

When the tension was at its height he went to see Mr Euston, and urged that a reconciliation be effected because it was bad for members of the community always to be involved in fights. His acquaintance with Mr Euston was confined to their common membership of the Association (i.e. was one-stranded) and Mr Euston was inclined to think that this visit was unwarranted interference in his affairs even though 'Mr Hadley is an educated man'.

2. *Links through mutual friends:*
   a. When Mr Hadley's approach to Mr Euston appeared to have failed, Mr Armstrong urged Mr Games to approach Mr Euston. Mr Games was reluctant to do so, as he said he 'did not really know Mr Euston except in the . . . club'. Eventually he did agree to 'drop a word to him at the game on Saturday'. This did not appear to have any immediate effect either.
   b. Eventually, when Mr Donen had intimated to Mr Carruther that he had reconsidered his stand, Mr Carruther suggested to Mr Donen that he urge both Mr Euston and Mrs Forward to withdraw also. Mr Donen who was eager that amicable relations should be restored as quickly as possible went to see Mr Euston and asked him to stop the quarrel. Mr Euston agreed to do this, but he immediately tendered his resignation. The public reason he gave was that he had been elected to an office in another formal voluntary association and needed to devote more time to that and other committees.

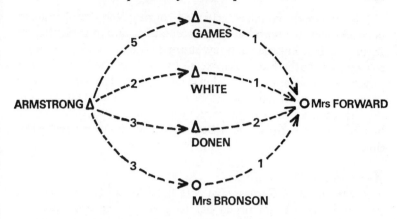

——————— Kinship relationship

- - -3- - - Network relationship showing number of strands in the relationship

- - - - -> Direction in which influence was brought to bear

FIGURE 12

Armstrong–Forward

Armstrong-Forward

Mrs Forward had always been the most vocal of the group of young challengers, and was invariably its chief spokesman, but she was not its leader. She had arrived in Middlebury relatively recently and her network was very small-range indeed. She had joined a sports club soon after her arrival but the Association was the first formal voluntary association of wide prestige to which she had been elected.[1] Her network bonds with most of its members were tenuous, since this was the only situation in which she was in contact with most of them. She was thus much more insulated than Messrs Donen and Euston from the strictures of general gossip as well as from specific pressures from people who were intermediary between herself and the established leaders.

[1] I have no information on how she was elected or who elected her. The fact that she had a professional training of high status may have had something to do with it. She was not, however, employed in a job commensurate with her training.

The network contacts activated during the campaign to persuade her to withdraw her accusations are represented in Figure 12. Her kinsmen and few intimate friends, were unknown to members of the Executive except by sight. It was therefore not possible to avoid approaching her directly, although the Executive agreed at an informal discussion, that 'this is a mistake because then there may be a fight to your face, and you don't know how to greet each other when you meet on the street after that'.

Approaches to Mrs Forward

a. Mr and Mrs Games gave Mrs Forward a lift to work one day, and Mrs Games urged her to give up her opposition to Mr Armstrong because this had caused a breach on the Association and this reflected badly on the community. Mrs Forward said that she would continue to oppose Mr Armstrong as 'a matter of principle' because she felt he had 'had his own way for too long' She implied that Mr Games was only interested in getting their investigations of the Association's affairs stopped because he was himself involved.

b. Mrs Bronson, who had recently retired from the committee, but who was still informed about its affairs agreed, on the urging of Mr Armstrong and Mr Games, to visit Mrs Forward and 'talk the whole matter over'. This did not appear to influence Mrs Forward to change her attitude, either.

c. Mr Armstrong and Mr Carruther then approached an influential European member of the Association and urged him to see Mrs Forward. He said that he only knew her through the Association but said that he would very reluctantly go and see her and 'urge her to get back on to friendly relations with the committee, so that people can get on with the real job and not waste all this time on unimportant personal rows'.

d. Although worried by the evident unanimity of the opposition which the attack had aroused, Mrs Forward was not prepared to make a gesture of reconciliation until she was approached by Mr Donen, who had been her ally. Mr Donen spoke to her only after he found that her continued opposition to the Executive was endangering his own attempts to restore peaceful relations. Mrs Forward was anxious to preserve peaceful relations with Mr Donen because he was influential in the sports club to which she belonged. She said that everybody seemed to be 'talking against' her and she would have to think about the whole matter. Possibly she had 'misinterpreted what was happening, and had not been justified on this occasion'.

General comments
There are striking parallels between this description of the processes by which pressures were brought to bear on a dissident group within society and that of Colson in her paper 'Social Control and Vengeance in Plateau Tonga Society' (1935b). She comments that 'various people . . . cannot see how controls can function in what seems at first glance to be an essentially unorganized society without clear-cut lines of allegiance to affiliate people to definite local groups' (1953b: 199). She points out that controls are exercised through the operation of a number of cross-cutting ties, for example, 'while the women were sending pleas to their relatives to settle the case in a hurry, their husbands were counselling their own kinsmen to accept a settlement' (1953b: 208). She describes how after relationships had been re-established it 'was again possible for Eland and Lion people to meet and partake in the same rituals and in the same gatherings without danger of immediate hostilities. Each group had had good reason to desire this result, and each had been under considerable pressure from outsiders to settle the case' (p. 209). This is because a permanent breach 'would lead to a general community disruption, affecting those who must live in the midst of the turmoil and are not directly concerned with it. Permanent bad relations then are only possible when the groups involved do not have kinsmen living together in the same local groups, and where they are not tied by the network of kinship and affinal ties to the same matrilineal groups' (p. 210).

Although the Tonga are remote rural agriculturalists, and the Coloured community of Middlebury is urban, industrial and literate, both societies are 'unstructured' in the sense that their members do not have unequivocal ties of allegiance to definite interest groups. In both societies too, the personal relationships of many members are multiplex and people are forced into mutual interdependence.

As a result, although these societies are in many ways very unlike one another, and the idiom through which issues are expressed is different, nevertheless many of the underlying political processes are the same.

The public resolution of the conflict

As soon as all three young leaders had agreed to withdraw their accusations the normal activities of the Association could be resumed. At an informal meeting members of the Executive decided that although it was important to recreate a public image of the Association as a unified group the matter had been so widely discussed that some kind of public statement would have to be made about it. It was agreed that all Mr Armstrong needed to say was that there had been a minor dispute between members of the Association which had been much exaggerated.

Several techniques were employed in this process of minimizing overt conflicts between individuals who are inescapably interdependent upon one another.

1. When the next formal meeting of the Association was held the resignations of the Executive which had been tendered early in the proceedings were ignored. (When I enquired about this privately I was told that these offers had been made at an informal meeting between friends, and were not therefore valid.)

2. The Chairman was thus able to refer to the matter as 'a storm in a tea-cup' which arose out of 'misunderstandings' of the decisions of the Association. He then went on to state his views on how these misunderstandings could be avoided. He particularly emphasized the value of regular and attentive attendance at meetings, which would prevent misinterpretations of decisions taken (it must however, be noted, that at the height of the storm it had been made clear to all members of the Association that the young leaders were, in fact, well aware of what decisions had been taken, and why, and had still continued to criticize them. At that time members of the Executive had emphasized that it was their irresponsible and persistent opposition which had forced the Executive to tender their resignations); the *proper* performance of assigned duties; and particularly when handling the Association's money; and frank and open dealings between members of the Association without recourse to 'street talking behind people's backs'.

Although to an outsider this speech would have appeared to be simply a general homily on the ideas of behaviour on committees, everyone present was well aware that it was directed at the young dissidents.

3. When in due course the Chairman returned to the normal agenda, under the minute 'Incoming Mail' the Secretary said that 'a letter had been received from a certain club which contained certain allegations about the functioning of the Association'. These were not elaborated upon and it was agreed that the club should be asked for an explanation and an apology. The consequent minute simply said that 'A letter from the . . . Club was noted'. The Executive of the club itself disowned the letter in private conversation, and the matter was not referred to again in either association.

4. Within a very short time the affair was 'forgotten' by participants in it. The White member of the Association who had reluctantly agreed to talk to Mrs Forward about it, was described by both factions as 'interfering in our affairs, trying to get Europeans back into all the important jobs in the community'. He was aware of this gossip and of the fact that he was being used as a scapegoat or 'stranger' (Frankenberg, 1957) in this matter.

5. Mr Euston who had been the leader of the dissident group resigned, and the bookkeeping techniques which had been recommended earlier, and to which he had objected so heatedly, were adopted.

6. Mr Donen did not attend a few meetings, and his part in the conflict was quickly forgotten. He then returned to the Association with much the same status as he had enjoyed before.

7. Mrs Forward, who found that people on the Association were still avoiding her (she seemed always to sit alone at meetings), later made a speech which referred only in very vague terms to this row but which amounted to tendering her apologies to members of the Association (unspecified), whom she had unintentionally maligned. A misunderstanding had arisen which was now put right, she said. In due course she also was accepted back into full participation in the Association's affairs.

When the public observed that an open row had not developed at the next full meeting of the Association, interest in the whole affair quickly lapsed. Within a short time even the participants were reluctant to discuss the issues or sequence of events in any detail. After the passage of a couple of months people appeared to retain only a generalized sense of grievance against the other side, and this was revived only when they again came into conflict with one another, on specified issues.

Within a short period this row on the Association was eclipsed by one involving almost all the people and organizations in the community who played or supported sport. The Association reluctantly became involved because it ran the sports fields, and on this occasion the Executive was divided, as were the young leaders. A vertical cleavage based on common sporting interests, rather than a horizontal one based largely on seniority, emerged.

I was told that there had been 'a lot of rows in this Association, its almost gone dormant quite a few times', and shortly before I left the field yet another set of divisions was beginning to emerge. In all the formal voluntary associations which I observed at any depth this same process of conflicts more or less successfully held in check by successive counterbalancing cleavages, was evident. This is part of a more general social process which I analyse in greater detail later. As a rule, the incentive to resist this frequently destructive process is greater in those associations which have material resources to administer or enjoy, such as some sports clubs, churches, welfare associations, and of course, the Association which I have described here. Many other associations, which lack these incentives, are ephemeral.

Conclusions

Several points of interest emerge from the analysis of this case:

1. *The personal status of the participants.* By the time the crisis had abated the issues it raised and the personalities involved had been discussed by a considerable proportion of the adults in the community. Certainly it had been a topic for comment in at least four sports clubs, in one church group, in two women's voluntary associations, and in a great many private homes. Commentators who were remote from any of the protagonists received and passed on a number of differing accounts of the quarrel. It was accepted that all the participants would suppress information which was unfavourable to their case, so interested observers made it their business to talk to informants on both sides, and to analyse the information they were given for contradictions and inconsistencies. All the influential people in the community to whom I spoke about this form of competition, decried it. Yet I observed that in fact these conflicts provided an essential platform

on which leaders could be seen to be active and exerting influence, and their public performance could be observed, assessed, criticized and praised. Thus, the effect of this controversy and confusion was to keep the relative social positions of the chief participants constantly before the public eye.

2. *Community Identity and Formal Voluntary Associations.* As I noted in the introduction to this paper, the political organization of the Coloured community has three important characteristics: many aspects of the life of its members are controlled by outside agencies; within the community there are no clearly-defined sources of power and authority; although it is urban and industrial the community is so small, and mobility in the caste society is so limited, that multiplex relationships between its members are common. In all societies individuals identify themselves with different and sometimes conflicting formal and informal groups in response to different situations. But it appears that the frequency and range within which individuals and small groups are able to shift these allegiances differs from one society to another, and appears to be most marked in societies with the kind of political organization I have described above. Van Velsen (1964: 313) when describing the Lakeside Tonga of Malawi, who are a 'chiefless society' says: 'Alignments are continually shifting. Groups thus emerge and disappear with ease because of the predominance of flexible relationships between individuals and very small groups.'

This process of constantly shifting allegiances is facilitated by the fact that the norms which people cite to validate their actions are, in most fields, very ambivalent. People, particularly when they wish to criticize their enemies, frequently do so in terms of a model of ideal behaviour which is based on 'what Europeans do'. (My observation is that this ideal is probably as unrealistic for Whites as it is for Coloureds.) But in most situations people invoke vaguely-defined norms derived from the interpretation of 'how *we* do things', which is current in the effective section of their networks.

In the Coloured community formal voluntary associations such as the Community Civic Association, which have control of and responsibility for capital installations, survive these divisive processes, but smaller and less prestigious associations often 'go dormant' as a result. When an association is described as 'going dormant' this does not imply that there was an open row between its members but rather that members ceased to participate in the association's affairs, and it faded away. Such associations are often revived later by some of the people who withdrew during the earlier phase. This form of social organization has been observed elsewhere. Dickie-Clark (1966: 137–41) describing the Coloured community of Durban, sees it in almost entirely negative terms: 'The helplessness of Coloured organizations in the face of White dominance and the resultant tendency for many of them to be short-lived or to have long dormant periods, makes the assessment that... "coloured organizations don't really get very much done", and the fear that they "sometimes lead to trouble and quarrels among the people" . . . realistic.' He says later (p. 139) '. . . the association showed a good deal of inefficiency and muddle. . . . Under such circumstances, there was ample opportunity for criticism, and ample criticism was made.'

'Again, in the actual running of the association the members knew well enough how such enterprises ought to be run, and were to the point in their criticisms of the organization's shortcomings. But poverty, too little leisure and the dearth of educated and experienced personnel along with other efforts of exclusion, frustrated their attempts to make the Ratepayers Association more efficient' (p. 141).

He ascribes this to the Coloured's marginal situation: 'Essentially the marginal dilemma in Coloured formal associations is that their White culture . . . requires them to publicly express sentiments and demands to set specific goals and general aspirations which are unrealistic in the face of their social exclusion' (p. 140).

But he then goes on to say 'None the less, the proceedings of the association were . . . clearly enjoyed by the members. In fact, one got the strong impression that the participants at meetings did not really expect to get very much done and it was the business of holding a meeting and enjoying reputable and satisfying interaction with one's fellows that was of primary importance to them.'

I would argue, instead, that these recurrent crises have an important positive function because, whatever their outcome, during these conflicts the participants and the people in their personal networks become involved in formulating and discussing the distinct interests of the community as a whole, or of groups within it. Thus the conflicts are themselves a source of unity, however ephemeral, between the people in a particular interest group, whatever its order. This definition and discussion of the special interests of Coloureds is not always confined within the limits of the community. In many really major conflicts some of the participants take the issues to the newspapers, and they may receive considerable publicity in the wider society. In the last fifteen years this has happened when there have been intra-community quarrels about the relative status of Coloureds and Eurafricans, and particular leaders; and inter-community quarrels with sections of the dominant White society about the standards of the Council housing provided, and what has been described by prominent members of the community as 'European interference in our affairs'.

Thus the very social process which is an important part of the maintenance of a feeling of identity within the Coloured community, is seen by outsiders as evidence of their lack of community identity. This has a positive function too, since the White conviction that Coloureds are 'helpless and hopeless' contributes to their willingness to afford Coloureds a protected economic status.

3. *The function of networks.* Coloureds are regarded, both inside the community and by outsiders, as jealous and quarrelsome. But the frictions which are commented on are, nowadays, not often permitted to reach the point where they permanently disrupt social relations between individuals and groups. An underlying cohesion is maintained through the operation of the network relationships of many people interacting with one another with differing degrees of intensity. Van Velsen (1964: 313) describes this process amongst the Tonga in the following way:

'Overall social and political cohesion is achieved through a wide network of relationships between individuals and small kin groups rather than through a structured ranking and co-ordination of clearly defined and permanent local or kinship groups.'

During my field work I observed the day to day operation of these social networks. Discussions of community affairs and personalities took place between people whose acquaintance with one another varied from the very intimate to the almost completely impersonal, and it soon emerged that a very clear distinction was usually made between 'talking frankly to real friends' and 'just chatting to somebody I don't know well'. When I analysed the character of the personal relationships of individuals it emerged that 'real friends' were people whom Ego saw regularly in three or more different social contexts. I have used Epstein's typology (Epstein, 1961) and allocated these three-or-more stranded relationships to the effective section of Ego's network. Individuals whom Ego sees in only one or two social contexts (who are often described as 'people I just know') I have described as falling within his extended network.

Effective network relationships differ from extended ones in several ways. They tend to be confined to Ego's peers; they are likely to persist despite vicissitudes; and they include the people with whom Ego gossips with most freedom and intensity, and with reference to the explicit formulation of moral norms. In this paper I have been particularly concerned with analysing the formulation and communication of norms, and how people who are deviant in a particular situation are persuaded to conform to norms.

4. *Pressures to conform.* The underlying cohesion of this kind of social system is maintained, in part, through the pressures which are brought to bear on dissidents to force them to conform. These pressures are more likely to be accepted by an individual who is deviant in a particular situation if they are brought to bear by a member of his effective network, or by somebody of high status. For example, Mr Carruther was more successful than Mr Games in persuading Mr Donen to withdraw his accusations against the established leaders (p. 165). And Mr Donen was more effective in influencing the attitudes and the actions of Mr Euston and Mrs Forward than any of the other people who tried to do so (pp. 168 and 170). Mrs Forward was also more susceptible to pressure from a high status White than from Coloured people with whom her relationship was equally remote.

5. *The formulation of norms.* All societies have, as part of their ethos, models of ideal moral behaviour. In the Coloured community many of these ideals have been taken over from White culture. But, since the social and political organization of the community, and its position in the total caste society is very different from that of Whites, people may acknowledge that some White ideals are inappropriate. This has to be done with care however, particularly by leaders or influentials, because if they were to suggest to mere acquaintances that certain ideals

were inappropriate, this might open them to later accusations of abandoning 'civilized standards'. Thus, the discussion of what is realistic rather than ideal behaviour in a given situation takes place between people who are members of each other's effective networks.

An example of this is the discussion between the Armstrongs and the old men (p. 164) in which it was acknowedged that friction between the members of associations was common, and techniques by which it could be limited were extensively discussed. One of the conclusions they reached, which was that members of associations should not quarrel *publicly*, was discussed in the extended networks of all the members of the Association and was specifically conveyed to Mr Donen. Other discussions in which actual behaviour was assessed, and realistic norms evolved, took place between Mr Carruther and Mr Donen (p. 166) and between Messrs Armstrong, Hadley and Games (p. 168). The modified ideal which was formulated in these discussions between close friends was that young people should be ambitious, but they must learn how to run things properly first, and not quarrel with their more experienced elders. This view was widely disseminated through the extended networks of the people concerned in the issue.

Thus, the many disagreements which are characteristic of Coloured social organization are not an indication of social disintegration; they are rather an aspect of the integration of a society of this kind. These often seemingly trivial disputes serve to emphasize the important personal and inter-group relationships of the moment, and provide an occasion for the consideration and emphasis of values and norms.

This form of social organization is, in Southern Africa, frequently regarded as resulting from the racial heritage of the Coloured community. I would argue, however, that it is determined by sociological and not genetic factors. Frankenberg (1957) in his analysis of politics and football in a small Welsh village, discusses very much the same kinds of social process, though in much less detail.

Elias and Scotson (1965: 146–73) in their study of a small suburban community in the English midlands observe that it is continually divided by jealousies, and note that although critical gossip and conflicts are endemic in the community they are more acrimonious amongst the newcomers who live in a recently completed section of the suburb and have not yet established clear-cut interest groups and institutions. I have already referred to Colson's work on the Plateau Tonga (p. 171). As a result of an earlier fieldwork experience amongst the Makah (1953 (a)), a small American Indian group in the Pacific North West, she commented on the same phenomenon.

All these communities, and many others which have been described have several important characteristics in common. The first is that they are small enough for people to meet one another frequently, in diverse situations, and hence develop many multiplex relationships in their personal networks. Secondly, they are relatively isolated, and their members are hence forced into a degree of mutual interdependence in a number of successive situations. The isolation may be the result of a degree of geographical separation from other communities, as in rural Wales, Washington State, or Central Africa. However, an equally effective social isolation of the Coloured community has resulted from the operation of a system of racial discrimination and exclusion as it is practised in Southern Africa. Many Coloureds would like to escape into White society, but are unable to do so, and thus the community, poised between mutually antagonistic colour groups, must necessarily be more close-knit than most urban societies.

CHAPTER VI

Norms and-the Manipulation of Relationships in a Work Context[1]

by
B. Kapferer

Introduction

The argument presented in this paper depends heavily upon the concept of *social network*. Numerous meanings have been attached to the term *network* ranging from the purely metaphorical to the highly specific. I prefer the more specific definition of the term in that I define a network as egocentric; this preference does not deny its effective use as a metaphor or its application according

[1] The fieldwork on which this paper is based was carried out with the support of a British Commonwealth Scholarship and while I was a Research Affiliate of the Institute for Social Research, University of Zambia, between March 1964 and March 1966. Most of the material presented here would not have been collected but for the co-operation of the Zambia Broken Hill Development Company. This paper is a much revised version of a paper read before a seminar chaired by Professor Mitchell at the University College, Salisbury, Rhodesia, in January 1965, and later re-read at the June 1966 seminar of the Department of Social Anthropology and Sociology in the University of Manchester. More people than I have named here have contributed freely of their time, advice and criticism during the writing of the paper. In particular I am indebted to Professor J. C. Mitchell, Dr G. K. Garbett, Dr Martin Southwold and Wesley Sharrock who gave unstintingly of their time and ideas during the development of this paper. I would also like to thank Professor Max Gluckman, Dr J. van Velsen, Dr Norman Long, Dr Bryan Roberts, Dr Chandra Jayawardena, David Boswell, Basil Sansom, and my other colleagues in the Department of Social Anthropology and Sociology at Manchester University. For special thanks I would single out Professor Mitchell, whose ideas and subsequent guidance as to the potential of a 'social network' approach in urban African research stimulated my work in the urban field from the beginning. Without the continual assistance and perseverance of my wife Judith, this paper could not have been written. It cannot be overstressed how grateful I am for the acceptance I received from all the Cell Room workers and for the extreme patience with which they bore all my enquiries.

Finally, I record a debt to Professor J. A. Barnes for the stimulation I received from reading a copy of his paper in this symposium before I had written this paper in its present form.

to other definitions. Indeed, to insist on one definition of a net-work and one only, may invite confusion and hostility, not only within the ranks of social anthropology, but also from those in other sections of the social sciences, some of whom can probably stake a stronger claim to the use of the term. For this reason I suggest the substitution of the term *reticulum*[1] for that part of a total network where network is defined egocentrically. There-fore, throughout this paper I will make reference to *reticulums* rather than to networks. As a working definition of a *reticulum* I refer to the direct links radiating from a particular Ego to other individuals in a situation, and the links which connect those individuals who are directly tied to Ego, to one another. These minimal criteria for the definition of a *reticulum* are sufficient for present purposes but in the context of later analysis additional properties of *reticulums* will emerge, and these will relate speci-fically to the nature of the ties encompassed within a *reticulum*. Finally, although I have isolated *reticulum* as the major analytic tool by which the data and analysis for this paper will be presented, and some theoretical propositions derived, I do not wish to view it as divorced from other analytic procedures. In particular, it should become obvious as the paper progresses that the method of data presentation and analysis, as well as many of the assump-tions included within this analysis, is dependent on 'situational analysis' and the theory of social exchange developed by Homans (1961) and Blau (1964).

The problem I have set in this paper is the general one of 'explanation'. Without becoming involved in philosophical argument concerning the nature of explanation I think it is fair to state that with the tools the sociologist presently has at hand, we can describe reasonably accurately the structure of the various societies which we examine and the norms and values which are part of them. But too often we pass over what I regard as a neces-sary adjunct to successful analysis. This is, given that in any society individuals are provided with a number of alternatives for action,

---

[1] The word *reticulum* has its root in the Latin *rete*, *retis*: net, network (see Nybakken, 1959), commonly used in the biological sciences. Throughout the text I have preferred the English plural to the Latin. An additional advantage of the word which I have not exploited here is that there are numerous closely associated words, such as *reticle*, *reticulation*, *reticular*, etc., which could be used to apply to different aspects of the total network.

why on specific occasions should these individuals choose to behave in one way when they could have behaved just as legitimately in another? Frequently we shy clear of analysis which attempts to arrive at explanations for this type of behaviour on the grounds that it is 'psychologistic'. Even an interest in the particular may be rejected with the assertion that it is not the sociologist's responsibility to be interested in the particular, but merely to paint with a thick brush on a broad canvas. Thus structural–functional analysis often seeks out the regularities in behaviour concentrating mainly on that social action which is consistent with the overall perceived morphology of the social system. Because of this, structural analysis often disregards behaviour which is irregular and not consistent with the general structure of the society studied. As van Velsen states, 'Norms, general rules of conduct, are translated into practice, that is, they are ultimately manipulated by individuals in particular situations to serve particular ends. This gives rise to variations for which the writer does not account in his abstractions. He may not consider these variations particularly relevant and he will therefore not state that they exist or explain how they fit into his frame of general principles of wide validity. Alternatively, he may mention that there are variations but ignore them as being accidental or exceptional. In this way, too, variations are not fitted into the structural framework. However, labelling this category of observed data "exceptional" or "accidental" does not solve the problem for, after all, they occur within, and are part of the same social order which the ethnographer has set out to study and describe' (1964: xxiv).

I do not wish to deny the efficacy of other forms of analysis for the type of explanation I attempt to give in this paper, for I draw on them, but merely to suggest and perhaps demonstrate the additional use of *reticulum* analysis for achieving this type of explanation. Therefore, with the aid of reticulum analysis I will attempt to assess, through one dispute I observed during my fieldwork, why specific individuals and not others were initially involved in the dispute, why certain issues and not others achieved prominence, and why this particular dispute should have resulted in a settlement in favour of one disputant and not the other.

I will begin the paper with a description of the setting in which the dispute occurred, and will then give an account of the dispute and its normative background. The analysis then leads into a description of the reticulums of the various individuals involved in the dispute, from which, I hope, some solution to the problems outlined above will emerge.

The setting

The dispute occurred within a group of African mine employees of the Anglo-American Corporation's Zambia Broken Hill Development Company, who are engaged in surface work in the Cell Room of the Electro-Zinc Plant of the mine. Broken Hill is a town situated on the line of rail 86 miles north of Lusaka, the capital of Zambia, and 120 miles south of Ndola, the administrative centre for the Zambian Copperbelt. Broken Hill[1] as well as being the administrative centre for Broken Hill District and the Provincial headquarters for Zambia's Central Province, is an important regional headquarters for the Zambia Railways and the headquarters of Central African Road Services, the largest road transport organization in Zambia. But it is on the Mine that the economy of Broken Hill largely depends. At the time of the study the majority of Broken Hill's 40,570 African population (Government of Zambia Report, 1964: 47) lived in separate housing areas according to the economic sector in which they were occupied. Thus Africans employed in the administration and in commerce lived in housing areas apart from those employed by the Railway, and those working for the Railway lived in a separate residential area from those who worked on the Mine. All the African mine employees of this study lived in the Mine African Township or on the Mine Farms surrounding the township. Both are located on Mine property. Generally, over the period of my fieldwork European, Asian and Coloured inhabitants of Broken Hill (who constituted the remaining 5,540 of Broken Hill's total population of 46,110, see Kay, 1967) were residentially separated from Africans but this was beginning to change with Independence.

The main minerals mined at Broken Hill are lead and zinc and the Cell Room is the section of the mine where the mined zinc

[1] For those who wish to gain a more adequate impression of Broken Hill than I give here, Godfrey Wilson's (1941–42) classic study of the town made twenty-seven years ago is still remarkably up to date. My own (1966) account of the results of a social survey gives some recent information, but is relevant only for the Municipal housing areas of the town. Further information on the sociological aspects of urbanization in Zambia can be gained from Epstein (1958), Mitchell (1956) and McCulloch (1956).

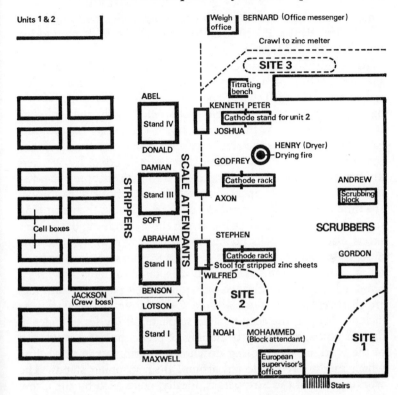

FIGURE 13

A schematic drawing of the cell room showing in detail the work area of unit 3 and the approximate working positions of those cell room employers who are engaged for most or part of their time in unit 3

passes through its final stages of purification before being placed on the world market. The zinc, after being reduced to a zinc sulphate solution in another section of the mine, is pumped into the Cell Room where by an electrolytic process purified zinc is deposited on both sides of an aluminium cathode and is separated from the sulphate which passes to a lead anode.

From Figure 13 it can be seen that the Cell Room is divided into three sections or units, and it will be with those people who spend all or part of their working day in the area of Unit 3 that this paper will be concerned. Fifteen workers (Crew Boss, Titrators, Strippers, Scrubbers and a Dryer) spend all their working time in the vicinity of Unit 3, whereas eight (Scale Attendants, a Block Attendant and an Office Messenger) divide their working time between the three units.

Although there are slight differences between Units 1, 2 and 3, the organization of work and the production process to be described for Unit 3 is broadly the same for the other units. Unit 3 has four double rows of cell boxes filled with zinc sulphate solution, each row with nine cell boxes containing 24 cathodes each. Every 48 hours the zinc is stripped from the cathodes in one row of each of the four double rows of cell boxes by workers known as Strippers, two being allotted to each stripping stand in the Unit. It is the Strippers' duty to lift one lot of eight cathodes at a time out of a cell box and to pull them down to their stripping stand. Here the zinc is stripped off the cathodes and the zinc sheets placed on blocks behind the stripping stand. (As the zinc is deposited on both sides of a cathode 16 zinc sheets are stripped off at each operation.) After eroded or dirty cathodes have been removed and new or cleaned ones put in their place, the cathodes are then replaced in the cell box. Other duties of the Strippers include cleaning the accumulated sulphate off the lead anodes in the cell boxes, and at the beginning of break time and at the end of the working day, hosing down and clearing away any refuse which might have collected around their stripping stands. The working rate of the Strippers is, ideally, controlled by the Crew Boss who blows a whistle, marking the time when they begin to remove the cathodes from the cell boxes and again for their replacement after all 16 zinc sheets have been stripped. After break when the Strippers' work is nearing completion, the Crew Boss's attempt at controlling the working rate is usually completely disregarded and an undisciplined race begins.

When the zinc sheets have been stripped and stacked on the blocks they are collected by the Scale Attendants who take them to the Weigh Office and then place them on small rail trucks to be pushed to the Melter where the zinc is melted into slabs. There are only six Scale Attendants and they serve all three Units. An additional man, known as a Block Attendant, oils and keeps in good mechanical trim the pulleys and lifting gear used by both the Strippers and the Scale Attendants.

As mentioned earlier some cathodes become eroded or dirty, and this results in a failure of the zinc to adhere to the cathodes properly. In such cases the Strippers place the cathodes in the cathode racks to be dealt with by the Scrubbers. It is up to the Scrubbers, one of whom is allotted to every two stripping stands, to decide whether the cathode is beyond repair or can be scrubbed clean. If the latter is the case, it is cleaned and replaced by the Scrubber in the cathode rack in readiness for re-use by the Strippers. If a new cathode must be sought, then it is the responsibility of the Scrubber to get a new one and place it in the cathode rack.

Some zinc sheets, when stripped, are wet with sulphuric acid and it is the duty of the Dryer (there is only one in each Unit) to dry them next to a fire before placing them with the already stacked zinc sheets in readiness for removal by a Scale Attendant. The Dryer's work also includes stripping difficult zinc sheets from the cathodes which have defied the previous efforts of the Strippers. He is also generally involved in helping with the cleaning and hosing down of the floor space in his Unit.

Near the Weigh Office is the titrating bench. The Titrator must continually check and keep constant the concentration of the various chemicals in solution in the cell boxes. If this is not done and the mixture of the chemicals in solution become disproportionate, a very thin layer of zinc is deposited on the cathodes and the job of stripping is made more difficult for the Strippers. When this happens more work is also created for the Dryer and Scrubbers. The Strippers now pass a greater number of cathodes than is usual to the Dryer to be stripped of their zinc sheets. In addition small pieces of zinc often remain attached to the cathodes even though the majority of the zinc has been stripped from them, resulting in more cleaning work for the Scrubbers.

The Crew Boss is directly responsible to the three European supervisors[1] in the Room and it is through him that the latter control the work in the Unit. The Crew Boss's activities are chiefly concerned with supervising the work of the Strippers. He not only controls the work rate of the Strippers but also sees that they do not replace dirty or eroded cathodes in the cell boxes. The Crew Boss is also generally responsible for the supervision of all who work within the domain of his Unit. Occasionally he assists the Strippers and often he cleans around the stripping

[1] All the Europeans employed in the Cell Room are in supervisory positions and are under the authority of the General Foreman.

stands when the Strippers have not done their job satisfactorily. Finally, the Office Messenger is mainly involved in carrying messages and information from the European supervisors to the Crew Boss and other individual workmen.

Important to an understanding of the Cell Room situation, is that, with the exception of the Office Messenger and the Titrators, all other African employees including the Crew Boss, are employed on a task work basis. Work commences at 7.00 a.m. and, with a break period which lasts from 9.15 a.m. to 10.00 a.m., work generally finishes at about 11.00 a.m., or when the Strippers have stripped their daily quota of cathodes. The Office Messenger works from 7.00 a.m. to 3.00 p.m. and the Titrators are employed on an eight-hour shiftwork basis, working around the clock, one Titrator being present in the Unit at a time.

According to the Mine Company, the classification of the African Cell Room employees is as follows: Regarded as Staff and also the highest paid are, in order of pay rates, the Crew Boss and the Titrators.[1] Then come the Strippers, who although not considered as Staff are in the same wage category as the Titrators, they are followed by the Scale Attendants and the Block Attendant, and then finally by the Scrubbers and Dryer. At the time of fieldwork the Office Messenger was regarded as Staff. He was formerly a Titrator but because of his age he was made an Office Messenger, though retaining his previous job classification. Normally, an Office Messenger is on the same rating as the Scale Attendants and the Block Attendant. The status accorded by the workers to the various jobs in the Room, follows roughly the Company's rating of the occupations in the Cell Room.

It is clear that each job is closely interconnected with other occupations in the general work and production process, and because of this tension can be easily engendered between persons occupied in different but interdependent tasks. The failure of a worker to carry out his work properly can severely upset the whole production process. Thus, a Scrubber who keeps an insufficient supply of clean cathodes up to the Strippers slows down the latter's speed of work and can lead to hostility between the Strippers and the Scrubber concerned.

As much of the argument in this paper is dependent on the type

[1] In August 1965 the Crew Boss and Titrators were reclassified as non-staff, but retained the same rate of pay.

of relationships which the Unit 3 workers establish with one another in the work context, it is important that direct interaction between pairs of individuals is not necessarily the result of the initial attraction of the participants to one another but is a product of the external conditions established by others, in this case the Mine Company. For example, the contact of particular workers with other Unit 3 employees is determined by the demands of the production process. Thus in the course of his duties a Scrubber must come into some contact with at least four Strippers, and, similarly, a Scale Attendant will be brought into association with all the Strippers. (Unlike Scrubbers, Scale Attendants do not work for specific Strippers but will collect zinc sheets from the blocks behind all the stripping stands during the course of their working activities.) In addition, the type of job a person has will affect the number of people with whom he comes into direct interaction. For instance, a Stripper's duties tie him to one area within the Unit and involve him in almost constant activity allowing him comparatively little time to move around the Unit, talking to friends, although this does not prohibit friends engaged on other work visiting him. In contrast, a Scale Attendant has a job which requires movement throughout all sections of the Room and this gives a greater opportunity for him to develop an extensive number of direct relationships with individuals in the work situation.

However, while admitting the influence of a person's job and his position in the production process on the type and number of individuals he has direct relationships with, these are not the only factors affecting interaction in the Cell Room. Workers have relationships with other employees which are not demanded as part of the production process. Some individuals whose work imposes restrictions on their movement have a wide variety of direct contacts in the situation, whereas other workers whose job is associated with freedom of movement throughout the work place include only a small number of persons within their direct set of relationships. These considerations suggest the influence of other factors which may inhibit or facilitate interaction between workers in the Cell Room. Thus various social characteristics such as those of tribal background, age and religion or the possession of power and/or authority in the work context affect the degree to which individuals come into contact with one another.

Table IV

Occupation, Tribe, Age and Religion of Unit 3 Employees

Name	Religion	Age	Occupation	Tribe
Jackson	Roman Catholic	48	Crew Boss	Lamba
Bernard	Roman Catholic	56	Office Messenger	Bemba
Peter	African Reform Church	40	Titrator	Nsenga
Kenneth	Roman Catholic	39	Titrator	Chewa
Simon	Methodist	29	Titrator	Ila
Maxwell	Nil	66	Stripper	Kaonde
Lotson	Roman Catholic	37	Stripper	Bemba
Abraham	Nil	58	Stripper	Bemba
Benson	Roman Catholic	52	Stripper	Lozi
Soft	ex-Jehovah's Witness	33	Stripper	Lala
Damian	African Reform Church	57	Stripper	Chewa
Abel	Roman Catholic	44	Stripper	Bisa
Donald	Jehovah's Witness	36	Stripper	Bisa
Joshua	Roman Catholic	34	Scale Boy	Bisa
Godfrey	Roman Catholic	34	Scale Boy	Bisa
Stephen	Roman Catholic	50	Scale Boy	Bemba
Noah	Roman Catholic	26	Scale Boy	Swaka
Wilfrid	Jehovah's Witness	36	Scale Boy	Lala
Axon	Free Church	52	Scale Boy	Lozi
Mohammed	Muslim	55	Block Boy	Aushi
Andrew	Nil	52	Scrubber	Nsenga
Gordon	Roman Catholic	36	Scrubber	Chewa
Henry	Roman Catholic	31	Dryer	Lala

Table IV gives the basic social characteristics of the workers who are the focus for this study. I will only make reference to the social characteristics of the Unit 3 employees where I consider it crucial to an understanding of particular interactional relationships. As a final point of information: all persons who are employed in Unit 3, with the exception of the Crew Boss and Titrators, are members of the Zambia Mineworkers' Trade Union. All these workers as well as those in similar job categories in other sections of the Cell Room and who are members of the Z.M.T.U. are represented by an elected union official or shop steward who is Lotson on Table IV. Lotson is also the Treasurer of the Broken

Hill Branch of the Z.M.T.U. At the time of fieldwork the Crew Boss and Titrators had no effective union representation.[1]

In order to present my approach to reticulums adequately as well as to draw out some meaningful conclusions from this analysis the scope of this paper must remain limited. As Devons and Gluckman have stated, '. . . any social scientist has to confine what he studies within certain limits: he cannot include the whole of complex reality. This limitation is vital if his study is to be manageable. The limitation can be of various kinds—a limitation in time, in space, or in the aspect of phenomena which is studied' (1964: 13). The ensuring analysis is based upon material collected during the months from September, 1964, to January, 1965, and is restricted to behaviour observed within the area of Unit 3.

The dispute and its normative background
The following is a brief account of a dispute which broke out between two co-workers of the same occupational status in Unit 3. It tells of Abraham's objection to the fast working pace of a fellow Stripper, Donald, who works at Stand IV with Abel (see Figure 13); Donald's brief period of angry opposition to Abraham's suggestion that he should slow down his work rate; and, finally, his eventual acquiescence to Abraham's demands.

The normal clamour and hum of the Cell Room is suddenly broken by Abraham who shouts across to Donald at Stand IV, '*Buyantanshe* (Progress), slow down and wait for us.' A hush now settles on the Unit. For a while Donald takes no notice and Abraham calls '*Buyantanshe*' once more. This evokes a reaction and Donald retorts that he is not to be called by his nickname as he already has a proper name. Abraham replies that he only knows Donald by his nickname, '*Buyantanshe*'. His blood up, Donald shouts, 'We young men must be very careful about being bewitched.' Abraham assents, 'You are quite right, you will

---

[1] Prior to fieldwork Staff had been represented by the Mine African Staff Association. This union was disbanded with the formation of the United Mineworkers' Union in October 1963, which purported to represent both Staff and non-Staff African mine employees, and which rivalled the power of the Zambia Mineworkers' Trade Union (then the Northern Rhodesia African Mine Workers' Trade Union). Largely because of the U.M.U.'s failure to gain the recognition of the mining companies, by the time of fieldwork it had lost much of its influence. In Unit 3 the Crew Boss and Titrators did not belong to U.M.U. and therefore did not even have the very minimal representation which U.M.U. could then afford.

be bewitched if you don't respect your elders.' Donald is now almost beside himself with rage, and goes straight to lodge a formal protest with the Shop Steward, Lotson, against what he considers to be Abraham's threat of witchcraft. This done he then goes down the stripping stands reporting the matter to the Strippers and those Scale Attendants working nearby. He is just passing Stand III when he hears, as do others close at hand, Soft's very audible comment to Joshua that Donald must be drunk or else they (the Unit 3 workers) should not be seeing such behaviour. Donald storms across to Soft, and the latter, in an attempt to pacify him and to persuade him to return to his stand, says, 'I didn't mean *you* when I said that.' Jackson, the Crew Boss, who has hitherto been amusedly observing the dispute from the sidelines, now steps in and orders Donald to return to work, which the latter does, muttering angrily all the way back to his stand, 'I don't wish anyone to call me *'Buyantanshe'*, I have my own name, Donald.'

Work now returns more or less to normal. Occasionally small clusters of workers collect to discuss or enquire about the dispute; but the event is once more brought fully to the attention of the Unit workers when Soft comes to seat himself near Lotson at break time. Lotson asks him why he has quarrelled with Donald at work. 'It's my own business; Donald didn't hear me properly,' mutters Soft. Others who are seated near Soft and Lotson now stop whatever they have been talking about and crane forward to listen. Damian and Jackson come from where they have been standing near Stand I and hover at the outskirts of the group surrounding Lotson and Soft. Soft now elaborates, 'Donald has taken too much beer and this is what has caused him to behave like this. Surely we all call him by his nickname!' Donald, who has been listening nearby, and prior to this had been discussing his version of the dispute with two of his friends, Godfrey and Stephen, impatiently breaks in, 'In my case please, I don't want anyone calling me *Buyantanshe* as I have my proper name, Donald. Drinking doesn't enter the case—the quarrel was caused by Abraham who insisted on calling me by my nickname and instead of answering properly to my protests, threatened to bewitch me.' At this Lotson bursts out with a disbelieving laugh and asks Donald for the real reasons behind his outburst: 'Was it because Soft called you a drunk? If so, this is not a real case.' Soft now intervenes and states that Donald has reacted in such a way because the comment came from a young man. 'Really,' he declares, 'there is no excuse for Donald's behaviour.'

Abraham, who is seated near Stand I calls across to Donald to join him where he is sitting. (He addresses the latter as 'Donald'.) Everybody seated with Donald urges him to go, and after much prompting he does so. Lotson, Abel and Soft joke together that now Donald need not fear being bewitched any longer. Immediately on Donald's arrival at Abraham's seating place, Abraham asks him to go and sharpen his stripping hook. After having completed this service Donald returns the hook to its owner and then joins a group of Scale Attendants and Titrators who are seated near the Weigh Office.

For most workers in the Unit, including Abraham, the dispute seemed to be at an end. But that this was not so for Donald, was demonstrated a few days later. Donald again accused Abraham of witchcraft and used his suspicions of Abraham's malevolence as a pretext for applying for a transfer from the Cell Room to another section of the mine. His application was successful and he was transferred to underground work.

It is immediately apparent that the various individuals involved in the dispute invoked a number of norms in the situation to support their own particular stand. These expressed norms also relate to the varied social factors, interests and beliefs which lie at the root of all Cell Room relationships. Thus in an attempt to obtain a clearer understanding of the processes involved in the dispute and the issues at stake, these expressed norms must be placed in the context of the social mosaic formed out of the intermeshing of Cell Room relationships.

The dispute between Abraham and Donald was precipitated by Abraham, who in shouting across to Donald to slow down his working rate called him *Buyantanshe*.[1] Donald took no notice of Abraham's words and did not slacken his pace, but instead made an issue out of being addressed by his nickname. Thus the major issue which had been introduced at the very start of the dispute was Abraham's implied accusation that Donald was a 'ratebuster'.[2]

[1] *Buyantanshe* means 'progress,' and Donald allegedly acquired this nickname because when he reads a newspaper passers-by hear him exclaiming 'Progress! Progress!' The nickname also has the effect of reminding Donald that he is one of the fastest workers in the Unit and in some ways it has a marked similarity to the nicknames of 'Cyclone' and 'Phar Lap' applied to the fastest workers in the Bank Wiring Room (Roethlisberger and Dickson, 1941: 463). Nevertheless, as indicated by the reason for its origin, the application of the nickname need not always imply reference to Donald's fast work. Many workers of all ages in the Unit prior to this dispute had regularly referred to Donald and addressed him by his nickname without eliciting the type of reaction which Donald on this occasion had shown towards Abraham.

[2] The notion of 'ratebuster' is very common to industrial sociological literature. Other terms have also been used to apply to much the same phenomenon such as 'job-spoiling' (Lupton, 1963: 118) and 'gold-bricking' (Roy, 1952).

Therefore, at this stage of the analysis it is important to explain the formal and informal controls which operate to restrict the work speed of Cell Room workers (in this case particularly of the Strippers) and the interests which are protected through the operation of these controls. In the first place, Management, through the Crew Boss, imposes a restriction on the work speed of the Strippers, for, as was described at the beginning of this paper, it is the duty of the Crew Boss to see that the Strippers work at a steady and equal rate. But this control over the work rate of the Strippers stems not so much from a desire on Management's part to slow the speed of work down, but rather from the belief that well regulated work is more efficient. An interest in a slower work rate is therefore a necessary by-product of Management's prime emphasis on regulated and efficient work. For example, if a Stripper hurries with his work, he may be tempted to replace soiled and eroded cathodes in the cell boxes, rather than go to the trouble of completely removing the cathode and replacing it with a clean cathode from the cathode rack. If a dirty or eroded cathode is replaced in a cell box after stripping, the quantity of zinc which deposits on it will be severely reduced. But within the restriction imposed by the desire for regulated and efficient work, Management does have an interest in speeding up the time in which the task of stripping can be completed. Although I do not wish to discuss its full implications, it is important to an understanding of Management's attitude to work speed, and the Cell Room workers' reaction to fast workers, that there is an informal agreement between the Management and the Union. This 'agreement' is that Strippers and other Cell Room employees can complete their daily work shift after only four hours if they have been occupied in work to which they are normally accustomed. However, should any worker finish his accustomed task well before the four hours are up, he can be allocated another task which could extend his working time to the full eight hours. By getting Cell Room workers to do tasks in addition to their usual ones, the Company hoped to wean them on to a full eight-hour day and thus bring the Cell Room into line with the rest of the Mine's employees. There is every reason why the Cell Room workers concerned should oppose the Management's efforts. If they worked eight-hour shifts they would receive no increase in pay as the Company maintains that they are already receiving the equivalent of eight hours' pay for four hours' work. Apart from the reduction in the number of hours they would be able to spend at leisure, some of the workers are involved in small side trading and business ventures which net them extra cash. If they converted to an eight-hour day the amount of time spent on these ventures would be reduced. It is evident that any worker who completes his accustomed task too quickly will give Management an opportunity to set him another task which could create a precedent for the eventual conversion of all Cell Room workers from a four-hour to an eight-hour working day.

It is not surprising that there should be an informal norm, which serves to regulate the time taken to strip the cathodes of their zinc to approximately four hours, operating amongst the Strippers and further reinforced by other Cell Room workers such as Scale Attendants, Scrubbers and Dryers, whose work rate and time of task completion is largely dependent on the work speed adopted by the Strippers. The existence of this norm could be seen as sufficient explanation for the accusation being levelled against Donald in the first place, and his seeming isolation from the sympathies of the other workers, some of whom could be regarded as his friends, during the course of the dispute. By working fast Donald had threatened the continuance of advantageous working conditions for many of the Cell Room employees, conditions which the Management was interested in changing. Although these considerations should be seen as influencing an understanding of the course of events, in the light of other information the existence of this norm does not provide sufficient explanation for the nature of the dispute. There are two factors which might reduce the apparent seriousness of Donald's offence. On occasion the Company manages to get individual workers to do tasks other than the ones in which they are normally engaged. When the cell boxes in Unit 3 were being overhauled the Unit 3 workers who were momentarily jobless, i.e. the Crew Boss, Strippers, Scrubbers and Dryer (the Titrators and Scale Attendants continued to work in the other units), were put on other tasks. But even though the Company has been able to do this it has been totally ineffective in making the employees concerned continue at work for longer than four hours. Donald's action was, in fact, no more likely to provide the Company with a

precedent for future policy than the behaviour of other workers
before him in the Room, whose fast work on previous days had
resulted in their engagement on other tasks, but who had not
had such an accusation levelled against them. Moreover Donald's
fast working pace had not placed him and his co-worker Abel, so
far ahead of the others that they were likely to finish more than
about ten minutes earlier. By referring to these other considerations relating to Donald's work speed I do not wish to deny
entirely an element of norm breaking in Donald's work behaviour
as a possible influential factor for the course of the dispute; for
Donald had done what many fast workers before him had not:
he had been working fast, disregarding the pace-setting of the
Crew Boss, before break time.

Before break the regular work rate imposed by the Crew Boss
is generally agreed to by the Strippers in their own interest and
in the interest of others in the work place. But the work regulating
norm which operates among the Strippers before break gives way
to another norm which permits fast work in the threequarters
of an hour following break, each pair of Strippers racing the
Strippers on the other stands in an attempt to finish first. Although
in one sense speed of work is a matter of disapproval, in another
it is a source of approbation. The possession of great physical
strength and skill in specific tasks are highly regarded qualities
among the Cell Room workers. The most effective way by which
the combination of these qualities can be demonstrated to a
worker's peers is through fast work, and through fast work prestige accrues to the worker. This attitude, which also influences
the pattern of work behaviour, may on the surface appear to
contradict the generally accepted norm which serves to regulate
work speed, and Donald, by operating in terms of one valued
attitude, could be seen as being forced into the position of
breaking a seemingly contradictory norm in the situation. But
that this latter norm ceases to be a potent factor controlling work
after break, permits this attitude to exist alongside it. In the threequarters of an hour following break it is unlikely that a worker
would have enough time at his disposal to get too far ahead of his
workmates on other stripping stands. Nevertheless the time is
sufficient for him to demonstrate his skill and strength over and
above that of his work companions. Therefore, to a certain extent
Donald had broken the rules of the game, which may be taken

to state that a Stripper can pit his skill and strength against those of the other Strippers by racing them in an attempt to finish first, but he must not jump the starter's gun, which in this case is the Crew Boss' blowing of a whistle for the recommencement of work after break.

However, with qualifications, the existence of an attitude which approves of a fast work rate provided an alternative according to which others involved in the dispute could frame their reactions to the issues raised at the outset. On the one hand, no contradiction need have been seen between the attitude which approves of the fast worker and the norm which seeks to regulate the work rate. Donald had simply broken an informal rule which only permits fast work after break, and as such must have had his attention drawn to this fact. On the other hand, it could have been possible for others in the work context to have sympathized with Donald. His fast work before break may have infringed the implied rule which serves to prevent such behaviour, but although his behaviour should not have been praised it did not seem to deserve retribution. As explained earlier, his 'crime' was not excessive; his work speed would not have resulted in his finishing more than ten minutes or so ahead of the other Strippers, and it was unlikely that he would have been placed on another task which could have given the Company a precedent for the implementation of a policy converting the Room workers to an eight-hour day. Furthermore, Donald's reputation as a fast worker could have been viewed by the other workers involved as a desired quality. Although Abraham used Donald's nickname, *Buyantanshe*, in a scolding way warning him, in Abraham's eyes, of his norm breaking behaviour, the nickname could have been seen by others as complimentary. Certainly as the account of the dispute illustrates, some of the workers could have been puzzled by Donald's reaction to the use of his nickname which to them might have appeared as flattering. For instance, this is evidenced in Soft's remark in reference to the use of the nickname when he states that he cannot understand Donald's behaviour as most people in the Room address him by it. Therefore, to many of the workers, as indeed was expressed by them, Donald's reaction on the basis of Abraham's calling him by his nickname could have seemed unreasonable.

It is possible that Donald's infringement of the norm regulating work speed before break could have influenced both Abraham's making the accusation against Donald in the first place and the eventual isolation of the other workers from Donald as the dispute proceeded. But in the expression of their various attitudes to the case, no worker, apart from Abraham, made reference to Donald's work speed. Rather in what appeared to be their support for Abraham, they either emphasized the unreasonableness of Donald's response to Abraham or invoked other norms which arose out of the dispute as it progressed. If the other workers involved in the case were opposed to Donald's ratebusting, why then did they not state it as a reason for their seeming alignment against him? It is clear that the discussion of the dispute has not provided us with any satisfactory answer towards an understanding of the process of events. Therefore it is necessary to delve more deeply into the norms and attitudes surrounding the case.

Abraham's reference to Donald's 'ratebusting' has an edge to it other than the implication that Donald by working fast was generally threatening the Cell Room workers position in relation to Management. The accusation had another purpose, that of protecting the interests of the older workers against the younger workers in the Room. This is revealed in the altercation between the two men which ensued after Donald's first reaction to being called *Buyantanshe* and which involved Donald's shouting across to Abraham, 'We young men must be careful of being bewitched.' The norm which serves to regulate the work speed of the Strippers operates more in the interests of the older than the younger Strippers. Many of the older Strippers in Unit 3 are nearing retirement age and it is a very real fear among them that if their work noticeably flags behind the rate of the younger Strippers they would run the risk of being sacked or retired.[1] In addition Figure 13 illustrates that with the exception of Stand IV where two relatively younger workers, Donald and Abel, are employed, all the young workers are paired with older workers. Some of these older workers, as for example, Damian, Maxwell and Abraham, because of their age, find the work very taxing physically, and are dependent on the younger men on their stands, in those instances where they are paired with them, to take

---

[1] During the study Abraham and Maxwell *were* approached by the European General Foreman who informed them that they were under consideration by the Company for retirement.

some of their load as well. Thus in a sense the younger men may have an interest in breaking the norm in an attempt to get rid of the older workers some of whose work they must on occasions assist with. However, because of the nature of the work it is not easy for a young Stripper paired with an older Stripper to rate bust. The exception is Stand IV where two relatively young Strippers are paired and it is therefore significant that they should be involved in the norm breaking. Also, because the stand at which Abraham works is the one in the Unit where two older workers are employed may explain why the accusation should come from this stand. These facts are given greater force when it is realized that for a number of days prior to the dispute, although they had not been working fast before break, Donald and Abel had been finishing their work well ahead of the others. In addition, from information collected over a period of twenty-six days before the dispute the two older Strippers, Abraham and Benson on Stand II, with only three exceptions were the last to finish. Not only had Donald and Abel been working fast but they had also been demonstrating very convincingly the greater speed in which a task can be completed when both the Strippers are young, than when the stripping pair consists of at least one older worker, or in Stand II's case, two older workers. Therefore a number of further considerations in relation to the case must be stressed. The norm which regulates work speed can be interpreted in one sense as protecting the interests of all workers concerned in the Cell Room, but in another way it could be seen as really having its main efficacy in protecting the interests of the older workers in the Room. In certain cases some of the young Strippers have to carry the weight of a very much older worker's work and may, in fact, have as much reason to break the norm as to maintain it. By breaking the norm they may be able to rid themselves of the older workers, thereby lightening their work load. Thus Donald by working fast could have been seen as doing the other young workers in the Room who are saddled with much older work partners, a service; and by showing up the latter's lack of suit-ability for the work he may well have merited the receipt of support in the dispute.

Another point is also worthy of attention. In certain circum-stances, as fast work can be regarded by Cell Room workers and particularly the older workers as being ratebusting threatening the maintenance of their present working conditions, so slow work could also be viewed as a similar threat. By 'dragging the chain' as Abraham and Benson might be regarded as doing, a Stripper will hold up the time of task completion of others in the work situation. The speed of work of Scrubbers and Scale Attendants is largely dependent on the rate set by Strippers. If a Stripper's work speed is slow this extends the time taken to complete the tasks of Scrubbers and Scale Attendants well beyond the accepted four hours work time in the Cell Room. This could cause considerable inconvenience. Not only does it shorten the leisure time of the persons concerned but if they are involved in other economic ventures outside Mine employment the necessity to stay at work could seriously upset their satisfactory operation. It was largely because of Abraham's and Benson's slow work that at least one Scrubber and some of the Scale Attendants had to work overtime for which they received no extra payment.

In the analysis of the various norms and attitudes so far relevant to the dispute it is clear that a variety of interpretations can be placed on them. The dispute cannot be explained simply in terms of Abraham's view that Donald was a ratebuster; for upon closer examination Donald's offence does not seem as serious as it might have first appeared and it is even possible that some case could be made out in support of his action. However, the analysis of the factors involved in the dispute to date does provide a partial explanation of at least some of the characteristics of the case. In the first place it can be understood why the accusation of ratebusting should come from a person working on Stand II and why it should be directed at a man on Stand IV. Secondly because it has been shown that some sympathy could be generated for Donald's action it is conceivable that no other worker involved in the dispute should raise the issue of ratebusting. But other problems remain or are raised. Why, for instance, was Abraham the accuser and not Benson? Why was Donald accused and not Abel, as the latter on this occasion was just as guilty as the former? Why, if some case can be made out to support Donald, was he deserted by the workers in the Unit who apparently threw in their support for Abraham? Perhaps by examining the other issues which entered as the dispute progressed some solution to these problems may be found.

Donald expressed a fear to Abraham that the latter might sanction his disapproval of Donald's behaviour by the use of witch-craft. Abraham jokingly replied that this was a possibility as Donald had shown disrespect to an elder. Here two additional norms which govern workers' behaviour in the Cell Room must be discussed: as Abraham pointed out and Donald realized, Donald had disregarded another norm in the situation which is that respect must be shown by younger to older men in the work context. Age is a factor together with other social characteristics such as seniority of service in the Cell Room and occupational status which demands deference from younger and more junior employees. Although these factors are subject to varied interpre-tation according to the particular persons involved, Donald's subordination to Abraham was institutionalized in a fictitious 'father-son' relation recognized by themselves and by others in the situation.

Donald rarely comes into contact with Abraham except to exchange greetings on arrival at work, but when they do greet each other Donald often addresses Abraham as '*tata*' (father) and Abraham reciprocates by calling Donald '*mwana*' (son). In the Cell Room a large number of kinship terms and occasionally other forms of address terms are applied by the employees to one another.[1] Also, as in Abraham and Donald's occasional adoption of kinship terminology in their address to each other, the use of kin terms between workers does not in general imply an actual kinship connection. But as is usual when specific kinds of kin terms are used between pairs of persons in any context, irrespect-ive of whether an actual kin link exists or not, a certain mode of behaviour is expected between them. In town and in the Cell Room, as in the rural areas, the terms for 'father' and 'son' denote both respect and social distance and indicate the one's dominant position over the other.[2] Ideally a son should be subordinate to the wishes and demands of his father and should not show the

[1] Kinship terms as a form of address between workers tend to be used irrespective of the tribal background of the workers. Most of the kin terms used are in fact intelligible to all Cell Room workers even though many of them have different tribal and linguistic origins. However there is a slight tendency for kin terms not to be used between people who are not of the same broad tribal and linguistic categories; these may use other terms of address such as *mudala*, *kalamba* (big man) and *mune* (equal).

[2] The father-son relationship is easier among matrilineal peoples like the Bemba and Bisa, than among patrilineal tribes.

latter disrespect. A further point must also be noted. The usage of certain types of address terms (kin or otherwise) between workers not only expresses the nature of their relationship to the particular persons involved but also communicates its character to others in the work situation. Therefore, by their use of particular kin terms in the address of one another the position in which Donald stood in relation to Abraham and the ideal mode of behaviour which could be expected between them was communicated to the other workers in the situation. Thus their expected behaviour towards each other was public knowledge in the Unit. Donald, by reacting strongly to Abraham's use of his nickname and by not slowing down his work speed, had breached another norm which frames behaviour in the Cell Room, viz. that a younger man should show respect to an older man; a norm reinforced by the fact that a recognized 'father-son' relationship existed between them. Donald's breach of this norm might have tipped the balance of the scales more in Abraham's favour, and more clearly defined the terms on which support for Abraham could have been based. It might also appear to answer one of the previously stated problems, as to why, when no other person took up Abraham's accusation of ratebusting—there even seeming to be a case for some support for Donald, at least from the younger workers—all the support flowed towards Abraham. For example, it was when Abraham drew his attention to Donald's disrespect of an older man that Soft seemingly gave his allegiance to Abraham, suggesting that Donald must be drunk to behave in such a way.

But in his realization of his disrespect for Abraham, Donald made reference to a much more serious issue, the threatened use of witchcraft.[1] What made matters worse was that Abraham endorsed Donald's claim by stating that his future use of witchcraft was a possibility if Donald did not come to heel. Most workers believe that witchcraft can cause grave personal misfor-

---

[1] Turner (1964) argues that there has been some confusion in the distinctions made by anthropologists between witchcraft and sorcery. I follow Turner in that I am not concerned 'with the proper pigeon-holing of beliefs and practices of either "witchcraft" or "sorcery" ' but with the relevance of these beliefs and the accusations which stem from them (whether they be witchcraft or sorcery), for the understanding of the dynamics of social action within a specific social context (p. 314).

tune such as illness, death, work accidents or premature retirement, or delay promotion to the benefit of other seemingly less
qualified members of the Room. Not all illness, accidents, retire-
ments and delays in promotion etc. are regarded as the result of
witchcraft. Witchcraft is only sought as an explanation for such
misfortune when no other immediately evident explanation is
available.[1]

It is widely accepted in the Cell Room that witchcraft which
is harmful to others should not be used, not only because it is
dangerous to the persons against whom it is directed but also
because its use drives a wedge, as the workers perceive it, between
people who must co-operate both at work and in their dealings
with Management. However, the very nature of the work
situation strengthens the belief in the existence of witchcraft in
the Cell Room and fosters witchcraft accusations between the
workers. The skill to perform various tasks within the Cell Room
is acquired easily and quickly, employees being transferred from
one job to another without any special induction training, except
in the case of titrating. In fact when workers, due to illness or some
other personal crisis are absent from work, men normally occupied in different tasks within the Cell Room will be momentarily
transferred to fill vacancies occasioned by such absenteeism. This is
particularly so when a person involved in a critical task on which
the production process depends, such as stripping, is absent from
work. In this instance, an employee who is a Scale Attendant or
Dryer, both tasks that are less critical in that slightly fewer men
doing these jobs does not greatly impede the work flow, will be
transferred to perform the task in the Stripper's absence. Because
of the ease by which employees can be transferred from one job
to another, no man can regard himself, or be considered by the
Company, as indispensable or providing difficulties for replacement. A considerable feeling of insecurity is thereby generated,
and it is felt, not without cause, that an illness or accident which
prevents attendance at work for any period of time could cost a
man his job. Furthermore there are wage differences operating
between the various Cell Room tasks, workers in high-grade
tasks such as stripping, receiving higher wages than employees in

[1] Witchcraft as a theory of causation has been clearly described for the
Azande by Evans-Pritchard, E. E. (1937) and more generally examined in an
African context by Gluckman, M. (1960).

lower-grade work. Short of combined Union action for general wage increases covering all Cell Room jobs, and perhaps the Mine Plant generally, the only way by which workers can increase their pay is to seek promotion. But the only time when a worker can hope for a promotion is when a vacancy arises in a higher-grade job.[1] These are few and far between as no new jobs are being created by the Company in the Cell Room at higher levels, and the rate of labour turnover is low, the latter undoubtedly being conditioned by the attractiveness of the Cell Room work conditions. Therefore employees who can be promoted in terms of the Cell Room work structure will compete with each other for promotion when a vacancy occurs: this competition is all the more fierce because the Cell Room workers are competing for scarce resources. Men with apparently similar qualifications for promotion to a specific task will compete, with only one man being successful. It is not surprising that the use of witchcraft in such a case is suspected as an aid to a successful promotion, and accusations of witchcraft in these instances are not uncommon. In addition to witchcraft accusations flowing between people of the same wage grade, particularly when they are thrown into competition with each other for promotion, accusations also flow between workers of different wage grades. Because of the limited number of jobs which fall vacant, people in higher paid jobs suspect the operation of witchcraft against them by lower paid workers to induce illness, accidents and even death in an attempt to create vacancies. This results in another pattern of witchcraft accusations when certain illnesses or accidents occur for instance, flowing from employees in highly-paid jobs to workers in low-paid tasks.

Witchcraft is also believed to be used by specific individuals at work as a sanction to reinforce their power and authority in the Room and to warn other workers in the work place against forms of behaviour which might threaten these former individuals'

[1] Except for the positions of Titrator and Crew Boss, where some education including knowledge of written and spoken English is required, no special educational achievement is needed for promotion. Other factors such as length of service, behaviour at work and the physical strength to carry out the heavier work often demanded in the higher job grades are influential in the Company's choice as to who is promoted. However it is important that it is not always clear what factors influence promotion when it occurs.

security. Although all men are thought capable of exercising witchcraft in the Cell Room it is generally believed that some of the older men, largely because of their age and supposed familiarity with 'traditional' witchcraft practices are the most dangerous and skilful exponents of the art. When accused of witchcraft they will deny the accusation vehemently, passing it off as ridiculous, 'for who would wish to bewitch a workmate?' But it must be stressed that the old men are not loth to foster the belief in their witchcraft powers amongst the younger men. The belief in their extraordinary powers is an important weapon in their hands, for the constant threat of its possible use is a valuable sanction with which the older men can control certain forms of work behaviour such as Donald's, which could threaten their continued employment in the Cell Room. In Unit 3 Abraham, Maxwell and Damian are the most feared for their witchcraft powers. On one occasion considerable consternation spread throughout the Room when Damian appeared at work with his green boiler suit covered in yellow clay. The clay happened to be of the same colour as that in the Broken Hill cemetery and it was thought that Damian had visited the place the previous evening for the purpose of robbing corpses of their vital organs for the practice of his witchcraft. In fact Damian had only been cultivating his gardens on the outskirts of the Mine township.

The use of witchcraft is strongly condemned by most workers in the Cell Room. Because of its seriousness no accusation involving witchcraft should be made lightly. In a sense it can be just as much an offence to level a witchcraft accusation when other explanations are feasible, for such an accusation needlessly provokes tension and hostility. But Donald's accusation against Abraham was not without foundation, for Abraham had in public admitted to his possible use of witchcraft to bring Donald back into line. With this public admission Donald had a very good case upon which support for him in the dispute could rest, and indeed he was well aware of the worth of his case. This is evidenced in his immediate reporting of Abraham's threat to the Shop Steward, Lotson, and his further reference to the witchcraft threat at the break-time hearing of the dispute. Donald's breach of the norm which demands that a younger man show respect to his elders in the work situation, a norm which in this instance found additional strength in that the two major disputants had a recognized 'father-son' relationship, could have been said to have balanced the outcome of the dispute in Abraham's favour. However, the admitted possibility of Abraham's use of witchcraft could have tipped the scales in Donald's direction, and might have been a useful basis for him to recruit support in the dispute. Why then did the other participants in the case refuse to seize upon this issue of threatened witchcraft? It could be argued that they regarded the crime of ratebusting as more serious on this occasion, but I have already shown that there was no reason why many of the workers involved should think so. In any case no other person in the Unit raised the issue of ratebusting as a basis for supporting Abraham. Instead they based their seeming alignment with Abraham against Donald through reference to much less important issues such as Donald's objection to Soft's suggestion that he was drunk, or Donald's reaction to being addressed by his nickname. These were regarded by the persons immediately involved in the dispute in Unit 3 as trivial issues not proportionate to the type of angry behaviour evinced by Donald. It is this attitude which is interesting. Not all the issues were in fact trivial: Abraham's accusation of ratebusting was not, nor was Donald's counter accusation of Abraham's possible use of witchcraft. Neither one of the issues was taken up; instead other people involved in the dispute tried to maintain the issues surrounding it at the trivial level. Witness, for example, Lotson's ignoring of Donald's mention of Abraham's threat of witchcraft, insisting that the latter's anger was because Soft called him a drunk.[1] I

[1] Soft's mention that Donald must have been drunk to behave in the way he did was more a reference to the unreasonableness of Donald's behaviour rather than to the possibility that he was drunk. Both to Soft and to others present at the time Donald was obviously not drunk. A number of factors influenced Donald's angry reaction to Soft's suggestion. An accepted ruling among members of the Jehovah's Witness sect, of which Donald is an adherent, is that they should not drink alcoholic beverages. Soft as an ex-Jehovah's Witness was aware of this and his suggestion could thus have stung Donald, in addition to the fact that Soft's utterances declared to Donald that Soft was throwing in his support for Abraham; a move which could have upset Donald as the latter regarded himself as being friendly with Soft and deserving of his allegiance. Furthermore, Soft's statement, as became clear when Lotson later questioned Donald, was viewed by Donald as an attempt to shift attention away from consideration of what to him appeared to be the main issues in the dispute.

Seen in another way reference to the possibility of Donald's being drunk could be viewed as an attempt to slander Donald in the eyes of his peers, and,

suggest that the others concerned in the case had an interest in maintaining the issues at a trivial level. Why? Perhaps the various workers involved in Unit 3 wished to reduce the open outbreak of hostilities and tensions within the section to a minimum. If the issues of ratebusting and witchcraft had been the major foci for the alignment of individuals and groups in the dispute, then the Unit could well have been split into two opposing factions, the older workers becoming allied against the younger workers. But this is not a completely satisfactory explanation, for at other times when similar disputes have occurred over similar issues the Unit 3 workers have shown no great reluctance to form themselves into opposing factions.

Before I continue the analysis which will be partially devoted to an attempt to solve the above problem, I shall summarize both the answers which have been provided by the analysis so far, and some of the problems not solved by the analysis, as well as the additional problems which have arisen out of the analysis itself. The analysis to date has explained why certain types of accusation should occur in the Cell Room situation. Some understanding for instance, has been obtained as to why an accusation of fast work should come from Stand II to Stand IV in Unit 3, and why Donald should suspect Abraham of invoking a witchcraft sanction against him. Abel and Donald's fast work threatened the security of the older Strippers in the Unit, and in particular, Abraham and Benson who had been regularly finishing last. But the problem as to why Abraham and Donald were the major personalities in the dispute is not solved. The reason why the issue of ratebusting was not seized upon as a major one determining the support of Abraham, can be partially explained by the possibility of others in the work situation not regarding the nature of this particular norm breach as being very serious, and the likelihood that some of the workers at least, may have had some sympathy with Donald. This being so, why did some of the workers, especially the younger employees like Soft, choose to isolate them-

---

more importantly, those in authority such as the Crew Boss. The Mine Management forbids its employees to appear at work drunk and a worker guilty of this offence is open to dismissal. But most of the Cell Room workers regard the ability to consume large quantities of alcohol to be more a virtue than a vice. On occasion workers have arrived in the Cell Room drunk and have consciously emphasized their condition to their fellows.

selves from Donald? On the balance of issues raised it might seem
that many of the workers had stronger cause to support Donald
rather than Abraham. Donald's breach of the norm of behaviour
governing relationships between older and younger workers, for
instance, appears to be a much weaker issue in terms of which to
frame one's support, than the threat of witchcraft. In fact, when
the focus of Donald's anger shifted momentarily from Abraham
to Soft, as the latter himself implied, some of Donald's anger was
to be expected, as the voiced suspicion that Donald was drunk
came from a younger man. Here it could be argued that Soft had
shown disrespect to an older man, but on this occasion the norm,
the breach of which appeared to work previously in Abraham's
favour, was not invoked later in Donald's. Perhaps some of the
answer lies in a wish of the Cell Room workers concerned to
maintain the issues defining the nature of the dispute at a trivial
level. Donald's objection to being called *Buyantanshe* and Soft's
suggestion that he might be drunk, coupled with Donald's
reaction to this, provided the other persons involved in the dispute with a number of opportunities which enabled them to do
this. But why should the various personalities concerned wish to
keep the issues of the dispute minor? As already explained, there
were frequent disputes of a similar nature in which there seemed
no desire to keep the issues surrounding a case trivial.

In this discussion I am not trying to assert that the process and
final outcome of the dispute is decided by reference to one guid-
ing norm, value or attitude. Obviously in any situation of conflict
a number of norms, values etc. will be relevant together with any
possible number of interpretations of them. But as there are many
norms, values, attitudes and beliefs which are crucial to the understanding of any situation, it is never certain which norms and
values etc. and their various interpretations will be called upon to
support individual action in times of conflict. In these situations
the norms and values which people hold to be important guides
to their behaviour, and which are often observed to be so by the
researcher, will on other occasions appear to be less important,
even though the situation may to outward intents and purposes
seem to be broadly the same. However, some detailed knowledge of the types of relationships which the people in a dispute,
for instance, have with other people in the situation, and the
character and extent of these people's relationships with each

other, could provide some additional insights into the nature of social process. It is possible that the patterning of social relationships in Unit 3, and the position in which Abraham and Donald stand in relation to each other, and to other workers (as well as the relationships those Unit 3 workers concerned have to one another) within this pattern of relationships, will give some clues which will enable some of the problems posed in the preceding analysis to be solved. To examine these relationships I will use a form of network, or as I prefer, reticulum analysis.

The reticulum and the mobilization of support
Prior to an analysis of the various reticulums relevant to the dispute some remarks must be made as to the orientation of the subsequent analysis. One way in which I have attempted to assess the many norms, values etc. expressed or implied in the conflict as it progressed was in terms of their utility for the rallying of support to the cause of one or the other parties involved. I was thus concerned with the mobilization of support. But at the risk of overstressing my position, I now want to suggest that the general norms, values, attitudes and beliefs which are overt in a situation of conflict are more the banners under which people act: they do not necessarily betray the underlying reasons for their action. Other norms and expectations which are more restricted to the governing of behaviour in the relationships between specific *pairs* of individuals will also influence the particular nature of the mobilization in a conflict situation. Norms which are general and accepted by most people in a situation better facilitate the communication to others, the reasons for an individual's action or alignment, than those norms and expectations which are restricted to the relationships operating between certain pairs of actors. Therefore, in the remaining part of this paper I will argue that the amount of support a person achieves in a situation will be conditional on the structure and nature of his direct and indirect interpersonal relationships. My approach to the dispute is closely related to that which Adrian Mayer (1966: 115–18) would term an analysis of an 'action-set', that is, I am concerned in relation to a particular event or occasion, with the degree to which an individual mobilizes his set of direct and indirect relationships in relation to other individuals who may be mobilizing against him in the same situation and who may be competing for the support

of the same individuals. By examining the sets of relationships in a dynamic or mobilizing situation, people, in the sense that they are to a degree all tied to the major competitors in the situation, will have opposing loyalties. But an important factor which will contribute to a decision for their support of one or another of the major parties involved will be the extent to which one of the parties is more 'strongly' linked to them and encompasses their set of relationships within the domain of his own ties. (By 'strongly' is meant that one disputant will be able to exert a greater pull and influence over the persons to whom he is tied than his opponent can over the individuals to whom he is linked.) In other words the process of individual and group action and the outcome of this action may not necessarily be seen in terms of the greater worthiness or weight of the issues ranged to uphold one or the other side in the dispute, but in the nature of the linkages which the opposing parties have to individuals over whom they are competing for support.

The analysis of an 'action-set' raises other points of interest in addition to the problems which have already arisen from the preceding discussion. The mobilization of an 'action-set' provides an occasion for the re-defining of relationships in the situation. An individual mobilizing support in relation to a specific dispute or event will utilize his relationships to other individuals in the situation to build up his support. The extent to which an individual can mobilize persons to whom he is either directly or indirectly linked is determined by the amount of support which his opponent can muster against him. Prior to this mobilization an individual in the normal course of his social activities is by and large operating his relationships with these individuals independently one from the other and is not calling on the persons to whom he is tied for unified action in his support. In a mobilizing situation once an individual must call on this support he tests the effectiveness of his relationships to other individuals relative to their relationships to his opponents. The degree to which an individual's relationships are effective for the mobilization of support for him will determine the future of these relationships—whether they will be strengthened or whether they cease to be active. An event around which people mobilize may also regenerate old relationships which for a variety of reasons have become inactive, or establish new relationships. In analysing the mobilization of an 'action-set', I am thus concerned with the dynamic aspects of the patterning of social relationships; for an individual's current set of social ties—as, indeed, is the existing pattern of all social relationships in a situation—manifests the effect of all the past mobilizations of all kinds.

The ensuing analysis will demonstrate that the course and nature of the dispute depended largely on the character of the relationships of the others involved in the dispute. It should also become evident that the type of mobilization arising out of the dispute altered the pattern of relationships within the Cell Room; the character and pattern of relationships in the situation not being the same after the conflict had subsided as before it.

Through an application of reticulum analysis various important aspects of the dispute will be thrown into relief. As defined at the beginning of this paper a reticulum is egocentric and it includes only those individuals to whom Ego is directly linked. In essence it corresponds to Barnes' primary zone (*supra*, p. 59). The analysis of reticulums falls into two parts, the *interactional* and the *structural*. In the former approach I concentrate on the actual nature of the interactional bond which ties Ego to each of the persons to whom he is directly linked. I am thus primarily concerned with the internal qualities of a reticulum and the varying degrees to which Ego interacts with the individuals in his reticulum. But in the *structural* analysis of reticulums I suggest a method by which some of their basic components can be abstracted and reticulums typified and related to others in the situation. With the latter approach the emphasis is not laid on the differential degree to which Ego is tied to specific individuals in his reticulum but rather on the broad characteristics of a reticulum which allow for comparisons with the reticulums of other individuals in the work context.

Interactional aspects of the reticulums
Before I describe Abraham and Donald's relationships to the individuals in their respective reticulums, it is necessary to outline the basic criteria by which I will analyse each of the interactional relationships in the reticulums. Three major properties of the interactional bonds between Ego and each of the individuals in his reticulum can be isolated for analysis and are: (a) the exchange content in the interactional relationship, (b) the degree of *multiplexity* of the exchange content within the relationship, and,

(c) the *directional flow* of the exchange content in the relationship.

   a. *Exchange content.*[1] By exchange content I refer to the overt elements of the transactions between individuals in a situation which constitute their interaction. For the purpose of this paper I have extrapolated from my observation of the face-to-face interaction between the workers employed in Unit 3 of the Cell Room some of the major elements which *regularly* appeared in these interactions. The exchange contents presented here are an attempt on the part of the observer to categorize the many forms of interaction which took place and are, therefore, not exhaustive; for each exchange content or element of a relationship which I isolate here can be broken down into further elements. However, the five exchange contents in interactional relationships I present here are, I consider, an accurate summary of all kinds of interaction observed. They are *conversation, joking behaviour, job assistance, personal service* and *cash assistance.*

   By *conversational exchange* within a relationship I refer to the mutual sharing of information, gossip, opinions etc. Sometimes, but by no means always, a relationship is characterized by joking exchanges only, though like most other exchanges discussed, it can appear in conjunction with other forms of exchange. Within this category of *joking exchange* I have included both institutionalized tribal joking and joking behaviour which is not part of such a recognized tribal joking relationship. For example, as has been discussed by Mitchell (1956: 35ff.), members of different tribal categories in town recognize an institutionalized form of joking—frequently obscene—between each other. There are workers in the Cell Room whose tribal membership places them in an institutionalized joking position in relation to each other and whose only observed form of interaction was the sharing of jokes, generally at one another's expense. A similar pattern applies to the other exchanges of work assistance and personal service, either one of these exchanges appearing by itself and not associated with any other form of behaviour. The one exception is cash assistance which always appears in conjunction with another type of exchange. By *work assistance* I refer to the practice of some

---

[1] My usage of the term *content* is different from the suggested application of it by Mitchell (supra, 20–22). I concentrate on the characteristics of the interaction between pairs of persons. Therefore, to distinguish my usage from Mitchell's I refer to this as *exchange content.*

employees' assisting others with their specific tasks in the work context. Within the exchange content of *personal service* I have encompassed the observed behaviour of workers performing services for each other such as the collection of drinking water for others and the giving of cigarettes and food. *Cash assistance* refers only to the giving of money to other workers. All these exchange contents recorded apply strictly to those observed and effected within the environment of the work place, and I have for the purposes of this analysis excluded exchanges which have occurred between work companions outside the work area. Finally, all these exchanges within relationships refer to the voluntary action of the individuals in the situation and not those enjoined on them as a necessity arising out of the demands of the work process. Thus I have excluded from this analysis conversation and work assistance, for example, which are essential for the successful operation of the production process.

b. *Multiplexity.* This simply refers to the number of exchange contents which exist in a relationship. In this case a relationship becomes multiplex when there is more than one exchange content within it, the minimum amount deemed necessary for a relationship to exist. In the terms of this paper the maximum degree of multiplexity occurs in a relationship when all five exchange contents previously discussed appear in it; the minimum amount of multiplexity obtains when only two exchange contents have been observed in it. The assessment of the degree of multiplexity in a relationship provides an index of the strength of the relationship. Thus, I make a basic assumption that those relationships which are multiplex linking pairs of actors are 'stronger' than those which are uniplex (or single-stranded). By 'strength' and 'stronger' I mean that an individual will be able to exert greater pull and influence over the persons to whom he is multiplexly tied. It may be that certain types of uniplex bond like the behaviour which stems from an institutionalized tribal joking bond, for instance, may be stronger than some forms of multiplex relationships, in particular those multiplex ties which combine only two exchange contents such as conversation and job assistance or personal service. But, as a general rule, I think it can be safely assumed from my observations that those relationships which have a multiplex exchange are stronger than those which are single-stranded.

c. *Directional flow.* This applies to the direction which the exchange takes in the relationship and for my analysis only has meaning for the exchanges of joking, work assistance, personal service and cash assistance. For a regular conversational exchange to persist in a relationship both the actors concerned must contribute. But the other exchanges need not be bi-directional. An individual may give work aid to another worker in the situation as well as personal services to him without having these reciprocated in kind. For example there is a pattern in the Cell Room for workers in low-status positions who generally lack power in the situation to give goods and services to other workers who are often of higher status and powerful in the work place in return for the latter's patronage. There is an element of reciprocity in the relationship but the reciprocity is not in terms of goods and services of like kind. As Blau states with reference to the social exchange concept it 'involves the principle that one person does another a favour, and while there is a general expectation of some future return, its exact nature is definitely *not* stipulated in advance' (1964: 93).

In the Cell Room these three aspects of interaction—exchange content, the multiplexity of exchange and the directional flow of it—are affected by many factors. Work position and the nature of the work process brings workers into contact with others and may stimulate the growth of a relationship between pairs of persons which extends beyond the bounds set by the production process. This major factor influencing social interaction within the work context apart, it is obvious that numerous other social characteristics will also affect the pattern of social relationships. These other social characteristics intervene to inhibit the development of strong interactional relationships between persons who need not come into contact as a result of their everyday working activities. It is clear that a host of social characteristics which various employees may or may not share in common with others at the work place will be influential to their interaction. These characteristics range from an individual's power position in the Cell Room, seen in terms of his ability to control and influence the action of others, through to his possession of certain social attributes such as those of age, occupation, religion and tribe, which serve to associate him with or differentiate him from others in the situation.

The crucial point which must be stressed at this stage, is that through an analysis of the exchange content in a relationship, and, particularly the degree of multiplexity and directional flow of this exchange content, some indication is given of the extent of the social investment which an individual has in those persons to whom he is directly connected relative to other persons who are linked to the same persons. On an occasion of dispute when an individual is forced to mobilize support to his cause the degree of his social investment in other individuals seen in the degree of multiplexity of the exchange in his relationships with them could determine the extent they feel obligated to his support rather than to others in the situation.

Reticulum characteristics of the disputants
With the above points in mind I will now turn explicitly to an analysis of Donald's and Abraham's direct relationships within their reticulums. The material on which this analysis is based is drawn from data collected in the Cell Room in the months I was there before the outbreak of the dispute between them. There is no significant difference between the two men in terms of the number of individuals included within each of their reticulums. Donald is linked directly in regular interaction with eight other workers, whereas, Abraham is tied to nine (see Figure 14). There are four individuals in Abraham's reticulum who are not directly linked to Donald and likewise three individuals in Donald's direct set of ties who are not directly connected to Abraham. This means that within both men's spheres of direct relationships there are five individuals who are commonly tied to them by direct links. I will examine the extent to which these individuals are differentially tied, if at all, to the two men, and thus assess the degree to which either Donald or Abraham could expect to exert the greater pull over them. Similarly, starting with Abraham, I will analyse their relationships to the men who are not common to both their reticulums.

Three of the four men to whom Abraham is linked but who are not tied to Donald, Maxwell, Damian and Andrew, are also multiplexly connected to Abraham. The exchange in Abraham's relationships with Maxwell and Damian exhibits well the closeness of the bond which Abraham has with them; for he talks regularly with them sharing a diverse range of opinion and

B. Kapferer

information about work and town life in general. Abraham also frequently shares cigarettes with them and on those occasions when they or Abraham bring food to the work place to eat at break, the food is shared between them. This mutual exchange of conversation and goods of like kind between them reveals clearly the feeling of friendship which Abraham has for them and they

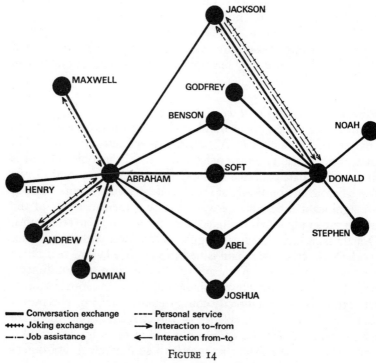

FIGURE 14

The direct relationships of Donald and Abraham

for him. The closeness of the tie which Abraham has with the two men is most certainly influenced by the common position in which they find themselves in the Unit. Although, belonging to tribes with different cultural and linguistic backgrounds (see Table IV) all three are old men and as Strippers are subject to similar insecurities and pressures deriving from their old age and the competition of younger, more physically active men in the Unit. But Abraham's tie with Andrew must be viewed in a different light. Andrew converses with Abraham on similar topics as those discussed by the latter with Maxwell and Damian. Abraham also has a personal service exchange content in his relationship with Andrew, but unlike his relationship with Maxwell and Damian the personal services involved in the relationship such as the fetching of drinking water and the giving of cigarettes flow from Andrew to Abraham, the latter to my knowledge never reciprocating in kind. In addition the two men regularly exchange jokes at one another's expense, their joking based on the institutionalized joking relationship which is recognized to exist in town between the members of the two tribal categories to which they belong. Although their age and their institutionalized joking behaviour might lead one to suspect the existence of a close emotional tie between them, as is evidenced in Abraham's relationship with Maxwell and Damian, the nature of the exchanges in their tie reveals what I think is the most important characteristic of their relationship. Andrew is a Scrubber, an occupation which is regarded by other workers in the Room as being of low status, whereas Abraham occupies a high-status position as a Stripper. By performing small personal services for Abraham and manipulating a tribal joking relationship with him,[1] Andrew thus ties himself to a man who has status as well as some power and influence in the Unit, Andrew perhaps receiving in return Abraham's patronage.

The fourth person to whom Abraham is tied, but Donald is not, is Henry. There is only a conversational exchange within this relationship. Relative to Abraham's other links already discussed I regard it as weak, not only because the relationship is uniplex, but because in comparison with the other links, conversational exchanges are seldom made. But, nevertheless, as in Abraham's relationship with Andrew, Abraham is the dominant partner in the relationship. It is always Henry who initiates the conversation and I regard this as an attempt by him, as a low status and

[1] One factor which influences the presence or absence of joking is the membership of tribes which have an institutionalized joking relationship. However, it is not only the fact that two men stand in a tribal joking relationship to each other that is important but also the nature of other factors conditioning their relationship—for example, a tribal joking relationship can be manipulated as in Andrew's instance to establish a tie with a higher status person in a situation, or, alternatively, to alleviate tensions and strains produced by the work context. Not all people who stand in an institutionalized tribal joking relationship to each other joke.

comparatively uninfluential man in the situation to establish an association with a much higher status and more powerful man in the Unit.

In contrast to Abraham, Donald is more 'weakly' linked to the three persons to whom he is connected and with whom Abraham has no tie. All three of Donald's relationships to Stephen, Noah and Godfrey respectively are uniplex, conversation being the only content exchanged in them. Stephen, Noah and Godfrey are all Scale Attendants and come into contact with Donald in the course of their work activities but Donald regularly joins them at break when they seat themselves near the Weigh Office (see Figure 13). Although Donald is superior to them in terms of his occupational status, he does not show any dominance over them in his relationship with them, as for example, Abraham does in his relationships with Andrew and Henry. None of my information suggests that these individuals associate with Donald out of a desire for his patronage; if anything it may well be the opposite as it is Donald who most frequently initiates the conversation with them.

Of the relationships discussed above connecting various individuals either to Abraham or Donald, Abraham's ties are multiplex whereas Donald's are uniplex. In terms of their social investment in their relationships with Abraham, coupled with their sharing of common interests arising out of their age and occupational position, it may be expected that Maxwell and Damian would be obligated to support Abraham. Abraham, in addition, could be expected to have some control, though admittedly limited, over the soliciting of support from Andrew and Henry. It could be surmised that a refusal to support him would be more disadvantageous to Andrew and Henry in the long run as it could result in the withdrawal of Abraham's patronage. At the very least, however, Abraham could expect support from Maxwell and Damian. But Donald could by no means be as confident, for as shown in the uniplexity of the content in his relationships with Stephen, Noah and Godfrey, they are not as heavily obligated to his support as for instance, Maxwell and Damian are to Abraham. It could be argued however, that as young men and because of the sentiments arising out of their membership of the same tribe, Noah and Godfrey would be tempted to sympathize with Donald. But equally, Stephen, who was not observed in any interaction with Abraham, could, on this occasion, have supported the latter because they are of the same tribe and as older men in the Unit have many of the same interests. As events were to demonstrate, possibly for some of the reasons outlined, Abraham did receive support from the three persons to whom he is multiplexly linked, Maxwell, Damian and Andrew. Henry remained neutral. Stephen, Noah and Godfrey took very little action on Donald's behalf. Stephen and Noah made no move to support either party in the dispute, while Godfrey, far from aligning with Donald, commiserated with Soft over Donald's reaction to Soft's calling him a drunk.

One reason for examining Abraham and Donald's links to the individuals within their reticulums who are not jointly tied to both of them, was that these relationships involved persons who are least likely to be faced with a decision of making a choice between their support of one or the other of the main disputants in the case. As they are directly linked to only one of the two parties they do not have to make a choice between opposing loyalties and obligations which would arise if they were involved in social relationships with both Abraham and Donald. This is not so with the other individuals in their reticulums to whom they are both directly linked.

With the exception of Jackson, the Crew Boss, who has a multiplex relationship with Donald but not with Abraham, all the remaining direct ties which Donald and Abraham have jointly to the same individuals are uniplex. Donald could be regarded as having a close tie with Jackson, for they exchange services with each other, as seen in Jackson's assistance of Donald at work and Donald's fetching of drinking water for Jackson. In addition Jackson and Donald joke with each other, though this is not part of a recognized institutional joking relationship, and they regularly engage each other in conversation. For these reasons Donald might have expected Jackson's support in the dispute. This did not happen, Jackson even appearing to align with Abraham through his action in sending Donald back to work when the latter was venting his anger against Soft. The obvious explanation for Jackson's behaviour is that he was acting according to the requirements of his job. But Soft also had stopped work and in fact had caused Donald's anger—Jackson could also have exercised his authority on Soft. An additional consideration which may further explain Jackson's action is the nature of his ties generally in the Unit. Jackson has many ties with other workers in the Cell Room similar to those he has with Donald. He uses these ties in an instrumental way, for by establishing close multiplex bonds with workers he eases his task of supervision and the exercise of his authority.[1] If Jackson had supported Donald he might very well have jeopardized his ties with other persons in the situation, and so reduced the effectiveness with which he could perform his job.

This type of explanation, which depends on the nature of social ties to individuals other than the two main disputants, needs to be more clearly demonstrated, not only to explain Jackson's apparent opposition to Donald, but also the seeming desertion of Donald by Stephen, Noah and Godfrey. Furthermore some explanation may be given as to why the other workers to whom Abraham and Donald had ties of equal strength supported the former and not the latter, especially when on the surface it would appear that men like Soft, Abel, Godfrey and Joshua, who isolated themselves from Donald during the dispute, had more interests in common with Donald than they had with Abraham. All can be classed as younger men, and three of them, Abel, Godfrey and Joshua, are of the same tribe as Donald (see Table IV): a common bond which conceivably could have influenced their support of him.[2]

Although this examination of Abraham's direct links in relation to Donald's reveals the former's as stronger, at least in terms of the number of multiplex links which Abraham has compared with

[1] Moreover, because Jackson has multiplex relationships with a large number of the Unit 3 workers, he exposes himself to pressures from them. Thus he intervenes seemingly against Donald when the tide of opinion and support is obviously beginning to turn in Abraham's favour.

[2] It may be considered that Donald's being a Jehovah's Witness could have influenced the attitude of other workers to him. At the time of fieldwork there was considerable conflict between the United National Independence Party, to which the majority of the Cell Room workers belonged, and the members of the Jehovah's Witness sect, which does not permit the participation of its members in political activities. However, Jehovah's Witnesses do take an active part in trade union affairs. No evidence appeared before, during or after the dispute to indicate that Donald's membership of this sect had any bearing on the attitudes of his fellows. The issues which were raised referred specifically to the work context and did not involve the wider considerations of political party and religious sect affiliations.

Donald, it does not provide sufficient explanation for the outcome of the dispute. Not enough evidence has yet been advanced which could adequately explain the apparent extent of Abraham's support and Donald's seeming isolation, let alone which could provide solutions of the earlier problems as to why Donald was accused of fast work and not Abel, or why trivial issues achieved prominence and not the more important ones of ratebusting and witchcraft. I have already suggested with reference to Jackson that some explanation could be given if the nature of ties to others apart from those to Abraham and Donald are examined. It will, therefore, be the purpose of the following analysis to examine the types of relationships which connect the individuals within the two reticulums to each other, and to other workers who were influential for the course of the dispute.

Structural aspects of reticulums
Inasmuch as I regard the foregoing description of the direct relationships which the two main disputants had to others at the work place as *interactional*, focusing on the exact nature of each relationship in the reticulums such as the content of the exchange, multiplexity and directional flow of the exchange in the relationships, the following analysis is *structural*.

In order to examine some of these structural aspects I will concentrate on four characteristics of reticulums in the hope of drawing up an elementary typology, thereby enabling comparisons to be made between the various reticulums in the Unit. Therefore, one of my first concerns at this stage of the analysis will be to deal with some relatively simple ways which can be used to measure relevant aspects of reticulums. I will not deal with all or indeed consider all the possible aspects of reticulums which are amenable to measurement.[1] Instead, I will only be concerned with measures which are relevant to the particular context I have

[1] For example, I do not deal explicitly with *reachability* or *criticality*. Because the Cell Room is such a restricted space with a relatively large number of persons working in it, I do not consider it very fruitful at this point to examine the problem of *reachability*, by *reachability* meaning the number of steps each person must go through to reach everyone else in the Room (see Harary, Norman and Cartwright, 1966: 121–22, for a precise definition of *reachability* in terms of digraph theory). Most people, should the need arise, can reach anyone else in the Room by at most a two-step path. Despite this, I would not minimize the significance of examining *reachability*, particularly in the sphere of such

chosen to examine. Nevertheless, some important properties of reticulums to which I draw attention in the analysis of Abraham's and Donald's relationships will not fall within the scope of this section. Thus, although crucial to the understanding of the structure of reticulums I will not analyse, using measurements, the nature of the exchange in the observed relationships, or the directional flow[1] of this exchange. My main reason for this important omission is that I wish to keep the factors I take for measurement to a minimum. There are only 23 work situation reticulums available for examination and a proliferation of factors could render the results of the exercise meaningless because of the small number of cases. Some degree of control over the error created in my analysis resulting from this omission will be achieved by introducing the aspects of exchange and direction where I think they are important for understanding the analysis.

But my interest at this stage of the discussion is not purely in measurement. Once some reticulum measure is obtained the task of comparing reticulums is facilitated as is also the ability to assess the differential degree to which each worker is tied into the set of relationships in Unit 3: a problem the solution of which is important to a more complete understanding of the process of Abraham's and Donald's dispute.

---

problems as communication; generally, however, the measurement of reachability may be of more interest when a *total* reticulum (spanning *all* the social contexts, including the work situation, neighbourhood etc. in which people are involved) is examined.

Criticality refers to the degree to which a person or a number of persons within an individual reticulum are crucial to it. Two major aspects of *criticality* can be distinguished: (i) the extent to which a person (or persons) is a major point connecting the other people in the reticulum to each other, thus providing an additional bond between them, other than their common relationship to Ego, and (ii) the degree to which a person (or persons) connects Ego to other people in the situation to whom in the terms of this paper he is either not directly connected or who, if zones other than the primary zone are considered, occupy a point on a path which is Ego's only route of access to certain individuals in the situation. The idea of *criticality* has a distinct affinity with the concept of strengthening and weakening points in digraph theory (see Harary *et al.*, 1966: 233–39).

[1] Harary, Norman and Cartwright (1966) show some interesting methods by which the directional flow within a reticulum may be measured. Other matrix measures such as that proposed by Hubbell (1965) might also be useful for this purpose.

Finally, although in the preceding analysis Abraham's and Donald's relationships were the major focus of interest, their sets of relationships will now be seen in relation to other Unit 3 workers' relationships. By drawing attention to some of the main

Table V

The Structural Types of 23 Unit 3 Reticulums

Name	No. in Retic-ulum	Types				Percentages			
		Span	Den-sity	Star Mult.	Zone Mult.	Span	Den-sity	Star Mult.	Zone Mult.
Damian	12	+	+	+	+	50·9	68·2	41·7	55·6
Godfrey	13	+	+	+	−	57·1	65·4	46·2	49·0
Soft	15	+	+	−	+	42·9	67·3	20·0	59·5
Mohammed	11	+	+	−	+	42·0	65·5	27·3	61·1
Lotson	12	+	−	+	+	56·3	64·1	61·5	50·0
Jackson	16	+	−	+	−	68·8	50·8	56·3	39·3
Joshua	19	+	−	+	−	87·5	46·2	47·4	36·0
Andrew	17	+	−	+	−	83·0	55·9	64·7	38·2
Henry	15	+	−	+	−	68·8	59·0	53·3	45·2
Abel	15	+	−	+	−	66·1	56·2	40·0	44·1
Bernard	11	+	−	−	−	37·5	56·4	36·4	41·9
Gordon	7	−	+	+	+	22·3	85·7	42·9	88·9
Maxwell	7	−	+	+	+	23·2	90·3	57·1	63·2
Wilfrid	2	−	+	+	+	2·7	100·0	50·0	50·0
Abraham	9	−	+	−	+	31·3	72·2	33·3	53·8
Peter	6	−	+	−	+	16·1	80·0	00·0	50·0
Stephen	8	−	+	−	+	25·9	75·0	25·0	66·7
Axon	9	−	+	−	−	30·4	69·4	11·1	36·0
Noah	7	−	−	−	+	16·1	52·4	00·0	63·6
Benson	8	−	−	−	−	23·2	64·3	12·5	44·4
Donald	8	−	−	−	−	23·2	64·2	12·5	38·9
Kenneth	1	−	−	−	−	·9	00·0	00·0	00·0
Simon	1	−	−	−	−	·9	00·0	00·0	00·0

structural characteristics of other reticulums in the Unit as well as Abraham's and Donald's, their relationships are now placed in proper perspective relative to the structure of other's relationships in the work situation.

There are three structural elements of reticulums which are relevant in this analysis. These are *Span*, *Density*, and the *Degree of Multiplexity*. The last structural element is divided into two parts: (i) that which is concerned only with Ego's direct links to members of his reticulum and which I shall call *star multiplexity*, and, (ii) that which relates to the ties connecting each of the individuals in a reticulum, excluding Ego's direct links to them, and which I shall call *zone multiplexity*. I will now explain each of the structural elements at greater length.

1. *Span*. By span I refer to the number of links out of the total viable links operating between actors observed in the area of Unit 3 captured by Ego as a result of including specific people within his direct set of relationships. Thus the measure of span presented in Table V was obtained in the following way: $\frac{100(E + Na)}{S}$, where $E =$ the number of direct links between Ego and other individuals in Ego's reticulum, $Na =$ the number of links between each of the individuals to whom Ego is linked and $S =$ the total number of links between all individuals in the situation, which in this case is Unit 3 of the Cell Room. For example, take the points in the hypothetical reticulums A and B in Figure 15 to represent all the individuals in a situation and the lines connecting the points to indicate all the relationships existing between the individuals in the situation, which in Figure 15 totals sixteen. Therefore, the span of A's reticulum would be as follows:

$$E = 5, Na = 0 \text{ and } S = 16 \ldots \text{Span} = \frac{100(6 + 0)}{16} = 37 \cdot 5 \text{ My}$$

main interest in focusing the measure of span on the number of links involved in a reticulum rather than the number of individuals is to distinguish the differential quality of the span of people's reticulums. For example, in the two hypothetical reticulums A and B on Figure 15 it is seen that both have the same number of individuals in them but the number of links which each of them includes in their reticulums differs, B's reticulum in terms of span being more significant than A's. B's direct links to his reticulum members, in contrast to A's ties, are reinforced by secondary and tertiary links through the persons to whom he is directly tied to other persons to whom he is directly linked (B's span = 68·8). A number of instances of this are borne out in my material. The percentages for span on Table V show that Donald and Stephen have the same number of individuals in their reticulums but the number of links which each of them includes in their reticulums is different. Again, Joshua, Andrew and Jackson show a very small difference between each other in terms of the number of individuals which they include in their reticulums but some marked differences in the number of links involved. Generally, however, the ordering of the 23 reticulums according to type shown on Table V does not alter whether my suggested measure for span, which focuses on the number of links, is used or that which merely counts the number of individuals. This is

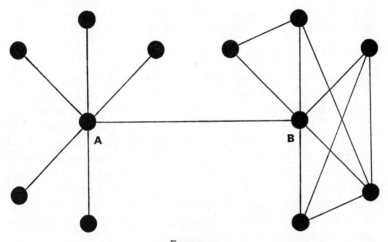

FIGURE 15

Two hypothetical reticulums, (A) and (B) illustrating span

important when I turn to an examination of the types of reticulums observed in Unit 3. Obviously span is affected by the degree of access which an individual has to others in the Unit by virtue of the sharing of various social attributes, the nature of the work (whether it involves frequent or limited movement about the Unit) and the type of authority and/or power he wields in the work context. Joshua, for example, both shares a number of social attributes with a relatively large number of Unit 3 workers and is in a job which permits regular movement around the work area. Jackson, because he is the Crew Boss, is placed in an authority position which demands a relatively large amount of contact within Unit 3. He also possesses a number of social attributes in common with other Unit 3 workers (see Table IV) which further facilitates the establishment of a considerable degree of contact within the Unit.

2. *Density.* The measure for reticulum density is the same as the one used by Kephart (1950) but I have excluded from it Ego's direct relationships to his reticulum members concentrating only on the degree of interlinkage between the persons to whom Ego is directly tied. This particular measure may be regarded as having some similarity to the concept of completeness in graph theory. Reticulum density is found by dividing the actual number of interlinkages between the individuals in a reticulum by the possible number of interlinkages. This is expressed by the following formula: $100 \times \left(\dfrac{Na}{N(N-1)/2} \right)$ where $Na =$ the number of actual links and N the total number of persons in the reticulum.

There is a clear tendency for reticulums with a high span to have a low density and *vice versa*. Nevertheless, a few reticulums do not conform to the general pattern of a high span and a low density or *vice versa*. In addition to degree of span, common social attributes, the amount of movement associated with the job and the authority and/or power of the respective actors in the situation which affect a reticulum's span also affect its density. Lotson and Damian who have a high degree of span to their reticulums and are also powerful and influential men at the work place also have a high density to their reticulums.

3. *Degree of multiplexity.* The measure of degree of multiplexity is simply obtained by dividing the number of relationships which are multiplex (i.e. two or more exchange contents) by the total number of *all* relevant relationships and expressing the result as a percentage. Therefore, in order to find the degree of star multiplexity I have divided the number of multiplex relationships which Ego has to each of the persons to whom he is directly linked by the total number of all his direct relationships (uniplex and multiplex). Zone multiplexity excludes Ego's direct relationships to his reticulum members and is found by dividing the number of multiplex links connecting the reticulum members to each other by all the relationships (uniplex and multiplex) connecting them.

By examining the degree of multiplexity of relationships, further information is provided which is of assistance in assessing the importance of the other measures of span and density. Thus taken together the measures of star multiplexity and zone multiplexity will distinguish reticulums which score highly on the basis of span but which differ in that whereas one reticulum includes links which show a tendency towards multiplexity, another's relationships tend to be uniplex. In terms of density the measure of zone multiplexity will evaluate the extent to which the ties linking members of a reticulum to one another (excluding Ego's direct relationships with his reticulum members) tend towards multiplexity. Similarly, the measure of star multiplexity will assess the degree to which Ego's direct links to his reticulum members tend to be multiplex or uniplex. This provides an index for gauging the extent to which Ego is strongly or weakly tied to the individuals in his reticulum and the degree to which they might be obligated to support him. For example, Ego's reticulum members could be densely interlinked by mainly multiplex bonds but Ego himself could be tied to the individuals in his reticulum by only uniplex ties. That Ego has few multiplex relationships to his reticulum members places him in a weak position in relation to them. This could reduce the degree of influence Ego may be able to exert on his reticulum members and could affect the extent to which he can build up valuable alliances should he be involved in a situation of dispute: for his reticulum members would be drawn to other individuals to whose reticulums they also belong but to whom they are linked by multiplex rather than uniplex ties.

These measures of span, density and of multiplexity have been used, as indicated on Table V, to typify the reticulums observed in the area of Unit 3. The degree to which the percentage for each structural element of span, density and multiplexity is above or below the median for each measure is indicated by a (+) or (−) respectively. Therefore, a response pattern of (++++) would indicate that the reticulum of a particular worker in comparison with other workers' reticulums in Unit 3 is above the median for each of the measured aspects of span, density and multiplexity.[1]

---

[1] For each of these measures I have employed a matrix technique based on a specially adapted card system. There are certain advantages to this system, especially for a small number of cases; one advantage is that it eliminates the problem of cycling within a matrix which otherwise requires fairly complicated mathematical procedures to overcome. This method was developed in association with Professor J. C. Mitchell and Dr G. K. Garbett. A much improved method incorporating different principles, which allows for the solution of many problems using graph theory, has been developed by Dr Garbett, and some information on it appears in Garbett (1968).

For the purpose of the analysis in this section of the paper I regard both star and zone multiplexity as of no interest unless they appear in association with one or another of the two major reticulum structural elements of span and/or density. One of the main interests of the paper generally and of this section in particular is to gauge the differential involvement of workers employed in the area of Unit 3 in the set of existing Unit relationships. Both the measures of span and density deal explicitly with this aspect for, as previously described, span has to do with the extent to which the observed social relationships extant in Unit 3 are included in a specified reticulum, whereas density measures the degree to which Ego's reticulum members are linked to one another resulting in Ego's either being part of a 'close knit' or 'loose knit' set of relationships. As already stressed, multiplexity has to do with the strength of relationships and has little relevance of itself, it being seen as only important supplementary to the existence of span and/or density being characteristics of a reticulum. It is, therefore, significant with reference to the material presented in Table V that there is only one reticulum, that of Noah recorded in Unit 3 which falls below the median in terms of span and/or density but which is above the median in relation to either star or zone multiplexity. Therefore, not only may I argue that multiplexity should only be seen as relevant in reference to span and/or density but it can generally be surmised that a high score of multiplexity tends to occur in association with a high score for span and/or density. But a high score for span and/or density need not imply multiplexity, although multiplexity appears to imply span and/or density.

It can be expected that star multiplexity has the most relevance for span, as this measure includes Ego's direct relationships, while zone multiplexity has relevance both for span (as it also includes the aspect of connection between Ego's reticulum members) but more specifically for density as this refers to the degree of inter-linkage between the reticulum members exclusive of their connection with Ego. The expected pattern does in fact appear in the data set out in Table V. For instance, star multiplexity appears mainly in association with span, there being only three reticulums where a high score for span, in relation to the other Unit 3 reticulums, is not associated with star multiplexity. Similarly, zone multiplexity mainly occurs in connection with density, there being only three reticulums in which a high density score as a structural element is not associated with a marked degree of zone multiplexity.[1]

It is clear that the presence or absence of a high measure for any one or a number of these structural elements of span, density and multiplexity in a reticulum, will serve to associate it with, or separate it from, in terms of structural similarity or dissimilarity, other reticulums in Unit 3. The 23 reticulums observed fall into eleven combinations (out of a possible 16) of the four structural elements measured. Of these eleven combinations, four account for the majority (15) of the workers (see Table V). Obviously, as was stated in the discussion of the reticulum measures, the degree to which a structural element is significant in a reticulum in relation to others in Unit 3, will depend on the extent to which each particular Ego shares social attributes with other Unit 3 workers. However, persons with generally similar social attributes differ in the degree to which certain structural elements are significant in their reticulums.

The extent to which there is a presence or absence of certain structural elements in their reticulums is a measure of the Unit 3 worker's differential involvement in the total set of social relationships operating within Unit 3. Persons who have high measures of span and density as structural characteristics in their reticulums are more included in the set of Unit 3 relationships than those persons who lack one or both of these qualities. But people who have both these reticulum structural features (Damian, Godfrey, Soft and Mohammed) can be ordered one in relation to the other in respect to the extent to which either star multiplexity and/or zone multiplexity are also important elements of their reticulums. Of the two multiplexity measures, I consider star multiplexity to be the more important, as it has to do, as previously described, with Ego's direct links with people in his reticulum and his control over them. Therefore, in terms of involvement in the Unit 3 set of relationships, I regard Damian as being involved in them to the greatest degree, followed by Godfrey, Soft and Mohammed.[2] In instances where either span

[1] Although not demonstrated in the material as presented, there is also some evidence to suggest that those persons to whom Ego is connected by multiplex links are also tied to each other by multiplex links.

[2] I have only used these measures in terms of the problems set by this paper.

or density is absent as a marked structural feature of an individual's reticulum I regard span as being the more important, for this is specifically concerned with a person's inclusion within the Unit 3 set of relationships. Density only relates to the degree to which those people to whom Ego is tied, are also linked to each other, thus it is relevant to the strength of Ego's involvement in the Unit's set of relationships, but is not as specific to it as span. Using star and zone multiplexity in the same way as they were used to differentiate between Damian, Godfrey, Soft and Mohammed: Lotson, Jackson, Joshua, Andrew and Henry can be ordered above Abel, Bernard, Gordon, Maxwell, Wilfred, and so on. The individuals whose reticulum structure indicates a marked lack of involvement in the Unit's set of relationships are Benson, Donald, Kenneth and Simon.[1]

Reticulum structure and the competition for support

Now that the character of Abraham and Donald's direct links has been described, and some assessment of the structural type of their reticulums and those of the other workers in the Unit has been reached, some solution to the problems preventing a satisfactory analysis of the process of the dispute should be achieved.

In Figure 16 I have drawn Abraham and Donald's direct links in the situation, the heavy lines indicating multiplex relationships and the light lines uniplex bonds. The figure is skeletal in that not all the ties between the many actors have been included, only those relationships which I consider important and illustrative of the general pattern of relationships with reference to Abraham and Donald being drawn. Beside each actor I have placed the structural type of his reticulum.

It is immediately clear from the figure, on information recorded, prior to the dispute, on Abraham and Donald's relationships, as well as those of other workers concerned, that Abraham's

However, seen in another way, the structural types presented here appear to bear a direct relation to the status and power position which the various actors have in the situation.

[1] Here I have been concerned with the extent to which the measures of span, density and multiplexity can be of assistance in determining the differential involvement of various Cell Room workers in the Unit 3 set of relationships. When other considerations are taken into account, such as the exchange contents in the relationships and the directional flow of these exchanges, some reordering of the above individuals in relation to each other would be necessary.

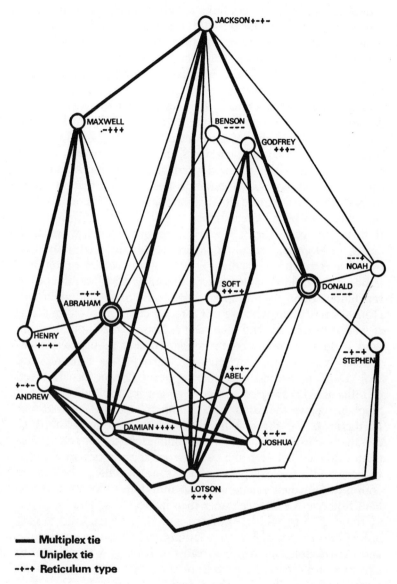

━━ Multiplex tie
── Uniplex tie
-+-+ Reticulum type

FIGURE 16

Direct and indirect links connecting the main actors in the Buyantanshe case
Links in diagram represent regular interaction only. Donald's link with
Abraham is one of occasional greeting only.

reticulum (and his indirect links to other people's reticulums) is
much stronger than Donald's. Thus a pattern which was beginning to emerge in the discussion of Abraham's and Donald's direct
relationships is now more distinct. Although, relative to the
other workers in the Unit, Abraham is not the most strongly
tied into the work situation set of relationships, he is more involved in them than Donald. Despite the fact that Donald and
Abraham include almost the same number of individuals within
their reticulums, Table V demonstrates that of the measured
reticulum structural characteristics, no factor appears to any
marked extent within Donald's reticulum in comparison with
other Unit employees. Abraham's ties in the situation cover
individuals who are more closely interconnected with one another
than those to whom Donald is tied, these interconnections tending
to be multiplex in Abraham's reticulum, but uniplex, where they
occur, in Donald's reticulum. Moreover, if the relationships of
the persons to whom Abraham is directly connected by multiplex
bonds are examined, it can be seen that they draw into their own
reticulums, often by multiplex links, some of the individuals in
Donald's reticulum who are not directly connected to Abraham,
as well as other powerful men such as Lotson, the Shop Steward,
who is directly connected to neither by any regularized interactional relationship. For example, through his multiplex tie
with Damian, Abraham is able to draw Lotson into his web
of influence. Likewise, Andrew, through his multiplex tie with
Stephen, draws the latter into Abraham's set of relationships.
Furthermore, of those individuals who are jointly linked to
Abraham and Donald, and who would seem to have their allegiance divided between the two parties as their ties are uniplex
to both (with the exception of Jackson) all tend to be heavily
committed in their relationships to individuals caught in Abraham's sphere of influence rather than in Donald's. Thus, in terms
of the degree to which Abraham and Donald are differentially
linked into the set of Unit 3 relationships, Abraham's reticulum
and the relationships which spread out from it is more open to
effective mobilization. Apart from the issues, norms and values
which were involved in the situation it was predictable that
Abraham should mobilize more support than Donald.

The structure of Abraham's and Donald's reticulums, and of the
other workers' reticulums, could also explain why the accusation

of fast work should pass from Abraham to Donald and not involve other combinations of workers employed on the two stands. Abel was equally as guilty of ratebusting as Donald, but when their reticulum structure is compared Donald has by far the weaker set of ties. Abel's ties cover a wide span of relationships in the Unit, and, although the factors of density and multiplexity are not significant in his ties relative to other workers, he is strongly linked to some powerful men in the situation, in particular Lotson. By not reproaching Abel, Abraham was not embroiling himself with a man who could have had the potentiality of mobilizing effectively against him. His reprimand of Donald was likely, however, to have more certain success. Similarly, Benson could have met with some difficulties if it had been he who had initially reproached either Abel or Donald. He would have been in a much weaker position in relation to Abel but by operating his ties through Damian and Abraham, for example, he could have conceivably mobilized effectively against Donald. Later in the dispute he did voice his support for Abraham, but that he was not the initiator of the dispute could be explained by the fact that he and Donald had some social investment in each other, as is demonstrated by the regular conversation exchanged between them. If he had told Donald to slow down his work speed he could have seriously infringed this relationship. At any rate, he did this later in the dispute by siding with Abraham, but this was more brought about by the stronger pulls exerted on him by Abraham, especially through other links such as his multiplex ties with Damian to whom Abraham was also multiplexly linked. The process of events meant that he had more to lose by not aligning with Abraham than if he had remained neutral or supported Donald. The strength of his ties lay through his connections with such persons as Abraham and Damian rather than with Donald. Therefore, by reproaching Donald rather than Abel, Abraham was playing from a position of strength. Being, of the two men on Stand II, the more strongly linked man into the situation, Abraham was the better placed to warn Donald against his fast work.

This argument is strengthened when it is realized that the Unit employees are not ignorant of the character of other people's ties in the situation. For example, the small groups of individuals which regularly form at break and which vary little in composition from day to day, give an impression to the workers in the

Room of others' main acquaintances at work. Thus Maxwell, Damian and Abraham regularly sit together at Site I (see Figure 13) at break; Lotson, Abel, Joshua, Soft and many other younger workers cluster at Site 2; while Donald and some of the Scale Attendants such as Noah and Stephen group together at Site 3 near the Weigh Office. It can be inferred therefore that Abraham, prior to the start of the dispute, knew roughly which people were involved in Donald's set of ties.

I have explained why Abraham should have received support in the dispute, and why it should be he rather than Benson, for instance, who should initiate the dispute. But no solution has been provided as to why some of the major issues involved in the dispute were not taken up and why there should even appear to be an interest in focusing on the seemingly more trivial issues. So that some reasonably satisfactory explanation for this can be presented it is necessary to examine more closely the process of mobilization in the dispute. The nature of Abraham's ties could be said to have had a cumulative effect which was to operate to Donald's disadvantage in the mobilization of support during the course of the dispute. Abraham was connected to individuals who in turn drew others to them, frequently by virtue of their multiplex links and so drew away from Donald any support he might possibly have hoped for. Donald's actions in fact facilitated part of this process as shown in his attack on Soft. Soft's position was difficult. His work position on Damian's stand placed him between two influential and committed men in the dispute, Damian and Abraham, and to have supported Donald could have infringed his work relationship with Damian. The difficulty of his work position could have contributed to his support of Abraham but, whatever the reason, his suggestion that Donald was drunk brought Donald's wrath down upon him. This reaction influenced Godfrey, with whom Soft is tied by a close bond, to commiserate with him, an action which aligned Godfrey with Soft, and therefore, by association, with Abraham.

This instance of Godfrey's support of Soft against Donald emphasizes an aspect of the various alliances which built up to support, seemingly, Abraham's position. Although the major issues raised in the dispute are important to an understanding of some individual behaviour (for instance, Damian and Maxwell's support of Abraham) they could cloud other factors which might also be important to understanding the support mobilized against Donald. It could be that for some of the individuals who were involved in this dispute that many of the issues raised were secondary to other considerations. Everyone did not enter the dispute at once, rather they were gradually drawn into it as other persons with whom they had close bonds, became involved. Their seeming alignment with Abraham grew out of the discharge of their obligations to specific individuals to whom they were closely socially committed, as evidenced by the multiplexity of content in their relationships.

The process of mobilization

The above suggests that there are numerous ways by which people can be committed to a common alignment. Although I do not exhaust the possibilities, I discuss three kinds of mobilization which relate to this case. Firstly, people can be mobilized to the support of one or other of the parties in the dispute on the basis of issues, norms and values raised during the course of events. Secondly, they could be mobilized, like Soft, for instance, because of the formal position in which they are placed in the production system. Thirdly, mobilization in the support of a disputing party may arise out of the necessity for individuals to fulfil the obligations involved in the nature of their close relationships with others in the situation. It was the interplay of all these three factors which gave rise to Abraham's successful mobilization against Donald.

But, despite the importance for the consideration of the train of events in the dispute of the first two factors affecting the alignments, I consider the last factor to be the most important for understanding both the build-up of Abraham's support in the dispute and the reason why the issues involved were maintained at a trivial level. In the description of Abraham and Donald's direct links it was shown that Abraham had more multiplex direct links than Donald. This apart, however, Abraham as well as Donald in comparison with other workers in the Unit, had a limited span and multiplexity of direct links in their reticulums. This limitation to their reticulums meant that both men could not reach a significant amount of support through their own direct links but were dependent on indirect ties, and, in particular, those relationships which were multiplex, through individuals to whom they were directly connected in their reticulums. In fact it was the nature of these workers' ties which primarily was to determine the success or failure of Abraham's or Donald's respective mobilization. Because of this dependence on them by both Abraham and Donald, these persons, to whom they were directly connected and who were the points through which they could gain access to other individuals, had control over those issues which were important, not Abraham or Donald. Earlier in the paper I made the point that the issues of ratebusting and witchcraft, if they had been seized upon, would most likely have divided the Unit into opposing factions, and that one explanation why they were not taken up was to prevent this. I regarded this explanation as not completely satisfactory as it did not lead to any understanding of why on other occasions when these issues again were involved in a dispute, they *were* taken up. The nature of the mobilization around the dispute I have been analysing and the degree of control which Abraham and Donald had over this mobilization may provide some solution to this problem.

For example, with regard to the successful man in the dispute, Abraham, some of the key men who contributed to the effectiveness of Abraham's mobilization were Damian, Andrew and Soft. In turn it was their links to powerful individuals like Lotson which led to the dispute's being settled very much in Abraham's favour. Here were people who had differing interests in the situation. Although Damian had reason to sympathize with Abraham's concern over Donald's ratebusting, if he had openly expressed support of Abraham on this issue he could have alienated other workers to whom he was connected but who had other interests in the situation. Thus he could have deprived Abraham of valuable access to other influential people in the work place and also have threatened the continuance of some of his own close ties which he had built up. To align himself effectively and also to influence the support of others to whom he was tied (and in fact make the discharge of their obligations to him easier), Damian had to appeal to a norm which was least likely to relate to a source of division within the Unit and which would not threaten the basis of his own relationships. Thus in his conversation with other workers who visited him at his work stand, and in his conversation with Maxwell and Lotson on the neighbouring stand, he remarked on Donald's lack of respect for an older man, keeping well clear of the potentially explosive issue of ratebusting. Likewise, Lot-

son's attitude had much to do with the outcome and alignments which were to be formed during the process of the dispute.
Much of his power and influence in the Unit and Cell Room
generally, as well as his ability to maintain this power and
influence, stems from his ability to include relationships within
his reticulum which tend to be multiplex and which cover a
relatively large number of individuals who are densely interconnected (see Table V). As with Damian's, Lotson's reticulum
also includes many individuals who have divergent and in some
cases opposed interests in the work situation. To have grasped
at the issue of witchcraft or ratebusting could have seriously
endangered the future of many of his relationships and thus have
upset his position of power in the Room. It was not surprising
therefore, that he should try to transfer the focus of the dispute
to the relatively minor issues which emerged over Soft's *contre-
temps* with Donald, and insist that it was the former's statement
that Donald was drunk which really lay at the root of the dispute.
In so doing he tried to keep the grounds of the dispute trivial,
thereby adopting a course of action which would result in the
least damage to his own set of relationships and powerful position
in the Unit.

I suggest then that because the effectiveness of the mobilization
in relation to the dispute lay in the hands of key individuals like
Damian and Lotson, and was not in the control of the major
disputants themselves, that the issues of the dispute were kept at
a trivial level. The importance of their successful attempt to play
down the more divisive issues of ratebusting and witchcraft which
were raised, was to preserve intact their relationships as much as
possible. On other occasions when issues such as witchcraft and
ratebusting have played a more dominant part throughout a dispute people like Damian and Lotson have had less control over
the course of events. At these times the major disputants have
themselves had a wide span of multiplex relationships and have
managed to keep the issues over which the dispute was initiated,
more in the forefront.

Some explanation has been given for the reason why Abraham
should receive support in the dispute and not Donald, why it
should be Abraham who accused Donald initially of ratebusting
and why despite the seriousness of some of the charges, the issues
surrounding the dispute were kept at a minor level. But what was

B. Kapferer

238

the result of this mobilization? The obvious effect was that the dispute between Abraham and Donald was settled in Abraham's favour. It was Abraham who produced the opportunity whereby the dispute could be settled by calling Donald to join him where he was seated, at the same time offering a concession to one of Donald's objections by addressing him as 'Donald' and not 'Buyantanshe'. Some of Donald's acquaintances in the Unit such as Abel, Soft, Joshua and Godfrey urged him to accede to Abraham's request. This Donald eventually did, and Abraham then asked him to carry out a personal service for him by sharpening his stripping chisel. In doing this service for Abraham, Donald publicly expressed an acknowledgement of Abraham's dominance in the situation and re-established an expectation accepted by most men in the Unit that a younger man should show respect and deference to an older man. Thus a norm which had been momentarily broken was now reaffirmed. Also Abraham, by requesting that Donald sharpen his stripping chisel established a relationship with Donald, based on his dominance within it, which had not existed prior to the dispute. By developing a relationship with Donald, initially through a personal service tie, the ground was prepared for an eventual more multiplex bond to be created between the two men. This meant that, in future, instead of working through other individuals in the situation to bring pressures on Donald and to control his behaviour at work, Abraham could now operate controls on Donald's behaviour to protect his own interests through a multiplex link. But another result of the mobilization in this dispute was to render unnecessary Abraham's attempt to build an effective direct tie with Donald.

In the eyes of the other Unit workers Abraham had emerged in a stronger position from the dispute than he had been in before it, whereas Donald had his isolation and the ineffectiveness of his current set of relationships in the Unit dramatically demonstrated to him. A few days later, Donald asked the European supervisor in the Unit to arrange his transfer to another section of the Mine Plant and a job underground, which was lower paid than his Cell Room task, was then found for him. Stephen and Noah, for example, remained neutral throughout the dispute and Godfsey supported Soft against Donald. Others, such as Soft and Jackson, whom he considered to be his friends, did not support him either. Donald was particularly angered by Soft's support of Abraham.

Although Soft was connected to Donald by a uniplex bond only, he was regarded by Donald as a close friend in the work place. Another person from whom Donald expected support was Jackson. He was the one person with whom Donald had a multiplex relationship. Both regularly talked about their experiences in the township after work, both men jested with each other, and Donald occasionally carried out some small personal services for Jackson while the latter occasionally assisted Donald with the stripping. As I have previously argued, this relationship can be seen as serving an instrumental purpose for Jackson, enabling him to perform his task of supervision more effectively. Additionally, in that Jackson has a number of similar instrumental links with other persons in the situation (see Table V), he could have damaged these other ties by supporting Donald, thereby making his task of supervision all the more difficult. But his establishment of such a strong relationship with Donald might have led the latter to expect some support when he needed it. The only part Jackson played in fact was seemingly to intervene on Soft's behalf. It is significant that when Donald applied for transfer he gave as his pretext his suspicion that Jackson was assisting Abraham to bewitch him, Abraham having given Jackson a sweet to be taken to Donald. Thus not only did he recognize a break in his relationship with Jackson, but perceived Jackson as aligning in a hostile way against him.

The mobilization surrounding the dispute was not only immediately advantageous for Abraham, in that he was able to control Donald's behaviour, but also his success demonstrated to others in the work place the power and authority he could command. The dispute aligned with him people to whom he had no previous regularized interactional bond of a multiplex nature, and provided a basis for him by which such multiplex ties could be developed in the future. In the weeks after the dispute a tendency emerged for others to whom Abraham had been only uniplexly connected to develop multiplex relationships with him. This was particularly noticeable with Jackson and Soft. Moreover people with whom Abraham had had no regular interactional relationship before the dispute, subsequently began to enter into more frequent contact with him. Lotson, for example, started to cultivate a regular conversational relationship with him. A result of Abraham's successful mobilization therefore, was to lead to a change in the nature of his direct relationships and to a certain extent, the ties of others in the situation.

As Abraham emerged in a stronger position from the dispute, Donald's position had been weakened. He chose to sever his ties in the Unit and transferred to another job. Thus the mobilization around the dispute which led to this action of Donald's also served to change the pattern of relationships within the Unit. Although he was not a significant member of the reticulums of those to whom he was directly tied, his opting out of the situation did alter the structure of these reticulums. The dispute and the various actions of the Unit workers redefined their relationships to one another and to the major disputants.

Conclusion

I have restricted the application of a network or reticulum approach to an analysis of the social process surrounding one dispute. The account of the dispute, following a short description of the industrial setting in which it took place, showed that the individuals involved in it, and the major disputants themselves, appealed to many norms and values in an attempt to define the normative basis in terms of which the conflict was to be resolved. This led me to make a brief description of the norms and values etc. which provided some understanding as to why certain types of accusation such as those of fast work and witchcraft could be expected. But although this description gave some broad impression of the structure of relationships and the general norms and values pertinent to the context, various aspects of the dispute could not be explained. For example, I was interested in such problems as why a particular worker should accuse one specific fellow worker of fast work when he could, just as legitimately, have accused another. The difficulties of explanation became more pronounced when I turned my attention to such problems as why the workers in the situation should select certain types of norms and not others in defining the, for them, important aspects of the dispute, and therefore the framing of their own reactions to it. This related directly to the question why, when the mobilization of support around the disputants was considered, this should result in the total isolation of one of the parties to the benefit of the other. The decision to support one or other of the disputants was by no means clear-cut in terms of the norms and values which appeared to be relevant, it being possible for a strong case to be made out for either one.

But the process of norm selection resulted in the more trivial aspects of a worker's behaviour being emphasized (to his disadvantage) and the comparatively more important norms, such as those relating to fast work and witchcraft, which largely occasioned the dispute, being pushed into the background. I suggested the possibility that witchcraft and fast work were potentially divisive issues, related to a separation of interests between older and younger workers: and if individuals' reactions to the dispute had been defined by the norms and values pertaining to fast work and witchcraft, then the workers could have divided into opposing factions on the basis of age. Although I do not disregard this possibility, this explanation was not completely satisfactory, as at other times of conflict the same workers, faced with similar alternatives, have not been loth to divide in this way. The need for further solution to these problems was necessitated by the realization that in the isolation of one disputant from the other workers (which was the result of this particular mobilization) many individuals aligned with, and by so doing appeared to reaffirm, norms, values and attitudes which protected more the interests of other workers than their own. In fact, by appearing to support an older against a younger man, many of the workers who had interests in common with the latter seemed to act against their interests.

I then suggested that the focusing upon general norms and values, although these are influential to the course of social action, tends to obscure the more specific norms and expectations which relate to the interaction between particular pairs of individuals. One of the most noticeable features of the conflict described was that those involved appealed to various norms and values in an attempt either to rally support to their cause or to justify their own actions. Here my attention focused primarily on the mobilization of support, though rather than discuss the mobilizing potential of the general norms and values referred to by the participants, I turned to an examination of the mobilizing potential of the sets of interpersonal relationships, the efficacy of their manipulation and the exertion of pressures through them to other individuals for the winning of support in such a conflict.

In any situation individuals are differentially tied to others, and the extent of their obligation and commitment to these others varies. Thus the degree to which an individual will fulfil the norms and expectations governing his relationship with another will depend on the extent of his social investment in this other individual, and the returns on the investment should he act according to norms and expectations arising out of the relationship. It was at this juncture that a form of network or reticulum analysis was introduced as an additional approach to those already pursued in an attempt to explain some of the particular aspects of the process of the dispute. Therefore my first exercise in the application of a reticulum analysis was to examine the direct interactional relationships of each of the major disputants to the individuals in their reticulums, concentrating on such qualities of the relationships as exchange content, multiplexity or uniplexity, and directional flow of the exchange contents within them.

The analysis yielded some *index* as to the form of commitment which the actors in the situation had to the disputants, and the likelihood of the fulfilment of their obligations to them. Although a few of the alignments observed in the dispute fitted well with what could have been expected, many of the alignments, from the information presented up to then, could not have been anticipated. In particular this referred to those individuals who were jointly tied to the disputants and were involved in similar forms of exchanges with them. This led to a qualification of the earlier proposition which stated that the degree to which an individual is likely to fulfil the expectations specific to a relationship with another is dependent on the extent of his social investment in that other, and the returns on this investment should he choose to fulfil these expectations. But the nature of a social investment in a relationship with *one* other person, and the expected returns on this investment, which condition the likelihood of fulfilment of the norms and expectations in the relationship, also depends on the kinds of social investment and expected returns which an individual has to *other* persons in the situation. Therefore the alignment of an individual with one disputant cannot be seen in terms only of his relationship with this person, but has to be seen also in terms of his relationships with other individuals in the situation. Commitment to one disputant may not only involve the breaking of ties with another disputant but could also result in the severing of relationships with others. In addition to the loss or gain by supporting one disputant, actors appear to weigh the extent of the loss of their investment in other individuals which would be incurred by taking a specific line of action. A basic assumption then, is that persons will align themselves in a dispute in such a way as to incur the least loss to their investments in the total set of relationships in the situation. But the strategic placement of individuals for mobilization within the total set of relationships will differ, this strategic placement varying, of course, relative to the major disputants concerned. Through the application of various measures relating to span, density and multiplexity, some indices were produced to show the degree to which the workers were differentially tied into the situation and the extent of their social investment in each other. Thus some indication was gained of the pressures and forces which could be exerted through the relationships in the work context to influence and explain certain patterns of behaviour relating to a particular dispute.

The result of the analysis which used the concept of network or reticulum was to provide an explanation for why one specific worker should accuse another, and why the ensuing mobilization should end with the isolation of one disputant. Added to this was a solution to the problem why certain divisive issues should not receive prominence when more trivial issues defined the terms of the dispute. Individuals selected the issues (and the relative norms and values) which allowed them to discharge their obligations to others without incurring too great a loss in their social investments built up over a period of time. If the issues of the dispute had been defined in terms which showed the disputants as representing opposed interests which divided the Room (in this case fast work and witchcraft) the loss to others of their social investments could have been too great. Furthermore, the ability to define the dispute in terms of less divisive issues was greatly facilitated because defining the issues perceived as relevant largely lay outside the power of the disputants themselves; this definition was more controlled by others to whom the disputants were directly or indirectly linked. It was on these others also that the disputants depended for the effective mobilization of support. Possibly, as appears to be the pattern in other similar disputes, if the major disputing parties had had more control over the process of norm selection and mobilization in the dispute others may have been forced, at least momentarily, into opposing factions.

Although, through reference to the general structure and norms and values of the situation, many of the workers may have been seen in their alignments to have opposed their own interests, an examination of the interpersonal sets of relationships indicates the reverse. A reticulum or network approach, which concentrates on a close examination of such interpersonal relationships, accounts for the selection of issues and norms, and variations in the manipulation of these norms to serve particular interests in a specific context.

CHAPTER VII

Personal Crises and the Mobilization of the Social Network[1]

by
D. M. Boswell

Since Barnes's article of 1954 there has been a growing interest in attempts to analyse informal urban social relationships, particularly through the use of the concept of the social network. This paper seeks to categorize the main zones of recruitment to such networks in Lusaka and the ways in which network ties may be used to mobilize support in situations of personal crisis, in this case the period of death, mourning and burial. In doing so it attempts to demonstrate both the use of the network concept in situational analysis and the relativity of the term *effective* (Epstein, 1961: 57) to the type of social situation under consideration, which influences the membership of the core of the social network.

The fieldwork setting

Although Lusaka is a new town dating, for the purposes of studying African urban social relationships, only from the decision to

[1] This paper is based on one presented to Professor J. Clyde Mitchell's Sociology fieldworkers' seminar in January, 1965, at University College, Salisbury, and I should like to express my gratitude to the participants for their comments and criticism, and especially to Professor Mitchell, Dr Jaap van Velsen, and Messrs Norman Long and Bruce Kapferer.

I am indebted to Mr Titus Musonda and Mrs Rosemary Mwezi, whose indefatigable attention to detailed observation in addition to my own helped me to build up the detailed case studies presented here.

I should like to acknowledge, with gratitude, the assistance received from the following bodies:

The Commonwealth Scholarship Scheme.
The Research Fund of the University of London,
The Institute for Social Research, Lusaka, Zambia, which made available the services of their research assistant, Mr Titus Musonda.

Finally I should like to express my sympathy and gratitude to those who were willing to accept our presence at such a time and later to answer certain crucial questions. Pseudonyms have been used throughout in order to preserve anonymity.

administer the country from a central position in the communication system and the shifting of the capital to it in 1935, it has from the beginning felt the stabilizing effects of government employment with designated urban married quarters, though this may have affected only a sector of the population. In 1943, 67·1 per cent of the adult male population was recorded as being married (Govt of Northern Rhodesia 1944, Appendix 6: 42), 32·7 per cent adult male population was estimated as living in Local Authority Locations and 71·3 per cent of the latter were married (Govt. of Northern Rhodesia 1944, Appendix 8: 43). It should be noted however that the majority of these families were living in one-room dwellings. By the time of the 1954 and 1957 surveys Lusaka had grown enormously and the percentage of married-accompanied men had fallen considerably, especially in the older locations represented in the 1943 estimate. By 1963 this drop seems to have been reversed and single men's huts to have again become married quarters though I do not possess sufficient information to demonstrate this as the results of the Census and the housing lists are not comparable.

Table VI

Percentage of the Adult Male Population who were married and resident in Local Authority Locations in 1943–54–57

	1943 %	1954 %	1957 %
Local authority locations[1]	71·3		
Matero and Chilenje[2]		57·4	62·6
'Other municipal suburbs'		42·4	47·4

[1] Source: Govt. of Northern Rhodesia 1944, Appendix 8, p. 43. An estimated figure.

[2] Source: Bettison, 1959, pp. 41 and 43. A breakdown according to the type of residential area. The areas designated 'other municipal suburbs' are similar in style to those referred to in[1] as Local authority locations.

In 1943, 41·2 per cent of the estimated adult male labour force were employed by the Government and the Local Authority. Over the years these clerks, office messengers and domestic servants have obtained conditions of service including periods of accumulated leave based either on their own service or that of their employers. This, with the system of monthly payment and

the scarcity of all accommodation and of jobs, may have encouraged the stabilization of the working population and the
establishment of urban family life. At any rate the contrast between
the stabilization indices of the Copperbelt in 1951 (Mitchell, 1954:
15) and those of Lusaka in 1957 (Bettison, 1959: 83) is apparent in
Table VII.

Table VII

Percentage of Time Spent in Town[1] by Males over 15 years of age

PLACE	a. 77·6–99·9	b. Total time	c. Over 77·6 (a + b)
Roan Antelope Copper Mine	9·6	11·8	21·4
Other Luanshya (urban areas)	11·3	26·3	37·6
Ndola	9·5	22·3	31·8
Lusaka[2]			
Matero/Chilenje	11·1	30·2	41·3
All other townships and unauthorized locations	8·5	18·0	26·5

[1] Sources: Mitchell, 1954, p. 15; Bettison, 1959, p. 83.
[2] The range for the index for the Lusaka suburbs is 80·0–99·9 and not 77·6–
99·9 as in the other townships. This discrepancy probably does not affect the
distribution materially. If anything it would increase the percentages shown in
the Lusaka suburbs.

In view of Epstein's analysis in terms of the *atomistic* structure
of the municipal townships (Gluckman, (Ed.) 1964: 93), the
greater degree of urbanization of their inhabitants may be of
added significance, as is shown in the other Luanshya and Lusaka
(Chilenje/Matero) figures of 26·3 and 30·2 per cent. It may further
help to explain the 'multiplicity of different groupings, each
catering for a different set of interests'. In the municipal townships
of Luanshya and in the two largest in Lusaka the degree of
stabilized residence in town is so high, relative to mine, private
and unauthorized compounds, that more than 37 per cent have
spent over 77·6 per cent of their time in town over the age of
fifteen. I think one can call such people urbanized in that their
working life, if not their retirement, is almost entirely spent in
urban surroundings and their norms of behaviour and aspirations

Table VIII

Percentage of the Population of Lusaka living in various Types of Residential Areas[1]

	1954		1957		1963a		1963b	
	Pop.	%	Pop.	%	Pop.	%	Pop.	%
Municipal suburbs	22,017	46·0	31,542	48·7	51,822	54·0		47·4
Private compounds	7,357	15·4	8,917	13·8	11,564	12·1		10·6
Unauthorized compounds	11,886	24·9	12,361	19·1	11,457	11·9		10·5
Domestic servants	6,533	13·7	11,934	18·4	21,096	22·0		19·3
Peri-Urban area							13,361	12·2
Total population	47,793		64,754		95,939		109,300	

[1] Sources: Bettison 1959, pp. 19–20. May/June 1963 (as corrected 1965) Census of Africans; Lusaka District. Columns 1963 a, b. respectively represent the population of the city excluding and including the peri-urban area as it is not clear how much of the latter was included in the two previous surveys.

are potentially determined by an urban environment. This is also true of their children. This big difference between the Mining and Municipal townships at that time is, I suggest, an additional reason for the difference in social structure characterized by Epstein as *unitary* and *atomistic*. Not only is the company town monolithic in an administrative, occupational and residential sense, but its residents may not have had the opportunity of time to establish interest groups and other more intimate forms of association, which were the sole form of social organization possible in the municipal townships.

In addition there is a marked difference in Lusaka between the Municipal Townships of Chilenje and Matero and the rest of the municipal areas and 'unauthorized locations'. Lusaka has experienced the greatest proliferation of haphazard self-built housing areas in Zambian towns (see Table VIII). This is due to the variety of land tenure around and within the municipal boundary (much of it ex-agricultural land in individual private hands), the constant flow of unskilled would-be labour into this central capital, the fact that its position in the transport system makes it a staging post for migrants to and from Malawi, the Eastern Province and more recently Barotseland, and the only recently reversed contraction of the construction companies. Being unauthorized they are also unrecognized for all administrative purposes except the collection of rent. Survey work in one of these areas suggests that there is a relatively stable core of house-owners and a shifting population of tenants. In 1954 the inhabitants of the various unauthorized areas numbered 11,886, 24·9 per cent of the urban population. Since then, apart from some increase by 1957 and since 1963, the numerical population of these areas has remained fairly constant, though it has represented a declining percentage of the total population, as municipal construction has increased.

Both the Bettison Report (1959: 115) and the 1963 Census (Govt. of the Rep. of Zambia (1964), p. 47 as corrected by 1965 circular) indicate the large number of residential areas in Lusaka of almost every classification. Outside the municipal suburbs of Chilenje and Matero the majority of the African population, 109,300 in 1963, live in a sprawl of municipal suburbs, townships and locations, private compounds and unauthorized areas, numbering no more than 6,000 inhabitants each. My own fieldwork has been concentrated on an area between the African market at

Luburma, the Central Hospital and the Kafue road, and in particular on the three housing areas of New Kamwala, an improved
municipal suburb, and Kapipi's[1] compound, an unauthorized
compound largely built since 1962, and Old Kabwata, a municipal
location built in the early 1940s.

At the time of a 10 per cent sample survey I conducted in
March 1964, the male population of New Kamwala, the first of a
series of fully-serviced housing estates paying from £6.9.4. per
month rent, consisted of senior officials, clerks and drivers employed by the political parties, government and commercial companies, earning between £20 to £40 a month. The domestic
servants, labourers and office messengers living in Kabwata, a
location of thatched rondavels built nearly 30 years ago were
earning £5 to £14 a month. Kapipi's compound dates from 1959
but has grown rapidly since 1962 and contains a large number of
self-employed marketeers and other business men and women, as
well as those who have moved there for the security they feel
it offers in its undivided allegiance to their own, opposition
party.

These three places, together with smaller adjoining areas, may
be seen as forming a social region because of the way in which the
women use the same shops and markets, the men drink at the
same bars and beerhall, the children go to the same schools, and
its churches and other associations draw on the same population
for membership. This is not to suggest that the combined population comprises a homogeneous community, merely that it constitutes a roughly defined socio-geographical area. Only in the
unauthorized area can there be said to be any embracing institutional structure. This is due to the identification of the capitaos
with the dominant local political organization. Apart from this,
however, the fragmentation of associational activity is comparable to that in the municipal townships, socially characterized
as *atomistic* (Epstein, 1958: 154).

The African population of the town of Lusaka originated from
the labourers hired by the traders, the clerks and messengers in
government offices and the domestic servants who were employed
by the Europeans who ran all these. Although no racial land-

[1] This is a pseudonym for the settlement. Such compounds are usually called
after the name of the owner of the land, in most cases a European, or some other
personality associated with them.

apportionment legislation was ever enacted, lack of economic opportunity effectively kept Africans out of *town*, as the low-density, predominantly European, residential area is still called, except as servants. The Townships' Ordinance made it illegal for non-Africans to live in or enter African townships without permission. African townships were sited on the flat, ill-drained land to the west of the town centre, and the ridge of government offices and European residential settlement, and were intended to service the industrial and other zones of employment.

Even now people talk of the two ends of Lusaka as having a different character from each other: Chilenje being a quiet, well-behaved suburb of government employees in stable jobs who played 'safe' during the political struggle. Matero, however, is said to be 'commercial' and most like the Copperbelt, where those with money demonstrate their affluence and where life is noisy, manners are bad and unemployment always imminent, and which was renowned for its 'toughness' during the Independence movement. Both places have populations of over 12,000, accommodated in a wide variety of house-types, according to occupation and income, the rents being paid by their employers. Their social caricatures were based on their categories of employment while those of the three areas in which I did fieldwork were based on length of residence and social status. Old Kabwata was 'a place that people entered but never rose out of', New Kamwala a suburb 'for people a little bit up' which was 'quiet', and Kapipi a dangerous compound inhabited by a shifting population of criminals and the unemployed as well as some old people and petty-tradesmen. These social caricatures do highlight important differences between the areas, as seen by local residents, but there are other significant aspects of social organization left unmentioned.

Zambia achieved self-government in 1964 after a general election on January 20th based on full adult suffrage. The victory scored by the United National Independence Party marked the culmination of four years of party political rivalry with the African National Congress, from which the leaders of U.N.I.P. had seceded in 1959. Throughout that period the pattern of social organization throughout the country was fundamentally changed and this is clearly marked in Lusaka. During this time party political organization was articulated at Regional, Constituency,

Branch and Section levels among both men and women. However after self-government and Independence this organization was affected by the occupational and residential mobility of the leadership, the result of which was most marked in the first of the new suburbs to be built by the Municipality, New Kamwala. This became the throughway for those rising in social status. The impact of these developments was least felt among the ranks of both parties in the poorer urban areas.

Although both parties have a considerable following in Lusaka, in most residential areas one or other is dominant. This cannot be said to be true of any other association. The 'established' Mission churches and the 'independent' African churches are essentially sectarian and regional due to their foundation in one tribally and linguistically homogeneous rural area. What tribal and burial societies there are have a similar regional basis though these do not play an important part in the organization of social activity in Lusaka. In only a few occupations, such as the teachers or the bus-drivers and single-firm industries, are trade-unions important outside the specific work situation and most of the big national unions have their head-quarters on the Copperbelt rather than in the capital. In fact, apart from a general political and/or religious affiliation, associational activity, as in so many urban areas, played a small part in the lives of most of Lusaka's citizens.

Being divided into many relatively self-contained residential areas, most of them with populations of less than 6,000, Lusaka had the characteristics of only a small town. This was reflected in the importance of neighbourhood and kin relationships and in the prominence of categorical divisions based on occupation (and therefore education and income), and tribal or regional origins. The most important public centres of social intercourse were the shopping streets and markets for women, and the bars and beer-halls for men from all social strata. Considerable differences existed, however, in the family life of men of differing social status, those in Old Kabwata and Kapipi spending most of their leisure time in informal recreational and drinking groups outside the home, whilst it was common for New Kamwala householders to entertain their friends in their own sitting rooms. Women of all strata however tended to draw their friends and acquaintances from their neighbours and only went further afield to visit close kin. Constant variety was added to most homes by the frequent arrival of passing kinsmen, *en route* to other towns or rural areas, attending school, seeking medical treatment or employment or coming to assist in certain familial crises such as the birth of a baby.

Because the lack of any particular system of house allocation and the considerable amount of time spent by the residents in Lusaka or other towns, there was a tremendous variety of social configurations linking people to one another and to associations, although these were circumscribed by age and occupational status. Although these social networks were in the main drawn by both men and women from certain categories of kinsmen, tribesmen, neighbours and workmates, the choice within these categories available to individuals was wide, except for the members of ethnic or other self-conscious minorities, such as the Southern Rhodesians, the A.N.C., the Jehovah's Witnesses, or the ruling élite. The social structure was *atomistic* but the categories from which these configurations might be drawn were defined and similar at all levels of society, though they were of course different for every individual and family.

The social network

Since the research of Mitchell and Epstein there has been a concentration on the nature of urban social relationships in Central Africa. Tribalism in town was analysed as 'a significant category of social interaction within the field of African-to-African relationships' (Mitchell, 1956: 34). Following the lead of Barnes (1954) and Bott (1957) Epstein made an important attempt to analyse the structural form of the informal social relationships of individuals (1961). The concept of the social network has provided the means for the analysis of urban social relationships as such without recourse to quasi-tribal or quasi-associational terminology, with its assumptions of a period of adaptation as a stage in urbanization in which rural or tribal values predominate or associational membership acts as a means of acculturation, alleviating the harshness of the confrontation with urban norms and styles of life (P. Mayer, 1961: 199). By using the concept of the social network one can analyse informal urban social relationships in a way which admits both the various channels of recruitment to them and their potentially transitory character. It is, of course, applicable to rural situations too, but there some regularity exists in the ways in in which status is ascribed and social relationships structured according to the more or less regular co-existence of tribe, clan, kinship and a system of authority. In town, however, the concept is capable of the wide flexibility required for the analysis both of relationships between individuals, such as friends or neighbours, and of those between all of the members of a defined population, such as a congregation or a work-group.

In his article of 1961[1] Epstein explains 'that part of the total network which shows the greatest degree of connectedness, I propose to speak of as forming the *effective* network: the remainder constitute the *extended* network'. 'In the *effective* network the tendency is of course for status differentiation to be minimized; but in the *extended* network, although interaction takes place between approximate social equals, the likelihood of some status differentiation being recognized is much greater because of the different social categories from which the network is recruited.' This division is fundamental to his analysis of the leisure-time movements of Chanda, and by implication to an understanding of the basis of most social interaction in other situations. 'The *effective* network, then, consists of clusters of persons fairly closely knitted together' (Epstein, 1961: 57). It is at this point that there is a danger of giving rigidity to a flexible concept. If the candidates for membership of an individual's *effective* network are those with whom he *moves*, and with whom he forms almost a clique, this suggests the paramountcy of intense leisure-time association. What matters as much as the intensity of the relationships and the interconnectedness[2] of the members of the network is the content of those relationships, i.e. *effective* in what situational context. In the case of a funeral, outsiders must be found because the bereaved may not undertake certain tasks.

During his life an individual's social network will be liable to expansion due to recruitment from different social categories, and be further influenced by social and geographical mobility. It will also be affected by changing familial status as marriage and parenthood close and open paths to future inter-action. Links with the past members of an *effective* network may remain dormant unless activated by a change of circumstances.

[1] Reprinted above as Chap. III.
[2] Epstein, 1961, p. 57, uses the term 'degree of connectedness'. See pp. 110–11 above.

Nevertheless, at any one time the members of the social network are in the potential position of being mobilized to deal with a problem-situation. Depending on the gravity and type of the latter, links long dormant may be brought into an instrumental relationship again. An understanding of the ways in which the set of relationships, analysed as the social network, may be used is crucial to the understanding of how problems are met and solutions reached. Writing in the recent past on African urbanization has tended to emphasize the importance of formal associational membership in the socialization of the urban immigrant (Little, 1957; Banton, 1957; Dubb as cited in P. Mayer, 1961; Fraenkel, 1964; Gugler, 1965). The social network encompasses the general structure of informal relationships as well as those operating within defined associational structures.

As already stated it is the purpose of this paper to use the concept of social network in the analysis of crisis situations in town. In rural and small communities it has been possible to isolate the various duties and obligations vested in certain individuals who stand in a particular political, kinship or economic relationship to those involved. The potential fluidity of urban society largely prevents such an analysis in town, because the availability of kin and 'big men' to every family may be completely different and no common pattern of duties emerge for various categories of kin and others. In town the general overarching institutional structure exists at a level more remote from the lives of individuals. Furthermore the fields of individual social-interaction beneath it are more numerous and exclusive of each other.

The crisis situation
Crises have tended to be studied for their bearing on the personality and deviant behaviour but I am not concerned here with anything so sophisticated or individualistic. In a recent article Rapaport expressed her concern as being with 'the critical transition points in the normal, expectable development of the family life cycle: getting married, birth of the first child, children going to school, death of a spouse or children leaving home. These too are seen as points of no return' (R. Rapaport, 1963: 69). Although my approach is similar it is more general and I am particularly concerned with the way individuals deal with the immediate situation in which they find themselves.

Crises have been defined in two ways: firstly, situations seen by the participants as ones of great stress, usually with which they cannot cope alone, and therefore differing in type and degree for each case; secondly, as situations defined as potentially critical by observers, which one set of participants may be able to deal with on their own but which will require extra-familial assistance for others. In a socio-economic sense life itself is potentially critical, particularly for those with no security of employment or a substitute for it, and some live in a state of mental, physical or economic stress from which they are never withdrawn. However, I have been more concerned with those periodic but normal situations where an individual or family is thrown into dependency on others by the nature of events; that is crises according to the second definition.

These situations may be grouped as follows:

1. Child-birth, puberty, marriage and death representing necessary stages in the life cycle.

2. Matrimonial and family disputes which develop to such an extent that others are called in to effect some form of solution.

3. Unemployment and debt which may affect the members of different economic strata unevenly, the unskilled experiencing long spells of unemployment whilst the better educated and more well-to-do may have shorter spells, which their higher wages and savings may tide them over, but be encumbered by more persistent and socially destructive debts. Although common neither may be seen as necessary to life as is the case with 1.

4. Sickness and, often associated with it, witchcraft, which may be seen as the reason for any misfortune and give rise to disputes in 2 above (Mitchell, 1952 and 1964). Although frequent in incidence the experience of either by different individuals is unequal.

5. Other demands which may be made on the individual and be due to the misfortune and disabilities of others, and which, in town, often lead to the provision of money or accommodation.

A variety of individuals and organizations may be called upon to assist in the alleviation of these crises but, except in the case of a small number of administrative institutions, even organizations and associations are primarily involved through the existence of personal connections with individual members that give rise to their obligations. I shall attempt to enumerate the various tasks to be performed if one particular crisis, death, is to be dealt with efficiently and in a socially acceptable way, so that one can see the way in which the social networks of both the deceased and the bereaved were mobilized to fulfil them.

Bereavement in Lusaka

The sequence of events at death in Lusaka follow a set official pattern from which only certain deviations may be made. They are followed by almost all, with the exception of some babies who die at home and are buried privily at night. If possible, relatives ensure that death takes place at the hospital as they are then relieved of police investigations and official interference. Those who die at home, in hospital or in accidents are transferred to the mortuary, which is situated outside the main entrance to the surgical wards of the central hospital, for *post mortem* examination if necessary. A death certificate must be obtained from the doctor and presented to the Administrative Office for the District Secretary to authorize the collection of the body by the municipal hearse and its transfer to the municipal cemetery in Chingwele, where an undertaker's room is provided, a self-employed coffin-maker allowed to operate his business, a grave already dug and a number plate provided from the cemetery office. By such a procedure the legal, medical and municipal authorities ensure the ascertainment of the cause of death and the hygienic disposal of the body, with a 5s. hearse fee only.

Assuming that those involved are residents of one of the central suburbs or unauthorized areas it can be seen that to comply with these legal and administrative requirements various journeys adding up to over 20 miles are entailed. Three days are given to the bereaved to arrange the rest of the funeral and mourning and, although this may differ widely, there is a normal pattern followed. One relative or friend will take charge of preliminary arrangements and contact those kin who live close to Lusaka and those closest genealogically, wherever they live. Others will gather at the house of the deceased and may contribute to the collection of money for food, or, in the case of women, contribute maize meal. No definite arrangements can be made until the arrival of the next of kin. Another takes charge at the mortuary in order to display the deceased to those who come to mourn, which they do by day. As soon as those relatives with authority arrive precision is given to the arrangements, a day fixed for the funeral itself and the necessary documents collected. Mourning starts in earnest and the gathering reaches its maximum at the mortuary by day and at the house of the deceased by night.

Except in the actual course of transportation the position and roles of men and women are segregated. At the mortuary men congregate to the north and women to the south side of the entrance. All organization is left to the men, whilst the women, 'who are weak', are left to keen and those closest to the deceased to lament. Depending on the size of the house men and women unrelated to the deceased sit outside in separate groups, the men on chairs and boxes and the women on sacks or the ground. The men may be asked to contribute money whilst the women are responsible for all cooking and cleaning.

On the day of the burial, transport must be arranged to take the relatives and mourners to the cemetery where the same segregation is re-enacted. The mourners sit apart and, depending on the sex of the deceased, a male or female kinsman prepares the body for burial. The men complete the construction of the coffin whilst others locate the grave. When the coffin is ready to be nailed down all the women present and some of the men file past again and the coffin is carried to the graveside by relays of men in a *cortège* of men followed by women, and lowered in. Prayers are then said and brief speeches made by close kin or others, to the mourners in thanks and in praise of the deceased. Something personal to the deceased is smashed and left on the grave with the number as a means of recognition. The gathering disperses to meet again, either immediately or in the evening, at the house of the deceased. On the following morning the kinsman who was in authority gives a short speech thanking those who have assisted in the funeral, which he declares closed, and the site is cleared up. After travel arrangements have been made there is a general dispersal and only the close kin of the deceased remain to discuss inheritance and the ritual *succession*[1] of the widowed spouse.

Here the differences between individual cases become greatest as decisions may only be finalized if all the important parties are present and often this is not the case as many important elderly

[1] This is the local English translation of *ukupyanika*. By this ritual intercourse the bereaved spouse is released from the marriage bond to the dead and forced to remarry the one chosen by the kinsmen of the deceased or any outsider.

kinsmen may be inaccessible in rural areas. In any case on return to the village senior kinsmen will recount to those unable to come to town how the death took place and how the funeral was arranged, and mourning will be held as in town. About three weeks after this, beer is brewed and the spirit of the dead is cleared and the period of mourning terminated. Succession and inheritance disputes may then continue until the ritual *succession* and final beer is brewed (Stefaniszyn, 1964: 131–33). Although I visited the area where these Lala originated none took place whilst I was there so I was unable to attend any rural period of mourning, *chililo*, in Serenje, but I have been in urban households at the time of a rural death and in these cases a short period of mourning has been the occasion of the visits and gathering of friends and kin.

This generalized description of the activities to be undertaken and roles to be played will serve as a basis for the three cases that form the rest of this paper, which is concerned with the sources of recruiting the participants and their place in the social network of the deceased and his kin. All three cases are of bereavement in families belonging to the Lala, a matrilineal tribe from Serenje and Mkushi districts. They are presented in order from the most disconnected in terms of kinship relationships to the most interconnected. Whereas in Case 1, little attempt has been made to preserve anonymity, this had to be done in the subsequent cases for reasons of sympathy and propriety but no essential data have been omitted. In each case I shall refer to the participants by names beginning with the letters indicated in the *dramatis personæ*, Tables IX, X and XI.

1. *The case of the lonely escort*

Alice, Barbara and Catherine all came to Broken Hill (Kabwe since 1966) hospital via the clinics at Fiwila Anglican Mission and Mkushi Boma and were sent down as escorts with their patients to Lusaka Central Hospital. There they took up a position in the central courtyard beside the main cluster of Bemba and Nyanja-speaking women, who were resident escorts visiting patients in the surgical wing.[1] Both

---

[1] A feature of the Zambian hospital scene is the congregation of clusters of women and some men who gather as resident escorts to patients and camp out in the vicinity of the hospital. In Lusaka they numbered 155 women, 37 men and 66 children at the time of a survey I conducted in August 1964. The permission of the Medical Superintendent and the Hospital Secretary are gratefully

Table IX

The Case of the Lonely Escort (see Figure 17)

Code	Fig. 17	Tribe	Sex	Age	Ed.	Church	Place of Origin	Occupation	Relevant Data
Alice	A	Lala	F	68	Nil	Anglican	Fiwila Mission, Mkushi, B. Hill	Escort	Daughter in surgical ward
Barbara	B	Lala	F	60	Nil	Nil	Serenje, B. Hill	Escort	D. in surgical ward
Catherine	C	Swaka	F	49	Nil	Anglican	Mkushi, B. Hill	Escort	D. in surgical ward
Dorothy	D	Nsenga	F	35	Nil	R.C.	Broken Hill	Escort for 5 mths.	B. in surgical ward
Edith	E	Nsenga	F	62	Nil	Nil	Petauke	Escort for 2 mths.	S. in surgical ward
Florence	F	Lala	F	29	St. 4	Anglican	Fiwila Mission	Teacher, Escort	Child in surgical ward H. is Headmaster
Gracie	G	Kunda	F	38	St. 1	Anglican	New Kamwala	Escort for 7 weeks	Child in S. ward
Hosca	H	Nsenga	M		St. 6	Anglican	Church near Hospital	Priest	Car. Arrived 4 days before
Isaac	II	Kunda	M	35	Fm. 2	Anglican	Chilenje	Clerical Officer	Secretary of E. P. Burial Soc. Lay Reader
James	J	Lala	M			R.C.	Chilenje	Teacher	T.U. official
Keith	K	Lala	M			Free Church	Chilenje	Teacher	
Lawrence	L	Swaka	M			ex-Anglican	New Kamwala	Teacher	Chilenje School
Mary	M	Nsenga	F			Anglican	Matero		
Nora	N	Nsenga	F			Anglican	Matero		
Orlando	O	Bemba	M				Chilenje	Party official	
Patrick	P	Lala	M		St. 6	Anglican	Lusaka Hospital	Medical trainee	
Queenie	Q	Bemba	F	27	St. 6	R.C.	New Kamwala	Research Assistant	Ed. at Fiwila

the old women relied on the use of Catherine's cooking pots in order to cook the little food Barbara had (Alice had nothing except a blanket), and what they were given by Florence, when she was at the hospital. At the critical moment Catherine had to withdraw her participation as her baby caught measles and died soon afterwards.[1] Alice and Barbara were left on their own to deal with the mourning for Alice's daughter, who died after a few days. In her lamentation Alice repeatedly idealized her daughter and expressed her feelings of total isolation now that she had died. 'I am thinking of my daughter very much as she is the one who supports me. She was buying me things like blankets and clothing and I sleep on bedsheets because of her. I was not suffering from hunger or anything because of you. I shall have no one to support me.' It emerged later that the other children had died or rejected their mother and that she was convinced that her kinsmen had bewitched her daughter who had been favoured by the chief because they were jealous of them both.

Barbara tried to persuade Alice to eat and mourned with her at the mortuary. Dorothy who had been five months resident at the hospital attending her husband also tried to activate Alice and Barbara into collecting wood with her as Catherine had ceased to do so due to her own preoccupations. Dorothy, who sat with her husband's old mother, is Nsenga and frequently joked with the other long-term escorts who were Bemba-speakers. She knows Lusaka well as she was born there.

Florence and Gracie sat apart from the rest. Florence is the wife of the headmaster at Fiwila Mission in Mkushi, and Gracie is married to a head-clerk in the Government, who is a polygamist living in New Kamwala. Florence has to attend the hospital at regular intervals for a week at a time with her child who is lame as is Gracie's child. Both are practising Anglicans coming from two of the four U.M.C.A. missions in Zambia. Alice, Barbara and Catherine also come from the same area around Fiwila though only Catherine had had regular contact with the mission. When the position became desperate and the possibility loomed of a burial without ceremony by the sanitary department, Florence took over and was shown the nearby Anglican Church by Gracie, whose child was released from hospital on the same day.

Florence took Alice across but the priest was out. On their return

---

acknowledged. In December, 1965, I published a preliminary report. See Boswell (1965).

[1] Catherine came to the hospital accompanied by two small children as well as the patient in the surgical ward. The youngest contracted measles whilst in the courtyard and died soon afterwards in the isolation ward. His mother left the cluster to wait beside the door of the isolation ward.

they met a policeman leaving the hospital, who took them both to the social welfare office in the centre of *town*, where a letter was obtained to inform the hospital doctor that financial assistance would be provided for the burial. Alice did not trust this letter, however, and called Florence to visit the Anglican priest again.[1]

On their second visit they found Hosea, the new priest who had only arrived four days before. Hosea contacted Isaac, his lay-reader and church-warden, a long-term Chilenje resident who was a clerical officer in the local courts office, a potential heir to a chieftaincy and the Secretary of the Eastern Province Burial Society. It is possible to see this relationship between Isaac/Hosea and Alice/Florence as a demonstration of the Nyanja/Bemba-speaking people's joking relationship, *ambuye*, but unlike the two other Lala funerals, where this was repeatedly emphasized, no mention was made of this and instead constant reference made to the duty to help other church members. The tribe of Hosea was unknown to Alice and Florence before they met and there is no evidence to suggest that there would have been a different reaction had the deceased been a Tonga from Mapanza.

Once the initial contacts had been made Isaac became the centre of the remaining organization. Up to this point Alice, seemingly alone, had been able to activate her own, often tenuous, contacts. Whilst at the hospital she had been operating within a network of contacts based on the accidents of the situation. From this moment however she was to remain inactive and the initiative was taken over by Isaac, whose own position and responsibilities had given him both wide contacts and experience in dealing with similar situations. He was able to collect crates for the coffin from one of his regular sources, the Government Printer, and, in passing him on the road, hailed Orlando, a U.N.I.P. official in Chilenje, 'as the party like to be informed of their members in need'. But although Orlando came to the mortuary nothing further came of this connection.

Isaac made a point of calling on the Lala teachers at Chilenje Upper and Lower Schools and in particular James, who is a senior official in the Union of Teachers and likes to be kept informed of Lala events. James assisted Hosea in driving his new car to collect the Boma certificate and back to the hospital, whilst Keith, Lawrence and Orlando

[1] This aspect of official contacts and processes has been left out of the analysis as they were not in fact used because Alice did not trust the impersonality of letters and offices and gave them up when the doctor did not appear immediately on receipt of the letter, although others had explained the doctor's hours to her. If there had been some social worker attached to the hospital the whole situation would probably have been different. One has been seconded for such duties by the City Council since this research was completed.

cut up the crates into suitable lengths. Florence enlisted Patrick, an Anglican Lala student medical assistant, to help and together with him they took the crates to the cemetery.

By a variety of routes in car, bus and bicycle, all except Orlando arrived at the cemetery through the afternoon. Hosea and Isaac made the coffin, assisted by Patrick, and Queenie, my Bemba lady-interviewer, helped Alice to prepare the dead for burial. Except for Patrick, whose sex precluded him, it is difficult to see who might otherwise have helped in preparing the dead for burial as all the escorts at the hospital had to remain there in order to visit their patients. By the time the coffin was ready, however, two Nsenga women, Mary and Nora, had arrived from Matero, having heard that a member of their church had lost her daughter and had no one to help and that the Anglican Church had helped with the coffin and everything. Mary said 'You know, this old woman is unlucky. Her daughter passed away on Saturday. This is Wednesday. If she had gone to Father on Sunday or Monday, he would have sent messages to all the churches telling them of this. We should have collected some coins to help her. You should have seen so many people attending the funeral, but this time it was too late for Father to inform everyone.'

Patrick helped Queenie to prepare the coffin. All the men, including Hosea then carried it out, taking it in turns to relieve each other, and Alice followed behind lamenting, supported by Queenie, with Mary and Nora. All the men lowered the coffin into the grave. After Hosea had said prayers and a short burial service and Alice had 'buried' her daughter with a handful of soil they filled the grave in. As they shovelled the teachers joked about the territorial army and how those who had joined under the influence of a certain headmaster had got drawn into the operations against the Lumpa sect. In conclusion Alice placed a broken mug and bowl on the grave which had been the personal property of the deceased, and left clutching the blanket which Queenie had persuaded her to keep for protection from the cold.[1]

On the following day Alice was taken in hospital transport to collect her travel requisition and left for Broken Hill, where she intended to stay with her brother's daughter, who had been unhelpful on her way down. At this point the set of people who had been welded together in this particular crisis situation parted, never to co-exist in the same form again although the precedent was used on the following day to deal with the funeral of Catherine's baby.

---

[1] The cup and bowl were left to mark the grave both for the bereaved and the spirit of the deceased, and broken to guard against theft and their use in sorcery (see Stefaniszyn, 1964: 125).

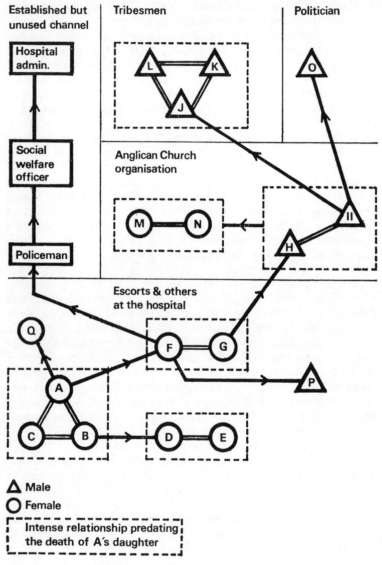

Established but unused channel
Tribesmen
Politician

Anglican Church organisation

Escorts & others at the hospital

△ Male
○ Female

Intense relationship predating the death of A's daughter

FIGURE 17
The Case of the 'Lonely' Escort.
Lines of communication between members of various recruitment categories.
(See Table IX)

This case does not show the operation of a pre-existing social network in the solution of a particular problem. It shows the formation of a temporary action set in a particular situation. based on bonds of common origin in tribe and district, on those of proximity in the cluster of escorts, and of common concern for their sick kinsmen, with the interconnecting strands that bound these individuals to an equally personal but more enduring Lusaka network, centred on a leading churchman and his acquired characteristics of education, Lusaka familiarity and experience, that were instrumental in enabling this situation to be met by a lonely old woman. Although associational ties were important in opening certain lines of communication the recruitment of helpers was largely based on personal contact. It is possible that the Anglican Church might have acted in a more corporate capacity had there been more warning, as indicated by the two Matero women. It is clear however that the bare essentials for this situation could be met with or without this organization.

The following cases involved clusters of individuals who were instrumental in carrying out similar tasks in far larger funerals attended by hundreds of men and women, and considerable numbers of close kinsmen, who were conspicuously absent in the first case. All were concerned with the mourning for adults, who had died outside the nuclear family setting. In Case 1 the daughter was divorced and far removed geographically from her home. In Case 2 the wood-cutter was estranged from his family and divorced but assimilated into another group of work-mates and neighbours. In Case 3 the politician's sister was divorced but otherwise living in familial surroundings. In mourning for a spouse the situation may be very different. It often is in the case of the death of a child or of a woman in childbirth because of the suspicion of guilt falling on the spouse and the tension arising from this between the affines.[1]

The individuals and clusters which are pulled in may be drawn from the personal network of the deceased, or the bereaved as with the escorts in Case 1, or they may be drawn from the

[1] I refer here to the widespread acceptance of this interpretation of the reasons for a difficult labour, which differ only in details throughout the country: that these difficulties are due to the adultery of one of the spouses during the pregnancy and may only be relieved by the confession of the guilty party under pressure from kinsmen or women.

Table X

The Case of the Run-down Wood-cutter (see Figures 18 and 19)

Code Fig. 18		Tribe	Sex	Relationship to Abel or others	Place of Residence	Occupation	Market Membership	Party Office
Abel	A	Lala	M	(Deceased)	Kapipi's	Wood-cutter	Member	A.N.C.
Bota	B	Lala	M	Elder B.	Serenje	Settlement Head		U.N.I.P.
Chisenga	C	Lala	M	Elder BDH	New Kamwala	Senior Executive Officer		U.N.I.P.
Duncan	D	Lala	M	Z younger S.	Broken Hill	Nil		U.N.I.P.
Eustace	E	Lala	M	Elder B. younger S.	Kitwe	Bus Inspector		U.N.I.P.
Fred	F	Lala	M	Z elder S.	Ndola	Policeman		U.N.I.P.
Gregory	G	Lala	M	Elder B. elder S.	Police Camp Lusaka	Policeman		U.N.I.P.
Helen	H	Lala	F	MBD	New Kanyama	(Husband is a member)		
Ison and family	II	Lala	M	Matrilineal kin	John Howard	Nil		U.N.I.P.
John		Lala	M	Works near C	Old Kamwala	Boma Messenger		U.N.I.P.
Kabamba		Lala	M	Works near C	Old Kamwala	Boma Messenger		U.N.I.P.
Luke		Bemba	M	Colleague of C	Chilenje	Civil Servant		U.N.I.P.
Mwale		Ngoni	M	Colleague of C	New Kamwala	Civil Servant		U.N.I.P.
Ngosa		Lala	M	Tribesman	Kapipi's	Nil		

Name	Tribe	Sex	Tribesmanship	Location	Occupation	Membership	Office
Offisi	Ngoni	M	Joking tribe	Kapipi's	Capitao		A.N.C. Branch Chairman
Paul	Chewa	M	Joking tribe	Kapipi's			Vice Chairman
Quotani	Nsenga	M	Joking tribe	Kapipi's	Nil		Sub-branch Chairman
Rebeccah	Ngoni	F	Joking tribe	Kapipi's			Chairwoman
Sarah	Ngoni	F	Joking tribe	Kapipi's			Officer
Teresa	Nsenga	F	Joking tribe	Kapipi's			Officer
Ursula	Kaonde	F	Neighbour	Kapipi's			
Vyvyan	Ngoni	M	Joking tribe	Kapipi's	Vegetable Seller	Member	A.N.C.
Wallace	Ngoni	M	Ate from Abel	Kapipi's	Nil		A.N.C.
Christian	Nsenga	M	Joking tribe	Matero	Storekeeper	Chairman	A.N.C.
Yotam	Bemba	M		Chilenje	Lusaka Mkt. Co.	Manager	A.N.C. official
Z	(Various)	M	(mainly Joking tribe)	(Various)	Tradesmen	Officials	A.N.C.
Adam	Tonga	M		Kapipi's	Af.-Doctor	Member	A.N.C. Branch official
Boniface	Zezuru	M		Matero	Transport contractor	Member	A.N.C.
Chibeka	Bemba	F		Matero	Seller of *Chimela* for brewing beer	Member	Constituency Chairwoman U.N.I.P.
Doris	Bisa/Nsenga	F	Claimed Tribesmanship	Old Kabwata	Shebeen queen	Long term Lusaka resident	A.N.C.
Elias	Ngoni	M	Joking tribe	Old Mumbwa Road (John Howard 1965)	Funeral expert	ex-member	A.N.C.

networks of others as with Isaac in Case 1. This sort of crisis situation calls forth all the human resources that can be mustered by the bereaved from their own *effective* and *extended* networks, but the nature of the response may be related to the past history and status of the deceased and his family as well as to important kinship and neighbourhood ties. It is at this point that the relativity of the term *effective* is apparent. Because of the way in which an individual's network may change in membership it is quite possible that friends or others who were in his *effective* network in the past, but for various reasons are no longer in such a relationship with him may, in a crisis situation, resume their intense relationship with him whilst his leisure-time associates remain on the side. During the crisis situation a new or renewed central cluster of interconnections may be formed, though this need not endure beyond it. Case 2 will make this point clear because of the way in which sections of Abel's network operated separately from each other in dealing with different parts of the mourning period with a minimum of cooperation. It is even more apparent in Case 3.

2. *The case of the run-down wood-cutter*

Abel was a Lala who lived alone in Kapipi's compound. He was a miner and recently adopted as a pensioner by the Pneumoconiosis Board. Apart from a brief visit to Serenje when he retired in 1953 he had avoided close contact with his kin and in Lusaka had neither visited them nor been visited. He was an early member of the Lusaka Market Association and a staunch member of the African National Congress, now the opposition party, whilst his kinsmen are all U.N.I.P. He had the reputation of being a self-sufficient tradesman, who was very good to his joking-tribesmen, Market members and Kapipi's residents who were from the Eastern Province, and his friends were Ngoni and Nsenga. He was knocked down by a car early in the morning on his way to the market and a political murder was suspected on the grounds of inaccurate information about the driver of the car. He died soon after reaching hospital. He was able to mention the name of a relative but no more. When word of this reached a Lala student medical assistant, he got a message through to Chisenga, whose name Abel had mentioned. Chisenga is a senior executive officer at present stationed in Lusaka and the husband of Abel's elder brother's daughter. Both he and his wife, who was absent at the time of the funeral, have had very little contact with their Lusaka relatives since they came to Lusaka in 1964, a fact of some influence on later events. Chisenga obtained two days leave and telephoned Serenje to have a message passed to his wife's father, Bota, Abel's elder brother and the head of the family settlement, as well as Eustace and Fred in Kitwe and Ndola. He also arranged for two Boma-messengers, who are Lala, John and Kabamba, to take charge of operations at the mortuary. This Chisenga was able to do due to his official position. Gregory heard of the accident through police channels as he works in the Lusaka headquarters,

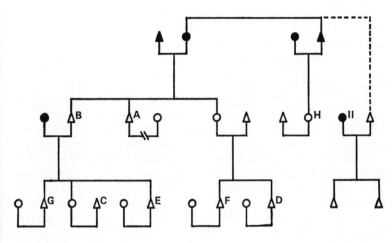

--- Putative matrilineal link
⌐ Divorce

FIGURE 18
The Case of the Run-down Wood-cutter.
Skeleton genealogy of Abel showing those mentioned in the case. (See Table X)

and took on the responsibility of forcing through the police enquiry into the cause of death. Helen heard of the accident late in the day after her husband called at the market on business. She lives in one of the western site-and-service schemes, New Kanyama. Other more distant relatives heard of it through rumours that circulated through Kapipi's compound and reached the nearby unauthorized area, John Howard, where they live. They are represented by Ison and family (II) as 'Matrilineal kinsmen', in fact an old Lala man and his two sons. It is already apparent that the kinship network did not operate as a corporate unit but through a series of disjointed channels of communication which only brought its various members together for the period of mourning. The existing tensions within the family were expressed in various ways during the course of the next few days and persisted afterwards.

As the accident happened at the time the marketeers arrive, early in the morning, and because many of them live in Kapipi's compound, the news reached both places very quickly and by the following morning Christian and Yotam, the chairman and manager of the Lusaka Market Company Limited had made arrangements with their other officers for the buying of a coffin, hiring transport at half-price from Boniface, to take the mourners to the cemetery, and collected money from the members of the market to pay for the funeral. When they heard that Abel had relatives in Lusaka a message was sent to Chisenga asking him to call at the market, where he was informed by Christian that the marketeers would 'look after the box and all that' and that he 'could do the rest'. Chisenga was much impressed with their organization and officialdom, as he was supposed to be. The manager told me during the course of the funeral: 'We hope to gain members by showing them what we can do for them. At present we have 290 members and 172 non-members.[1] We want to start a burial society for everyone in the country to be based on the Market Company. The —— Burial Society is dying and they select whom they will help. Abel's funeral will show what we can do.' As far as the market officers were concerned Abel's funeral presented the ideal opportunity to demonstrate the value of being a Market member, to provide and advertise the launching of their new burial society, and to take advantage of the respect in which Abel was held by various sections of the community to project their new image. The last point is important because the Market officials, who had themselves been colleagues of Abel in the market and the party, were not just taking advantage of the situation. The opportunity to make a show suited their purpose well but it is unlikely that they would have done the same for someone held in less esteem (they have had no other funerals like it since) and therefore the importance of Abel's work situation and associational contacts remains.

In Kapipi's, the senior capitao had just heard of the death of his sister in Fort Jameson[2] and was himself in mourning. His eldest son had been told by an African-doctor in Kitwe that he should not attend funerals

[1] Since November, 1956, the Lusaka Market has been run by the traders themselves, following a boycott in that year of the municipal premises. It started as a cooperative, became an independent association and in 1964 the Lusaka Market Company Limited. Membership is by subscription and confers the privilege of paying lower stand rentals daily. For further details see Nyirenda, (1957) and Miracle (1962). I intend to publish a paper on the later history of the Market up to the time that the City Council resumed direction in October, 1965.   [2] Renamed Chipata in 1966.

or his epilepsy would return. Due to these disabilities his family took little part in the mourning ceremonies. In fact, had Abel not died at this time it is likely that there would have been a gathering at the senior capitao's house with him. However, the senior capitao of New Kapipi, who is also the chairman of the local A.N.C. branch, Offisi, and Quotani, the chairman of the sub-branch, organized money collections and Rebeccah, Sarah and Teresa, who are all women officials of the same branches, collected maize-meal. Rebeccah and Sarah took charge of the cooking and domestic arrangements for the three days of the mourning. The money was used to buy relish and maize-meal. On the first day no one in Kapipi's knew that Abel had any relatives at all and Ngosa, an unemployed Lala living in the compound who was not a close friend of Abel but his only fellow-tribesman, took charge of Abel's house, which had no lock on the door, and received those who came to mourn. Ngosa explained that he was guarding the house until he could hand over to Abel's relatives when they came. (By this time the news of the Market officials' meeting with Chisenga had reached Kapipi's.) Ngosa and some of the other Kapipi's mourners were worried by the fact that, although Abel was a single man with a successful business, he had not even left a suitcase of clothes in his house or put a lock on the door. Another friend of his, at whose house Abel had called on the morning he was knocked down, had noticed that he did not have his money-bag with him and when he came to the house found that it was not there either. Conspicuous by their absence were Vyvyan and Wallace, Ngoni from the Eastern Province who were intimate friends and joking-partners of Abel. They lived next door and had often eaten from his food. They were suspected of being at least implicated in the disappearance of his money-bag and belongings. However the residents of Kapipi's were intent on keeping their suspicions concealed from Abel's relatives and this mystery was never solved. Four months later Duncan, who came to live in the house, had heard nothing about it. The result, however, was that during the period of mourning Abel's closest leisure-time associates were absent and members of his *extended* network moved to the forefront.

It is noticeable here that the mourners were almost all his tribal joking-partners, *ambuye*, and that those of his own tribe, such as Ngosa, were treated as quasi-kinsmen by the mourners from the Eastern Province. This will be considered in greater detail later in the case. It contrasts with the situation in Case 3, the well-provided family, where many fellow-tribesmen fulfilled the roles of funeral friends, *bali*, corresponding to their clan membership. In that case almost all the mourners were Lala and, except, at one stage, tribal joking-relationships did not enter into the situation.

After the arrival of Bota all decisions were left for him to take and Ngosa ceased to play any further part in the organization once he had handed over to Gregory the accounts book in which he was recording the contributions of individuals and party sub-branches. Offisi and Paul, the Kapipi's party leaders, bought the food but after that also ceased to play a conspicuous part in the organization. Exceptions were at the burial itself, when Paul carried a black flag, emblazoned with a white A.N.C., which they had made. He and Adam sat in the truck as it carried the coffin through the streets of Lusaka with the flag unfurled and planted it in the grave mound to mark the grave as the mourners left. And on the last day Paul was responsible for supervising the clearing-up operation. Apart from Ngosa there were no other Lala or Northern Provincials present from Kapipi's and the only mourner who was not from the Eastern Province and who played an active part was Ursula, a Kaonde neighbour of Abel. She made a major mistake on the last day when she asked for money in payment for helping to clear up the site. Helen and Doris, kinswomen of Abel, and Rebeccah and Sarah, the leaders of the A.N.C. joking tribesmen, reacted angrily to Ursula's justification of her demand on the grounds that in Chibolya (an old site-and-service compound), she had seen the 'owners of the funeral' pay the sweepers money. Helen called to them, 'Don't talk so much. Oh, leave her. Our *ambuye* (joking tribesmen) will do it.' Ursula withdrew. In a situation where urban tribal joking-relationships were being played out in funeral responsibilities she was an outsider who had not acclimatized herself to the prevailing atmosphere, however correct her knowledge of what went on in Chibolya.

As soon as Bota arrived Chisenga was obliged, as his daughter's husband, to assist him in the arrangements left to the kinsmen; obtaining the death certificate from the Government offices, collecting clothes for the burial (which were found to be missing because there was no suitcase in Abel's house), and in collecting the relatives as they arrived and transporting them to Kapipi's. Chisenga had never been to Kapipi's before and was alarmed by the thought of going there at all. (Unauthorized areas have a reputation for violence, vice and political deviance.) Chisenga was not only unwilling to sleep at the house of the deceased himself but tried to persuade Bota to return with him. There was a difference of opinion with Gregory over such 'uncustomary' behaviour and Chisenga returned to his house alone with his friend, Luke, who was driving him. Gregory supplanted Chisenga. Bota spent the second night after Abel's death (his first in Lusaka after arrival) at Kapipi's with Gregory and the rest of his kinsmen who had arrived. Early the following morning they walked to the hospital mortuary, and when Chisenga arrived to collect them he found they had already left. There had been some misunderstanding about the time of the burial and Chisenga was blamed for being late in collecting them for food before it. He was sent off to collect clothes from Kapipi's and drive to the cemetery. As already mentioned there were none, but he brought a blanket. As they had not found any themselves, however, Bota and Gregory had already bought a new blanket which they used instead, rejecting the one Chisenga had brought. Gregory had not been in touch with the marketeers himself and when they did not arrive at the expected time he arranged for a truck to come from his place of work to transport the mourners from the mortuary to the cemetery. In fact, there had been a confusion of the time of collection and the time of the burial. The result was that those kinsmen and residents of Kapipi's who had walked to the hospital were taken to the cemetery on the side of Matero suburb called Chingwele in Gregory's truck, whilst the remainder of the residents of Kapipi who wanted to go and the marketeers went in trucks hired at half-price from Boniface and another contractor.

However, once the chairman of the Market Company, Christian, had arrived at the cemetery in Boniface's *Chevrolet*, Gregory was also supplanted and Christian, with his market colleagues, took charge of the direction of the mourning, the preparation for burial, the funeral procession and the burial itself. Bota and other kinsmen actually prepared the dead for burial as he was a man and decisions were ostensibly left to them, such as when Bota was called on to arbitrate in a dispute between Christian and Chibeka, a political opponent who insisted on the correct procedure of taking farewell of the dead before the closing of the coffin. He decided in favour of Chibeka. For the rest Bota followed the directions of Christian. At the burial Bota and Gregory were asked to make speeches and to cast earth into the grave 'to bury' the dead, and Chisenga's Ngoni colleague was called to say the prayers. Bota was told where to stand, when to act and when to get back into line. Once this was done Christian gathered the Market officials on a nearby mound and, after the grave was filled in, gave an oration in praise of Abel and, with the help of the treasurer's report, explained in addition the projected role of the Market Company in burials and the bonus (dividend) payable to Abel the day he died. 'Abel died at a quarter to six from a motorcar on the 21st December. He has been a member of the Lusaka Market Company Limited since 1948 and has been a very good man. If someone was in trouble he would loan them 10s. if they needed it. He was a well-known man and a man who did not want to quarrel with friends. During my work at the market Abel has never given me any trouble. He was a cheerful man and I wanted to hand him his bonus of 1s. 6d. on Monday but he never touched it.

He died at a quarter to six and I was supposed to give it to him at seven o'clock. Now all those who had debts with Abel or from whom Abel borrowed anything should come to my office and complain. I am going to refund them. If it is 6*d.* or wood worth 6*d.* you come to the office and I will try to pay you back.'

Throughout this period Christian was advised by Elias, one of Lusaka's long-term residents, who has buried so many that he is regarded as an authority in the matter. He was particularly attentive to the behaviour of the mourners and the sequence of events and ended the ceremony by singing one of the Dutch Reformed Church hymns lustily. At only one stage were Christian and Elias challenged successfully. As already mentioned, when Christian wanted to prevent the final viewing of the dead Chibeka strode forward objecting 'Let the people see him. That's our custom.' Christian was forced to concede when Bota agreed with her. Thereafter Chibeka, who is as staunchly and prominently U.N.I.P. as the rest are A.N.C., redirected all orders given to the women mourners by Christian but intervened no more. The most prominent woman mourner, who belonged to Abel's own tribal group, was Doris, who, because of her part-Bisa ancestry and long acquaintance with Abel deemed herself a relative and acted accordingly.[1] She was prostrate at the burial, and on return to the market went over to lament at Abel's woodpile followed by all the other women, before she went out to Kapipi's where she sat inside the house of the deceased with the other kinswoman, Helen. It was conspicuous that Chibeka had no role to play as an organizer and that though a tribal-group member she was not a prominent mourner. Had this been a U.N.I.P. mourning ceremony the situation would have been different but here she was present, as far as everyone else was concerned, as a market member and no more. She did not come to Kapipi's.

After the burial Christian and the marketeers as an association withdrew from corporate participation, after arranging with Bota who should succeed to Abel's bonus and stand in the market, 'provided he becomes one of us'. After a short family discussion it was decided that Abel's sister's younger son should succeed as he was unemployed. Offisi, on behalf of Kapipi's, completed this by asking Bota to recommend a successor to Abel's position and residence in Kapipi's. Duncan was again recommended and accepted. For one more night the mourners gathered at Abel's house and on the following morning Bota gave a speech of thanks to those who had mourned his younger brother's

---

[1] The Bisa and the Lala come from adjacent districts and are often classed together, particularly by outsiders such as in tribal joking-relationships as in Case 3, or, as in this case, in the relative absence of full fellow-tribesmen.

death and helped during the period of mourning. The neighbours and
fellow party members returned home and the marketeers to work.
The kinsmen remained for an hour to have a final meal before their
journeys and to complete their own arrangements. Gregory was left
with the duty of pursuing the police enquiry. Bota went to stay with
Chisenga and laid claim to Abel's bicycle. And Duncan took up residence in Abel's single-roomed hut, took over his business and the rest
of his effects.[1]

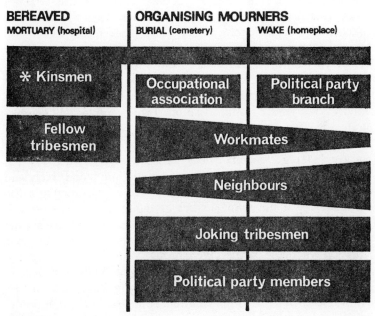

BEREAVED	ORGANISING MOURNERS	
MORTUARY (hospital)	BURIAL (cemetery)	WAKE (homeplace)
* Kinsmen	Occupational association	Political party branch
Fellow tribesmen	Workmates	
	Neighbours	
	Joking tribesmen	
	Political party members	

 Indicates membership of both but predominance in one part (See Table X)

* Senior kinsmen were instrumental in the taking of most decisions in all
parts of the *Chililo* after their arrival.

FIGURE 19

The Case of the Run-down Wood-cutter.
Recruitment categories making up the membership of the three organizing
bodies and parts of the *Chililo* for which they were responsible

---

[1] Six months after the accident Gregory reported that the court case had gone
no further once it had been established that there was no murderous intent and
that the driver was a young lad who was not qualified to drive. Duncan had
little knowledge of his neighbours even after this time, due, he suggested, to the
fact that until four months had passed he had not been joined by his wife and

The importance of this case lies, not so much in the numbers of people involved, as in the categories of relationship from which the main participants were recruited. Due to the hitherto unknown kinship links of Abel, the relatively well-organized political-party and occupational associations to which he belonged felt they had both a responsibility and an opportunity to do something to give him a renowned mourning ceremony which would not only demonstrate their respect for Abel but also establish themselves in the public eye at a time, just after the country's Independence and the reformation of the market, that was critical for their organizations. These associational ties, however, closely coincided with those of residence and intertribal joking-relationships which gave a greater intensity to the associational ties and by contrast made tribal-group and kinship-group membership almost synonymous in this situation. Two examples will demonstrate this. An *nsima* (stiff, maize-meal porridge) seller from the Eastern Province lamented, 'I am now going to suffer. My *ambuye* (joking tribesman) has passed away. My *ambuye* has been helping me very much. He was giving me wood freely and he was joking very much with me. When he was buying *nsima* from me I was not selling it but giving it freely. *Ambuye* was buying tea for me while I was in the market.' At the market the intensity of the reciprocal joking-relationship was formed in a situation where the partners were brought together as workmates. In Kapipi's women were crying, 'They have killed our *ambuye* (joking tribesman). Our *ambuye* was very good to his *ambuye*. He was known even to the children. If he was in the compound and he wanted to go to one of the groceries children were following him saying, "*Ambuye! Chitumbo!*"[1] When he hears so he takes them all to the grocery and buys them sweets.' Hostility to the other political party, the joking relationship and neighbourliness were all strands in this relationship with Abel. In particular situations such as this members of Abel's *extended* network were instrumental in giving him a fine mourning ceremony. The good-

lived alone, working every day until dark at the market and eating there. He had not joined in the political activities of his deceased mother's brother, Abel, and for the first few months had found it difficult to re-establish Abel's business as he was unknown to potential customers.

[1] Abel had a very corpulent figure which was accentuated by his loose clothing. He was widely known as *Chitumbo*, Tubby.

will which was felt towards him had created an intensity of feeling which only his death brought into action. However due to the added presence of associational organization the situation was dealt with by these people in their corporate party and company capacity. Each was concerned with different aspects of the period of mourning and in terms of organization only the presence of a third category, the kinsmen, gave a semblance of unity to the arrangements although their tasks were different also. At one point one of the market organizers expressed distaste at the way the Kapipi's A.N.C. branch were taking advantage of the transport and carrying their flag, saying that they had hardly collected anything because they were 'poor people' but that none of the organizers had said anything because they did not want any quarrels at a 'sorry time'. The common membership of one political party did not prevent this distinction between the two associations and their rivalry. I suspect that the total amount collected was falsified in Kapipi's in order to bear comparison with that collected by the richer Market Company. It was reported as being £11 11s. 6d. The market contribution was £17 10s. 11d. in addition to which the Company itself spent even more on the coffin, mourning cloth, and transport. However a general unity was preserved by the co-existence of traders, fellow party-members and joking tribesmen.

3. *The case of the well-provided family*

This case provides a contrast with the previous two in that, although Agnes was divorced when she died, she was surrounded by members of her family and her brother, Basil's friends.

Agnes was a Lala school-teacher, the sister of a local politician, Basil, and the daughter of Chalwe, a younger sister of one of the Lala chiefs of the *bena Nyendwa*, vulva clan, who is divorced from David, a retired headmaster who was at the 'Free' Church Missions. Agnes was married to Edson but a divorce was arranged when she was advised not to have any children for six years after the death of her third Caesarian baby. There was no hostility between the families and Basil used regularly to stay with Edson on his frequent visits to Lusaka. Edson was in fact negotiating a reconciliation in order to regain the custody of his two children, Fanny and Godfrey, whom he wanted to benefit from education facilities in town at the time when Agnes died. She died suddenly in hospital in Lusaka, where she had been brought by Basil to undergo her fourth Caesarian operation. She had been made

Table XI

The Case of the Well-Provided Family (see Figure 20)

	Code Fig. 20	Sex	Tribe	Clan	Relationship to Agnes or others	Usual place of residence	Where staying at time of death	Place of Education	Occupation	Other Attributes
Agnes	A	F	Lala	Nyendwa	(Deceased)	Serenje	New Kamwala	Free Church Mission	Teacher	(Deceased)
Basil	B	M	Lala	Nyendwa	eldest brother	Serenje and New Kamwala	Serenje	Free Ch. M.	Ex Teacher Snr. Politician	Car
Chalwe	C	F	Lala	Nyendwa	Mother	Serenje	New Kamwala			Chief's sister
David	D	M	Lala	Nsoka	Father	Serenje	Serenje	Free Ch. M.	Retired Teacher	Divorced from C
Edson	E	M	M is Bemba Lala	M is Nkashi F is Tembo	ex Husband	New Kamwala	New Kamwala		Clerk	Car
Fanny	F	F	Lala	Nyendwa	D of A + E	Serenje	New Kamwala			
Godfrey	G	M	Lala	Nyendwa	S of A + E	Serenje	New Kamwala			
Hermia	H	F	Lala		Wife of B	Serenje				
Ibbotson	II	M	Clrd		Cousin of A	Lusaka	n 'Town			Car
Anson	AA	M	Lala	Nyendwa	M elder ZS	Kitwe		Free Ch. M.	Police	
Benson	BB	M	Lala	Nyendwa	younger B	North Western Province			Clerk	
Changwe	CC	M	Lala	Nyendwa	youngest B	Kitwe staying with AA		Free Ch. M.	Nil	
Doreen	DD	F	Lala	Nyendwa	younger Z of C	Serenje				
Jelita	J	F	Lala	Tembo	MBD (Cross Cousin)	Nr. Lusaka				
Kunda	K	M	Lala	Mfula (Bali)	MBDH	Nr. Lusaka		Free Ch. M.	Teacher	

Name		Sex	Tribe	Descent	Relationship	Location		Free Ch. M.	Occupation	Notes
Lazarus	L	M	Lala	Nguni F is Bl (Sister Clan to Nyendwa) M is Nkashi	W is Nyendwa	New Kamwala		Free Ch. M.	Teacher	Once taught by D
Mark		M	Lala			Chilenje			Teacher	Car
Norman	N	M	Lala	M is Nguni (Bali)	MMZSS of J (Cross Cousin)	Lusaka	in 'Town'	Free Ch. M.	Snr. Teacher	
Oliver		M	Lala	Mwanso (Bali)	W of O	Near Lusaka		Free Ch. M.	Clerk	
Patsy		F	Lala	Ngandu	ex colleague	Near Lusaka				
Quentin		M	Swaka		'Friend'	New Kamwala		Free Ch. M.	Teacher	Car
Rabson		M	Lala		Colleague of B	Serenje			Snr. Teacher	Driver of R's Car
Samuel		M	Bemba		Colleague of B	Serenje			Snr. Politician	Driver of B's Car
Tylo		M	Lala	F is Ngoma M is Nguni (Bali)		Serenje			Driver/Party Official	
Unwin		M	Lala		Jnr. Employee of B's Party	Serenje			Party Driver	Driver Party Land-Rover
Vumbe		M	Kunda		Snr. Colleague of B's Party	New Kamwala			Snr. National Politician	Came in Party Car
Walter		M	Lala	Besa	Wife of W	New Kamwala		Free Ch. M.	Clerk	Car
Christina		F	Lala		Friend of B	New Kamwala	in 'Town'			
Yuwiti		M	Lala		Joking tribe	Lusaka			Gov. Official Social Welfare Worker at Lusaka Hospital	
Zebedee		M	Yao			New Kamwala				
Xerxes		M	Yao		Joking tribe	Matero			Leader of Group of mourners	Mourning at own *Chillo*
Youngson		M	Ngoni		Joking tribe	Matero			Teacher	

pregnant by Rabson, her occupational superior, under the threat of blocking her salary increment. She was rushed to hospital in an ambulance and only Edson and Lazarus were immediately aware of her death besides Chalwe, as her brother was absent in Serenje.

At this point the *effective* and *extended* parts of the family's network were mobilized to deal with the crisis, as almost all of Agnes's kin were absent in Serenje or the other places where they work and only her elderly mother, Chalwe, was staying with her at Basil's house. Due to the complexity of the arrangements and the fact that most of those involved do not fall into simple categories as in Case 2, it will be necessary to follow the sequence of events closely as it is only in this way that the communication links demonstrating the ties between individual Lala and their ramifications will become apparent. Again it is not helpful to separate the network into parts as other duties often override those of friendship and those on the periphery of the *extended*, leisure-time network are often in the centre of the funeral organization, performing necessary tasks and filling defined roles.

Throughout the early stages of preparation for the period of mourning, four men were pre-eminent; Edson received the news from the

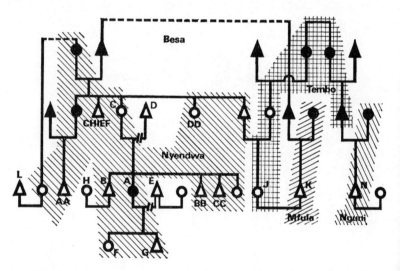

▬ ▬ ▬ ▬ Putative clan link

FIGURE 20

The Case of the Well-provided Family.
Genealogy of Agnes showing kinship and clanship. Inclusion in hatched areas indicates common clan membership. *Nyendwa* is the clan of most chiefs of the Lala tribe. (See Table XI)

hospital at 5.00 a.m. and came to tell Chalwe, whom he thought was staying with Lazarus, a former pupil of David's whose wife is of the same clan as Agnes, and Norman, an eminent and related tribesman. Lazarus obtained permission from his headmaster to be released from his teaching duties and walked around New Kamwala and to Emmasdale and Matero telling all the Lala from Serenje of his acquaintance of the death. By the time he reached Emmasdale School, some five miles away, he found that Norman who was in a car had got there before him. Lazarus then returned to take charge of the house in New Kamwala and told Chalwe not to go to the hospital to mourn until the next day by which time other relatives would have arrived. By 9.00 a.m. Kunda a 'funeral friend' of the *Mfula* (rain) clan[1] had come in from his school outside Lusaka, where he had received a telephone call from Norman. With Edson they discussed the collection of money by Lazarus and Walter, and firewood. Jelita, Kunda's wife and a cross-cousin (*mufyala*) to Agnes, and Christina and Patsy collected maize meal from the other Lala women they knew and some of Agnes's

---

[1] Father Stefanizyn's account of *Funeral Friendship in Central Africa* (1950) is particulary relevant here as his material is drawn from the Ambo of the Luangwa valley whose ties with the Lala are very strong. He indicates both the stages of the funeral itself, and the clans which are 'funeral friends' of other clans. From the material which I was able to collect whilst on a short fieldwork tour in Chief Kafinda's area of Serenje in 1963, and in Lusaka from Lala informants from Chief Mailo's area I was able to find out the clans which have this relationship to the *bena Nyendwa* in these two areas. Mr Norman Long, who completed an extensive research tour in Serenje in 1964, has kindly given me further information relating to Serenje as a whole which considerably extends and confirms what I had found and has advised me on my presentation of the Lala ethnography, but for any errors I alone am to blame. Without going into detail it is important to point out that the *bali*, funeral friends or joking clansmen, may be divided into three: Those 'general' clans like the *bena mfula*, rain, and *bena mbulo*, iron, which joke with many other clans as well; those that have a special relationship with the chiefly clan for historical reasons like the *bena Mbushi*, goat (Munday, 1961: 13 and 17), or due to their involvement as objects in the burial ritual like the *bena Ngoma*, drum; and finally those that for reasons of physical dependence or association are paired with the *bena Nyendwa*, vulva, like the *bena Mwanso*, penis (see Table XI for clans in this case). Stefanizyn's paragraph (1964: 6) is relevant to the Lala as well as the Swaka. The Ambo regard these as sister clans. It should be noted that the *bena Mfula* have special funeral duties towards the particular chiefs in this case, and also that one of the few Lala chiefs that is not of the *bena Nyendwa* is of the *bena Bi*, anus (see Figure 20). Since this paper was first written, Fr. Stefanizyn's book *Social and Ritual Life of the Ambo of Northern Rhodesia* has been published (O.U.P. for I.A.I. 1964). This gives a full account of Death, Succession and Inheritance in Chapter Six.

Bemba-speaking friends. The latter included some of the officials of
the women's brigade of U.N.I.P., the party of which Basil is a senior
member, but no organized collection was made by the brigade as an
association.

In the meantime Edson had telephoned Tylo at his workplace in
Serenje who then told Basil of his sister's death. Basil left for Lusaka
immediately, driven by Tylo, arriving at 5.00 p.m. Samuel waited to
send off the party Land-Rover to collect David with other relatives
and party officials from various parts of Serenje district. He then commandeered Rabson's car and reached Lusaka at 8.30 p.m. with Rabson
and four prominent party women. The Land-Rover arrived at
10.00 p.m. In Serenje the occupational links in Basil's network had
been instrumental in achieving what was required, whereas in Lusaka
this had been done by his affines and educational ex-colleagues, who
had grown up with him and his sister at the same mission schools at
which his father, David, was a teacher.

Throughout the night Lazarus and Quentin led the women in singing hymns, whilst the rest of the men sat outside talking and drinking
chibuku, a commercial brand of maize beer, which had been bought
from the money collected. This only amounted to £1 16s. 0d. Those
who were not related were reluctant to contribute on the grounds that
they were poor men whilst Basil was enjoying the new riches of
political office. Lazarus remained in general control of the household
arrangements for the mourners and the distribution of beer and
cigarettes. He led the singing, which he explained was intended to keep
up the spirits of the women who would have been physically endangered by constant weeping. On the following day he collected the
grave number plate and made a note of it before leaving the cemetery
in order to tell late comers, and on the evening after the burial led
a jocular conversation with the men who were gathered outside.

The preparation of food was undertaken by Hermia, who came
down from Serenje with her husband, Basil, by Jelita and by Patsy, the
wife of one of the prominent 'funeral friends'. The latter two women
were responsible for the washing of the body at the cemetery with the
help of an elderly kinswoman of Chalwe.

On the morning after their arrival the relatives decided to go over
to the mortuary. As no large transport was available and central
U.N.I.P. assistance was ruled out by the preparations for the immanent
return of the Prime Minister, importance must be attached to the
attendance of car owners, Basil, Edson, Ibbotson, Mark, Rabson,
Unwin, Yuwiti, and one other teacher, whom I have excluded from
Table XI with several other Lala teachers in Lusaka in the interests of
brevity. There were in fact fourteen Lala teachers in the Lusaka area

at the time and six schoolmistresses. These cars made the movement of mourners easy. That there should have been as many as eight indicates the high status of those concerned in this mourning ceremony. It is characteristic of most functions involving residents of New Kamwala, where, according to a survey in March 1964, one house in every seven had a car.[1] Mark made a great display of his sports car, driving at high speed to the doors of the undertaking room carrying purchases of soap and black cloth. He took charge of one of the mortuary mourning parties and attempted to join Basil, Kunda and Samuel when they went to see the hospital doctor. His behaviour led to some hostile and mocking comment from, at least, the Serenje U.N.I.P. officials.

Kunda was primarily responsible for all arrangements both at the mortuary and the cemetery, acting after discussion with Basil and David. After obtaining the death certificate, Basil went off with Edson to buy a coffin and Samuel was sent to collect the District Commissioner's authorization. Although his car was commandeered Rabson was ignored and given no part to play. He was not given a lift to the cemetery and the black cloth he had bought to nail on the coffin was rejected. He made no attempt to help in carrying the coffin to the grave. After the burial he wanted to leave for Serenje that night but his car tyre was deflated to prevent this. However, Basil took care to prevent any open outbreak of hostility towards him during the period of the mourning saying that a family conference would decide what action to take after David's return home.[2] Probably fearing this hostility, Rabson did not spend the night at the house of mourning but with Norman, his previous superior. This fact may help to explain the relative inactivity of Norman during the period of mourning.

At the cemetery David gave all final orders and insisted, after a disagreement with Kunda, on being the first 'to bury' the dead, *ukushika* (to cast the first earth on the coffin). Administrative arrangements were however made between Basil, who spoke thanking the mourners, and Kunda, who gave a short homily on death and read prayers, after the burial. These three with the help of Edson, Mark, Quentin and Oliver, a 'funeral friend' of the *bena Mwanso* (penis clan), nailed up the coffin after the final leave-taking and carried it out of the undertaking room.

Up to this moment most of the tasks of the funeral had been carried

---

[1] This status-conscious man has rejected the clan name of his chiefly father, *bena Bi*, anus, and uses instead that of the sister clan, *bena Nyendwa*, which is that of the adjoining chiefs, from whom he claims direct descent. (For historical origins see Munday, 1961: 17.)

[2] Chalwe spent a week at David's village when they returned home although they have divorced and Basil took on the responsibility of dealing with Rabson. He was successful. Rabson was demoted and transferred.

out by occupational colleagues and ex-colleagues of Agnes and Basil, by prominent Lusaka Lala, and more specifically by those classified as affines, 'funeral friends' of appropriate clans, and cross-cousins. Now, however, another category of relationship became involved in a situation, which had hitherto been almost exclusively confined to Lala. Whilst the deceased was being prepared for burial, the funeral of an infant belonging to the Yao tribe was under way, the ceremony according to Islamic rites being the main topic of conversation of the Lala waiting around. One of their number, Xerxes, came over to tell David and Ibbotson, a coloured kinsman who was sitting with him that they would assist in the procession and the burial when their own funeral was over. This was the first time that the urban form of tribal joking relationship had shown itself during this period of mourning. The Yao have such a relationship with the Bisa which is justified by the story of how one of the Yao chiefs had died in Bisa country and had been buried by them. As the Bisa and the Lala are often classed together it was quite understandable that the Yao should do this in town for the Lala as well. What was particularly interesting was the fact that at the same time as the Yao were fulfilling their responsibilities to a specific tribal group, others from the Eastern Province were fulfilling theirs to the general Bemba-speaking reference group. When the coffin was brought out, the Yao group, numbering about a dozen, stepped forward to take it to the grave. They were relieved by Youngson and another Ngoni teacher, who had come as joking-tribesmen, together with many of the Lala, but not kinsmen. After the coffin had been lowered into the grave, Zebedee, a social welfare worker of the Yao tribe, who had heard of the death when visiting the hospital, jumped into the grave in order to put it straight and to remove the flowers to put on top. He even intervened to argue with Kunda about the correct sequence of events but was over-ruled by David. After the speeches he jumped into the grave again to shovel the earth around evenly whilst the other Lala and joking-tribesmen helped. As already mentioned David insisted on being the first 'to bury' the dead by casting in a handful of earth. He was followed by the rest of Agnes's closest kin, Basil, Benson, Changwe, Doreen and finally Fanny, and Godfrey whom Chalwe brought forward. Chalwe was prostrate with grief and was supported by Youngson.

Immediately after the burial, the Yao group went their own way and only Zebedee returned to the house of mourning. Just as this was happening the Administrative Secretary of U.N.I.P. Vumbe, arrived, with his own condolences and with a message from the Deputy Prime-Minister who was the Deputy National President of the Party. This was, however, the only point at which the National Headquarters of the Party participated in the mourning ceremony. The mourners then went back to the house in New Kamwala, some of them like Ibbotson to take their leave immediately, most to spend the night there. The same men and women were in charge of operations as on the previous night. Basil went off with Yuwiti, who had been unable to come to the burial, for an evening drink. The women sat inside as before, the closest matrilineal kinswomen in a room of their own. The men gathered in a circle around the fire with David in the centre introducing themselves to him so that he could trace their genealogical connections with each other. On the next morning, David thanked the mourners for coming and arrangements were made to take those from Serenje back again. Agnes's two children, Fanny and Godfrey, were divided between Chalwe and Basil and taken from their father, Edson, until a decision had been taken as to whether he should be given custody of them which he had been negotiating before Agnes's death. The decision was later taken in Serenje that he should not be given them but that on his frequent visits to Lusaka, Basil would bring Godfrey to stay with his father, Edson.

Except at the point of burial this crisis was dealt with almost entirely by the members of Agnes's and especially Basil's networks, which was composed of members of the educational and political mileux within which they had grown up, worked and lived, and which comprised members of their own tribe. Not only were these network members mobilized but also the kinship network members, some of whom were also in other categories. Classificatory affines, in particular sons-in-law (*bakweni*), and a cross-cousin (*mufyala*), were active at the most crucial stages. Not only does this sort of crisis call forth all the human resources an individual can muster, i.e. his social network, but the nature of the reaction and the categories involved demonstrate his past life history and status, and that of his whole family, as well as his kinship and neighbourhood ties. In such a situation people may be brought to the forefront whose frequency of contact may be slight and whose interests may not be in common with the central person. In Case 3 they were men from Basil's past *effective* network who play little part in his present one which is largely composed of his political associates, as was clearly demonstrated by Basil's movements a week later when he came down to Lusaka again for the Independence celebrations and spent the time with Samuel, Tylo and Unwin.

The analyses of these three cases have concentrated on the way in which the people concerned were recruited to carry out certain necessary tasks at the time of greatest organizational crisis. I have not been concerned with the more prolonged critical period for the bereaved following the main ceremonies of mourning. It was apparent, months after the death, that some of the kinsmen in Cases 2 and 3 were still deeply disturbed by what had happened. In Case 1 it was obvious that all the helpers tried to do was to give Alice's daughter a decent burial. Alice demanded no more of them and only Queenie tried to give any personal comfort. All three cases differ widely in the status groups involved, and this is apparent from the occupational columns of the tables. Whereas Alice in Case 1 was destitute with no status strings to pull, in Case 2 Abel was a well-known character in self-employed and A.N.C. circles with some high-status relatives who were not very welcome to the former because of their different political colour. In Case 3, Agnes came from a family which enjoys both high traditional and educated modern status. There was discussion as to whether to take her body back to Serenje for burial with the rest of the royal line. Transport could be obtained to bring down a considerable section of the family and make movements in Lusaka easy. Except for the Yao, whose presence at the cemetery was fortuitous, nearly all those involved were of high status including even Anson, a policeman who could not come but paid for Benson, who is unemployed, to come. That is to say they were all people who commanded some position of influence in the community in Lusaka or Serenje, though none except possibly Basil is pre-eminent. Finally, the different numbers of mourners attending these funerals should be noted as it will be a total with which to compare the figures of those active in their organization. The counts were taken by myself at the cemetery.

Table XII

Number of Mourners attending the Burial

Funeral	Men	Women	Total
Case 1	5	3	8
Case 2	112	102	214
Case 3	35	60	95

It will be seen that in Table IX all those at the burial are included, but only the organizers in Cases 2 and 3. The large number of men present in Case 2 is partly due to the fact that many of them are self-employed or unemployed, and that the Market Company laid on transport. It is also indicative of the Market Company's aims that they took a poll of their own which they reported to be 1580! In Case 3, many men who were at work were represented by their wives, including members of the ruling political élite. Others came at night to greet David and offer their condolences.

Choice of recruitment to the social network
From the foregoing cases it emerges that what matters as much as the intensity of the relationships and the inter-connectedness of the members of the network is the content of those relationships with reference to particular situations. That is to say, those who are members of the leisure-time *effective* network may not necessarily be within it in another situational context, and in such crisis situations as those concerning death, the use of the *extended* network concept as a recruitment field may be more helpful. The tasks to be carried out are more or less prescribed but the categories from which the participants may be drawn are numerous and, in town, not prescribed.

If the various means of recruiting members to an individual's network are considered this point will be clear. Whereas in a rural society such a network must consist largely of kin, clan and tribal members operating in a varying but enduring system of social relationships, in town there are more fields of social interaction and they may be less inclusive of each other. There is, for example, no reason why work-mates may not be quite separate from neighbours. The over-arching structure that does exist, the administrative and economic system, does so at a remote and less personal level than in a rural area or monolithic company town (see Epstein, 1958: 20, Diagram 3, and Harries–Jones, 1964, Diagram facing p. 31). There exists a theoretical possibility of an infinite variety of social contact between people. Individuals are not isolated in the urban mass, at any rate not in Lusaka. Although it is a large town, one only has to observe the main street at even the busiest times to see the knots of individuals of every age, sex and status which are gathered in conversation on the pavement. The concept of the social network is a useful tool to analyse the bases of these relationships.

Generally speaking bonds of kinship are enduring but actual relationships may become dormant and only be resuscitated at certain stages in the life cycle or in particular situations, as happened to the kinsmen of the run-down wood-cutter. Unlike many other urban personal relationships the bonds of kinship are not chosen by the individual concerned. They exist regardless of his attitudes. (I include such phenomena as *Ubwali*, the joking-clan-relationship here.) However, as in the rural situation where kinship relations may be classified according to prescribed patterns of status and intimacy, which connections are actuated and which are left dormant result from the reactions of the parties concerned (see van Velsen, 1964). Usually only fragments of the kinship universe are present in any one town, and the members may even then be widely scattered and in different occupations, especially in a place like Lusaka where even government employment is departmentalized, as Case 3 shows. But however scattered and however strained links may be between the members, their existence is known to one another and on such occasions as the birth of a baby or the death of one of them these ties may be utilized. Others may establish putative kinship links through the use of similar clan or geographical origins and so construct a web of kinship, as Ngosa and Doris did in Case 2. Whether putative or real these kinship connections are optative in as far as they are actuated. It is up to individuals to decide which contacts to use and which to ignore.

The same is true of tribal co-membership. As Mitchell (1960: 32) and Epstein (1958: 231–33) point out tribalism is a category of common reference in a multi-tribal society. Its strength as a single category lies in the relative scarcity of its members and its important characteristics are the mutual intelligibility of its languages and the similarity of its customary behaviour. The importance of tribe as a category of reference is demonstrated in the case of the 'lonely' escort, not only in her initial hospital contacts but in those extended by the Anglican lay-reader, Isaac. It has already been pointed out (Mitchell, 1956: 39) that broad regional, linguistic and cultural differences are what matter in town, not the distinction between, for example, Chishinga and Bemba tribal membership. In Lusaka, however, though Nsenga, Ngoni and Chewa may be classed together under the Ngoni name by others, so large a proportion of the population is drawn

Table XIII

Percentage of Adults belonging to the 18 Numerically (by Males) most numerous Tribes in Lusaka by Types of Settlement[1]

TRIBE AND SOCIAL TYPE	Chilenje/Matero %	Subtotal %	Other Municipal %	Subtotal %	Private Compounds %	Subtotal %	Unauthorized Compounds %	Subtotal %	Total Population of Both Tribes %	Subtotal %
Bemba	13·7		6·8		5·0		7·6		9·3	
Bisa	2·7		2·4		1·6		2·1		2·3	
Lala	2·5		—		—		1·5		1·3	
Northern Matrilineal		18·9		9·2		6·6		11·2		12·9
Kaonde-Ila	2·4		0·9		1·0		1·5		1·6	
Tonga	2·9		3·2		6·3		5·4		4·2	
Lenje	6·7		6·4		5·0		3·4		5·5	
Soli	2·9		2·4		5·4		5·1		3·8	
Central Matrilineal		14·9		12·9		17·7		15·4		15·1
Kaonde	4·7		3·2		2·4		3·3		3·6	
Luvale	0·8		0·9		0·4		1·8		0·9	
Western Matrilineal		5·5		4·1		2·8		5·1		4·5
Lozi	5·2		4·1		4·0		3·0		4·2	
Bilateral		5·2		4·1		4·0		3·0		4·2
Lungu	2·0		2·4		0·4		2·5		1·9	
Tumbuka	4·2		4·9		6·0		1·2		3·9	
Northern Patrilineal		6·2		7·3		6·4		3·7		5·8
Nsenga	17·3		25·6		17·5		24·2		20·5	
Chewa	11·2		14·6		19·1		14·3		14·1	
Nyanja	2·9		0·9		0·6		0·6		1·5	
Yao	2·9		1·5		1·2		3·3		2·3	
Eastern Matrilineal		34·3		42·6		38·4		42·4		38·4
Shona	2·8		3·0		2·4		3·2		2·9	
Southern (S) Patrilineal		2·8		3·0		2·4		3·2		2·9
Ngoni	12·6		16·9		21·7		16·1		16·0	
Southern (N) Patrilineal		12·6		16·9		21·7		16·1		16·0
Total Population of each type of settlement		10,040		4,688		5,072		6,526		37,985

[1] Source: Bettison, D. G., 1959, Table 38.P.65-66. Classified by social type according to Mitchell, J.C. Numerical code for Tribes in the Federation. Slightly more than 20 per cent adult population belong to the 54 other tribes but no indication is given as to how these might be distributed according to Social Types or regions of origin. My own sample surveys in 1964-65 of New Kamwala, Kabwata and Kapipi's confirm the contemporary relevance of this general picture. This is to be published shortly.

from their number, 58·3 per cent, that such designation is un-helpful and also perhaps confusing due to the different kinship systems operating. Eastern Provincials themselves tend to be more specific or to refer to themselves as coming from the Eastern Province or from 'Eastern Power'.

Broad classification by reference to certain predominant tribes is however particularly marked in the justification of tribal joking-relationships.[1] Eastern Provincials are classified as Ngoni and those from the Northern Province as Bemba, and joking freedom and obligations, such as those of burying one's joking-tribesmen, structured accordingly. However it may be possible to see both this general relationship and the more specific relationships between tribes, e.g. Bisa-Yao in Case 3, in operation at the same time. Failure to be aware of the general categorizations can lead to embarrassment as in the following example. A small number of rural authority councillors had gone out to a peri-urban bar during the middle of a fortnight's course in Lusaka. All had important local political posts but a varied experience of town life. The Chewa, who had lived in Lusaka intermittently for some years, joked with the Bisa, who had had similar urban experience, in front of the Lala, who had been out of town for eleven years. The Lala looked angry and checked with the Bemba friend pres-ent whether such conduct as the Chewa had shown to the Bisa was tolerable because at home he, the Lala, would have fought a man who said anything like that. The Chewa was not his *bali* (joking-clansman). He was told that this was all right because people from the Eastern Province acted this way with all who spoke Bemba, and were like Ngoni, that is *ambuye* (joking-tribes-men). Because of his long absence from town the Lala had for-gotten about the broader categorical tribal relationships operating there and was judging this situation according to his rural experience. However, because the Bisa man was not angry, he knew the behaviour of the Chewa was somehow all right and wanted to find out the reason for this in case he was addressed in a similar manner.

It is obvious that common tribal membership may, by its regional character, be the basis for, or rather yet another link between those who call each other 'homeboys', or who were at

[1] See Mitchell, 1956, p. 30. 'Tribalism on the Copperbelt thus refers to groupings made on the basis of broad cultural differences,' *et seq.*

school together or even members of the same church. These ascribed bonds of kinship and common tribe do, in most cases, form the basis for future encounters which tend to establish an individual's pattern of relationships for many years. A study of educated middle-income men and women in New Kamwala (Boswell, 1966) shows how bonds of lasting intensity, even without regular contact, have been established through growing up together and going to school together, and that if this has been in a rural area, as was so with the 'Free' Church Mission in Case 3, 'homeboys' and ex-schoolmates are also fellow tribesmen. An urban upbringing or extended secondary education may modify this but I think the general pattern remains similar.

Certain forms of associational membership also help to perpetuate this pattern. Their urban congregations naturally reflect the regional basis of most of the mission churches. This has complicated recent trends towards church unity.[1] The United Church, on the Copperbelt, consists largely of the Northern Provincial members of the London Missionary Society and 'Free' Church (now Church of Scotland) missions. In Lusaka, the church responsible is the Methodist and the superintendent comes from the Southern Province which, with the Central Province, is the area from which the Methodists come. However most of the prominent members of the congregation are from the L.M.S. and 'Free' Church areas of the Northern Province and the main services are conducted in Bemba. In national political terms the Tonga-speakers are aligned against the Bemba-speakers and belong to the A.N.C. Although this is also the church to which the Church of Barotseland members are affiliated when in Lusaka and some Lozis do attend, a self-organized branch of this Church was founded in Chilenje as a Lozi-speaking congregation. Few of the Shona, a large proportion of whom are Methodist, attend, although they make up 10 per cent of the population of the nearest housing estate, New Kamwala. Few of them understand Bemba. In Matero they have founded their own congregation. The bulk of United Church members from the Eastern Province and Malawi, who are members of the Church of Central Africa, (Presbyterian), attend the South African Presbyterian church

[1] I should like to acknowledge the help of Reverend Hugh Fielder in confirming and amplifying my initial impressions. The period referred to immediately predates the foundation of the United Church of Zambia in 1964.

further along the road, which uses their own language, Nyanja. This is an indication of the way in which education, religion, language and region of origin may all lead towards the natural continuity of so-called tribalism or ethnicity. The same is obviously true of tribally-centred associations and burial societies, but these do not seem to be flourishing as independent organizations in Lusaka, perhaps because of the way churches act in cases like that of the 'lonely' escort.[1]

These ramifications do not exist, and personal choice may not operate, in the other major fields of social interaction where the situation is clearly bounded: the work situation, trades union membership, residential allocation and political organization. In very few categories of occupation or housing are employees or tenants selected knowingly on a tribal basis. Even the night-soil scavengers of the municipality are now drawn from tribes other than the Luvale. These fields are all important sources of recruitment to an individual's network, which may less often lead back to his place of origin. Of course, some employers may have a preference for those from a certain place, and some influential man may build up a core of fellow-workers through the recommendation of his kin or 'homeboys', but this is not necessarily the case. Certain interaction is prescribed by the work

---

[1] The Anglican church in Zambia originated, as far as African missions are concerned, from the visit of Bishop Hine in 1910, though its arrival in Central Africa was a direct result of Livingstone's visit to Cambridge in 1857 (see Mackintosh, 1950). Four missions were established at Mapanza, Msoro, Fiwila and Chipili in the Southern, Eastern, Central and Luapula provinces but the strength of their church lay around the shores of Lake Malawi. In Lusaka the Anglican church for the Eastern suburbs uses Nsenga in its services. The membership of its council and influential lay hierarchy consists of: seven Eastern Provincials (Nsenga and Kunda) excluding the priest; four Malawians (the recently departed priest was also a Nyanja); one Tonga, who spent his working life in S. Rhodesia (the two others from the Southern Province are influential but not councillors and on the periphery of the congregation. Few originating from the Southern Province attend); one from the Central Province, who has lived much of his life in Southern Rhodesia; one from the Northern Province; two regional outsiders from Barotseland and Southern Rhodesia whom the lay reader has involved in affairs, with those from the Southern and Central Provinces, in order to get other language groups represented.

Mr Richard Chata, to whom I am most grateful for the above information, is a lay reader, the secretary of the church council and the secretary of the Eastern Province Burial Society.

process but there is considerable scope for choosing friends within the total membership of the work group, which is set up by an outside force, the management (see Kapferer, B. *supra* pp.214).

In a suburb or location, the situation is initially similar since the allocation of houses is determined by employers working through the Housing Officers of the Municipality, but, in the course of time, as some move out and others stay and their children marry within the suburb, the possibilities for choosing one's neighbours increases. This has happened in Old Kabwata. In an unauthorized compound, like Kapipi's, the opportunities for such personal choices are much greater and houses may be built in clusters based on kinship or other ties, such as Bettison's team found in the peri-urban area of Blantyre-Limbe (Bettison, 1958: 44. clusters and accretions). The establishment of neighbourhood ties with his joking tribesmen was a marked feature of the run-down wood-cutter's network. In New Kamwala, the relatively high educational standards of the residents implies past contact because of the small number of appropriate schools available until very recently. We have already seen, in Case 3, how the bonds of growing up at the same schools together or being taught by the same teacher had created a set of Lala who could be mobilized. This is also true of the Lozi, who form over 10 per cent of New Kamwala's population. It seems that this may be because they have tended to be drawn from the same upper-stratum of their society and to have gone to the same schools, because of the particular policy of the Paramount Chief and his special relationship with the Paris Evangelical Missionary Society and the foundation of the Barotse National School (see Mortimer, 1957). As neighbours, they do have much in common with each other or at any rate others near them. The neighbourly involvement of husbands and wives tends to differ, however. The wives are usually less mobile with fewer external sources of recruiting friends and with their activities centred on the kitchen and the yard which necessitates some neighbourly contacts. These may initially be established by their children. The husbands may draw on their work situation in a similar way. At the time of a period of mourning it is the women who contribute maize meal and make house-to-house collections. Only the men who attend are expected to contribute money. Though it may lead to some disapproval it is often the case that male neighbours do not get involved, but it would be much more difficult for women because they live together and are often dependent on each other for small household items.

Apart from the churches, membership of which tends to reinforce existing divisions in the community, except for the Roman Catholic church and the Jehovah's Witnesses who are universal, the only other major category of association is the political party. Whatever may be said about the regional, tribal or linguistic distinctions between the mass of rural supporters of the two parties, the same cannot be so confidently asserted for the two parties in Lusaka. Though it is certainly true that most of the Bemba are U.N.I.P. and most Tonga are A.N.C., the bulk of the support for both parties must come from the Eastern Provincials who are most numerous in Lusaka (see Table XIII), and the strength of the opposition party in the eastern half of the city is certainly based on its 'Ngoni' officials. In Kapipi's, for example, thirteen of the twenty-one adult officials are from the Eastern Province. This combination of party, neighbourhood and joking-relationship ties was the basis of the organization of the run-down wood-cutter's mourning ceremonies. Probably only kinship acts as a bond between the members of different parties and the strains inherent in political division were apparent in this case as well.

From this consideration of the categories of social encounter which may lead to the establishment of social relationships and inevitably limit an individual's possibilities of choice, it will be clear that the existence of an intense *effective* set of relationships must be related to the situations in which they become intense and *effective*. The leisure-time network is only one of these and may not be the most significant when it comes to taking important decisions or actions, e.g. those who meet all day at work but live distant from one another may discuss all they have to at work, including economic assistance. They need not meet out of hours. Others 'move' together all the time. The former may be the most interlocked in economic matters, the latter in leisure-time activities.

From these cases it emerges that the social network may be seen as representing a series and an ongoing set of social relationships. At various stages of an individual's life his network is composed entirely of kinsmen, to which are added schoolfellows, workmates, associational members, affines etc. At any one stage in life he may draw predominantly from one or other but a few from each are likely to survive throughout, and some connections are activated in certain conditions and some are dormant. There is a tendency to include in the intense *effective* network only those with whom an individual has an amicable relationship. However if one takes a confined situation such as the work group or neighbourhood it is obvious that hostile relationships are equally important and that there may be intense relationships which are disruptive. These tensions cannot be ignored if the individual plays a vital part in the work process, or the domestic life of the street or village is disturbed, or, for example, if ties of kinship conflict with those of political association. These tensions were most apparent in Case 2 where Gregory did not trust the marketeers' transport organization and in Case 3 where Rabson was clearly rejected because of the particular circumstances of his involvement in the death.

During the course of life an individual's social network will be liable to expansion due to recruitment from the categories indicated, as in Case 3 with Basil, the ex-teacher and politician, and be further influenced by his social and geographical mobility. It will further be affected by his changing familial status as marriage and parenthood open and close paths to future interaction. Links with many past members of earlier *effective* networks may remain dormant unless activated by a change of circumstances. Had Agnes, in Case 3, died in Serenje probably very little would have been done in Lusaka if Basil had also been away in Serenje. Nevertheless, at any one time, the members of the whole social network are in the potential position of being mobilized to deal with a crisis situation. Depending on the gravity and type of the latter, links long dormant may be brought into an instrumental relationship again, as in Cases 2 and 3, or even created on the grounds of categorical affinity, as in Case 1, where the lonely mother was able to mobilize her own tribeswomen and mission links. An understanding of the ways in which the set of relationships analysed as the social network may be used in such crisis situations as death is crucial to the understanding of how such problems are met and solutions reached. Recent writing on African urbanization has emphasized the importance of formal associational membership in the socialization of the urban immigrant (Dubb as cited in P. Mayer, 1961; Little, 1957; Banton, 1957 *et alia*). The social network encompasses the general structure of informal relationships as well as those operating within confined institutional and associational structures, and the concept has the flexibility required for the analysis of the development of interrelationships over time, in different places, from various categories, many of which may only be apparent during a crisis situation.

CHAPTER VIII

'Home-boy' Ties and Political Organization in a Copperbelt Township[1]

by
P. Harries-Jones

Introduction

The importance of the social category 'home-boy' for studying the formation of small groups in urban areas of Southern Africa has been ably demonstrated by Philip Mayer (1961) and Monica Wilson (1963). Mayer's work is of particular interest to the study of social relations in Zambian towns because of the criticism he levels at previous urban research in Zambia and of the importance he attaches to the study of urban networks to rectify what he believes to be the major flaws of previous research.

Mayer's argument, developed in an article in the *American Anthropologist* (1962: 576–92) is that Mitchell (1956) and Epstein (1958) in their justified concern to counter the then prevailing tendency of viewing urban problems as problems of 'detribalization' emphasized the on-going nature of urban institutions and the continuities of the urban 'social field' in which these institutions appeared. But in doing so, their heavy emphasis on 'town' as a series of overlapping institutions 'feeding back' into each other had produced a rather rigid notion of an urban-rural dichotomy. In their analysis the 'urban social field' was opposed to the 'rural social field' and while it was true that they had tried to align both by proposing that a migrant coming to town was able to switch from one 'field' to another, that is to say a migrant could play urban roles while he was in town and rural roles while he was in the country, this was not a sufficient understanding of social change. Mitchell and Epstein had presented a 'static and schizoid picture of the migrant's social personality', a picture which misinterpreted the real problem of social change, namely the shift of balance in the migrant's social personality

---

[1] My particular thanks are due to Mr A. A. Nyirenda for his help in collecting fieldwork data.

from the ties he maintains with his home village, through his 'home people', to the ties he develops within town, which are purely town oriented. A study of how country-born people can become townsmen in the sense of shifting their personal centres of gravity from their home areas to urban clusters, from 'extra-town ties' to 'within-town ties' opens up a new historical perspective for the understanding of social change on a comparative basis throughout Africa. At the moment, Mayer says, the peculiar treatment of Copperbelt material had rendered it unique.

Mayer's strictures on Mitchell and Epstein's concepts of 'social field' may well be sustained. Viewing town as some form of total social system, and town-based institutions as forms of sub-systems within the total system, involves peculiarly difficult problems of how the sub-systems articulate both with one another and with the system as a whole. Hence as Mitchell points out in the introduction to this book, one of the major advantages of network analysis is to abstract urban material in a different way, to trace the connection between the individual and partial, rather than total, systems, while still underlining the importance of pressures on individuals involved in conflicting expectations as a result of living in town. At the outset, therefore, application of network analysis to the Zambian urban scene could well lead to the sort of comparative data on the shift of balance between 'within town ties' and 'extra-town ties' that Mayer feels is so conspicuously lacking. But here one must protest that the Zambian material already published shows that so far as comparability is concerned, it is South Africa, rather than Zambia, that raises problems of unique material. First, as Wilson points out (1963: 180), the State in South Africa has acted for some years as the strait-jacket in which all local social groupings are welded, as it is the State, rather than any one group, that claims a man's total allegiance. Hence the decision to join one group or another is often artificial in the sense that the urban social system presents choices that are sharp, arbitrarily defined by white administrators, and often antithetical.

Second, the time scale of urban residence and experience of urban life in South Africa, particularly in Cape Province, has been much longer than most of the rest of Africa south of the Sahara. While it may be true that over a long period of time the migrant's shift away from 'home-boy' ties is a key study, in shorter periods of urban residence more typical of Zambia and the rest of Africa, the opposition Mayer draws between 'extra-town' ties and 'within-town ties' is not so clear cut. Of more importance for the study of social change are the varying emphases placed on 'home-boy' relationships. 'Home-boys' are important for mutual aid and services, but such mutual aid is not exclusive to this category. Equally, the situations in which ego will want to identify himself with 'home-boys' or accuse others of promoting 'tribalism' will vary. In the context of securing compensation for adultery, pressure brought by 'home-boys' may be crucial (Harries-Jones, 1964); in political organization identification among 'home-boys' is important in specific circumstances. On the other hand, it would be difficult to find a voluntary organization of long standing in which there was no evidence of clusters of 'home-boys'.

The Bemba word *bakumwesu*—'those that are from my home' —is equivalent to the Xhosa word *amakhaya*, translated by Wilson as 'home-boys' and by Mayer as 'home-people'. But the multi-ethnic compositions of the Copperbelt has made the term more flexible in use than its South African counterpart.[1] A Lamba whose village lay in the hinterland of Luanshya would attach the same significance to *bakumwesu* as his Xhosa counterpart; a Bemba might speak of *bakumwesu* as people coming from villages in his own administrative district, while others whose 'bomas' (administrative districts) included two or more tribes, such as those who live in the Luapula valley, might make little of their different tribal affiliations in describing themselves as *bakumwesu*.[2]

The relativity of the term is emphasized by the fact that in town

[1] Mayer says the term *amakhaya* 'is a term primarily applied to people from one's own rural location . . . (administrative unit under a headman). . . . The definition of home-people in town may be stretched to include, if necessary, people from these nearby locations', i.e. those who have ties resulting from marriage or those which have the practice of stick-fights, between respective gangs of boys (Mayer, 1961: 99–100) Wilson states: 'Home-boys are those who come from one neighbourhood (*isiphaluka*). The size of the area, which is important, varies with the number of men coming from it to Cape Town; often it is those from one rural village or "location" under one headman, but if the village is large, and many of its members are in Cape Town, the effective group for most purposes will be those from a section of the village . . . (but) All those from one magisterial district are recognized as home-boys in some sense irrespective of numbers' (Wilson, 1963: 47).
[2] But there are specific reasons for this. See Cunnison (1959).

only some from among several who could be chosen in any given context would be specifically recognized as *uwakumwesu* (sing. a person from home). This may depend on such factors as physical propinquity of one family to another, or even on emotional nearness.

My concern in this paper is to discuss the category *bakumwesu* in political organization of a single Copperbelt town, Luanshya. Luanshya was, while I was in the field, dominated by the presence of the United National Independence Party, its officials, active supporters, and sympathizers. In the 1962 and 1964 general elections, U.N.I.P. gained between 93 and 98 per cent of valid votes cast in the constituencies in which Luanshya was incorporated. Throughout both election campaigns and until I left the field at the beginning of 1965 U.N.I.P. officials both at local and national level exhorted its members to think in terms of the slogan 'One Zambia, One Nation.' Ethnicity and tribalism, race and colour were political straw-men constantly condemned as divisive and destructive of the aims of the Party, which presented itself as an all-embracing association working for the common welfare of every inhabitant of Zambia.

In view of the vigour of the politicians' denunciation, it is obvious that the appearance of *bakumwesu* ties in local organization of the party would not be immediately apparent, and that the formation of groups or factions within the hierarchy of the party through *bakumwesu* ties could be discounted as evidence of 'tribalism'. In order to examine their importance, therefore, I intend to contrast use of these ties in two different situations. In the first I will examine their significance in relation to the lowest unit of U.N.I.P.'s organizational hierarchy, the cell or 'section'. In the second situation I wish to consider their importance for M. and C., prominent local politicians. The first situation bears on territorially defined relations during the period of three to five months; the second relates to the interaction of a faction and a clique derived from two 'action-sets', a term which Adrian Mayer has proposed to describe an interacting series of people that have been purposively brought into a relation with each other by the action of a single individual, whose relationship to them is nevertheless ephemeral so that they in no way constitute a 'group' (Adrian Mayer 1966: 97–122).

In this paper I follow Mayer's use of the term with reservations.

I would wish to define more explicitly than Mayer the relation between 'action-sets' and ego-centred or 'personal' networks. Further, while accepting the usefulness of his term 'action-sets'. I would criticize the usefulness of his concomitant term 'quasi-group', to denote a series of action-sets built up by an individual over time. Connotatively the term 'quasi-group' is ambiguous, its ambiguity arising from the confusion of a discrete social phenomenon, *the group*, with a methodological technique, *network*. The ambiguities in the term become compounded when transcribing empirical relationships drawn from fieldwork material into graphs of these relations. In an appendix to this paper I have set out some formal objections to Mayer's arguments. Here, I would note that I have deliberately avoided the use of the term 'quasi-group' and that I view the relation between an action-set and a personal network as follows: an action-set is a series of links within a personal network which describes ego's communication for a specific purpose (in this case political influence) over a short period of time.

The basic technical terms I wish to employ in this paper are 'category', 'ego-centred' or 'personal' network, 'action-set' and 'link'. In addition I wish to use the terms 'total network', 'clique', 'faction', 'commune', and 'semi-path'. Each bears a relation to the other. 'Total network', 'personal network', and 'category', may be considered together. A 'total network' may be described as a set of elements (people) and a set of relations (links) in which the set of people may or may not be finite and the set of links may or may not be finite. Within 'total network' arises a 'category', which is a finite set of people and a finite set of links, the set of links between people being defined either by the observer in virtue of the set of people having at least a single social attribute in common, or defined by a multiple of individuals in virtue of their regarding the set of people as having at least a single social attribute in common. Within the 'total network' are 'personal networks'. A 'personal network' is a sub-set of a total network, the sub-set having a finite number of persons and associated links. The sub-set is termed an 'ego-centred' or 'personal' network if it has the property that an ego has a 'pole position' in the sub-set so that all other persons and their links are ordered with reference to this 'pole position'.

'Action-set', 'clique', and 'faction' may also be considered together. As defined above an 'action-set' is, like a personal network, oriented to ego and arises as a sub-set of ego's personal network. It describes an interacting series of people that have purposively been brought into relation by a single individual. An action-set over time will change. Though ephemeral, repetitive use may be made of its links in which case an action-set may result in the formation of a 'clique' or a 'faction'. A 'clique' is defined by the interaction of its participants in relation to the organization of the co-activity of the participants. A 'clique's' participants have considerable interaction and the pattern of their co-activity shows diffuse organization analogous to that of a group. However, a clique lacks the corporate and persistent characteristics of group activity and is hardly likely to survive changes in personnel. Like a 'category', a 'clique' may be formally recognized by the people themselves, or be identified by the observer. Following Adrian Mayer I describe 'factions' as 'units of conflict, activated on specific occasions rather than maintained by formal organization . . . "loosely ordered" and with "structurally diverse" bases of recruitment . . . they are made manifest through a linkage of personal authority between leader and follower' (Mayer, 1966: 116). Both cliques and factions may merge into formal groups, or arise within formal groups. This is particularly true in the political context and as Mayer points out, over time an action-set may become the basis of a political faction, which in turn becomes the basis of a branch of a political party. Below I cite such an example from my fieldwork. Equally, the process is reversible. Former leaders of a political branch may later form a 'clique' or become leaders of a faction within the party. At some other point of time, former political colleagues may be an important part of ego's action-set.

Finally, we may consider the terms 'link', 'semi-path', and 'commune'. Any 'link' or set of 'links' between people is defined in virtue of the content that either the actor or the observer gives to the 'link'. When transcribed to a graph of links between ego and others in a network, a link becomes a 'semi-path' describing a relation between ordered pairs of points which represent people. 'Commune' is a term derived from Harary, Norman and Cartwright (1965) to represent certain aspects of reachability in a communication network. Harary, Norman and Cartwright think of a 'commune' as a 'strong set' in a communication network, namely a maximal collection of people who can engage one another in two-way communication, so that if a message was transmitted to one member of this 'commune' all other members would be bound to receive it. As I wish to use the term, it would represent those who would be able to engage in a dialogue about political action, so that if ego transmits a message to A, B, and C, ego would know that A, B, and C are members of different 'communes' and that his message would be transmitted to all members of A, B, and C's respective 'communes'. Ego would thus be able to 'reach' people he may not even meet by maintaining communications with A, B, and C.

To summarize, the purpose of the paper is to assess the importance of a category of people known as *abakumwesu* for political organization in Luanshya by using techniques of network analysis. One of these techniques is the identification and use of action-sets in different situations over time. The other is to identify personal networks within a particular neighbourhood and to show how the presence of *abakumwesu* ties in these personal networks may affect the grass roots of political organization in Luanshya. But before I begin a detailed examination of both, I wish to make some assessment of *abakumwesu* as a source of recruitment of personnel for intended political action, and relate this to known changes in political organization.

'Abakumwesu' and political change

At the outset we may make a distinction between the types of social interaction ego may have with his 'home-boys'. There are the 'home-boys' of his neighbourhood (*chitente*) and the 'home-boys' who are important to ego in maintaining his ties with his rural home. The latter may be spread over several towns on the Copperbelt. Though there is no absolute distinction between the two, the 'home-boys' of his neighbourhood are recognized in purposive action of a political or economic kind, such as the establishment of mutual credit relations, and are essentially local ties of fairly short duration—the average length of residence in any neighbourhood being only two to three years. On the other hand, the 'home-boys' who are important for maintaining his ties with his rural home are usually near kin; the ties he has with these are often first established in ego's district of origin. These 'home-boys' are important to ego because, as may be supposed, he has a

continuing series of rights and duties towards them. The extent
to which these are maintained may be variable. Generally they are
stronger when he arrives in a new community that is, arrives for
the first time on the Copperbelt, or shifts from one town to
another on the Copperbelt. Compared with those whom he
defines as 'home-boys' within the neighbourhood, these latter are
his communication links with his rural home, and so long as links
with home remain important to him, contact with the latter type
of *abakumwesu* will remain.

The distinction I have drawn between 'home-boys' of the
neighbourhood and those 'home-boys' who are important to a
person for maintaining ties with his rural home is not one of kind.
In the past such a distinction was minimal as many rights and
duties of an *abakumwesu* were formally defined. In the past ego's
links with *abakumwesu* were at once political and economic as well
as involving him in specified obligations, such as hospitality and
participation in mourning. Formerly ego had a 'home-boy' who
stood as the representative of his rural chief in the urban area and
who, as a result, had authority not only over other 'home-boys'
but also over those of ego's own tribe. In some cases this 'tribal
elder' had extended authority over members of other tribes who
had no specific representative of their own.

The existence of these accepted leaders tended to channel
multiple 'home-boy' links both between town and rural area and
within town itself, in a direct path—with the Elder standing at
the nodal point. The Elder would arrange contact with 'home-
boys' when strangers came to town, and repatriation to rural
areas; he would hear domestic disputes and settle quarrels between
neighbours. The Elders saw themselves as 'fathers of the location'
and all people recognizing their authority as their 'children'. They
saw themselves as guardian of law and morals of the urban community whose function it was, through instruction and advice,
to re-affirm the values of rural society in town (Epstein, 1958: 58).
As late as 1953 Epstein noted a deep respect for Elders, and said
few in the township did not know who their Elder was.

Though Copperbelt anthropologists have spoken of 'tribal'
rather than 'home-boy' contacts in their analyses, some of their
comments regarding tribal cohesiveness also serve as an indication
of 'home-boy' cohesiveness. In 1951 a survey of drinking partners,
an important consideration as drinking is a main leisure time

activity, revealed that 88 per cent of the sample chose drinking companions from among their fellow tribesmen (Mitchell, 1956: 18). A concurrent analysis of dance teams, an equally important leisure time activity, revealed that the majority of single men (17 out of 23 observed) participating in the Kalela Dance could be described as 'home-boys'. There is also evidence that employers outside the big mining companies tried to hire labourers on a tribal basis, which would have increased the chances of 'home-boys' working together as 'home-boys' are the first to hear, under these circumstances about job vacancies. Finally, one of the clearest demonstrations of 'home-boy' solidarity on the Copperbelt was the way in which unmarried men congregated in 'single quarters' according to their district of origin. Mitchell's unpublished survey material of 1951–52 demonstrates this striking feature.

In general, therefore, the fairly widespread occurrence of 'home-boy' or tribal contacts at work and during leisure time suggests that any outward links from ego would, for the most part, be subsumed by links with other home-boys, particularly since those with 'domestic' authority, the Tribal Elders, espoused moral virtues of such contact. Further, it is likely that, if graphed, the structure of the links from ego, to 'home-boys,' to tribal elders, would accord with the observation that Barnes made about rural African societies, namely that of the many possible links that could lead away from ego to A to B to . . . N, in fact links lead back from N . . . to B to A to ego after only a few steps (1954: 44).

With the decline of the tribal elder system throughout the 1950s the overlapping ties linking *bakumwesu* in multiple activities also tended to decline. Unlike West Africa, new voluntary associations did not have a pronounced ethnic base. This was particularly evident in political organization and can be shown with reference to the appearance of a branch of the African National Congress in Luanshya, as documented by Epstein. The formal constitution of the branch was preceded by the appearance of a vitally important action-set initiated by C. I speak of a 'branch' but as Epstein noted, the word 'branch' was almost inappropriate since there was no membership bound by rules and no regular contributions planned. 'Congress organization,' he said, 'was built up through a large number of small nuclei . . . each designed to organize the community as a whole on some specific issue, for some specific purpose' (1958: 180). He then goes on to describe how each nucleus seized upon the possibility of utilizing political feeling for its own ends. The Chairman of the Hawkers' Association wanted to use Congress to advance his and his fellow Hawkers' cause of permitting Africans to open tea-rooms in one township and allowing Hawkers permits to trade in another. The Secretary of the Shop Assistant Union wished to use the new branch to get back at Banda, a member of the Urban Advisory Council whom he thought had double-crossed him. Epstein notes: (1958: 182)

> As secretary of the Shop Assistants' Union he was a leader in what was probably the strongest trade union in the (township). Nevertheless his influence was limited. So he decided upon the formation of a Congress branch since Congress was the one body which, since it cut across divisions created by occupation and tribalism, could give him the strength and support he required.

Another committee member of the Shop Assistants' Union, as well as being one of the first tribal elders to be elected in the township, also had a grudge against Banda on the ground that the latter had once accused him of neglecting his duties as a deacon in the church, a grudge he continued to hold because he thought Banda wanted the post.

In the years immediately following the butchers' boycott C, the former secretary of the Shop Assistants' Union, maintained and enlarged the action-set he had successfully established. Adrian Mayer would say that C was the focal point of a 'quasi-group', but Mayer's definition of a 'quasi-group' would suggest that the *same* people in C's initial action-set were used in successive periods to maintain his influence. However, though C stayed within the township, members of his initial action-set did not, and mobility within the township generally militated against the formation of a 'quasi-group'. The initial members of C's action-set were representatives of various groups and voluntary organizations in the township. Those who planned the butchers' boycott were representatives of the Hawkers' Association, the Shop Assistant' Union, the African Mineworkers' Union, the Presbyterian Church, Tribal Elders, and so forth. In the years following the boycott, C maintained contact with the organizations' new representatives, rather than his initial contacts, some of whom had gone. During any short-time period during the 1950s a visitor might describe C's relations with these revolving representatives as a 'clique', there being fairly frequent interaction and some degree of diffuse political organization. At the same time the term 'clique' seems inappropriate as their activity remained oriented to C. Hence a better way to look at C's communication with these representatives of various institutions over a long period of time is to speak of C keeping in contact with various 'communes'. By maintaining contact with these communes, C remained in political communication with a very much wider number of people than he was able to influence directly (see below pp. 335 ff. for further discussion).

As the African National Congress 'branch' in Luanshya continued to be dominated for some years by C's action-set this proved to be both its inherent weakness as well as its source of strength. For it was obvious that no one action-set, no matter how well interpersonal relations were manipulated within it, could ensure the continued massive, unquestioned response from the community that was necessary to force any significant political change. The 'branch' organized protest boycotts of the beerhall, held public meetings from time to time and tried to raise money for the party, but my own interviews with current political leaders in Luanshya suggest that the 'branch' made little impact in these years on those who would have been prepared to work for political independence. In fairness to the branch, the party leadership above it did little to improve the branch's impact. National leaders of the African National Congress made only infrequent visits to Luanshya, and when they did they spent much of their time with branch officials rather than concentrating on building up party membership in Mikomfwa township.

Formal organization of a Congress branch, as distinct from the complex paths of C's action-set, started in 1958 when Africans throughout the Territory were given limited executive powers in local authority areas. Elections to a local authority board on a ward basis returned a solid bloc of Congress candidates determined to use the limited executive powers to further the aims of the A.N.C. But the following year this bloc, in a dramatic move, defected from the ranks of A.N.C. and joined the rival United National Independence Party—now the ruling party of Zambia. From its inception U.N.I.P. showed itself capable of running a

chain of command from the national executive to the local
branches and from the local branches to the people. It quickly
proved that people would turn out when it called for a demonstration. At the same time the party realized that scattered or even
deliberately phased demonstrations alone were not enough. If the
party were to lead the country to independence against a largely
unified body of White voters who held institutional power, the
party's own organization would have to give the appearance of
massive strength. The party needed an urban population that
would not only demonstrate, but keep on demonstrating around
the clock, if need be. And, equally important, the party needed the
funds from the urban population to offset mounting costs.

As a result, in late 1961 the party established a series of cells or
'sections', as they were called, within each urban township.[1] In
Mikomfwa Township, Luanshya, 'sections' were established in
housing areas which corresponded roughly to those which had
been designated as wards for the 1958 local authority Housing
Board election. Specially selected political activists, chosen on the
basis of their attendance record at secret meetings during previous
months, were called to U.N.I.P.'s regional offices on the Copperbelt and instructed on section organization. Initially these activists were to return to Mikomfwa and contact those friends in
designated areas whom they knew to have attended some of the
recent 'secret' meetings of the party, relatives, and *bakumwesu*.
These friends, relatives and *bakumwesu* were then, in turn, to
contact more relatives and more *bakumwesu* until in each cell or
section ten to fifteen people had agreed to form a committee. The
political activist would then return to the section area and super-
vise elections of committees.

Section organization was conducted in an atmosphere of
secrecy and tension. Officials of the party at branch, constituency,
and regional levels spoke of the sections as being the 'heart' of
the party's political organization, and section members thought
of themselves as the 'eyes and ears of the party'. An atmosphere
of secrecy surrounding section deliberations and section decisions

[1] The previous discussion has left out consideration of the Zambia African
National Congress, the first splinter group from the African National Congress.
Z.A.N.C. was banned almost as soon as it was founded but the enthusiasm it
aroused carried over into the United National Independence Party, many
officials of Z.A.N.C. and U.N.I.P. being the same people.

lasted, in fact, not only during the whole of the organization period, but for many months after political independence. But there was a physical limit to secret deliberation. Section meetings, unlike public meetings, had to be held inside closed doors and the maximum attendance at such a meeting was the number who could squeeze into the standard two-room dwellings, that is approximately 50 to 60 people. If meetings showed signs of rising above this level, then the section split in two. Despite splits, there was no instance in Mikomfwa where *all* householders in a section area became constant political attenders. Officials tried to insure that a *significant* number came to section meetings, a number who by their presence in the meetings and loyalty to various tasks set them exerted enough pressure on the non-attenders to produce general conformity to section policy.

The systematic use of *bakumwesu* links by the political activists had both central and peripheral effects on the distribution of power in Luanshya. The immediate effects at the centre were short-lived, and, though structurally important, were unlikely to have occurred elsewhere. In Mikomfwa, political activists selected for the task of organizing the sections were themselves *bakumwesu* from Luapula. They constituted a third of the committee members at constituency level, had important 'home-boys' in the branch, and were able to extend their links into the 'sections' as a result of the opportunity given to them. But almost as soon as this action-set, initiated by M had been established, the political activists were cut off from the source of their potential power. U.N.I.P.'s regional office alleged that the Luanshya constituency had misappropriated a sum of money from the 'Freedom Fund' and all but one constituency official (who was not from Luapula) were removed from office. An uneasy relationship existed between the dismissed organizers and the new constituency officials for more than two years afterwards, the dismissed organizers still responding to the activities of M who managed to maintain his political prestige, if not his office. At a later date it is possible to demonstrate how M's action-set became crucial in organizing an anti-constituency faction.

In summary, this section has shown how the juxtaposition of political links and *abakumwesu* ties changed over a period of ten to fifteen years in Luanshya. Starting from a period when there was a formal organization of *abakumwesu* links through tribal elders—and such political action as was available to the inhabitants of the African townships was channelled through the tribal elders—recruitment of *abakumwesu* became increasingly less important for initiating political action. The heterogeneous content of C's action-set demonstrates this point. This situation was once more reversed when the United National Independence Party began forming its 'sections' or political cells in an effort to involve all the people of the townships in the struggle for independence, and not merely leaders who had influence enough to conduct scattered boycotts. The problem now is to gauge the extent of this reversal.

The political significance of 'abakumwesu' in the neighbourhood
Section organization imposed well defined territorial boundaries on blocks of householders whose awareness of territorial unity previously had mostly been confined to shared ablution facilities. Before section organization money loans, food collections, funeral arrangements, the settling of marital disputes and disputes with employers were handled through agencies in which the Church, the townships' Estates Office, the Tribal Elders, and trade unions all played their part. The section soon came to offer a single alternative outlet for such social action. At the outset the section behaved as if it were the 'eyes and ears' of U.N.I.P. Early section meetings were taken up with discussion of how best to 'instruct' people who showed little inclination to join the party, to denounce those opposed to section formation as African National Congress or United Federal Party 'stooges'[1] to report on the activities of White people who might be paying Africans to inform, and, in fact, to identify any strange or unusual activities that were seen or suspected within section boundaries. In short, the section was a mutual protection committee of U.N.I.P. supporters who felt strongly enough about the political situation to patrol their boundaries throughout the night, and to question all strangers during the day.

In the months prior to Zambia's independence (October, 1964) the mutual protection aspect of section organization began to die away and sections began to adopt the function of a 'friendly

[1] The United Federal Party was the party of the Federal Prime Minister, Sir Roy Welensky and during the 1962 election campaign purportedly tried to 'buy' African votes. For an account of this campaign together with an analysis of election returns see Mulford, David C., (1964).

society'. Some signs of this had been apparent since mid-1963. For instance, when a section attender was jailed for political offences, section leaders would organize the payment of house rent and see that a regular supply of maize meal went to the wife of the imprisoned man. Collections of maize meal also went from the section to the branch where unemployed youths, whose parents themselves were out of work, could come to collect free food. Perhaps most important of all, the sections, as from April, 1963, became responsible for the organization of burials in the community, regardless of whether the deceased was a section attender or not.

Active membership of the section became an option to be weighed for its advantages and disadvantages. To become or remain an active section attender meant the possibility of being elected a section official with the prestige attached to that post. It was also widely believed by section attenders that they and their children would secure priority in any benefits government decided to bestow on hardworking party members. This belief vied in the minds of section officials with any political principles behind their section work, such as 'working for the good of the country'. On the other hand section attendance meant an inroad into free time—at least four hours a week for section officials—as well as some financial sacrifice, since it was from political levies in these sections that much of the local branch and constituency business was paid for.

Section committees by 1964 had under their control a whole body of formal and semi-formal procedures of social control from settling marital disputes to arranging burials and the repatriation of widows. Thus the freedom of choice an individual had as to whether he should remain a section attender was limited, as he was unable to opt out entirely from the section's influence. It was true that, apart from burial arrangements, the section had no monopoly of these procedures. A householder could find means of settling disputes, or means of obtaining credit other than through the sections. When the occasion arose he could still visit church, Tribal Elder, trade union or Housing Estates Officer, if he wished. But it was no mere coincidence that section attenders spoke of their territory as *umushi*, 'the village', and the section chairman in a meeting addressed those present as *abene ba mushi*, 'people of the village', for in the short space of two or three years, householders' relationships had become more formally structured in virtue of political commitment.

However, unlike relations in a rural village, relations among members of a *chitente* did not mean that each had definite rights and duties towards each of the others. First, some members of the *chitente* were excluded from having to make any firm decision about political commitment. Second, the degree of cohesiveness resulting from opposition to section attendance was variable. At any given moment the decision the householder made with regard to attendance or non-attendance rested to a great degree on the balance between the relationship he had with his local section organizer in the neighbourhood and the strength of his ties with those whom he regarded as 'home-boys' in the neighbourhood. To illustrate the degrees to which links within neighbourhoods were structured by section organization, I have chosen to analyse in detail a particular *chitente* whose boundaries are cut by its division into parts of two different sections. The sections whose divisions meet within the neighbourhood, Sections 1A and 1B had above average attendance for section meetings during the period in which I was in the field. Average attendance for seven sections (i.e. half Mikomfwa's total number) was 26·24 householders per section, while Section 1A registered 28·28 and Section 1B 29·06 householders per section respectively.[1] That part of the neighbourhood which lay within Section 1B had the highest ratio of attenders to non-attenders of any neighbourhood within either of the two sections, and it is this area to which I will pay particular attention. Figure 21 represents the *chitente*, or neighbourhood.[2] It is bounded by the tarmac Accra Road on two sides; a dirt street, Lagos Street joins Accra Road and created the partition between Sections 1A and 1B. A small footpath runs beside houses 506 to 509 and leads to a bottle store; their front doors face the footpath as does the front door of house 521. Houses next to Accra Road, numbers 510, 511, 512 and numbers

[1] Figures were obtained from section secretaries in nine of the twelve sections in Mikomfwa, housing predominantly married couples. These figures were double checked with the Branch secretary's list and, as a result, two were discarded as unreliable. The figures listed here refer to the remaining seven sections.

[2] Note that from hereon personal names, house numbers and other physical descriptions are fictitious.

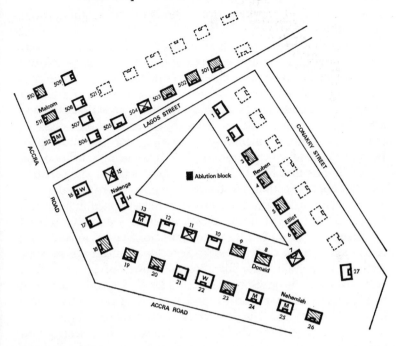

FIGURE 21
Map of neighbourhood

16 to 26 face towards the tarmac, but all other houses face towards each other across an open triangle of grass, near the middle of which is an ablution block for washing and showering. Identification of this *chitente's* boundaries is made easy by the triangular arrangement of the houses and the fact that front doors face inwards, but by no means all neighbourhoods are so distinguishable. Though the diagram gives a greater geographical precision to the neighbourhood than is perhaps understood by its inhabitants, only one house, number 27, not already included within the

area described, is important for a discussion of neighbourhood relationships.

During the early 1950s this and adjacent neighbourhoods were known as the best housing area in the municipal townships. Now it is regarded, by those who choose to differentiate, as accommodating the *bapanshi*, or 'low ones'. House rents at £2 2s. per month are among the lowest obtainable for married quarters and a high proportion of the residents are either labourers, charcoal sellers, hawkers or unemployed, earning, for the most part, between £5 and £11 per month. When the neighbourhood was originally organized by U.N.I.P.'s political activists, the partition which divided Section 1A from 1B along the route of Lagos Street did not exist. Both sections were incorporated into a much larger section of 525 households known as Section 1. Section 1 organizers for U.N.I.P. were householders 8, 26 and 511. After the branch had divided Section 1 into two separate sections, householder 26, Silas, became trustee of Section 1B, a position which is advisory. Householder 8, Donald, continued to organize Section 1B up to the Lagos Street boundary, while householder 511 continued to work for a while as organizer in Section 1A. Then householder 511, Malcom, was elected to a higher official position within the section. Just before the study of the neighbourhood began he became Chairman of Section 1A. He considered himself, therefore, as *uwapamulu* (top man) and felt that organization of the neighbourhood was no longer his task. This was work best left to those under him. But promotion did not dim the respect he held for his former co-organizer, Donald, and Malcom regarded the houses across Lagos Street as *umushi wa Donald*, Donald's 'village'.

Donald, a short, energetic man, was very conscious of his being an official of U.N.I.P. and of the position this gave him within the neighbourhood in terms of both respect and authority. He spoke of himself as the senior man of the neighbourhood and expected to be treated as such, cutting others short if respect was not given to him. Neighbours mostly gave him respect, not only because of his official party position but because he had lived in the neighbourhood longer than most, some five years. He regarded it as his duty to see that every person in his neighbourhood became a section attender and that there were none who could be called *balofwa* (loafers). To Donald 'everyone' did not mean every household, rather every 'eligible' household. He did not, for instance, try to approach the Malawians in the *chitente* because 'the Malawians have their own section meetings'. Nor did he try to organize members of Watchtower (Jehovah's Witnesses) whose religious convictions stopped their participating in any political activities. 'At the moment', said Donald, 'we are not worried about the Watchtowers. But the time will come when we shall be told by the branch what to do with them.' Donald also recognized that there were some householders in his 'village' who were often away on business and as impermanent residents these were also left unvisited on his periodic membership drives.

The exclusion of these three categories of people reduced the number of 'visits' necessary to keep pressure on actual or potential section attenders by about a third. Householders 7, 11 and 15 were all recognized, for reasons ranging from fish trading on the Luapula to frequent trips away delivering cars, as 'impermanent residents'. Three householders, 13, 24 and 25, were Malawians, while a set of two householders, 16 and 22, were Watchtower members. Another householder, 10, was also an objector on moral grounds to joining in any neighbourhood association. He was a Seventh Day Adventist who regarded the *chitente*—section attenders or not—as a neighbourhood of drunkards, and only kept company with Seventh Day Adventists from other neighbourhoods.

Of the categories of householders excluded from Donald's visiting, the most important were the Malawians. Their leader was Nehemiah, householder 25, a man of about 65 years of age who had been an adviser to his chief in Malawi in his younger days. He had come to Luanshya some 12 years ago and even before his active political participation in the Malawi Congress Party was known as a close confidant of the recognized 'elder' of the Malawi people in Mikomfwa. With the growth of the Malawi Congress branch in Mikomfwa, Nehemiah had assumed political prominence, together with his wife, who had become active in the Malawi Women's League. Nehemiah was the 'chief adviser' of the M.C.P. branch and M.C.P. meetings were often held at his home.

Despite the esteem with which he was regarded by Malawians, Nehemiah said that most other people in the neighbourhood regarded him as a foreigner. Nehemiah reciprocated this by recognizing a political and ethnic division between Malawians and Zambians in the neighbourhood. He and other Malawians had nothing to do with section or section meetings, he said, as those were for the people of Zambia. Though he recognized that some Malawians in other neighbourhoods attended Zambian section meetings, he was adamant that this was against M.C.P. policy. As with other members of the Congress branch he had tried to put pressure on those participating in U.N.I.P. section meetings to give them up. He wished to see all householders have one party card only, so it was clear where their allegiance lay. Those who held two cards did so 'because they were married to Zambian wives and their wives had influenced these to adopt Zambian ways', he said.

The distinction Nehemiah tried to draw between 'Zambians' and 'Malawians' was partly connected with his antipathy towards the neighbourhood U.N.I.P. organization. He regarded some of the local section and branch officials as 'foolish'. He disliked their jealousy of Malawians who were in good jobs and their policy that Zambians alone should have these jobs. Of all the junior U.N.I.P. officials, there was only one, Donald, whom he respected. Donald had been in the *chitente* as long as he, Nehemiah, had, and the latter thought Donald had earned his position within U.N.I.P. by hard work. But, Nehemiah held that his next door neighbour, Silas (householder 26) was typical of the lax moral standard of many U.N.I.P. officials: 'he changes wives like he changes his shirts'.

Thus for Nehemiah his 'home-boys', the Malawian householders numbers 13 and 24 together with householder 512 formed the most immediate (territorially considered) members of his personal network. Whenever financial help was needed they established credit among themselves—maize meal to make up for month-end shortages or cash to send their wives back on holiday to Malawi. Yet 'the Malawians' were by no means an isolated ethnic clique within the neighbourhood. The wife of one of their number, NaPhiri ran a shebeen at house 13 and as a result her social contacts cut across both ethnic and party attachments, bringing all Malawi households into active social contact with the rest of the neighbourhood. This was particularly true of 'the Malawians' relationship with Peter, householder 16, a member of the Watchtower. The latter usually joined the Malawians drinking at house 13, but since drink is supposed to be religiously prohibited to Watchtowers, Peter always stoutly maintained that he had not come to drink, but to 'preach the gospel of God' to his friends.

The self-conscious *bakumwesu* ties among members of Nehemiah's personal network was reflected in one other network of the neighbourhood. This might be described, from the observers' point of view as the 'non-attender' network, since the section attenders also had their own network centred on the position and influence of Donald in the neighbourhood. Both the 'non-attender' and the 'attender' networks were verbally antipathetic to one another, drank separately, and provided a mutual credit ring for their members. As much as Nehemiah spoke of the 'foolishness' of U.N.I.P. officials, so members of Donald's network said they had no time for non-attenders, whom they characterized as being either 'Watchtower' or 'non-Zambians'.

At the centre of the non-attender network was Soloman, a shebeen owner who had placed his granddaughter and her husband Edward in house 27 to look after his interest in Mikomfwa. All three lived together there, though Soloman would frequently spend a night or so away to check his other shebeen, run in the mine township by other near kin. His Mikomfwa shebeen was in a very suitable position, for though it was a house in a relatively poor area of the township, the *chitente* had Mikomfwa's most wealthy inhabitants living just across the Accra Road in Section 7, and was doubly fortunate in that this part of Accra Road lay halfway between the heart of the township and the light industrial area where many residents worked. As there were plenty of clients, Soloman was able to offer bottled beer as well as his own home brew, so upgrading his shebeen from the usual run of maize beer or *munkoyo* (root beer) sold in most shebeens throughout the township. Soloman's comparative wealth obtained from his trade enabled him to make loans to relatives of *bakumwesu*, a single feature that polarized the 'opposition' between section attenders and non-attenders more distinctively in this neighbourhood than in others in Section 1B.

The ramifications of the opposition between the set of non-attenders surrounding Soloman and the attenders surrounding Donald can best be described by tracing the former's real and putative kin links in the neighbourhood. These are shown in

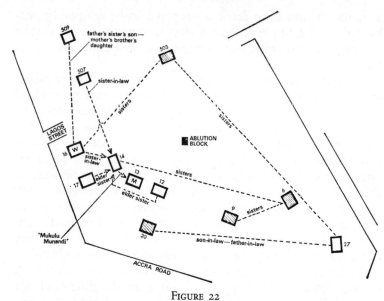

FIGURE 22

Maps of Soloman's real and putative kin links in the neighbourhood

Figures 22 and 23. Edward's wife had a putative sister at house 503, who in turn had a putative sister at house 16. Peter, the householder of No. 16 was, as noted above, a 'Watchtower', but his wife, a Lenje, kept close contact with those whom she identified as *bakumwesu* and did not share her husband's isolation. Her closest relationships were with her 'sister-in-law', the wife of householder 14 and with blood relations living at house 509, two sisters and her father's sister's son, the head of that household. The 'sister-in-law' relationship between the women of 14 and 16, was, if traced, a distant one, the husband of No. 14 being No. 16's mother's sister's husband's brother's son. But however tenuous it was sufficient to establish a firm *bakumwesu* relationship that within the alignments of the *chitente* was important for both. Here then is an indication of a difference of type between territorially defined *bakumwesu* ties and *bakumwesu* ties maintaining a person's communication links with his village of origin. *Bakumwesu* ties within an urban neighbourhood are more than that of a categorical similarity representing common 'ethnic interest'. They are important in mutual services from day-to-day. On the

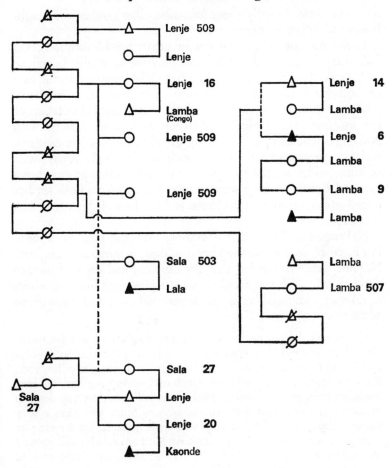

▲ Householder Section Attender
⚥ Householders living out of 'chitente'
--- Putative links

FIGURE 23

Genealogy of Soloman's real and putative links in the neighbourhood

other hand those *bakumwesu* who are important for maintaining ego's rights and obligations in his village of origin are contacted more formally, through visiting, or through agreements on the sharing accommodation of relatives who decide to stay in town

for some time. Usually these *bakumwesu* live outside the neighbourhood, often in other towns.

In the case of *bakumwesu* ties in urban neighbourhoods, kin
links may be fictionalized because they are mutually beneficial
or because they establish one in a beneficial position. In the case
of household 16, the wife, NaDorothy, had close relatives,
relatives who ensured that she did not share political isolation of
her husband. Her ability to establish an *uwakumwesu* tie with
NaLenga, wife of householder 14, greatly extended her range of
social contacts within the neighbourhood. For NaDorothy, wife
of householder 16, the *uwakumwesu* tie with NaLenga gave her a
close relationship with a woman who was respected both for her
sound advice on marital problems and her knowledge of African
medicines.

NaLenga's abilities carried authority in the neighbourhood.
For instance, on one occasion her next door neighbour's daughter,
NaPhiri, came to tell her that her husband had decided to take
another wife. 'Oh my daughter what a pity your husband wants
to take an additional wife,' exclaimed NaLenga and went on to
advise:

This is very dangerous, and you must be on the look out for medicines. I understand that your co-wife was once married to a polygamist and this makes it even more dangerous for you, my daughter.
She must know lots of medicines which may make your husband love
her more than yourself and probably even kill you. Anyway, leave it
to me for a while, and listen to my advice. Since you have a very
young baby I advise you to stay with your parents. Of course you
must get your husband's permission first, but I am sure he will be only
too willing to give it. While you're here we shall advise you what to
do when you go back to him.

NaLenga used the term 'daughter' because the young married
woman's mother referred to NaLenga as *mulongo*, sister. NaLenga
reciprocated this by referring to her Malawi neighbour as *mukulu
munandi*, in other words, an equal unrelated to her, but a possible
sister-in-law since her son might one day marry another of her
daughters. Respect for NaLenga seemed to influence two Lamba
wives of households 12 and 17 to refer to NaLenga as 'elder
sister', while another two housewives claimed blood or affinal
connections with her. NaChanda of house 6 traced common
ancestry with NaLenga back to great grandparents and claimed

that she called NaLenga 'sister' on the grounds that their respective husbands were 'brothers'; in fact, both husbands were Lenje, and *uwakumwesu* rather than 'brothers' would be a more accurate description of their relationship. The wife of house 507, Na-Button, a Bisa, said she was *mulamu* (sister-in-law) to NaLenga because her brother Tom had married one of NaLenga's cousins. But NaButton was not an intimate member of this sub-set of wives. She was disliked, not as a Bisa among Lamba and Lenje women with overlapping ties, but because she used to drink a great deal and when drunk was feared for her fighting ability.

Those wives calling themselves *bakumwesu* and expressing their relationship to each other in kinship terms was completed by houses 505, 508 and 502. NaLenga had a warm 'home-boy' relationship with the Lamba householder of 505 and this was reciprocated by his wife who, when NaLenga fell sick for a few days, was one of the first to come and comfort her. Household 508 had been in the neighbourhood for barely two months and while the wife was already participating to some extent in the Lamba-Lenje (non-attender) network, her husband still had most of his friends and those whom he called *bakumwesu* living in other neighbourhoods. Household 502 was a special case. The wife's contacts in the neighbourhood were clearly through her mother in house 2 and both had limited participation in the Lamba-Lenje network. Her husband, on the other hand, though he had registered as being a Lamba with the office supervising housing, admitted that he was Karanga from Southern Rhodesia. He felt that most people in the *chitente* were 'below his standard' and had most of his contacts in other neighbourhoods. However, he respected his father-in-law and drank with him on the occasions he returned from his w ork as a 'building contractor' to stay for a few days at home. The Southern Rhodesian also visited his neighbours, householders No. 1 and householder 503, both good friends of his father-in-law. His association with both 1 and 503 brought him into contact with Soloman of the shebeen in house 27.

For the most part, the relationships created among the women carried over to their husbands. But the example, above, is one of a husband who only partially followed his wife's links in the *chitente*; Peter, the Watchtower of No. 16, was more rigorously an exception as was NaButton's husband in house 507 who reciprocated friendship only with Malcolm, the Section Chairman of Section 1A and the Lamba household of 505, though everyone in the neighbourhood knew him as a long-term resident. The crucial exception was Elliot, the householder of No. 6, a Lenje who could have been very much at ease in the mixed Lamba-Lenje network—as was his wife—but associated with them neither at their shebeen in house 27 nor through his wife's ties with NaLenga. His reason for not doing so was specific. He was a section attender and on more than one occasion he declared that he did not associate with non-attenders. The strictness of this self-imposed rule was greatly aided by the fact that nearly all neighbours around him were attenders, except for householder 7, who was away much of the time in Luapula. Elliot's neighbours included both the organizing secretary of the section, Donald, and his brother-in-law of household 9. Elliot spent much of his time with both, all three being the best of friends, and frequently drinking together at house 9 or the shebeen at No. 13. At any one of these gatherings of Donald, Elliot, and Kaisala, his brother-in-law, other attenders would join, including householders 3, 4 and 5, and, sometimes, another Lamba attender who lived behind Elliot's house and next to the shebeen (house 27). The drinking session might well run over current section affairs, but even if they veered off current affairs, Donald was keenly listened to, his listeners addressing him as *bamadala ebene bamushi* (lit. village elder but in this context an acknowledgement of his leadership). After one such session Elliot remarked: 'We usually call on the old man because he is like our chief here and tells us all the latest news. That old man is very wise and behaves very properly. So does his wife, and that is why he is a friend of everybody in this area.'

It was significant that though Soloman (house 27) regarded Elliot as one of his *bakumwesu*, he recognized that Elliot had no interest in reciprocating this acknowledgement. Soloman's daughter put his lack of interest in her and other Lenje 'home-people' down to the fact that Elliot had contracted an intertribal marriage and that his wife would like him to be regarded as Lamba. But even if this were so, the overlapping links of Lamba and Lenje in the neighbourhood should have drawn Elliot into the non-attender network. Elliot's own rationalization for his behaviour was that when he came to live in the neighbourhood a year before he felt lonely because he did not know anyone. Then

Donald had visited him and discussed joining the section. Since Elliot had been a section attender in his previous *chitente* he had willingly agreed, and it was through the section meetings that he had come to know the friends he now moved around with.

If this argument had been put to Soloman, it is likely that the latter would have taken it as evidence proving, rather than contradicting, his point of view. Like his daughter, Soloman felt that Elliot was 'always with Lamba people', and, disregarding the fact that there were a significant number of Lamba who were among his own set of non-attenders, he categorized the Lambas in the neighbourhood as section attenders. 'No other of my *bakumwesu* are invited to U.N.I.P.'s "private meetings",' said Soloman, 'and section organizers never come to my house. They think we are African National Congress members but we are not. Though we are not invited to these private meetings, this does not stop us from attending big public meetings. Anyway, these private meetings are all organized *pachibululu* (on a kinship basis).'

To Soloman's Kaonde son-in-law, Sedi of house 20, who overheard the remark, this was a hard-headed attitude. If his father-in-law did not want to be thought of as being a member of the African National Congress, then he should prove himself to be a U.N.I.P. supporter by coming to section meetings—without waiting to be invited. Going to public meetings was not enough, Sedi admonished him, and in any case his father-in-law should not think in terms of 'tribe'. 'We are all Zambians,' said Sedi, and quoting one of the slogans constantly re-iterated in section meetings, continued, 'our President has always said "one Zambia one Nation". There are no Lozi, Bemba, Lenje or Soli— but all are Zambians.'

The exchange between Soloman and Sedi, father-in-law and son-in-law, is revealing in that Soloman saw the sections being organized on a kinship or *bakumwesu* basis, while indirectly admitting that those who did not go to the meetings were equally *bakumwesu*. Sedi, on the other hand, did not argue the pros or cons of his father-in-law's contention but objected to the fact that he had raised the subject in the first place since this was an observation totally against the aim of political unity. Partly because of the dual nature of Sedi's links in the neighbourhood, distinctions between attenders and non-attenders did not apply to him in the same way that they applied to Elliot. Sedi's

allegiance to Soloman was through his wife and was made stronger
by the fact that he wanted to move out of town eventually and
settle down in his wife's village at Mumbwa. At the same time
Sedi was *uwakumwesu* to three other households in the neighbourhood, one of whom, Ruben of house 4, persuaded the others to
become section attenders.

   Though Ruben was not a section official, he behaved as if
he were, moving around with the section leaders as they went
'visiting' members who had not appeared at meetings or trying to
persuade others to attend for the first time. Next to Donald,
Ruben was most convinced of his 'duty' to see that people were
committed to section participation, and his particular sphere of
duty lay with *bakumwesu*. Ruben met with success in recruiting
both Sedi and his workmate of house 18, also from Northwestern
Province, as well as influencing another who lived behind his
(Ruben's) own house in Conakry Street. He failed, on the other
hand, to induce householder 17 to attend. While Ruben recognized that the latter had a driving job that would make it difficult
to attend, he regarded this man as *mulofwa* 'a loafer'. Nevertheless,
Ruben contented himself with the opinion that his *uwakumwesu*
was an attender 'in spirit'.

   Ruben's enthusiasm for section participation and organization
seem to stem from his personal acquaintance with the Chairman
of Section 1B who, though living in a different neighbourhood,
was his *kapitao* (foreman) at work. But in return from his organizing efforts, Ruben received considerable respect from Sedi and
other *bakumwesu*, who regarded him as knowledgeable about
section affairs in much the same manner as Elliot regarded
Donald. Thus, though Soloman's remark about sections being
organized '*pachibululu*' seemed to be aimed against Elliot, it was
in fact more applicable to relations among his own 'kin' and
affines. In the case of other section attenders, their spatial relationship one to the other—with Donald's house as the centre of attraction—seemed as important as any real or putative *bakumwesu* links
they had. Affinal links between houses 6 and 9, Elliot and Kaisala,
had certainly influenced Elliot to join, but the nearness of his house
to Donald's and the fact that the latter was able to keep in constant
touch must also be taken into account. In the case of house 23 a
kinship connection was explicit since the householder was the
elder brother of the Section Chairman of 1B, but no such ties

influenced the decisions of houses 3, 5, or 19 to join the section. Of these houses 3 and 5 were firm section attenders, while house 19 was 'falling away'. Householder 3 came from the Congo but had no connection with householder 16, whom he knew came from the Congo but was Lamba and Watchtower. His wife, a Lala, had little contact with the Lamba-Lenje sub-set of wives and kept very much to herself and her neighbours. Householder 5 and his wife both came from the Luangwa valley and spoke Nsenga. Neither of them had any *bakumwesu* in or near the neighbourhood, and they kept close contact with their section-attending neighbours. Both householders were drinking partners of Donald and acknowledged his influence in persuading them to join the section.

Householder 19 was more unusual. Allen was a Lamba who had been living in Luanshya since childhood. He worked as a driver for a local milling company and rumour in the neighbourhood was that he was spending far beyond his means and was making up his losses by defrauding the company. The unsavoury nature of the rumour indicates the relationship between the neighbours and himself. He was disliked and he made it plain to his neighbours that he considered the people in the *chitente* as beneath him. He had even complained to the Estates Office on one occasion when he went to pay rent that the standard of his house was not good enough for him. Allen owned a car and made a great show of his wealth by taking his wife and other women around in it, entertaining them in the town bars and, according to his neighbours, returning home frequently drunk. During the fieldwork period Allen was involved in a major incident when a petrol bomb was thrown into his house late one night, the first incident of its kind in almost a year.

Soloman's reaction to it was immediate: 'You see, only a few days ago I said that if you do not attend section meetings they may mistake you for A.N.C. supporters and beat you. Attend these meetings and you can get on well with people. Look, that young man (Allen) thought far too much of himself and had no regard for other people in the section. And when it happened to him not many people came to his rescue.' Soloman was not to know that Allen was an attender. Allen's neighbours together with other section attenders, on the other hand, were concerned to show that the event was not politically inspired. They decided to hold a meeting the following evening to discuss the matter and to scotch any rumours that Allen's petrol bombing was related to a drive for membership recently launched by U.N.I.P. on a Copperbelt-wide scale. Allen's accident, they said, was a domestic matter. Allen's wife had gone 'on leave' to her parents' village some miles away and Allen had been 'entertaining' another woman in the interim period. The woman's husband had approached Allen and asked why he had abducted his wife. Allen had insulted the husband, calling him *uwapanshi* (low person) and telling him that he did not earn enough to keep a wife properly. The husband had walked away quietly and the neighbours had thought the incident finished until the petrol bombing.

Though Allen and his mistress were badly burned, none of the immediate neighbours came to help. Allen himself did not seek help from them either and instead ran naked to a house half a mile down Accra Road. The house was that of a well known Mikomfwa personality whose prowess at both soccer and beer drinking was widely admired. This person did not know Allen well, but both were frequent visitors to town bars. In Allen's *chitente* only NaButton and her husband of 507 came to his assistance. They removed Allen's smouldering furniture and helped his injured mistress. Later a municipal councillor with a car was roused and took Allen and his mistress to hospital. In perspective, the incident gives a far more complex view of the significance of section attendance than is immediately apparent. Section attendance did not, as Soloman supposed, guarantee that any person would auto-matically 'get on well with people' in the neighbourhood. By this remark Soloman was pointing to the rewards of belonging to a cluster of people who, as a result of their activity were free from gentle, or none-too-gentle external pressure, and who had certain common facilities available, such as the extension of credit to help them over immediate difficulties. But section attender or not, an individual had to have the more traditional virtue of *umuchinshi*, respect. Where such existed, as in the case of Donald and Nehemiah, recognition of the fact earned the individual a prestige that cut across the boundaries of any particular affiliation. Where there was no *umuchinshi*, the most an individual might achieve would be prestige derived from an official position, as in the case of Silas. Constant flouting of respect could lead, as in the case of Allen, to a form of social ostracism.

Political participation and the pattern of social relationships
We have dealt with how the presence of *abakumwesu* links in a neighbourhood may affect political organization at the lowest possible level. In this context it is important to realize that the section organization was imposed on pre-existing *bakumwesu* ties, not vice-versa.

Thus before the formation of sections a woman with a knowledge of African medicines and a reputed ability to give sound advice about marital disputes, and a man who was able to extend credit and supply beer would have built up extensive personal networks within the neighbourhood—both woman and man expressing social relations in their networks by use of the reciprocal term 'home-boy', whether the 'home-boy' tie was putative or real. Equally Donald's reputation as man with 'respect' and a knowledge of current affairs, or Nehemiah's close relationship with the recognized Malawi Tribal Elder may have been of sufficient social significance for men to seek their friendship. But section formation had the effect of differentiating the informal networks of the neighbourhood and categorizing relations between members of one network and another as 'strong U.N.I.P. men' 'Watchtowers' or 'Malawians'. The result was an awareness of opposition of interests between members of various networks which, although 'political', affected social relationships in the neighbourhood from day-to-day. Networks in these circumstances became more discrete. One included all those of disparate ethnic affiliation who felt bound together through common and repetitive experience of political discussion. The other two, one Malawian and one mixed Lamba-Lala-Lenje, arose as *bakumwesu* ties assumed an importance for each participant of the respective networks as they tried, in varying measure, to side-step political pressure. All three networks, noticeably, were able to provide for members facilities such as advice and credit, features which made relations in this particular neighbourhood unusually discrete.

Since it has been pointed out that sections were strongly influenced by existing *bakumwesu* ties in their formation, it would seem logical to conclude that each neighbourhood would have a cluster of *bakumwesu* significant among attenders, and 'opposed' to these, *bakumwesu* of a different tribal affiliation, who were the significant among non-attenders. Hence total section affiliation would correspond to a series of 'oppositions' among different ethnic groups in neighbourhoods throughout Mikomfwa. But though other neighbourhoods seem to be organized similarly to the one under discussion, the 'logical conclusion' is not reflected in the overall statistics on section attendance. This apparent contradiction becomes more understandable when Figure 23 is considered in relation to the margin of political pressure needed to make any one household change its mind and either become a section attender or 'fall away' from attendance. Figure 23 depicts the inter-relationship of nine heads of household, of which four were section attenders and five were not. Except for house 20, section attenders had putative rather than actual kin links with non-attenders. House 20 Soloman's Kaonde son-in-law is involved in two networks but other relations are such that a shift of allegiance from attender to non-attender, or vice-versa, would cause no radical disruption of interpersonal ties. Householders 6, 9 or 503 can enter freely into the non-attender network by stressing their putative ties equally as well as householders 27, 509, or 16 can assume *bakumwesu* relations with attenders. The restructuring of any one of these householder's relationships would be 'positional', that is, show changes of communication links within ego's network, rather than re-orienting the whole framework of his interaction. Structurally, therefore, the distinction between attenders and non-attenders in this neighbourhood, as well as in others, is not absolute. Since identification in network activities is related largely to a 'single stranded' link, that of political attendance at section meetings, the margin of pressure needed for a householder to move from attender to non-attender, or vice versa, is small. For instance, at the time of Allen's (house 19) 'accident' the sections were instructed to begin an intensive membership drive. The effect throughout the neighbourhood was rapid. Householder 1 was casual about the drive. He had been an attender once, he said, and now he felt it was time for him to join again. NaLenga's husband declared that he had been an attender for the past three months and that the section's listing of membership was wrong. NaDorothy, wife of householder 16, said that she was no longer so satisfied with the Watchtower faith as her husband, and that it was about time that she stopped being a member of this church. Edward, Soloman's son-in-law, said he would be glad to attend meetings. On the other hand, I have evidence from other sections in which comparatively small disputes have led to the dismissal of one of the section officials and where the end result is ego's dropping of section membership completely.

This 'positional' relationship of attender and non-attender households may be more closely examined by considering their links within the neighbourhood, total of all sets formed by attenders and non-attenders alike. For purposes of Table XIV, I have taken both husband's and wife's contacts into account, though I have pointed out in the text that in some cases the husbands' did not follow their wives' social contacts in the neighbourhood. The table has been compiled from constructing a digraph of the relations each household had and then considering the households to which they had most immediate contact (1-step paths) and the households to which they were joined by virtue of this immediate contact (2-step paths). If the further relationship of 3-step paths had been considered, almost all the 31 households considered would be seen to be in contact directly or indirectly with each other. The table shows that of the households which have two or more contacts in the neighbourhood, only eight of them at the primary or 1-step range have contacts which are entirely attender or entirely non-attender. At the 2-step range two households, 23 and 26, have their contacts entirely among attenders, but they both reach these through a single common primary link. Attenders therefore did not confine their relationships to other attenders, or non-attenders to non-attenders: there were some links between the two categories.

Finally consideration of husband and wife links together reveals that the networks of the three selected political leaders, Donald, Nehemiah and Soloman did not have the largest number of direct and indirect contacts in the neighbourhood. This distinction belongs to Ruben of house 4, NaPhiri, owner of the shebeen at house 13, and the respected household of NaLenga. It would seem in this example therefore that particular qualities such as organizing ability, closeness to recognized authority, or the ability to extend credit are more important in establishing a leader than a focal position of communication in any given neighbourhood. At the same time the regularity of communications flowing through section leaders as a result of their action-set becoming incorporated into the formal organization of the party is an undoubted

P. Harries-Jones

Table XIV

Links of Attenders and Non-attenders among Neighbourhood Home-boys

House No.	1–step paths	2–step paths
1.	502, 503	Nil
	2	16, 27
2.	502	503
	1	Nil
3.	4, 5, 6, 8, 9	18, (19), 20, 23, 26
	13	12, 14, 17, 24, 25, 512
4.	3, 5, 6, 8, 9, 18, 20	(19), 23, 26
	13, 17	12, 14, 16, 24, 25, 27, 512
5.	3, 4, 6, 8, 9	18, (19), 20, 23, 26
	13	12, 14, 16, 17, 24, 25, 512
6.	3, 4, 5, 8, 9	18, (19), 20, 23, 26
	13, 14	12, 16, 17, 24, 25, 505, 507, 508, 509, 512
8.	3, 4, 5, 6, 9, (19), 23, 26	18, 20
	Nil	13, 14, 17
9.	3, 4, 5, 6, 8	(19), 20, 23, 26
	13	12, 14, 16, 17, 18 24, 25, 512
12.	Nil	3, 4, 5, 6, 9, 18
	13, 14, 16, 17	22, 24, 25, 505, 507, 508, 509, 512
13.	3, 4, 5, 6, 9	8, 9, 18, 20, 503
	12, 14, 16, 17, 24, 25, 512	22, 505, 507, 508, 509
14.	6	3, 4, 5, 8, 9, 18, 511
	12, 13, 16, 17, 505, 507, 508, 509	22, 24, 25, 503, 512
16.	503	3, 4, 5, 6, 9, 18, 502
	12, 13, 14, 17, 22, 509	1, 24, 25, 27, 505, 507, 508, 512
17.	4, 18	3, 5, 6, 8, 9, 20
	12, 13, 14, 16	22, 24, 25, 503, 505, 507, 508, 509, 512
18.	4, 20	3, 5, 6, 8, 9
	17	12, 13, 14, 16, 21
19.[1]	(8)	(3, 4, 5, 6, 9, 23, 26)
	(Nil)	(Nil)
20.	4, 18	3, 5, 6, 8, 9
	27	17, 503
22.	Nil	503
	16	12, 13, 14, 17, 509
23.	8	3, 4, 5, 6, 9, (19), 26
	Nil	Nil

[1] Number 19 has been bracketed as the strength and quality of his relationships in the neighbourhood does not appear to be similar to other households under consideration, for reasons stated in the text. He has been included for completeness' sake.

House No.	1–step paths	2–step paths
24.	Nil	*3, 4, 5, 6, 9*
	13, 25, 512	12, 14, 16, 17
25.	Nil	*3, 4, 5, 6, 9*
	13, 24, 512	12, 14, 16, 17
26.	*8*	*3, 4, 5, 6, 9*, (*19*), *23*
	Nil	Nil
27.	*20*, *503*	*4, 18, 502*
	Nil	1, 16
502.	*503*	Nil
	1, 2	16, 27
503.	*502*	*20*
	1, 16, 27	2, 12, 13, 14, 17, 22, *509*
505.	Nil	*6, 511*
	14, *507*, *508*	12, 13, 16, 17, 505, *509*
507.	*511*	*6, 510*
	14, *505*, *508*, *509*	12, 13, 16, 17
508.	Nil	*6, 511*
	14, *505*, *507*, *509*	12, 13, 16, 17
509.	Nil	*6, 503, 511*
	14, 16, *507*, *508*	12, 13, 17, 22, 505
510.	*511*	Nil
	Nil	*507*
511.	*510*	Nil
	507	14, 505, *508*, *509*
512.	Nil	*3, 4, 5, 6, 9*
	13, 24, 25	12, 14, 16, 17

Note—Numbers in italics denote Section Attenders.

factor in maintaining their positions of leadership. Failure to pass messages, or to see that they were passed on, was a major consideration of section meetings and section leaders are acutely aware that once this communication flow breaks down, much of the section's political influence breaks down with it.

Political leadership and home-boy ties

To some extent a discussion of the relationship between 'home-boys' in a neighbourhood and the incorporation of individuals into political cells to work for the party overemphasizes a peripheral problem of political organization. A balanced assessment of the relationship between political organization and 'home-boy' ties must take into account the extent to which political leaders used their links with their own 'home-boys' to initiate or bolster their own political power. Leaders, in this context, I define as those who were committee members of sections, branch and constituency offices.

I have already given one example of explicit 'home-boy' ties among political leaders when I discussed M and those of his action-set who came from Luapula. These achieved prominence at the time of section organization when the closest cooperation was required among section organizers to create sections within the shortest possible time and with the maximum amount of secrecy. It is possible that through the vital part this set of leaders played in a critical period, the ramifications of their *bakumwesu* ties would have become an important consideration in the allocation of political offices throughout the constituency, branch and sections for some considerable time. But their removal from office effectively prevented an adequate assessment. Examination of the links between M and the numbers of officials in the 'eight-man cabinet' at branch and constituency levels, plus a varying number of committee members shows that those from Luapula were a strong contingent—filling between one-third and one-half of all committee posts. But this is not sufficient evidence. More revealing, perhaps, are figures drawn from the sections. I consider these more revealing because of the rapid turnover among officers at all levels of the party organization. Thus those initially recruited by M would, providing they retained interest in political affairs and attended meetings regularly, have a good chance of rising up through section and branch offices to constituency offices within the comparatively short period of two years. Hence if during section organization *bakumwesu* links were an important means of recruitment in the sections, this would later be shown in holders of branch and constituency offices. The more interesting question concerns the replacement of original section officials. Are *bakumwesu* links perpetuated in the lower offices, or are they simply a tie used politically in a single instance?

Table XV presents three columns of figures. The first column shows the total number of householders in seven political sections broken down by province of origin. The second column shows the number of section officials (members of the eight-man cabinet) and the third column shows the number of section attender households in seven sections, each household being counted if any of its male members attended section meetings regularly. It is clear from Table XV that, whereas people from Luapula constitute only 10·5 per cent of total householders and 8·9 per cent of section attender households, they contribute 20 per cent of the officials in these sections. This is to be compared with a similar over-representation among leaders from the Northern Province and a slight under-representation of officials from the Western Province. Western Province householders constituted 9·1 per cent of all households, 5·9 per cent of attender households, but only 2·9 per cent of section officials; Northern Province households constituted 26 per cent of total households, 30·2 per cent of attender households and 39 per cent of all officials. Luapula and Northern Province households, both Bemba-speaking, held between them 60 per cent of all section offices, though they constituted only 37 per cent of total households. Considering the uniformity of figures in all other columns I would consider this over-representation as significant as it is apparent.

Table XV

Political Attributes of Householders in Selected Sections by Province of Origin, 1964

	Total Householders[1] (Attenders and non-Attenders)		Section Officials[2]		Attenders[3]	
	No.	%	No.	%	No.	%
Northern	356	26·0	27	39·1	112	30·2
Eastern	296	21·6	13	18·8	97	26·1
Central	176	12·8	5	7·3	44	11·8
Luapula	144	10·5	14	20·3	33	8·9
Western	125	9·11	2	2·9	22	5·9
North West	79	5·8	3	4·3	21	5·6
Malawi	110	8·0	4	5·8	21	5·6
Other	86	6·3	1	1·4	22	5·9
Total	1372		69 3 others		372	

[1] For Seven Sections.
[2] The 'eight man cabinet' for Nine Sections.
[3] For Seven Sections

At the present stage of analysis of my fieldwork I am unable to give a full explanation of the over-representation of Northern Province section officials. Any fieldworker on the Copperbelt has a ready reason for expecting a high proportion of Northern Province officials in any voluntary association simply because of the Bemba 'presence' on the Copperbelt. Equally the political militancy of the Bemba in the Northern Province was unquestioned as was their close identification with the leadership of U.N.I.P. But I am not satisfied that general propositions of this type are entirely adequate as an explanation of the particular political circumstances in Luanshya and prefer to relate over-representation and under-representation to specific actions by specific political leaders. In the case of Luapula and Western Province the over-representation of one and the under-representation of the other may be directly related to action-sets initiated by M and C over a period of years.

M activated a number of people who assumed responsibility for political organization when normal political expression through public meetings was suppressed, namely during the months of 1959.

Links from M and the 'core' of his action-set K, W, H, and P to other *bakumwesu* shifted according to circumstances. Those officials in the sections or branch whom they had promoted as organizers before they lost office constituted one series of links; some of these were *bakumwesu*, some were not. Another series of links lay with those who for one reason or another had lost office and were disgruntled, and another series with organizations which were an integral part of U.N.I.P.'s political activity but which were not identified with election procedure in sections, branch and constituency, such as the U.N.I.P. Choir. A third series of links, more specifically 'home-boy' ties lay with the fish traders in the African market. However, many of these latter spent extended periods away from the Copperbelt travelling to and from Luapula valley.

Until such time as M with K, W, H, and P discussed the possibility of taking direct action against the leadership of the constituency, their links with others consisted largely of discussion of decisions made by the local leaders. Yet M managed to mobilize enough support at one stage to put himself back into an influential position by being nominated as a member of the constituency executive. Following this manoeuvre, M's action-set began to grow into a fully-fledged faction no longer centred entirely on the activities of M. Politicians in the constituency labelled the faction, the 'Kansengu Branch' and M himself denied affiliation with its activities. In Luanshya rules about the correctness of political behaviour were vague in many areas, such as in the handling of money, in the production of rumour, in the keeping of records, in the ability to organize. But one rule was clear: whatever differences that existed among leaders or between leaders and followers, the party must be united. Disunity, factionalism, 'tribalism' created opportunities for the 'neo-imperialists' to divide and destroy the party's accomplishments, and no public speech to party members ever went by without a reminder of this fundamental political rule. Hence when it was rumoured that members of M's faction had held a meeting 'in the bush' instead of airing their views in the constituency, it was generally considered that M had overreached his position. There was immediate political pressure to 'stamp out the Kansengu Branch' (the title *Kansengu* is an allusion to the fact that in order to discuss politics its members had to hide in the bamboo to do so) and to re-affirm the local party's belief in unity by prohibiting all those who were reported to have attended the meeting from access to political decisions.

My discussion here is not concerned with the ways in which the 'Kansengu Branch' tried to influence local party leaders or, alternatively, what methods local leaders used to discredit the faction. The point I wish to make is that of the series of links used by M, first among members of his action-set, and then by his contacts with others as their dissatisfaction with local political leadership increased, ties forged through common recognition of 'home-boy' were dominant.

By contrast let us reconsider the action-set initiated by C, one of the founders of the African National Congress Branch in Luanshya and a central figure in Luanshya politics for the past ten years. I am plainly not in a position to record all contacts of political importance that C has had over a ten-year period, but feel there is a technique available to present a partial evaluation of them. This is by tracing C's links with those who are members of a 'commune', rather any particular person, or, following the term of Harary, Norman and Cartwright (1965: 77), present a 'condensed digraph' of certain of C's relations over this period. A 'condensed digraph' is a summary of certain interconnections in any network; it is a diagram of *paths*[1] between communes so that path A B represents a relation between all those people with whom A can engage in two-way communication and all those whom B can engage in two-way communication.

Thus 24(a), 24(b) and 24(c) represent contacts C had with certain sets over a period of time. Figure 24(a) represents a summary of the information given by Epstein. The main links C has in Figure 24(a) are with trade unionists in the General Workers' and Shop Assistants' Unions. Significantly, C's links with *bakumwesu* and rural kin are tenuous. C is Lamba. His 'Tribal Elder' who would have acted as the focal point of activity for *bakumwesu* and his rural kin had C been of a different ethnic group is not living in town at all, but in the nearby rural area boma (Mpongwe as it then was, some 40 miles away). Thus the pyramid channelling of decisions usual between Tribal Elders and *bakumwesu* of other areas is absent. Lamba *bakumwesu* needing adjudication or advice referred their problems to elders or court assessors in their nearby rural area, not to a representative in town.

At the time of the butchers' boycott, C's action set was somewhat enlarged to include a number of Tribal Elders who took an interest in the growing political consciousness of Luanshya as well as the advance of trade unions. It also included members of the Hawkers' Association and a set of relatively well educated individuals who were interested in forming a branch of the African National Congress. Of these, members of the Hawkers' Association may have provided links with *bakumwesu*, though I have no direct evidence on this point. However Lamba vegetable hawkers have been an economic feature of Luanshya's for many years.

In the two or three years following the boycott, C's links with the trade union movement proved more central to his action-set than his links through the politically inactive branch of the A.N.C. (Figure 24(b)). The Hawkers' Association proved equally inactive, its former leader involving himself in the activities of the trade

[1] The emphasis here is on a *path* rather than a strict *semi-path*. Following the definitions of Harary, Norman and Cartwright, a semi-path orders pairs of points; a path is a sequence of distinct points.

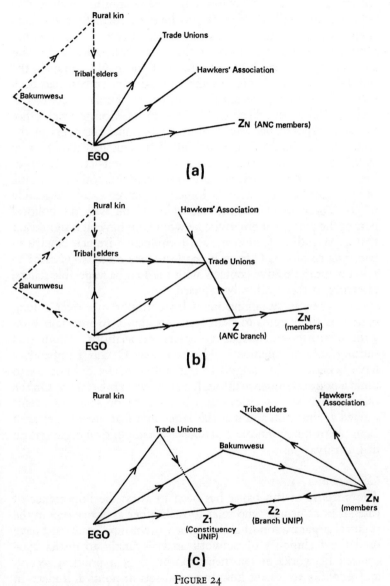

FIGURE 24
Diagrams of C's action-sets at certain periods 1952–1964

union movement. At this time C's career was interrupted by a
prison sentence and Figure 24(c) traces C's relationship following
the rise of U.N.I.P. in Luanshya and the establishment of section
organization. Tribal Elders are no longer a formally constituted
body, while the creation of sections had altered the relationship
between the political base of the party and officials. During
the time that C had been an official of the A.N.C. branch, the
link between branch officials and individual members had been
direct. This, in Figure 24(b), is shown as the line between Z
and Z_n. But as an official of U.N.I.P. in the Constituency office
C has interposed between him and individual members in the
sections, a committee of branch officials. This had the effect of
'splitting' the interlocking paths of C's action-set depicted in
Figure 24(c). It is in these circumstances that C chooses to make use
of his 'home-boy' ties with the loosely organized Lamba vegetable
sellers. These *bakumwesu* provide a direct link with the political
base of the party that otherwise he would not have. It is significant
that as M and his faction moved to influence Branch officials in
late 1964 to dismiss C from his constituency office, so C came to
rely on more positive contacts with the Lamba vegetable sellers,
referring to them as his 'bodyguard'.

C's success in sustaining his political importance over a long
period of time seems to stem from his ability to maintain links
with members of various voluntary associations, despite the
shifting rota of members. The fact that C was Lamba may
have benefited him originally but unlike M he did not try to
build a political presence through contact with *bakumwesu*. On the
other hand, he was clearly in a position to do so when events
moved against him and it is this latter case that gives the clearest
example of the significance of *bakumwesu* in political organization
in Luanshya.

Conclusion
The purpose of this paper has been to assess the importance of
categories of people who refer to each other as *bakumwesu* in the
political organization of a Copperbelt township. To do so I have
used the techniques of network analysis firstly to depict ego-
centred networks in one neighbourhood of a political section
and secondly to discuss links in action-sets of political leaders. In
both cases, my concern was to try to isolate those links which

could definitely be called 'home-boy' links as opposed to any
other social contacts ego might have with other people. Both the
example of the *chitente* and the action-sets of leaders demonstrate
that *bakumwesu* ties are significant but that political organization
does not rest on opposition between sets of *bakumwesu*.

Recruitment of *bakumwesu* seems important primarily to achieve
short-term objectives. This is clear in the case of the formation
of sections; it is clear in the case of opposition between activists
and non-activists within a political section. In the examples given
of recruitment for support of political leaders it is uncertain
how long M can rely predominantly on *bakumwesu* support to
achieve his campaign of dissent against other political leaders. It
might be that his faction is enduring, but would appear more
likely that it will survive only until the original objective is
secure. In the case of C recruitment of *bakumwesu* was more
definitely short term.

With the progressive elimination of institutionalized relationships between those in authority and *bakumwesu*, a feature of the
era of Tribal Elders, it is not surprising that their political significance should become intermittent. The fact that neighbourhood
bakumwesu mutually recognize each has claims on the services of
the other, means that each *uwakumwesu* has an available link
through which organization for specific purposes can be promoted. At the same time, given that *bakumwesu* of rural importance
are geographically dispersed, 'home-boy' ties do not appear
sufficient for sustaining prolonged tasks confronting political
organizers. More generally, this inherent limitation helps explain
one of the most puzzling features of the organization of voluntary
associations on the Copperbelt, namely, that despite the widespread existence of informal credit rings among *bakumwesu*,
mutal aid 'tribal associations' have been shortlived.[1]

The problem raised by Philip Mayer of the importance of a
shift in the migrant's social personality from 'extra town' ties to
'within town' ties as a comparative index for social change in
African communities seems to rely too heavily on the assumption
that each set of ties would, as in East London, create separate
systems of social control. If such were so, then, as Mayer rightly
points out in his most recent criticism of Epstein, it would be

[1] For an interesting comparative discussion of the existence of these small
credit associations see Ardener (1964).

important to distinguish between urban activities and associations which 're-inforce its members extra-town ties' and those which do not. Mayer feels that urban associations can be classed into those which are based on the bond of common home-place and which reflect their members 'extra-town' interests and those which are based, in town, on a more general categorical similarity of tribal interest (in Epstein 1967: 287). But the Copperbelt situation reveals that the 'bond of common home place' and the 'more general categorical similarity of tribal interest' are merged so far as organization of urban activities are concerned. The category *bakumwesu* and the activity resulting from social recognition of this tie reflects both 'ethnic' and 'home place' bonds.

The flexible use of the term *bakumwesu* on the Copperbelt means that residents could stress their 'home-boy' ties in situations which called for the rendering of mutual services, and indeed, recognition of 'home-boy' ties still implied reciprocal rights and duties upon those calling thjemselves *bakumwesu*. But 'home-boys' in the sense of 'near rura kin' did not engage in the sort of corporate activities which distinguished social relations among migrants in Cape Town or East London. On the Copperbelt voluntary organizations were inflected by *bakumwesu* ties rather than moulded by them. Home-boys were important for political organization, but only in specific instances were these ties responsible for the rise of factions among party members: a faction was not automatically 'home-boy' instigated. Perhaps the major difference between East London and the Copperbelt is that the nearness of the rural hinterland to East London means those 'home-boys' who are important for ego in the rural area are also the *same* 'home-boys' ego lodges with in town and the *same* 'home-boys' with whom he shares his leisure time activity in town. In Zambia those 'home-boys' who are important to ego to maintain his 'extra-town' ties are scattered throughout the various mine and municipal townships of the urban areas. These 'home-boys' are vital in domestic crisis but in married residential areas *different* 'home-boys', or those categorized as 'home-boys', are important for social and economic activity. Thus the East London situation of 're-inforcement' of rural values in the urban areas, which arises as a result circulating among the same members of ego's personal network in both town and rural area, does not occur on the Copperbelt.

Philip Mayer envisages a situation where a 'shift in the migrant's social personality' would result in a person's refusing to acknowledge a 'home-boy' tie in his personal network as a meaningful link between him and another person. Such people would obviously ignore an *uwakumwesu* in generating support for a particular plan of action. Throughout my fieldwork I came across only one political figure who specifically rejected a 'home-boy' tie as meaningful. Perhaps this informant is a 'pointer' towards the attitudes of future generations on the Copperbelt. At the same time I cannot help but think that my informant who rejected 'home-boys' as a meaningful category objected not so much to communication between them and him, but to social recognition of a tie which implied an obligation to render services. At a more general level recognition of 'home-boys' and inter- action between themselves is a badge of ethnocentrism which people willingly display. 'Home-boy' ties are not a specific phenomenon of East London, Cape Town and the Copperbelt but, I suggest, a common feature of personal networks in mobile populations.

The analytical problem posed by identification of 'home-boys' among mobile populations lies in their social significance— whether 'home-boys' are *obliged* to render mutual services to each other or whether 'home-boys' are merely a useful means through which ego can express social values, beliefs and experience in common with others. Obviously the range of social situations between the one and the other is very wide. East London is probably a limiting case in which there is complete 'incapsulation' of social activity among 'Red' networks of 'home-boys.' It is significant that this social situation should exist more than 100 years after the establishment of East London yet Luanshya, one- third its age, does not duplicate the latter. The analytical prob- lem therefore, is not, as Mayer suggested, a simple one to one correspondence with chronological time.

On the Copperbelt we have noted a change in the constrain- ing influence of 'home-boy' ties from a time when the authority of Tribal Elders positively sanctioned the recognition of reci- procal rights and duties among 'home-boys' to the present posi- tion where in voluntary associations, home-boys feel obliged to render mutual services in specific circumstances only. But to what extent this is a sufficient index for social change, as Mayer proposes, is doubtful. Certainly the structural framework in which choices have been made is not revealed by the mere identification of these choices.

Here then the study of personal networks must be complemented by wider considerations of how changes in social norms occur. Comparison of 'within town' ties and 'extra-town' ties, or of 'home-boy' ties at point one and point two is not in itself a complete study. Epstein (1967) has already identified other variables which ought to be taken into account, and of these of crucial importance in comparing East London and the Copperbelt are administrative decisions that have affected urban development and migration. The heavy emphasis that Mayer has given to tracing the social activities of migrant males whose main concern, even while working in town, is to bolster their status in their rural home, and the equally heavy emphasis Copperbelt anthropologists have given to married men and members of their households engaged in 'on-going' urban activities are in themselves a reflection of administrative decisions. Ironically, this double observer bias more than any other factor limits direct comparison of the material collected in the two urban situations, even granting—as this paper has tried to demonstrate—the significance to both of 'home-boy' ties.

Appendix
My main criticism of Adrian Mayer's conception of a 'quasi-group' is that he seems to draw too thin a line between empirical relations drawn from fieldwork material and the notion of a 'quasi-group' as a model of certain aspects of ego's communication patterns. Mayer's central point, on the other hand, is well taken. Mayer states that those previously using the term network have not distinguished its finite and infinite properties, namely the interacting series of people that have been brought purposively into relation by a single individual, which he terms an 'action-set' and the sum total of links a person may have within a field of social activity, which he terms a 'network'.

At the same time, in trying to define the content of the links that may be described as an action-set, Mayer suggests that the properties of these links, the relations ego has with members of his action-set, are different from the relations ego has with members of his network, thus the 'transactional element distinguishes action-set linkage from network linkage', 'transactions furthering in some way the interests of the parties concerned'. 'True, persons linked in a network may derive some benefit from their relationship; but this is not because of the very nature of the relationship, and many of these relationships have an only minimally interactional aspect . . .' Mayer (1966: 112–13). This suggests a discreteness between ego and his action-set whose ties are purposive and highly interactive as opposed to the relation between ego and his network, whose ties are non-purposive and minimally interactive. Barnes in his article in this book has further suggested, on the basis of Mayer's definition, that network ties are symmetric, while action-set ties are asymmetric. Therefore despite the incisiveness of Mayer's review of the literature, there are clearly problems of interpretation requiring solution.

I feel that interpretative problems are compounded rather than eased if the notion of a 'quasi-group' is retained. According to Mayer, a 'quasi-group' has the same pattern of linkages as an action-set and can be regarded as a successive series of action-sets superimposed on one another. This image is clear, but becomes less clear when Mayer tries to distinguish a 'quasi-group' from a 'potential group', or to distinguish a 'quasi-group' from a 'formal group'. The first is a classificatory 'quasi-group', which could also be seen as a 'potential group' or entities 'whose members have certain interests or modes of behaviour in common which may at any time lead them to form themselves into definite groups'. The second is the interactive quasi-group arising from action-sets. Yet the interactive quasi-group can, according to Mayer, develop a 'core' which 'may later crystallize into a formal group and so could be deemed a 'potential group', thus obscuring his initial distinctions. Mayer goes on to state that once this core becomes a clique or a formal group, it may be possible to take it, rather than ego, as the central unit of consideration. But I do not see logically, or in fact, how a formal group can be the central unit of a 'quasi-group'. 'Quasi-groups' by Mayer's own definition have no formal basis of membership. To have as the central unit of a 'quasi-group', a formally coordinated group would seem a contradiction in terms. The reverse situation would seem more applicable.

In fact the confusion in Mayer's argument seems to stem from lumping together in the concept 'quasi-group' two separate

considerations. The first is a consideration of how ego's informal
links can, in time, become formalized. In Mayer's terms this
would mean a progression in time from ego initiating his action-
set, to forming a 'quasi-group' and, later, to see the 'quasi-group'
emerge as the branch of a political party. Above I make reference
to a progression in Luanshya from action-set to political branch.
It is also apparent from the Luanshya material that this movement
need not be one way. A 'quasi-group' having formalized its
relations and become a group in the usual sense of the term may,
at a later stage, cease to be a group and revert to being a 'quasi-
group' again. Presumably it is possible that the reversibility of
this process goes even further. The individual orienting the 'quasi-
group' may, at a later stage, lose more of his influence, and find
that he is unable to activate former members.

The only question arising from this first consideration is whether
the notion of a 'quasi-group' is really necessary. Mayer considers
the concept to be a generic term to cover specific examples of
'quasi-groups' such as 'multiple uses of the same action-set' or
an 'action-set core', cliques, factions and so forth. 'Quasi-groups'
emerge in situations which are ephemeral and not persistent, in
such situations would it not be better to use the specific term to
cover the specific example, rather than a blanket term which may
give rise to loose terminological usage?

The second consideration that is lumped together with the first
is the notion of a 'quasi-group' as a 'model' of certain aspects of
ego's communications. Here more substantial queries arise and to
do justice to an analysis of this situation we must assume, contrary to Mayer, that 'quasi-group' links are *not* empirically
different from network links, but merely an abstraction and con-
densation of a universe of links in ego's network in order to
describe a particular situation.[1] In which case action-sets and
'quasi-groups' describe the effect of manipulation by ego of a
series of selected links in his network. They are, therefore, an
aspect of purposive communication and may be analysed as a
communication network. Empirically action-set links must be
coincident with network links, though the former may be abstracted from the latter, and this point may be clearly put in
notation form. Let us take A to denote the elements and links in an

[1] I acknowledge the help and the criticism of Mr R. Startup in the following
discussion.

action-set, E to denote 'quasi-group', N to denote ego's personal network (which is finite) and T to denote total network (which may or may not be finite). Then Mayer in his article makes the following statements:

$$A \subset E$$
$$E \subset T$$

the action-set is contained in the 'quasi-group' which in turn is included in an 'unbounded' or infinite Total Network.

But one cannot further make out from Mayer's argument whether he is saying (i) $E = N$ or whether (ii) $E \subset N$. If the first is true then a quasi-group would be the same as a personal network so that if $E \subset T \Leftrightarrow N \subset T$ but that the only elements of N are action-sets and their linkages.

$$\text{Thus } A \subset E \subset T \Leftrightarrow A \subset N \subset T.$$

In some cases, however, Mayer talks as if $E \subset N$ so that the elements and links of E are augmented by other elements and links ('lateral links' as Mayer terms them) and $N = E \cup L$ where L represents a set of lateral relations. Although he does not investigate the point we may suppose that in this case the two sets are not mutually exclusive so that $E \cap L \neq O$.

If the latter is so, which he suggests more strongly, is it the case that $T \supset N$, and thus $A \subset E$, $E \subset N$, $N \subset T$? In which case: all parts of E would be A;

$$N = E \cup L \text{ so that } E \cap L \neq 0$$

all parts of T would include N.

(i) In such a framework, Total Network, T, may be described as a set V of elements (people) and a set x of elements (links) in which the set V may or may not be finite and the set x may or may not be finite.

(ii) Two points are always joined at most by one line so that

$$x_1$$
$$V_1 \ldots \ldots \ldots \ldots V_2$$

(iii) If the points V_1, V_2 are joined by a link we write $r(V_1, V_2)$, that is, there is a relation between V_1 and V_2 and also $r(V_1, V_2) \Leftrightarrow r(V_2, V_1)$ i.e. the order is not important.

(iv) A relationship (path) joining V_1 and V_N is a collection of points V_1, $V_2 \ldots V_N$ and $(N - 1)$ lines so that

$$r(V_3, V_2), r(V_2, V_3) \ldots r(V_N, V_{N-1}), r(V_{N-1}, V_N).$$

(v) At the same time the symbol N describes a subset of T in which N is a *finite* number of persons and associated links. It is called a personal or ego-centred network as it has the property that ego (V_0) has a 'pole' position in the set of elements P consisting of

$$(V_0; V_1, V_2, V_3, V_4, V_1 \ldots V_N)$$

and that a path joins V_0 to each of $V_1 \ldots V_N$ and any of the elements $V_1 \ldots V_N$ to any of the other elements in the set.

The symbols A and E present problems of nomenclature. Action-Set would seem more permissible than 'Quasi-Group' in that our discussion so far of personal network, N, describes ego's communication with other people. The significance of ego's 'pole position' is that N is oriented—both empirically and in a 'model' of ego's relations—to ego. A as we have defined it is a specific aspect of N, that sub-set of N which describes purposive actions on the part of ego. L represents other communications. As a term E, 'quasi-group', is redundant.

One way to make such a comparison from the empirical data of ego's communications is to construct a digraph. A digraph is an abstraction from the personal network—a net that disregards relations that would lead to the construction of loops and parallel arcs (see Harary, Norman and Cartwright 1965). Mayer has in fact done this in presenting his material from Dewas. The only problem in his presentation is that he has constructed a non-reciprocal digraph, in that the links back to the candidate from the people contacted in the action-set are not shown, whereas the whole of his previous analysis refers to reciprocal relations involved in the term 'transactions'. Mayer describes the securing of voting support, initiated by ego, in return for all sorts of promised services which those voting for ego hope to receive later. From his textual analysis the reciprocity is clear: every indegree relation to ego would also have its appropriate outdegree.[1] But his non-reciprocal representation of the data through constructing an asymmetric digraph could, without necessary qualification, lead the reader to think of 'transactions' as being qualitatively different from reciprocal network links. This misconception may be effectively disposed of. It is possible in any empirical situation to

---

[1] 'Indegree' refers to links coming into a point; 'out degree' to links going out from a point.

see that elements and links in ego's personal network *N* will include both parallel ties and reciprocal relations. These could be graphed, but in abstracting these to construct a 'model' of paths between the elements (i.e. in describing relations) the anthropologist may simply neglect both parallel ties and reciprocal relations if he wishes. An asymmetric digraph will be the result.

Notes on Contributors

MITCHELL, James Clyde. b. 1918. S. Africa.

B.A.(Soc.Sc.), B.A.(Hons) Sociology. University of S. Africa. D.Phil. (Oxford). Professor of Urban Sociology, University of Manchester, formerly Professor of Sociology, University College of Rhodesia and Nyasaland, Salisbury, Rhodesia. Fieldwork in Nyasaland (now Malawi) and towns of N. Rhodesia (now Zambia). Author of *The Yao Village* (1956), *The Kalela Dance* (1957) and various papers on urbanization in Africa.

BARNES, John Arundel. b. 1918. England.

M.A.(Cambridge), D.Phil.(Oxford). Professor of Sociology, University of Cambridge; formerly Professor of Anthropology, Australian National University. Fieldwork in Northern Rhodesia (now Zambia) and Western Norway. Author of *Politics in a Changing Society* (1967), *Inquest on the Murngin* (1967) and various papers on politics and kinship.

EPSTEIN, Arnold Leonard. b. 1924. Liverpool, England.

LL.B.(Queen's University, Belfast). Ph.D. (University of Manchester). Professorial Fellow in Social Anthropology, Australian National University, Canberra. Fieldwork amongst the Bemba of Northern Rhodesia (now Zambia), in the towns of the Copperbelt, and more recently amongst the Tolai of New Britain. Author of *The Administration of Justice and the Urban African* (1953), *Politics in an Urban African Community* (1958); editor of *The Craft of Social Anthropology* (1967).

WHEELDON, Prudence, nee Craib. b. 1930. S. Africa.

B.A.(Hons.) Social Anthropology, University of Cape Town. Assistant Professor, Simon Fraser University, Vancouver. Formerly Lecturer in Sociology, University College of Rhodesia and Nyasaland. Fieldwork among marginal 'coloured' communities especially into formal voluntary associations and leadership and social networks in Central Africa; currently working on comparative studies in network and political processes in powerless groups and the concept of community in urban studies.

KAPFERER, Bruce. b. 1940. Australia.

B.A. Social Anthropology, University of Sydney. Lecturer in Social Anthropology, University of Manchester, England. Formerly Commonwealth Scholar at University College of Rhodesia and Nyasaland. Fieldwork in rural and industrial/urban areas in Zambia. Author of

The Population of a Zambian Municipal Township (1966) and *Cooperation, Leadership and Village Structure* (1967).

BOSWELL, David Mark. b. 1937. Sheffield, United Kingdom.
B.A.(Hons. History), Christ's College, Cambridge. M.Phil.(Sociology) London School of Economics. Research Sociologist, Department of Social and Preventive Medicine, University of Manchester. Formerly Commonwealth Scholar affiliated to the Rhodes-Livingstone Institute (now Institute for Social Research, University of Zambia), and Research Associate, Department of Sociology and Social Anthropology, University of Manchester. Fieldwork in Lusaka and other areas of Zambia, and subsequently in establishments of the mental health service in Lancashire. Author of *Escorts of Hospital Patients* (1965) and *Kinship, Friendship and the Concept of the Social Network* (1966).

HARRIES-JONES, Peter. b. 1937. Oxford, England.
B.A. Rhodes University, South Africa, B.Litt. (Oxford). Lecturer in Social Anthropology, University College, Swansea. Formerly Research Officer, Rhodes-Livingstone Institute (the Institute for Social Research, University of Zambia). Fieldwork among the Bemba of Zambia and on the Copperbelt. Author of 'Kasaka: A Case Study in Succession and Dynamics of a Bemba Village', *Rhodes-Livingstone Journal*, xxxiii (1963); 'Marital Disputes and the Process of Conciliation in a Copperbelt Town', *Rhodes-Livingstone Journal*, xxxv (1964).

Bibliography

Several papers bearing on the study of social networks are included which are not referred to in the text.

NOTE: Rhodes-Livingstone Papers, Journals, Proceedings and Communications were published at Manchester, by the Manchester University Press, for the Rhodes-Livingstone Institute, Lusaka, Zambia. This arrangement was continued during the years 1966 to 1970 when the Institute was known as the Institute for Social Research and will continue now that the name has been changed to Institute for African Studies, University of Zambia.

ADAMS, BERT N. (1967) 'Interaction Theory and the Social Network', *Sociometry*, xxx: 64–78.

ALDOUS, J. and STRAUS, M. A. (1966) 'Social Networks and Conjugal Roles: a test of Bott's hypothesis', *Social Forces*, xliv, 576–80.

ARDENER, S. (1964) 'The Comparative Study of Rotating Credit Associations', *Journ. Royal Anthro. Inst.*, xciv: 201–29.

BACK, K., FESTINGER, L., HYMOVITCH, B., KELLEY, H., SCHACHTER, S. and THIBAUT, J. (1950) 'The Methodology of Studying Rumour Transmission', *Human Relations*, iii: 307–12.

BANTON, M. (1957) *West African City*, London, Oxford University Press for International African Institute.

BARNES, J. A. (1954) 'Class and Committees in a Norwegian Island Parish', *Human Relations*, vii: 39–58.

—— (1962a) 'African Models in the New Guinea Highlands', *Man*, lxii: 5–9.

—— (1962b) 'Rethinking and Rejoining: Leach, Fortes and filiation', *Jour. of the Polynesian Society*, lxxi: 403–10.

—— (1969) 'Graph Theory and Social Networks: a technical comment on connectedness and connectivity', *Sociology*, iii: 215–32.

BATES, ALAN P., and BABCHUK, NICHOLAS (1961) 'The Primary Group: A Reappraisal', *Sociological Quarterly*, ii: 181–91.

BAVELAS, A. (1948) 'A Mathematical Model for Group Structures', *Applied Anthropology*, vii: 16–30.

—— (1951) 'Communication Patterns in Task-Oriented Groups' in Lerner, D, and Lasswell, H. D. (Eds.) *The Policy Sciences*, Stanford University Press, 193–202.

BEATON, A. (1966) 'An Interbattery Factor Analytic Approach to Clique Analysis', *Sociometry*, xxix: 135–45.

BEFU, HARUMI (1963) 'Network and Corporate Structure' in R. K. Sakai (Ed.) *Studies on Asia*, Lincoln, University of Nebraska Press.

BERGE, C. (1962) *The Theory of Graphs and its Applications*, London, Methuen.

BESHERS, JAMES M. and LAUMANN, EDWARD O. (1967) 'Social Distance: A Network Approach', *Amer. Sociol. Review*, xxxii: 225–36.

BEUM, CORLIN and BRUNDAGE, EVERETT C. (1950) 'A Method for Analysing the Sociomatrix', *Sociometry*, xiii: 141–5.

BETTISON, D. G. (1958) 'Migrancy and Social Structure in Peri-Urban Communities in Nyasaland' in Apthorpe, R. J. (Eds.). *Present Interrelationships in Central African Rural and Urban Life*, Proceedings of the Eleventh Conference of the Rhodes-Livingstone Institute.

—— (1959) *Numerical Data on African Dwellers in Lusaka*, Rhodes-Livingstone Communication No. 16.

BLAU, P. M. (1964) *Exchange and Power in Social Life*, London, John Wiley and Sons.

BOSWELL, D. M. (1965) *Escorts of Hospital Patients: A Preliminary Report on a Social Survey Undertaken at Lusaka Central Hospital from July–August, 1964*, Rhodes-Livingstone Communication, No. 29.

—— (1966 'Kinship, Friendship and the Concept of the Social Network', *Proceedings of the Annual Conference of the East African Institute for Social Research*, January 1966, Kampala.

BOTT, E. (1955) 'Urban Families: Conjugal Roles and Social Networks', *Human Relations*, viii: 345–85.

—— (1956) 'Urban Families: the Norms of Conjugal Roles', *Human Relations*, ix: 325–41.

—— (1957) *Family and Social Networks*, London, Tavistock Publications.

—— (1964) 'Family, Kinship and Marriage' in Douglas, Mary *et al.* (Eds.). *Man in Society: Patterns of Human Organization*, London, Macdonald: 82–103.

BOISSEVAIN, JEREMY F. (1968) *Netwerken en Quasi-groepen: Enkele beschouwing over de plaats van die niet-groupen in die sociale Wetenschapen.* (Networks and Quasi-groups: a survey of the place of non-groups in the social sciences). Inaugural lecture, University of Amsterdam, Assen: Van Gorcum & Co.

BUCKLEY, WALTER (1967) *Sociology and Modern Systems Theory*, Englewood Cliffs, Prentice Hall.

BUSACKER, R. G. and SAATY, THOMAS L. (1965) *Finite Graphs and Networks: an Introduction with Applications*, New York, McGraw-Hill.

CAPLOW, T. (1955) 'The Definition and Measurement of Ambience', *Social Forces*, xxxiv: 28–33.

CARTWRIGHT, D. and ZANDER, A. (Eds.) (1960) *Group Dynamics: Research and Theory* (2nd ed.). Evanston Ill. Row Peterson.

CHERRY, C. (1957) *On Human Communication: A Review, a Survey and a*

Criticism. New York: Technology Press of Massachusetts Institute of Technology and John Wiley and Sons.

COHN, B. A. and MARRIOTT, MCK. (1958) 'Networks and Centres in the Integration of Indian Civilization', *Journal of Social Research* (Ranchi) I: 1–9.

COLEMAN, JAMES S., KATZ, ELIHU and MENZEL, HERBERT (1957) 'The Diffusion of an Innovation among Physicians', *Sociometry*, xx: 253–70.

COLEMAN, J. S. (1960) 'The Mathematical Study of Small Groups' in Solomon, H. (Ed.) *Mathematical Thinking in the Measurement of Behaviour*, Glencoe: Free Press, 1–149.

—— (1964) *Introduction to Mathematical Sociology*, New York. Free Press of Glencoe.

COLEMAN, J. S. and MACRAE, D. (Jr.) (1960) 'Electronic Processing of Sociometric Data for Groups up to 1000 in Size', *Amer. Sociol. Review*, xxv: 722–7.

COLSON, E. (1953a) *The Makah Indians*, Manchester University Press.

—— (1953b) 'Social Control and Vengeance in Plateau Tonga Society', *Africa*, xxiii: 199–212.

—— (1958) *Marriage and the Family among the Plateau Tonga of Northern Rhodesia*, Manchester University Press for Rhodes-Livingstone Institute.

CUNNISON, I. G. (1956) 'Perpetual Kinship: A Political Institution of the Luapula Peoples', *Rhodes-Livingstone Journal*, xx: 28–48.

—— (1959) *The Luapula Peoples of Northern Rhodesia*, Manchester University Press for Rhodes-Livingstone Institute.

DAVIS, J. A. (1963) 'Structural Balance, Mechanical Solidarity and Interpersonal Relation', *Amer. Journ. of Sociol.*, lxviii, 444–62.

—— 'Clustering and Structural Balance in Graphs', *Human Relations*, xx: 181–87.

DEVONS, E. and GLUCKMAN, M. (1964) 'Introduction' in Gluckman, M. (Ed.) *Closed Systems and Open Minds: The limits of Naivety in Social Anthropology*, Edinburgh. Oliver and Boyd, 13–19.

DICKIE-CLARK, H. F. (1966) *The Marginal Situation: A Sociological Study of a Coloured Group*. International Library of Sociology and Social Reconstruction, London, Routledge and Kegan Paul.

DOTSON, F. (1951) 'Patterns of Voluntary Association among Urban Working-Class Families', *Amer. Sociol. Review*, xvi: 687–93.

ELIAS, N. and SCOTSON, J. L. (1965) *The Established and the Outsiders: A Sociological Enquiry into Community Problems*, New Sociological Library, London, Cass.

EPSTEIN, A. L. (1958) *Politics in an Urban African Community*, Manchester University Press for the Rhodes-Livingstone Institute.

—— (1959) 'Linguistic Innovation and Culture on the Copperbelt,

Northern Rhodesia', *South Western Journal of Anthropology*, xv: 235–53.

—— (1961) 'The Network and Urban Social Organization', *Rhodes-Livingstone Journal*, xxix: 29–62.

—— (1962) 'Immigrants to Northern Rhodesian Towns'. *Paper Presented to Section N of the British Association for the Advancement of Science, 31 August 1962.*

—— (1964) 'Urban Communities in Africa' in Gluckman, M. (Ed.) *Closed Systems and Open Minds: The Limits of Naivety in Social Anthropology.* Edinburgh, Oliver and Boyd: 81–102.

—— (1967) 'Urbanization and Social Change in Africa', *Current Anthropology* viii: 275–95.

EVANS-PRITCHARD, E. E. (1937) *Witchcraft, Oracles and Magic among the Azande*, Oxford, The Clarendon Press.

FALLERS, L. A. (1963) 'Political Sociology and the Study of African Politics', *Archives Europeannes de Sociologie*, iv: 311–29.

FARARO, T. J. and SUNSHINE, MORRIS H. (1964) *A Study of a Biased Friendship Net*, Syracuse, Syracuse University, Youth Development Center.

FESTINGER, L. (1949) 'The Analysis of Sociograms Using Matrix Algebra', *Human Relations*, II: 153–8.

FESTINGER, L., SCHACHTER, S. and BACK, K. (1950) *Social Pressures in Informal Groups*, Harper, New York.

FIRTH, R. (1954) 'Social Organization and Social Change', *Journal of the Royal Anthropological Institute*, lxxxiv: 1–20.

FLAMENT, C. (1963) *Applications of Graph Theory to Group Structure*, Englewood Cliffs, Prentice-Hall.

FORSYTH, E. and KATZ, L. (1946) 'A Matrix Approach to the Analysis of Sociometric Data: Preliminary Report', *Sociometry*, ix: 340–7.

FORTES, M. (1949) *The Web of Kinship among the Tallensi*, London, Oxford University Press.

FOSTER, C. C., RAPOPORT, A. and ORWANT, C. J. (1963) 'A Study of a Large Sociogram II Elimination of Free Parameters', *Behavioral Science*, viii: 56–65.

FRAENKEL, M. (1964) *Tribe and Class in Monrovia*, London, Oxford University Press.

FRANKENBERG, R. J. (1957) *Village on the Border: A Social Study of Religion, Politics and Football in a North Wales Community*, London, Cohen and West.

—— (1966) *Communities in Britain: Social Life in Town and Country*, Harmondsworth, Penguin Books.

GARBETT, G. K. (1968) 'The Application of Optical Coincidence Cards to the Matrices of Digraphs of Social Networks', *Sociology*, ii: 311–31.

GLUCKMAN, M. (1940) 'An Analysis of a Social Situation in Modern Zululand', *African Studies*, xiv: 1–30; 147–74.

—— (1955) *The Judicial Process Among the Barotse of Northern Rhodesia*, Manchester University Press for Rhodes-Livingstone Institute.

—— (1960) *Analysis of a Social Situation in Modern Zululand*, Rhodes-Livingstone Paper No. 28.

—— (1960) *Custom and Conflict in Africa*, Oxford, Blackwells.

—— (1961) 'Ethnographic Data in British Social Anthropology', *The Sociological Review*, ix: 5–17.

—— (1962) 'Les Rites de Passage' in Gluckman, M. (Ed.) *Essays in the Ritual of Social Relations*, Manchester University Press.

—— (1963a) 'Gossip and Scandal', *Current Anthropology*, iv: 307–16.

—— (1963b) *Order and Rebellion in Tribal Africa*, London, Cohen and West.

—— (Ed.) (1964) *Closed Systems and Open Minds: the Limits of Naivety in Social Anthropology*, Edinburgh, Oliver & Boyd.

GOVERNMENT OF NORTHERN RHODESIA (1944) *Report of the Commission Appointed to Inquire into the Administration and Finance of Native Locations in Urban Areas*, Lusaka, Government Printer.

GOVERNMENT OF THE REPUBLIC OF ZAMBIA (1964) *Second Report of the May/June 1963 Census of Africans*, Lusaka, Ministry of Finance.

—— (1965) *May/June 1963 Census of Africans Village Distribution District: Lusaka*, Lusaka Central Statistical Office.

GUGLER, J. (1963) 'The Relationship Urban Dwellers Maintain with their Villages of Origin' (unpublished manuscript).

—— (1965) 'Life in a Dual System', *EAISR Conference Paper*.

GUTKIND, P. C. W. (1965) 'Network Analysis and Urbanism in Africa: The Use of Micro and Macro Analysis', *Canadian Review of Sociology and Anthropology*, ii: 123–31.

GUTKIND, P. C. W. (1965) 'African Urbanism, Mobility and the Social Network', *Int. Journal of Comparative Sociology*, vi: 48–60.

HARARY, F. (1959) 'Graph Theoretic Methods in the Management Sciences', *Management Science*, v: 387–403.

HARARY, F. and NORMAN, R. Z. (1953) *Graph Theory as a Mathematical Model in Social Sciences*, Ann Arbor: University of Michigan, Institute for Social Research.

HARARY, F. and ROSS, I. (1957) 'A Procedure for Clique Detection Using the Group Matrix', *Sociometry*, xx: 205–15.

HARARY, F., NORMAN, R. Z. and CARTWRIGHT, D. (1965) *Structural Models: An Introduction to the Theory of Directed Graphs*, New York, John Wiley & Sons.

HARRIES-JONES, P. (1964) 'Marital Disputes and the Process of Conciliation in a Copperbelt Town', *Rhodes-Livingstone Journal*, xxxv: 30–72.

HELLMANN, E. (1949) 'Urban Areas' in Hellmann, E. (Ed.) *Handbook of Race Relations*, London, Oxford University Press, 229–74.

HENRY, JULES (1958) 'The Personal Community and its Invariant Properties', *Amer. Anth.* lx: 827–31.

HOCKETT, C. F. (1966) 'Language Mathematics and Linguistics', *Current Trends in Linguistics*, iii: 155–304.

HOMANS, G. (1961) *Social Behaviour: Its Elementary Forms*, London, Routledge and Kegan Paul.

HUBBELL, C. H. (1965) 'An Input-Output Approach to Clique Identification', *Sociometry*, xxviii: 377–99.

JAY, E. J. (1964) 'The Concepts of "field" and "network" in Anthropological Research', *Man*, lxiv: 137–39.

JONES, A. D. (1966) 'Social Networks of Farmers among the Plateau Tonga of Zambia' in Lloyd, P. C. (Ed.) *The New Elites of Tropical Africa*, London, Oxford University Press for International African Institute: 272–85.

KAPFERER, B. (1966) *The Population of a Zambian Municipal Township*, Communication No. 1, Institute for Social Research.

KATZ, ELIHU, LEVIN, MARTIN and HAMILTON, HERBERT (1963) 'Research on the Diffusion of Innovation', *Amer. Sociol. Review*, xxviii: 237–52.

KATZ, FRED E. (1958) 'Occupation Contact Networks', *Social Forces*, xxxvii: 52–55.

—— (1966) 'Social Participation and Social Structure', *Social Forces*, xlv: 199–210.

KAY, GEORGE (1967) *A Social Geography of Zambia: A Survey of Population Patterns in a Developing Country*, London University Press.

KEPHART, W. M. (1950) 'A Quantitative Analysis of Intergroup Relationships', *Amer. Journal Sociol.*, lv: 544–49.

LAPIERE, R. T. (1954) *A Theory of Social Control*, New York, McGraw-Hill Book Co.

LITTLE, K. L. (1957) 'The Role of Voluntary Associations in West African Urbanization', *Amer. Anthropologist*, lix: 579–96.

LOOMIS, CHARLES P. (1967) 'Change in Rural India as Related to Social Power and Sex', *Behavioral Sciences and Community Development*, 1: 1–27.

LOOMIS, C. P. and BEEGLE, J. A. (1950) *Rural Social Systems*, New York, Prentice-Hall.

LOOMIS, C. P., MORALES, J. O., CLIFFORD, R. A. and LEONARD, O. E. (1953) *Turrialba: Social Systems and the Introduction of Change*, Glencoe, Illinois, The Free Press.

LUCE, R. D. and PERRY, A. D. (1949) 'A Method of Matrix Analysis of Group Structure', *Psychometrika*, xiv: 95–116.

LUCE, R. D. (1950) 'Connectivity and Generalised Cliques in Socio-metric Group Structures', *Psychometrika*, xv: 169–90.

LUPTON, T. (1963) *On the Shop Floor: Two Studies of Workshop Organization and Output*, Oxford, Pergamon Press.

McCULLOCH, M. (1956) *A Social Survey of the African Population of Livingstone*. Rhodes-Livingstone Paper No. 26.

MACIVER, R. M. and PAGE, CHARLES H. (1962) *Society: An Introductory Analysis*, London, Macmillan.

MACKINTOSH, C. W. (1950) *Some Pioneer Missions of Northern Rhodesia*, Occasional Papers of the Rhodes-Livingstone Museum No. 8, Livingstone, Rhodes-Livingstone Museum.

MALINOWSKI, B. (1922) *Argonauts of the Western Pacific*, London, Routledge & Kegan Paul.

MAYER, A. C. (1962) 'System and Network: An Approach to the Study of Political Process in Dewas' in Madan, T. N. and Sarana, G. (Eds.) *Indian Anthropology Essays in Memory of D. N. Majumdar*, Bombay Asian Publishing House, 266–78.

—— (1963) 'Municipal Elections: A Central Indian Case Study' in Philips, C. H. (Ed.) *Politics and Society in India*, London, Allen & Unwin, *Studies on Modern Asia and Africa*: 115–32.

—— (1966) 'The Significance of Quasi-Groups in the Study of Complex Societies' in Banton, M. (Ed.) *The Social Anthropology of Complex Societies*, A.S.A. Monographs 4, London, Tavistock Publications: 97–122.

MAYER, P. (1961) *Tribesmen or Townsmen: Conservatism and the Process of Urbanization in a South African City*, Cape Town, Oxford University Press.

—— (1962) 'Migrancy and the Study of Africans in Towns', *Amer. Anthro.*, lxiv: 576–92.

—— (1964) 'Labour Migrancy and the Social Network', in J. F. Holleman *et al.* (Eds.) *Problems of Transition: Proceedings of the Social Sciences Research Conference held in the University of Natal, Durban, July* 1962. Pietermaritzburg, S. Africa, Natal University Press: 21–34.

MIRACLE, M. P. (1962) 'Apparent Changes in the Structure of African Commerce Lusaka, 1954–1959', *The Northern Rhodesia Journal*, v: 170–75.

MITCHELL, J. C. (1951) 'A Note on the Urbanization of Africans on the Copperbelt', *Rhodes-Livingstone Journal*, xii: 20–27.

—— (1952) 'A Note on the African Conception of Causality', *Nyasaland Journal* v, 2: 51–58.

—— (1954) *African Urbanization in Ndola and Luanshya*, Rhodes-Livingstone Communication No. 6.

—— (1956) *The Kalela Dance. Aspects of Social Relationships among*

Urban Africans in Northern Rhodesia. Rhodes-Livingstone Paper No. 27.

—— (1957) 'Aspects of African Marriage on the Copperbelt of Northern Rhodesia', *Rhodes-Livingstone Journal*, xxii: 1–30.

—— (1958) 'Types of Urban Social Relationships' in Apthorpe, R. (Ed.) *Present Interrelations in Central African Rural and Urban Life*. Proceedings of the Eleventh Conference of the Rhodes-Livingstone Institute. 84–87.

—— (1959) 'The Study of African Urban Social Structures' in *Housing and Urbanization*: Inter-African Conference, 2nd Session. Nairobi, Publication No. 47, CCTA.

—— (1960) *Tribalism and the Plural Society: An Inaugural Lecture*, London, Oxford University Press.

—— (1964) 'The Meaning in Misfortune for Urban Africans' in Fortes, M. and Dieterlen, G. (Eds.) *African Systems of Thought*, London, Oxford University Press for International African Institute: 192–203.

—— (1966) 'Theoretical Orientations in African Urban Studies' in Banton, M. (Ed.) *The Social Anthropology of Complex Societies*, ASA Monographs 4, London, Tavistock Publications: 37–68.

MITCHELL, J. C. and EPSTEIN, A. L. (1959) 'Occupational Prestige and Social Status among Urban Africans in Northern Rhodesia', *Africa*, xxix: 22–40.

MORENO, J. L. (1953) *Who Shall Survive? Foundations of Sociometry, Group Psychotherapy and Sociodrama*, Beacon, NY, Beacon House.

MORRIS, R. N. and MOGEY, JOHN (1965) *The Sociology of Housing: Studies at Berinsfield*, London: Routledge & Kegan Paul.

MORTIMER, M. C. (1956–9) 'History of the Barotse National School: 1907–1957', *The Northern Rhodesia Journal*, iii: 303–10.

MULFORD, D. C. (1964) *The Northern Rhodesia General Election 1962*. Nairobi, Oxford University Press.

MUNDAY, J. T. (1961) *Kankomba: Central Bantu Historical Texts*, Rhodes-Livingstone Communication No. 10.

MWEWA, P. H. (1958) *The African Railway Workers Union Ndola*, Rhodes-Livingstone Communication No. 22, Lusaka: Rhodes-Livingstone Institute.

NADEL, S. F. (1957) *The Theory of Social Structure*, London, Cohen and West.

NELSON, JOEL I. (1966) 'Clique Contacts and Family Orientations', *Amer. Sociol. Review*, xxxi: 663–72.

NYBAKKEN, O. E. (1960) *Greek and Latin in Scientific Terminology*, Iowa State University Press.

NYIRENDA, A. A. (1957) 'African Market Vendors in Lusaka', *Rhodes-Livingstone Journal*, xxii: 31–63.

ORE, O. (1962) *Theory of Graphs:* Providence, American Mathematical Society, Colloquium Publications, 38.

PAUW, B. A. (1963) *The Second Generation*, Cape Town, Oxford University Press.

PHILPOTT, STUART B. (1968) 'Remittance, Obligations, Social Network and Choice Among Montserratian Migrants in Britain', *Man*, iii (n.s.): 465–76.

POWDERMAKER, H. (1962) *Coppertown*, New York, Harper and Row.

RADCLIFFE-BROWN, A. R. (1952) *Structure and Function in Primitive Society: Essays and Addresses*, London, Cohen and West.

RAPAPORT, R. (1963) 'Normal Crisis, Family Structure and Mental Health', *Family Process*, II: 68–80.

RAPOPORT, A. and HORVATH, W. J. (1961) 'A Study of a Large Sociogram', *Behavioral Science*, vi: 279–91.

READER, D. H. (1964) 'Models in Social Change with Special Reference to Southern Africa', *African Studies*, xxiii: 11–33.

RICHARDS, A. I. (1937) 'Reciprocal Clan Relationships among the Bemba of North Eastern Rhodesia', *Man*, xxxvii: 222: 188–93.

ROETHLISBERGER, F. J. and DICKSON, W. J. (1939) *Management and the Worker*, Cambridge, Mass, Harvard University Press.

ROSE, ARNOLD (1962) *Human Behavior and Social Process: An Interactional Approach*, Boston, Houghton, Mifflin & Co.

ROSS, I. C. and HARARY, F. (1959) 'A Description of Strengthening and Weakening Members of a Group', *Sociometry*, xxii: 139–47.

ROY, D. (1952) 'Quota Restriction and Goldbricking in a Machine Shop', *Amer. Journ. of Sociol.*, LVII: 427–42.

SAMPSON, A. (1958) *The Treason Cage*, London, Heinemann.

SOMMERFELT, A. (1958) *Political Cohesion in a Stateless Society: Studies Honouring the Centennial of the Oslo Universitets Etnograliske Museum*, Oslo, A.W. Brøggers Buktrykker A/S.

SRINIVAS, M. M. and BÉTEILLE, A. (1964) 'Networks in Indian Social Structure', *Man*, lxiv: 165–68.

STEFANIZYN, B. (1950) 'Funeral Friendship in Central Africa', *Africa*, xx: 290–306.

—— (1964) *The Social and Ritual Life of the Ambo of Northern Rhodesia*, London, Oxford University Press for International African Institute.

TEW, M. (1951) 'A Further Note on Funeral Friendship', *Africa*, xxi: 122–24.

TURNER, CHRISTOPHER (1967) 'Conjugal Roles and Social Networks', *Human Relations*, xx: 121–30.

TURNER, V. W. (1957) *Schism and Continuity in an African Society*, Manchester University Press for the Rhodes-Livingstone Institute.

—— (1964) 'Witchcraft and Sorcery: Taxonomy versus Dynamics', *Africa*, xxxiv: 314–24.

UDRY, J. R. and HALL, M. (1965) 'Marital Role Segregation and Social Networks in Middle-Class, Middle-Aged Couples', *Journal of Marriage and Family Living*, xxvii, (3): 392–95.

VAN VELSEN, J. (1964) *The Politics of Kinship*, Manchester University Press for the Rhodes-Livingstone Institute.

—— (1967) 'The Extended Case Method and Situational Analysis' in Epstein, A. L. (Ed.) *The Craft of Social Anthropology*, London, Tavistock Publications: 129–49.

WILLIAMS, W. M. (1963) *A West Country Village Ashworthy. Family, Kinship and Land*, London: Routledge and Kegan Paul.

WILSON, G. B. (1941–2) *An Essay on the Economics of Detribalization in Northern Rhodesia*, Rhodes-Livingstone Papers No. 5 and 6

WILSON, M. and MAFEJE, A. (1963) *Langa: A Study of Social Groups in an African Township*, London, Oxford University Press.

WIRTH, L. (1956) 'Urbanism as a Way of Life', in *Community Life and Social Policy*, University of Chicago Press.

YOUNG, MICHAEL and WILMOTT, PETER (1957) *Family and Kinship in East London*, London, Routledge and Kegan Paul.

ZELENY, L. D. (1941) 'Measurement of Sociation', *Amer. Sociol. Review*, vi: 173–88.

Name Index

Adams, Bert. N., 2n
Aldous, J., 5
Aquina, Sister Mary, vi
Ardener, S., 339n

Back, K., 4, 36n
Banton, M., 255, 295
Barnes, J. A., v, 1n, 3, 4, 6, 8, 11, 12,
    14, 15, 19, 20, 24, 35, 36n, 39n, 45,
    48, 52, 53, 66, 72, 80, 109, 111, 117,
    122, 132, 181, 211, 245, 253, 305,
    343, 348
Bavelas, A., 4n
Beaton, A., 4n
Beegle, J. A., 31n
Berge, C., 56, 58, 63
Beshers, J. M., 3
Béteille, A., 1n, 24, 27, 28, 44, 45, 54,
    58, 73, 132
Bettison, D., 246n, 247, 248n, 249,
    289n
Beum, C., 4n
Blau, P. M., 49n, 182, 214
Boswell, D. M., vi, 7, 14, 25, 26, 32,
    39, 41, 181, 261n, 291, 349
Bott, E., v, 3, 6, 10, 11, 17, 18, 27, 30,
    36, 37, 48, 52, 54, 57, 61, 69, 71, 80,
    110, 111, 112, 117, 132, 253
Brundage, E. C., 4n
Buckley, W., 47n
Busacker, R. G., 12n

Caplow, T., 20n
Cartwright, Desmond, 4
Cartwright, Dorwin, 4n, 15, 15n, 33,
    34, 36n, 47n, 221n, 222n, 302, 335,
    336n, 346
Chata, R., 292n
Cherry, C., 56
Cohn, B. A., 57
Coleman, J. S., 4, 63
Colson, E., 112, 131, 171, 180
Cunnison, I. G., 100n, 299n

Davis, J. A., 47n
Devons, E., 191
Dickie-Clark, H. F., 176
Dickson, W. J., 193n
Dotson, F., 106
Dubb, A., 255, 295

Elias, N., 179
Epstein, A. L., v, 3, 6, 9, 10, 13, 17,
    18, 21, 25, 31, 32, 37, 42, 47, 48, 57,
    64, 71, 74, 79, 96, 102, 105, 107,
    117, 125, 126, 132, 134, 178, 184,
    245, 247, 249, 250, 253, 254, 287,
    288, 297, 298, 304, 305, 306, 339,
    340, 342, 348
Evans-Pritchard, E. E., 8, 203n

Fallers, L. A., 52
Fararo, T. J., 35
Festinger, L., 4, 4n, 36n
Fielder, H., 291n
Firth, R., 2
Flament, C., 34, 56, 66
Forsyth, E., 58
Fortes, M., 8, 52
Foster, C. C., 34
Fraenkel, M., 255
Frankenberg, R. J., 1n, 23, 48, 54, 56,
    128, 141, 156, 173, 179
Fry, P., vi

Garbett, G. K., vi, 1n, 34, 181, 227n
Gluckman, M., vi, 22, 24, 37, 38, 48,
    75, 124, 132, 181, 191, 203n, 247
Gugler, J., 255

Hall, M., 5
Harary, F., 4n, 15, 33, 34, 36n, 47n,
    53, 55, 58, 63, 64, 66, 221n, 222n,
    302, 335, 336n, 346
Harries-Jones, P. J., vi, 7, 14, 15n,
    23n, 25, 27, 28, 31, 32, 35, 38n, 39,
    42, 287, 299, 349
Hellman, E., 89

Startup, R., 344n
Stefaniszyn, B., 259, 263n, 280n, 281n
Straus, M. A., 5
Sunshine, M. H., 35
Swartz, M. J., 51n

Thibaut, J., 36n
Turner, C., 5
Turner, V. W., 74, 90n, 202n

Udry, J. R., 5

Van Velsen, J., vi, 1n, 9, 131, 175, 177, 181, 183, 245n, 288

Wheeldon, P. D., vi, 7, 14, 19, 22, 23, 25, 29, 32, 35, 38, 41, 348
Williams, W. M., 6n, 23n, 40n
Wilmott, P., 27
Wilson, G., 184n
Wilson, M., 297, 298, 299
Wirth, L., 89
Woods, R., vi, 1n

Young, M., 27

Zander, A., 4
Zeleny, L. D., 4n

Subject Index

Abakumwesu, see Homeboys

Abel, 268–71; instrumentality of extended network, 276

Abene Bamushi (people of the section), 311

Abraham: implies Donald is rate-buster, 193–94; opposition between older and younger workers suggested by, 198; 'father-son' relationship with Donald, 201; feared for witchcraft, 205; reticulum characteristics, 215–18; reticulum compared with Donald, 218–21; reticulum structure affects degree of control over process of dispute, 236–37

Accusations: pattern among Coloureds, 139; in effective network, 140; resolution of, 140–41; in Cell Room, 201–6

Action sequences, 69, 73

Action set, 7, 38, 54, 59–72, 209–11, 300–2, 342–46; content in, 21; defined, 209, 300–1, 342; Harries-Jones extension of Mayer's definition, 301; directionality, asymmetry in, 21, 25, 343; in Dewas, 346; in mourning, 263; in personal (ego-centred) network, 301, 302, 338, 339, 343, 345; and manipulation of personal network, 344; quasi-group and, 301, 342–46; and mobilization of support, 209–11, 265, 302, 305–7, 309; lateral links in, 39; political party organization and, 302, 305–7, 310, 329; of 'C', 336–37; of home-boys, 343; of Lamba-Lenje faction, 329; of 'M', 329; transaction in, 39; fieldwork use of, 303

Adjacency matrices, 33

Adultery: on Copperbelt, 114n, 119

Affines: duty of Chisenga to, 272, 275; role of, 280, 281, 282, 284;

classificatory, 285; life cycle of network and, 294

African market: in Lusaka, 249; women in, 252; Lusaka Market Association, 268; and news of Abel's death, 269; officers of, 270; membership and burial societies, 270; reformation of, 276; joking relationships at, 276; rivalry with party branch, 277; and fish trader's links, 334

African medicine: and marital problems, 320; and personal networks, 327

African Mineworkers' Union, 47; butchers' boycott and, 306; see also Zambian Mineworkers' Trade Union

African National Congress: Chanda and Crawford officials in, 87, 107; as representative of African interests, 107; basis for other relationships, 108; rivalry with UNIP, 251; recruitment to network and, 253; in Kapipi, 271; and Abel's funeral, 271, 272, 274; rivalry with market, 277; support in Lusaka, 294; in Luanshya, 305; and Hawker's Association, 306; and 'C's' action-set, 305–7, 335–36; and local authority board, 307; defection to UNIP, 307; accusations of membership of, 323

African Urban Court, 92, 102, 112; and marriage norms, 112; adultery cases in, 119

Age opposition: in Coloured community, 152; in Cell Room, 198–200, 201–2, 205

Agnes, 277–86; network of, 285, 295

Alice, 259–63; lack of status of, 283; apparent lack of contacts, 262

Allen, 325–28; social ostracism of, 328

Scrubbers: job description, 187; company classification and wage rate, 188

Second-order contacts, 69

Second-order star, 14; defined, 59

Second-order zone, 14, 63; defined, 60

Selection: of issues in disputes, 232–237; of norms in disputes, 208

Semi-cycles, 63, 71

Semi-path: definition of, 63, 302

Serenje: district, 259; communication with, 268, 269, 282, 283, 285; funeral friendship in, 280ff, party officials and kin from, 282; significance of situation in, 280, 285, 286

Seventh-day Adventist: political non-attendance of, 315; attitudes to drink, 315

Sex: Coloureds attitudes to, 139

Shebeen: and section attender network, 322; keeper's network, 329

Shona: tribe 291

Shop Assistants' Trade Union: in butchers' boycott, 306; use of party branch, 306; and 'C', 336

Simplex relationships: see single-stranded relationships

Single-stranded relationships, 15, 22, 75; characteristics of industrial societies, 48; defined, 182, 213; accusations and 142; index of 'weak' relationships, 213; of Donald compared with Abraham, 218

Situation: and context of network relationships, 287, 294; bounded, 292; and kinsmen's political attitudes, 323; range of social- and 'home-boys', 341; in which quasi-groups emerge, 344

Situational analysis, 182, 245; network studies and, 32; dependence on ecological and institutional background, 32

Small-scale societies, 8, 12, 74; and multiplexity, 24; and tight mesh, 24; and social integration, 46; in

contrast to urban societies, 77; of coloured community, 140

Social change, 297, 298; in African communities, 339; index for, 341

Social class: and networks, 67

Social control: systems of, 339

Social field: see field

Social investment: exchange content, multiplexity and direction as indices of, 215; in Abraham's relationships higher than for Donald, 218

Social redundancy, 23, 54

Social status: in African towns, 104ff, 115; criteria of, 105; difficulty of 'class placement', 106, 126; relative equality in networks, 111; element in gossip norms, 125; in the gossip set, 126; of coloured leaders, 134; and networks, 253, 254; in family and networks, 252, 254, 295, 326; and debt and unemployment, 256; and assistance to hospital escorts, 261; of deceased, 265, 268, 286; in rural areas, 253, 342; of housing areas, 251, 252, 293, 314; and official positions, 311, 326; and conspicuous consumption, 325; and education, 250, 265, 286

Social structure: Radcliffe-Brown's definition of, 2

Sociograms: similarity with networks, 4; and patterns of linkages, 4

Sociometric studies: restricted contents in, 20, 22, 31; use of questionnaires in, 31

Soli: tribe, 323

Soloman: centre of non-attender network, 317–19, 321, 322, 329; attitude to tribalism and section attendance, 322, 323, 326; and Allen's petrol-bombing, 325; son-in-law's network, 323, 328

South-Africa: uniqueness of situation, 298; longer experience of urban life, 298

Southern Rhodesia, 115, 253, 321

Whites—*contd.*

in Community Civic Association, 143, 144 156; relationship to Coloureds affects relations within Coloured community, 160–61; voters holding institutional power, 308; elections, 316

Witchcraft: accusations in Cell Room, 201–6; accusations and promotion, 204; and sickness, 256; against Alice's daughter, 261

Women: social contacts of, 250, 252, 293, 294; roles at funerals, 257, 258, 271, 281, 282, 287; Chibeka's re-direction of orders to, 274; female sitting at mourning, 274, 282, 285; joking-relationship to Abel; and mobilization in Case (1); gardens in town, 89; from Southern Rhodesia, 115

Work: accidents, 203; situation and trade unions, 252; situation of importance to Abel, 265, 270, 273, 274; and interaction, 292, 295; and friendship, 293, 294; and tribal recruitment, 292, 305; and recruitment through teachers, 261–63, 282, 293; divisions created by, 306; and neighbourhood politics, 324; zones of employment, 251; -mates and joking-relationships, 276; -mates and Case (3), 282, 284; -mates and life cycle of network, 294; and urban values and esteem, 89, 90; situation on Copperbelt, 90–92; structure of occupations in Lusaka, 250, 251

Work speed: see restriction of output

Yao: tribal joking-relationship, 284, 290; burial ceremony, 284; fortuitous presence of, 286

Zambia, Mineworkers' Trade Union: membership in Unit 3, 190; relationship of Z.M.T.U. to U.M.U., 191n

Zambianization: of good jobs, 316

Zebedee: role of social worker, 284

Zone multiplexity: see multiplexity